OFFICE FOR THE WEB MADE EASY

Free Productivity Apps in the Cloud

By James Bernstein

Copyright © 2021 by James Bernstein. All rights reserved.

All rights reserved. This book or any portion thereof
may not be reproduced or used in any manner whatsoever
without the express written permission of the publisher
except for the use of brief quotations in a book review.

Printed in the United States of America

Bernstein, James
Office for the Web Made Easy
Part of the Productivity Apps Made Easy series

For more information on reproducing sections of this book or sales of this book,
go to **www.madeeasybookseries.com**

Contents

Introduction 6

Chapter 1 – Getting Started 7
   Overview 7
   Signing up for a Microsoft Account 7
   Office for the Web vs. Microsoft 365 and Office 365 16

Chapter 2 – OneDrive 19
   Introduction 19
   OneDrive Plans and Features 19
   Using OneDrive 20
   Creating Folders and Uploading Files 28
   OneDrive Desktop App 32
   Sharing Files and Folders 35

Chapter 3 – Word 40
   The Word Interface 40
   Using Templates 41
   Tabs and Ribbon Items 45
   Basic Document Editing 83

Chapter 4 – Excel 86
   The Excel Interface 86
   Tabs and Ribbon Items 88
   Entering Data 125
   Number Formatting 127
   Sorting and Filtering 132

Functions and Formulas 141

Spreadsheet Formatting 146

Adding, Renaming and Hiding Sheets 153

Chapter 5 – PowerPoint 156

The PowerPoint Interface 156

Themes and Templates 159

Tabs and Ribbon Items 162

Adding New Slides and Slide Layouts 184

Transitions and Animations 188

Notes and Sections 193

Slide Shows 196

Chapter 6 – Outlook, Calendar and People 201

Overview 201

The Outlook Interface 201

Folders 205

Groups 208

Composing, Reading, Replying to and Forwarding Emails 211

Attachments 217

Outlook Calendar 221

People (Contacts) 229

Files 237

To Do 238

Email Rules 245

Outlook Settings 248

Chapter 7 – OneNote 255

    The OneNote Interface 255

    Tabs and Ribbon Items 258

    Adding Sections and Pages 269

    Adding Content to Your Pages 272

    Adding Additional Notebooks 276

Chapter 8 – Additional Apps 280

    Skype 280

    Forms 287

    Sway 298

    Family Safety 303

Chapter 9 – Sharing, Downloading and Printing Your Files 309

    Sharing and Collaboration 309

    Downloading and Exporting Your Files 320

    Printing and Page Setup 325

Chapter 10 - Extras 330

    Word Reviewing Mode 330

    Previous Versions 333

    Keyboard Shortcuts 336

    Add-Ins 337

    Office Apps on Your Mobile Devices 344

What's Next? 350

About the Author 352

Introduction

If you have been using a computer or smartphone for any length of time I am sure you have noticed how we are doing more things online in regards to work, school and even our everyday lives. And if you are not a regular internet user then you are missing out on a lot of things and might be feeling a little left behind!

Working in "the cloud" is nothing new but now we have many more options to help us decide how we want to go about using these technologies. When I say the cloud I am referring to working online using web based applications rather than using software installed on your computer itself. If you use an online service such as Dropbox or Google Docs then you are in fact working in the cloud.

Microsoft is no stranger to online applications and offers many technologies that can be used for anyone from home users to large enterprises. Of course these products vary in complexity and also in price. And just like with everything else, the more features you need the more it's going to cost you!

Fortunately for those of us who like free stuff that still offers plenty of features and usability, there is Office for the Web (formerly named Office Web Apps and also as Office Online). Office for the Web is Microsoft's online suite of productivity applications that anyone with a Microsoft account can use free of charge. One of the best parts of using online apps is that you can access them from any device at any location as long as you have an internet connection.

Office for the Web consists of many familiar apps such as Word, Excel, PowerPoint, Outlook, OneNote and Skype as well as additional features such as online storage with OneDrive and a daily planner called To Do. Rather than using these apps as you would with a program installed on your computer, you actually access them via your web browser and use them within the browser itself. As for storing the files you are working on, you generally keep them within your OneDrive online storage repository.

The goal of this book is to get you up and running with Office for the Web and show you how to use each app as well as share your files and properly use your free online storage to store and access these files. If you have used or currently use Microsoft Office software on your computer then it should be a fairly smooth transition to using these apps online. So on that note, let's head to the cloud!

Chapter 1 – Getting Started

Before I get started on how to use Office for the Web, you will need to have an idea of how it works because it is important to understand the technology behind it in order to get the most out of it. I'm not saying you need to be a cloud application specialist but if you can visualize how it works then it will save you some confusion and possible headaches once you start using the apps.

Overview
I mentioned in the Introduction that Office for the Web is a suite of productivity applications that you use via your web browser. This means that you will need to open your browser and go to the Office website in order to use these apps. You can't use them on your desktop like the standard versions of Word and Excel etc. that you might be used to.

When you open or create a document, spreadsheet, slide show etc. using these apps, you will be working on them within your browser but fortunately the way they look and feel will remind you of the Office software you are most likely use to using. You can even have multiple documents\files open at the same time in different browser tabs or windows.

Office for the Web also allows you to share your files with others in case you need to do some person to person or group collaboration. But instead of having to email your changed files back and forth, each person can edit the files and the others will then see the new changes. This makes it easier to ensure that you have the latest copy of the file rather than having to go through multiple email attachments or saved copies on your hard drive.

Speaking of files, Microsoft designed this version of Office so that you will store and access your files from your OneDrive cloud storage repository (discussed in Chapter 2) to ensure that you can get to your files from any location that has an internet connection, which is pretty much everywhere these days!

Signing up for a Microsoft Account
To use Office for the Web you will need to sign into the Office website at **office.com** with your Microsoft account. If you are a Windows 10 user then you most likely have a Microsoft account that you use to sign into your computer with unless you chose the local user account option when you first set up your computer.

Chapter 1 – Getting Started

If you are interested in learning about how Windows 10 works to improve your overall Windows skills then check out my book titled **Windows 10 Made Easy**.
https://www.amazon.com/dp/B08RZDL5CP

If you do have a Microsoft account that you use to sign into your computer but don't want to use that account for Office then you have the option to make a new account to use instead. Simply open your browser and type in the following URL in your address bar.
https://signup.live.com/

You will then be asked to create an account if you don't have one to sign in with.

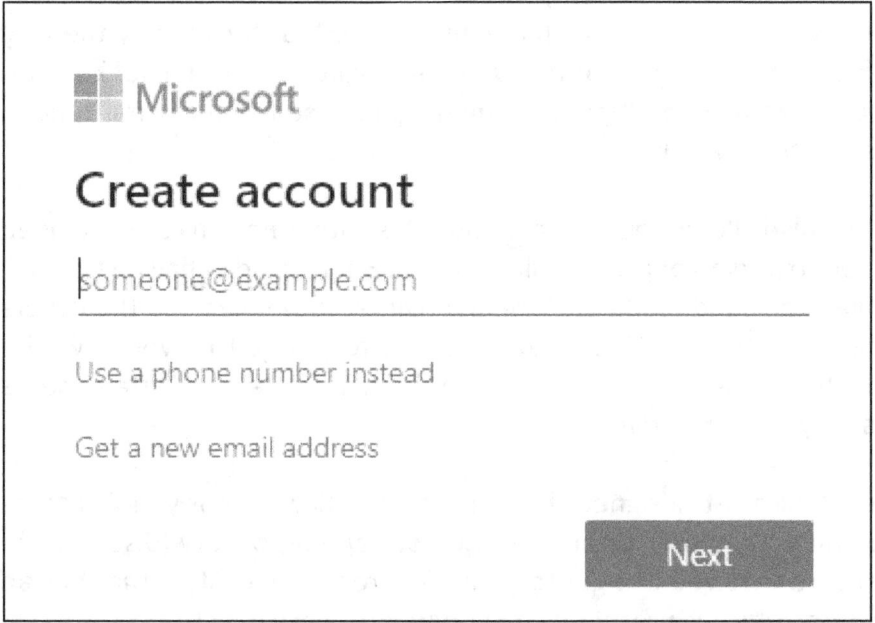
Figure 1.1

You don't need to use a Microsoft email such as **joe@outlook.com** to sign up for a Microsoft account. You can simply use any email address that you might have. You will then need to create a password and enter your name and date of birth. You don't need to add the real information here if you want a little privacy, but you might want to for file sharing purposes. You will then be sent a code to that email address that you will need to type in to verify your email address.

Chapter 1 – Getting Started

Once you supply all the information Microsoft asks for and verify your email address, you will be taken to the main Microsoft user account portal where you can do things such as add family members, connect additional devices to your account or change your password. There is even a place to sign up for a Microsoft 365 account (more on that later).

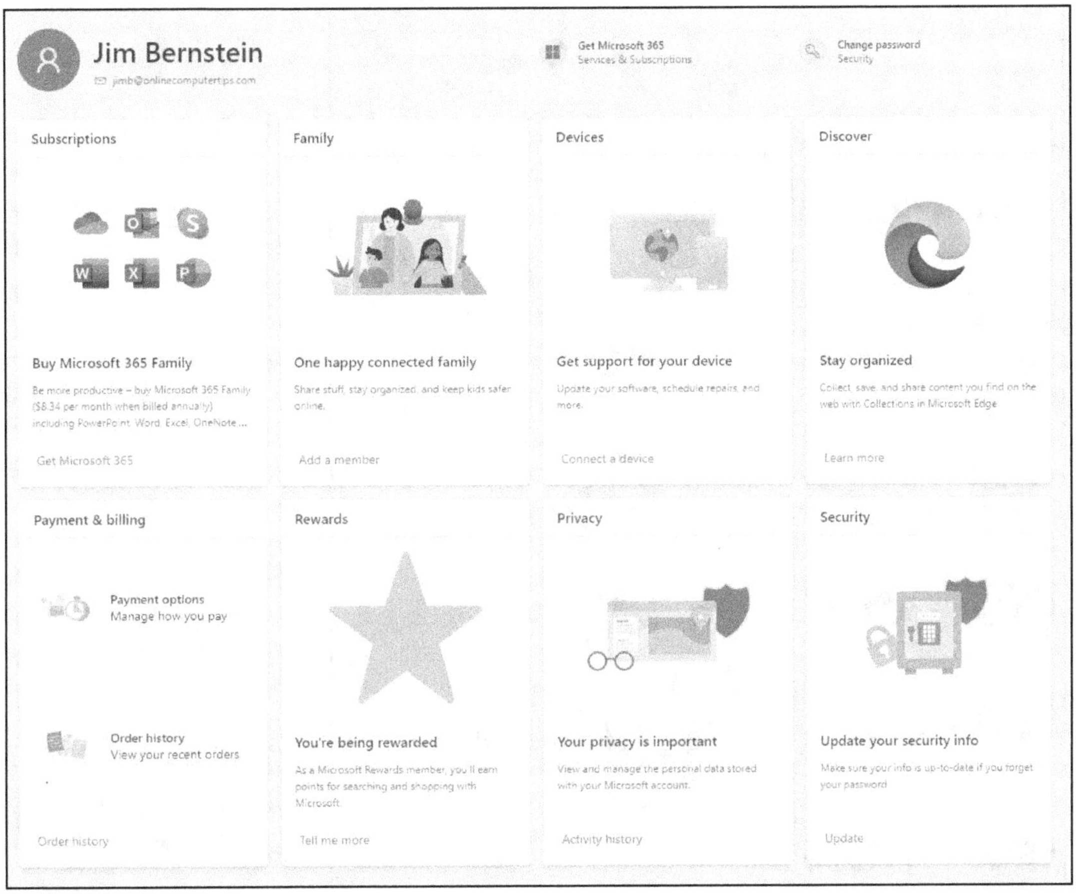

![Figure 1.2 - Microsoft account portal showing Subscriptions, Family, Devices, Discover, Payment & billing, Rewards, Privacy, and Security sections]

Figure 1.2

From there you can click on the icon with the nine dots next to where it says Microsoft account to bring up the Office menu as seen in figure 1.4.

Figure 1.3

Chapter 1 – Getting Started

If you look closely you will see that it says Microsoft 365 which is different from Office for the Web. I will be discussing the different versions of Office later in this chapter. What you need to do next is click on Office at the top right of the menu to go to the Office home page.

Figure 1.4

The first time you do this you might be shown some informational screens telling you how you can upgrade your Office type and also giving you information about Office itself.

Chapter 1 – Getting Started

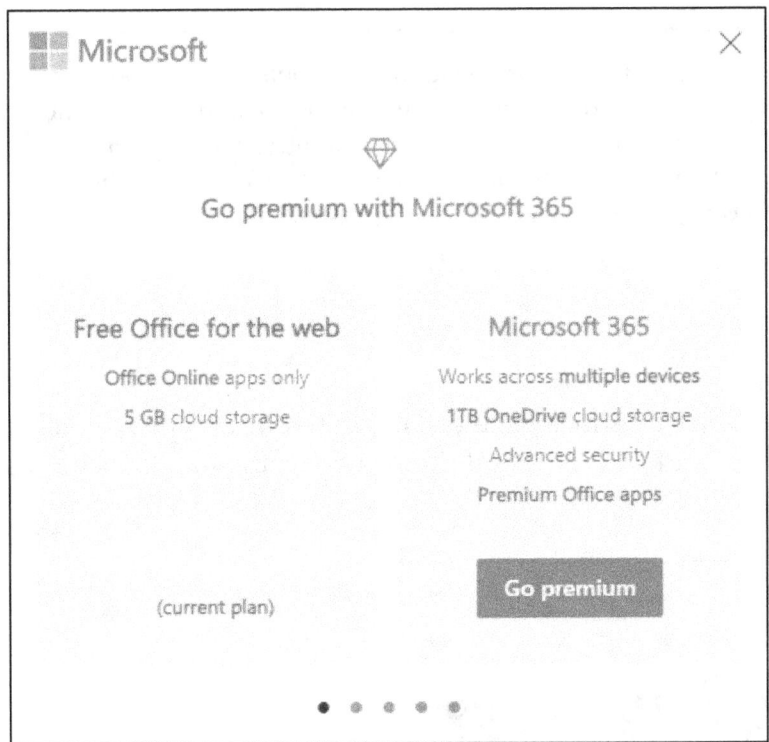

Figure 1.5

Figure 1.6

Chapter 1 – Getting Started

One problem that I always encounter with online applications and even websites is that they are always being updated and not always for the better! If you run into a situation where something doesn't look exactly the same while reading this book then its most likely because of one of these updates.

Office for the Web Interface

When you first go to the Office interface page you might be shown popups telling you about various features and where to find them such as the app launcher as seen in figure 1.7.

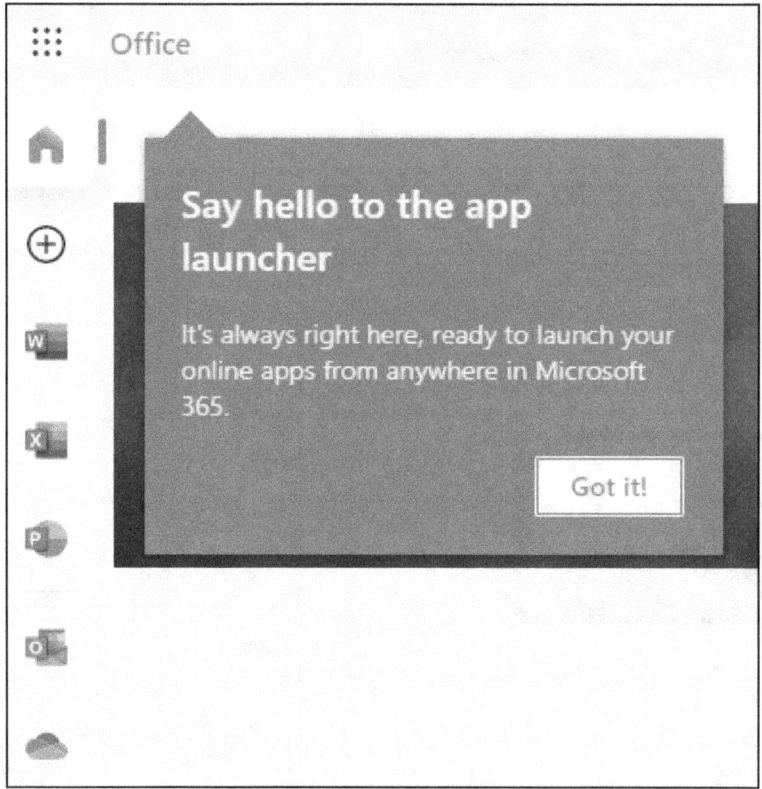

Figure 1.7

Figure 1.8 shows the main Office interface for a new account. You will notice how it says *no recent online Office documents* because there have not been any created yet. There is also a *Pinned* section where you can see commonly used files that you mark as favorites and then the *Shared with me* section where you will see files that other people have given you access to.

12

Chapter 1 – Getting Started

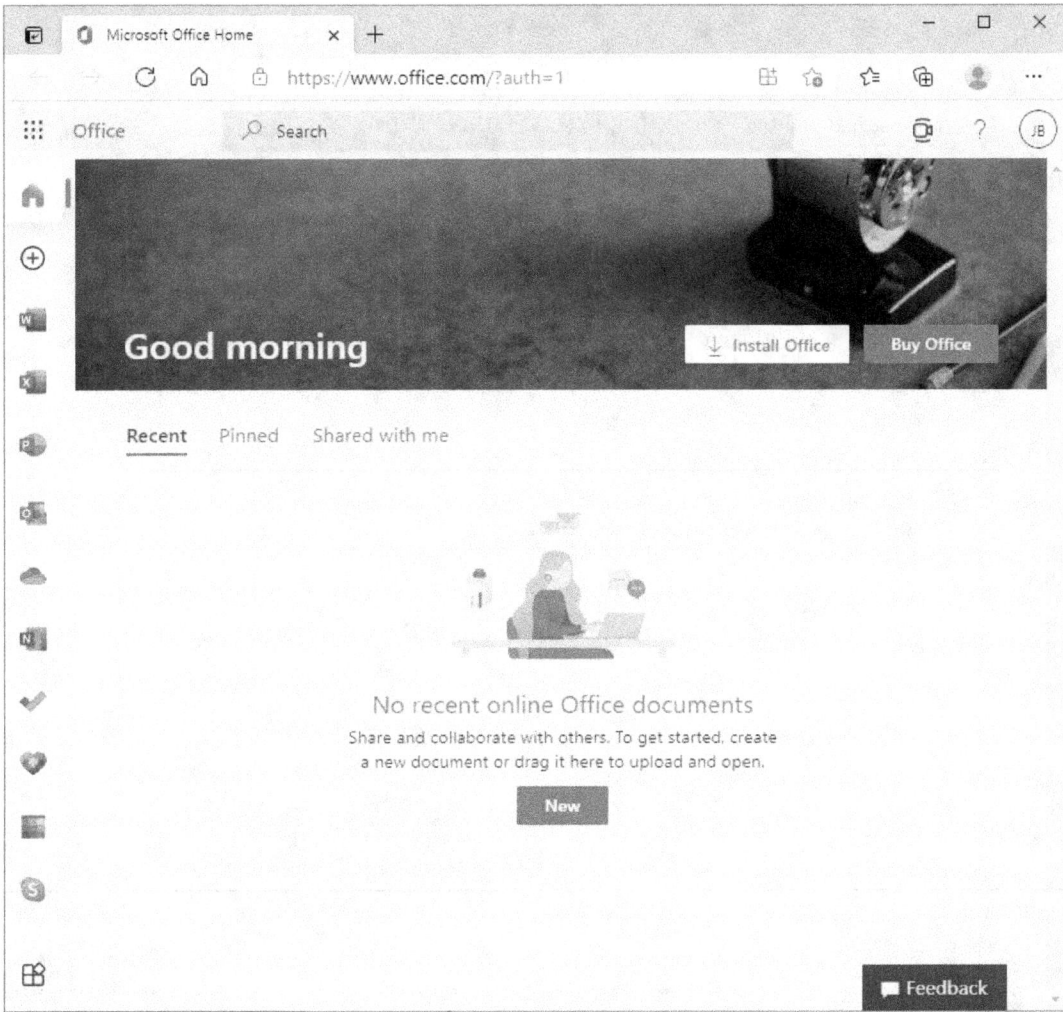
Figure 1.8

The left side of the page lists all of the available Office apps such as Word, Excel and PowerPoint etc. The **+** button will allow you to quickly add a new document, spreadsheet, presentation, form or page. You can also just click on whatever app you want to open by clicking its icon. The home button will take you back to this main home page any time that you click on it. At the bottom left corner you will find the *All Apps* button which will show you all the apps that are included with Office since the icon bar on the left generally shows the most popular or commonly used apps (figure 1.9).

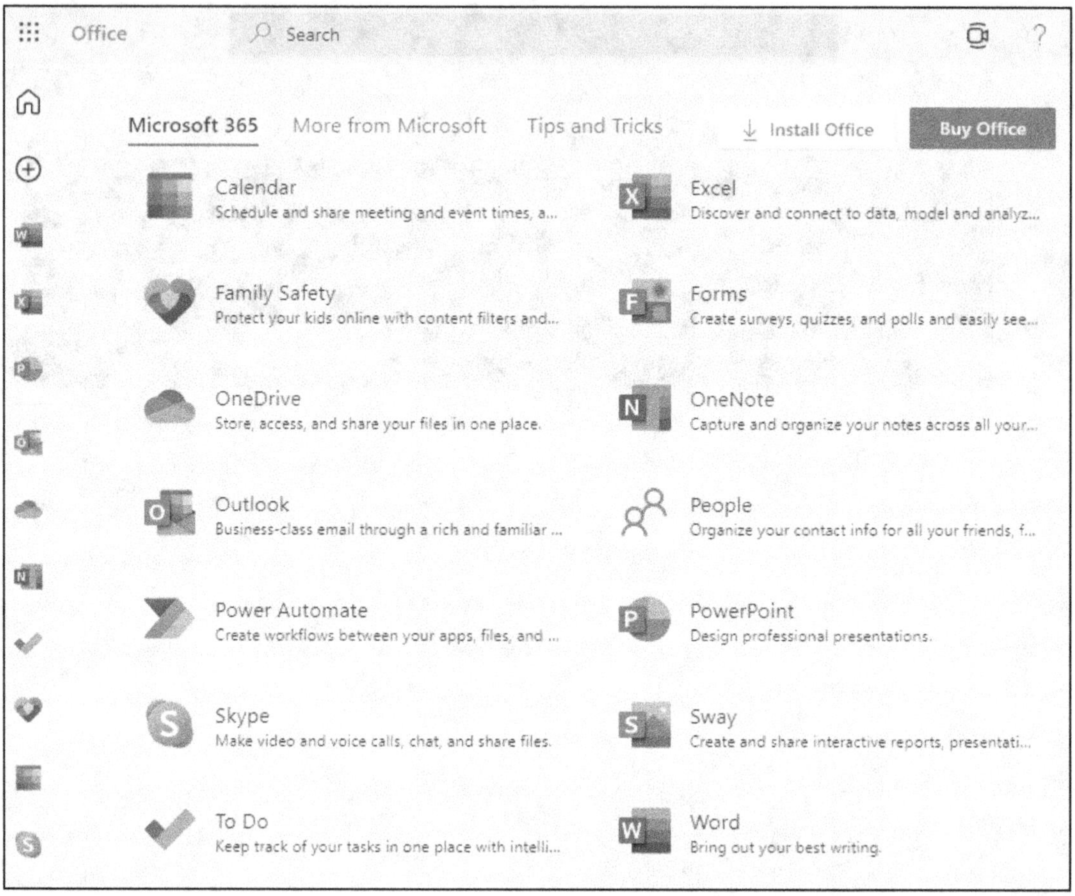

Chapter 1 – Getting Started

![Office web interface screenshot showing app tiles for Calendar, Excel, Family Safety, Forms, OneDrive, OneNote, Outlook, People, Power Automate, PowerPoint, Skype, Sway, To Do, and Word]

Figure 1.9

As you are using Office for the Web you will find that you are constantly asked to install or buy Office. This is because Microsoft wants you to use the pay for version rather than the free version because they make money that way. Keep in mind that you can't install office with the free version so simply ignore that button!

At the top right of the page you will see a question mark that will allow you to search for help by typing in a word or phrase related to the top you wish to find help on.

Chapter 1 – Getting Started

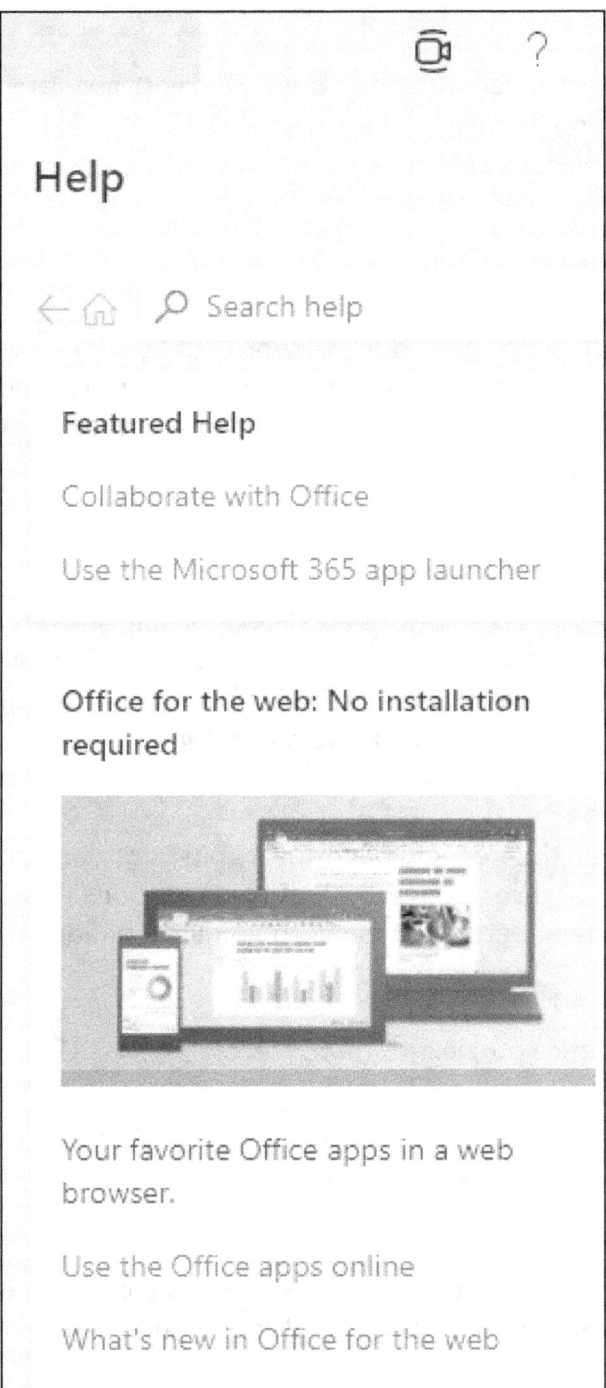

Figure 1.10

The video camera icon next to the help question mark will let you start a Skype online meeting so you can collaborate with your fellow employees or even have a virtual family reunion. I will be discussing Skype in Chapter 8.

If you are interested in learning how to use the most popular online meeting tools then check out my books titled **Zoom Made Easy** and **Google Meet Made Easy**
https://www.amazon.com/dp/B088B96YNK
https://www.amazon.com/dp/B08DFQPSD7

Finally, if you need to do things such as change your password, edit your name, add a profile picture, change your contact information and so on, you can click the *profile* button to the right of the help question mark to take you to your Microsoft account profile page.

Office for the Web vs. Microsoft 365 and Office 365
As I previously mentioned, you will always see buttons and links to install or to buy Office since Microsoft would prefer that you use the paid version of their apps. Once you start using the free version there is a chance that you will find that you need some additional features that the paid version offers and might eventually end up signing up for a subscription.

But what are the differences between the free and pay-for versions? I'm glad you asked! There are way too many differences between all of these versions to list here so I will be summarizing the main features of each, so you have an idea of what each one offers.

We can break down the Microsoft Office puzzle into three pieces.
- Office for the Web
- Office 365\Microsoft 365
- Office installed on your local computer

Office for the Web
This is the free and most basic version of Office you can use. This is competition for Google Apps which is also a free online suite of applications that perform similar functions.

Office for the Web offers the most commonly used Office apps such as Word, Excel, PowerPoint and Outlook but with reduced functionality compared to the higher end versions. For example, it is missing features such as advanced page layout tools and inserting videos in Word, advanced formulas in Excel, and fewer animations and transitions for PowerPoint. For most home users, these missing features will not be deal-breakers and you might not even notice they are not there if you don't use them.

You do have the ability to open Office files that were created on the desktop (installed) version of Office once you upload them to your OneDrive storage repository.

One important factor to consider when using this version is that you will need to have an internet connection to access your files or create new documents etc. On the other hand, you have the ability to use Office for the Web on almost any device that has a web browser and an active internet connection. There are even mobile apps available that you can install on your smartphone or tablet (discussed in Chapter 10).

Office for the Web also offers basic collaboration features so you can share your work with others as well as allow them to work on your files without having to email them back and forth to each other.

Office 365\Microsoft 365
Here is where things get confusing since most people are used to Office 365 and recently, it has been rebranded as Microsoft 365 even though you will still see references to Office 365. It can actually be kind of confusing since there are so many versions of their paid-for subscription based service.

Office 365 is the full featured version of Office that you use online and has additional applications that Office for the Web does not include. For example, you can use Office 365 with SharePoint and Teams which are enterprise collaboration tools. Microsoft 365 on the other hand includes Office 365 as well as Windows 10 and other business related services.

One of the big differences between Office 365 and Office for the Web is the ability to use the desktop versions of the Office programs on your computer. This will let you install the full featured programs that you can then use without needing to be connected to the internet. Plus you always get the latest version of the desktop software and support as long as you keep your subscription current.

There are several Microsoft 365 plans you can sign up for and here are a few examples.

Microsoft 365 Family - $100/yr.
- For use with up to 6 people
- 1 TB of cloud storage
- Premium Office apps
- Advanced security features

Microsoft 365 Personal - $70/yr.
- For use with 1 person
- 1 TB of cloud storage
- Premium Office apps
- Advanced security features

Microsoft 365 Business plans (based on users)
- <u>Microsoft 365 Business Basic</u> - $5 per user per month – Includes web and mobile versions of Word, Excel, and PowerPoint
- *Microsoft 365 Business Standard* - $12.50 per user per month - Includes Outlook, Word, Excel, PowerPoint, Publisher and Access apps plus several cloud services such as Teams, SharePoint and Exchange
- <u>Microsoft 365 Business Premium</u> - $20 per user per month – Includes the same Office apps as the Standard plan but comes with additional cloud services such as Intune and Azure

Office installed on your local computer
If you want to only use a locally installed version of the Office software that runs on your computer rather than online then you can use this option. Currently, the latest version of Office for the desktop is 2019 and it only runs on Windows 10 and Mac OS Extended or APFS.

With this type of installation you are limited to installing and using the software on one device and will only have the version that you purchased. So if a newer version comes out you will need to buy the upgrade separately. You also only get 60 days of support with your purchase.

There are no collaboration options with this version of Office unless you upload your files to your OneDrive account and share them that way. You can sign up for a OneDrive account with or without using any version of Office.

Chapter 2 – OneDrive

Before I get into the specific Office applications I would like to go over the OneDrive app since you will be using it with most of the Office apps. OneDrive is Microsoft's free, cloud-based storage service. (Of course, you'll have pay for plans with more storage space and other options, which I will get to shortly.) If you plan on using Office for the Web or Microsoft\Office 365, you should probably take advantage of the free space you get with OneDrive so you can be fully cloud integrated.

Introduction
OneDrive works the same way as many of the other cloud-based storage services. You have many ways to access OneDrive, such as with your web browser, desktop app, and mobile device app. One thing you will begin to notice as I go through all of these cloud providers is how similar they are to each other when it comes to their basic features. It will be the extra features that will make one service stand out from the rest.

With Microsoft OneDrive there are personal subscription plans as well as business subscription plans. I will list the plans with their pricing, as well as what you get with each one as of the writing of this book. For most home users the personal plans will be the way to go.

OneDrive Plans and Features
Personal
OneDrive Basic 5 GB - Free
- 5 GB of storage only

OneDrive Standalone 100 GB - $1.99 per month
- 100 GB of storage only

Business
OneDrive for Business Plan 1 - $5/user per month
- 1 TB of storage
- 15 GB file upload limit
- Advanced sync technology
- Mobile apps
- Web-based access

- Enterprise-grade security
- Secure Sharing
- Microsoft phone & email support
- Search & discover
- Photos
- Edit & annotate files
- Rich previewers
- Workflow
- Auditing and reporting
- API access

OneDrive for Business Plan 2 - $10/user per month
- 15 GB file upload limit
- Advanced sync technology
- Mobile apps
- Web-based access
- Enterprise-grade security
- Secure sharing
- Microsoft phone & email support
- Search & discover
- Photos
- Edit & annotate files
- Rich previewers
- Workflow
- PowerApps
- Auditing and reporting
- eDiscovery
- Data loss prevention
- In-place hold
- API access

Using OneDrive
To sign up for a OneDrive account all you need to do is sign up for a Microsoft account, and there is a good chance you already have one, especially if you are using Windows 10. Once you have your account configured, simply go to the OneDrive login page and sign in to access your OneDrive at:
https://onedrive.live.com.

Chapter 2 – OneDrive

If you have been using OneDrive, then you will see your files and folders that you have saved in your storage (as shown in figure 2.1). If you are completely new to OneDrive, then you won't have anything there except a few folders and maybe a file called *Getting Started With OneDrive* or something similar that you can open to read up on using OneDrive.

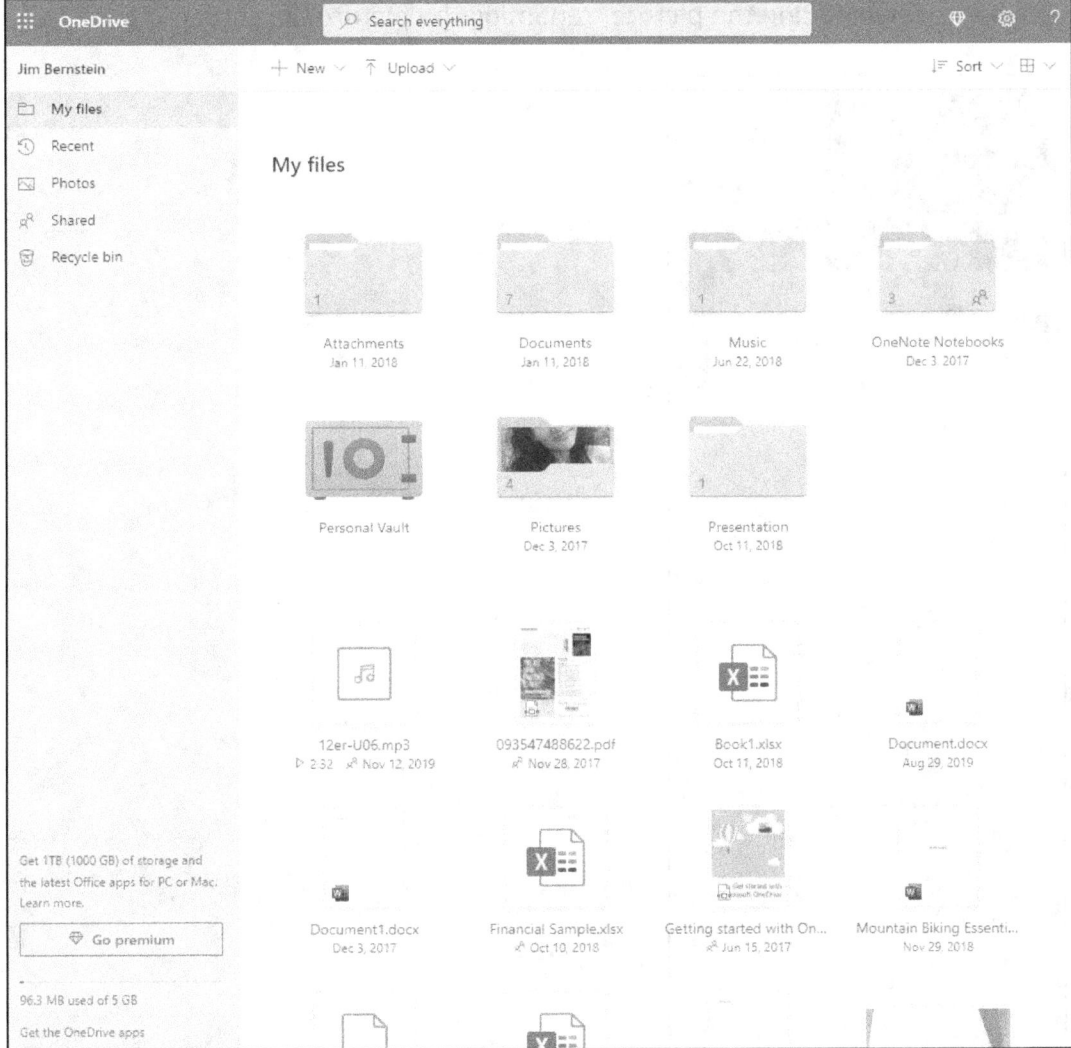

Figure 2.1

As you can see in my example in the *My Files* area, I have files and folders for different types of items such as documents and pictures and also a OneNote notebook folder.

The *Recent* section on the right will show you files and folders that have recently been added to OneDrive, so if you have a lot of files and are looking for something you just uploaded, then the Recent section is a quick way to find it. If you keep your pictures in the *Photos* area, then when you go into them they will be displayed by date and in a thumbnail view so you can see them without having to open each one individually. You can also create photo albums to categorize your pictures as well as add tags to images so you can search or view images by the tags later on. Right clicking on a picture will give you some options such as adding it to an album, downloading the picture, renaming the picture, and so on (figure 2.2).

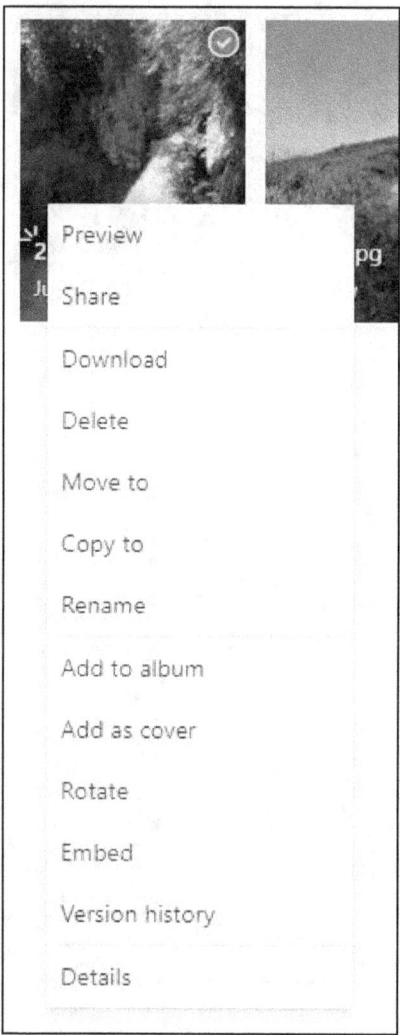

Figure 2.2

For files you have shared with other people, you can find them in the *Shared* section. However, just because it's here doesn't mean that this is where it's stored. OneDrive just lists shared files and folders here as shortcuts to the actual file or folder.

Chapter 2 – OneDrive

When you delete items they go into the *Recycle Bin,* just like they do in Windows. If you need to get them back, you can go to the Recycle Bin section, right click on them, and choose *Restore* to have them go back to their original location.

If you click on an Office file, such as a Word document or Excel spreadsheet, OneDrive will attempt to open it in your web browser using an online version of the program like shown with an Excel file in figure 2.3. It will even do this for things like PDF files or pictures that can be opened within a web browser.

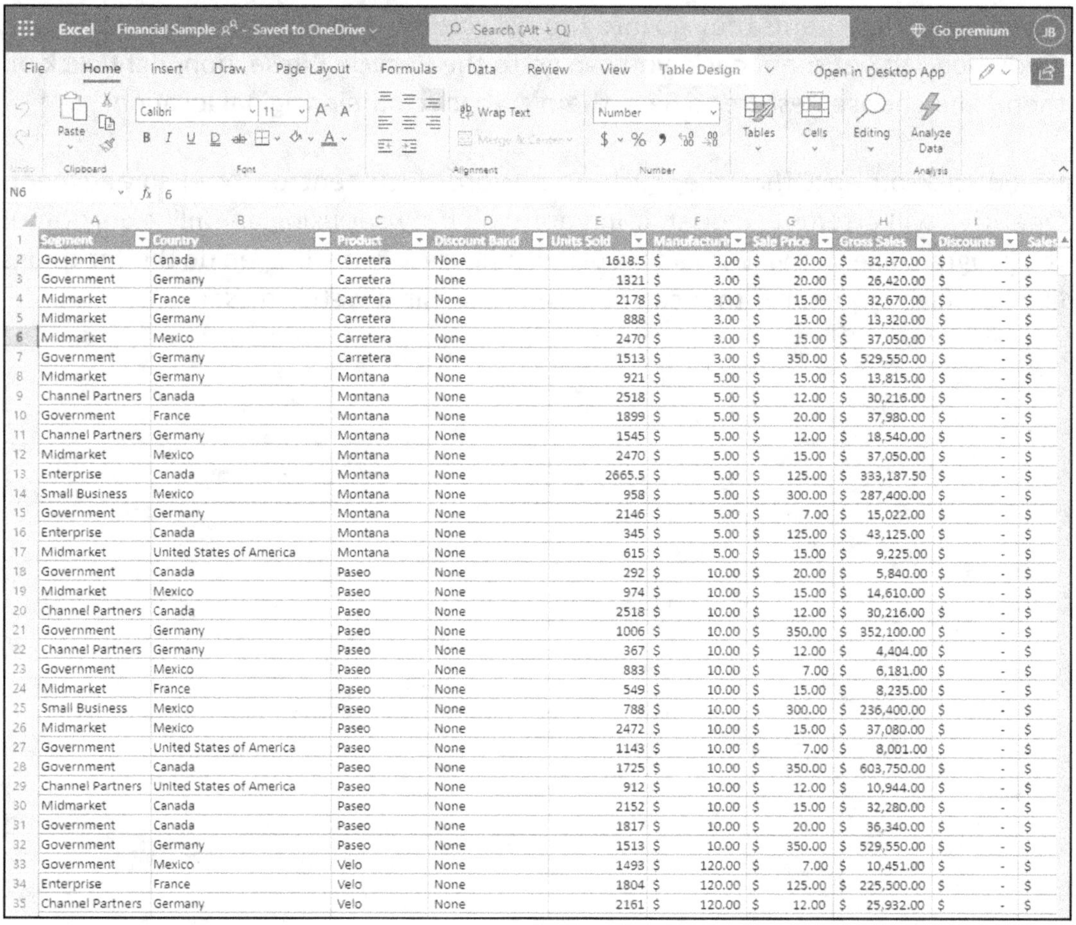

	Segment	Country	Product	Discount Band	Units Sold	Manufacturi	Sale Price	Gross Sales	Discounts	Sales
2	Government	Canada	Carretera	None	1618.5	$ 3.00	$ 20.00	$ 32,370.00	$ -	$
3	Government	Germany	Carretera	None	1321	$ 3.00	$ 20.00	$ 26,420.00	$ -	$
4	Midmarket	France	Carretera	None	2178	$ 3.00	$ 15.00	$ 32,670.00	$ -	$
5	Midmarket	Germany	Carretera	None	888	$ 3.00	$ 15.00	$ 13,320.00	$ -	$
6	Midmarket	Mexico	Carretera	None	2470	$ 3.00	$ 15.00	$ 37,050.00	$ -	$
7	Government	Germany	Carretera	None	1513	$ 3.00	$ 350.00	$ 529,550.00	$ -	$
8	Midmarket	Germany	Montana	None	921	$ 5.00	$ 15.00	$ 13,815.00	$ -	$
9	Channel Partners	Canada	Montana	None	2518	$ 5.00	$ 12.00	$ 30,216.00	$ -	$
10	Government	France	Montana	None	1899	$ 5.00	$ 20.00	$ 37,980.00	$ -	$
11	Channel Partners	Germany	Montana	None	1545	$ 5.00	$ 12.00	$ 18,540.00	$ -	$
12	Midmarket	Mexico	Montana	None	2470	$ 5.00	$ 15.00	$ 37,050.00	$ -	$
13	Enterprise	Canada	Montana	None	2665.5	$ 5.00	$ 125.00	$ 333,187.50	$ -	$
14	Small Business	Mexico	Montana	None	958	$ 5.00	$ 300.00	$ 287,400.00	$ -	$
15	Government	Germany	Montana	None	2146	$ 5.00	$ 7.00	$ 15,022.00	$ -	$
16	Enterprise	Canada	Montana	None	345	$ 5.00	$ 125.00	$ 43,125.00	$ -	$
17	Midmarket	United States of America	Montana	None	615	$ 5.00	$ 15.00	$ 9,225.00	$ -	$
18	Government	Canada	Paseo	None	292	$ 10.00	$ 20.00	$ 5,840.00	$ -	$
19	Midmarket	Mexico	Paseo	None	974	$ 10.00	$ 15.00	$ 14,610.00	$ -	$
20	Channel Partners	Canada	Paseo	None	2518	$ 10.00	$ 12.00	$ 30,216.00	$ -	$
21	Government	Germany	Paseo	None	1006	$ 10.00	$ 350.00	$ 352,100.00	$ -	$
22	Channel Partners	Germany	Paseo	None	367	$ 10.00	$ 12.00	$ 4,404.00	$ -	$
23	Government	Mexico	Paseo	None	883	$ 10.00	$ 7.00	$ 6,181.00	$ -	$
24	Midmarket	France	Paseo	None	549	$ 10.00	$ 15.00	$ 8,235.00	$ -	$
25	Small Business	Mexico	Paseo	None	788	$ 10.00	$ 300.00	$ 236,400.00	$ -	$
26	Midmarket	Mexico	Paseo	None	2472	$ 10.00	$ 15.00	$ 37,080.00	$ -	$
27	Government	United States of America	Paseo	None	1143	$ 10.00	$ 7.00	$ 8,001.00	$ -	$
28	Government	Canada	Paseo	None	1725	$ 10.00	$ 350.00	$ 603,750.00	$ -	$
29	Channel Partners	United States of America	Paseo	None	912	$ 10.00	$ 12.00	$ 10,944.00	$ -	$
30	Midmarket	Canada	Paseo	None	2152	$ 10.00	$ 15.00	$ 32,280.00	$ -	$
31	Government	Canada	Paseo	None	1817	$ 10.00	$ 20.00	$ 36,340.00	$ -	$
32	Government	Germany	Paseo	None	1513	$ 10.00	$ 350.00	$ 529,550.00	$ -	$
33	Government	Mexico	Velo	None	1493	$ 120.00	$ 7.00	$ 10,451.00	$ -	$
34	Enterprise	France	Velo	None	1804	$ 120.00	$ 125.00	$ 225,500.00	$ -	$
35	Channel Partners	Germany	Velo	None	2161	$ 120.00	$ 12.00	$ 25,932.00	$ -	$

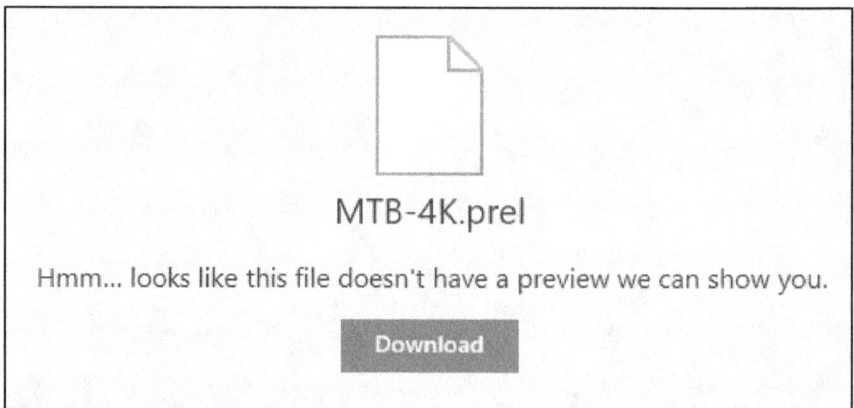

Figure 2.3

If you click on a file that OneDrive can't preview in a browser, then you will get a message like the one shown in figure 2.4, and you will have the option to download the file and try to open it directly from your computer.

Figure 2.4

Chapter 2 – OneDrive

When you select a file or folder you will have some options as to what you can do with that file or folder. To select a file or folder, click in the circle on the top right of the file to put a check mark in it like shown in figure 2.5. If you are viewing your files in a list view, then the circle will be to the left of the file.

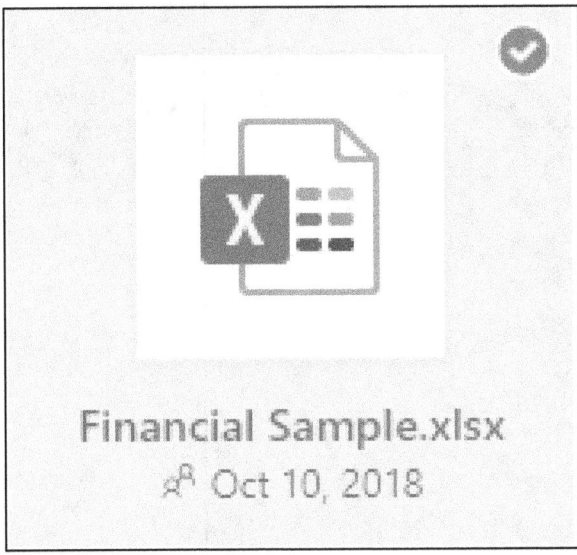

Figure 2.5

Once you have a file or folder checked there will be some options that appear at the top of the page that you can use with that file or folder (figure 2.6).

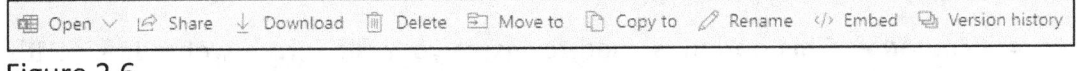

Figure 2.6

Most of them should be obvious, but I will go over the ones that might not be.

- **Move to and Copy to** — This will allow you to move or copy the file to a different folder within your OneDrive account. When you click on one of these choices you will be given a choice as to where you want to move or copy the file to based on your available folders.

25

Chapter 2 – OneDrive

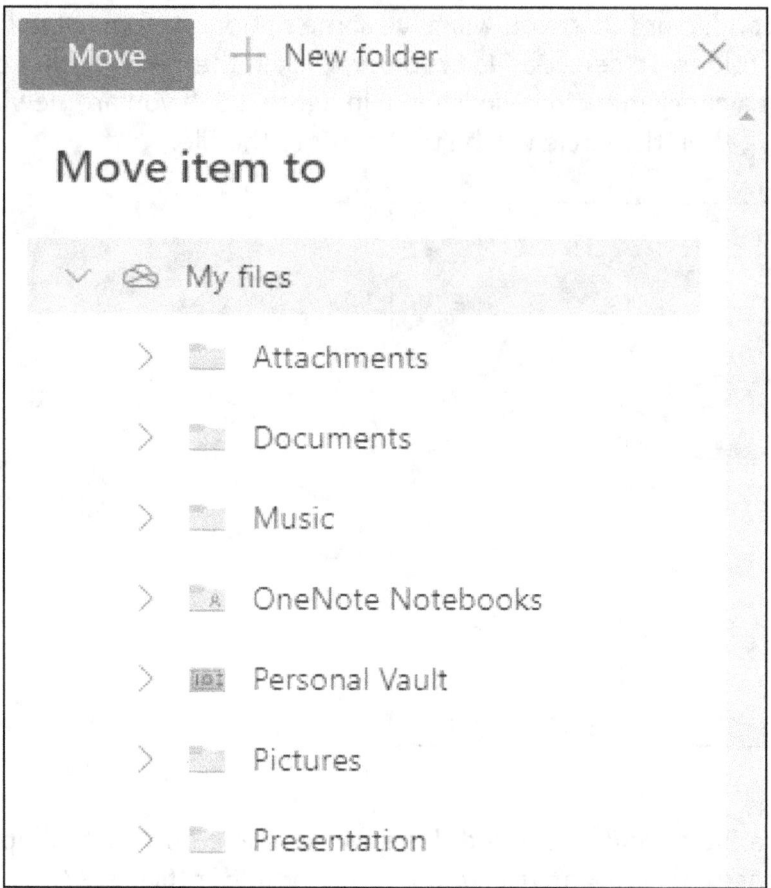

Figure 2.7

- **Embed** — This option is used to insert your file into a web page, so it's integrated with the page itself (figure 2.8). OneDrive will convert the file into HTML code that you can copy and paste into your web page editor and then upload to your website.

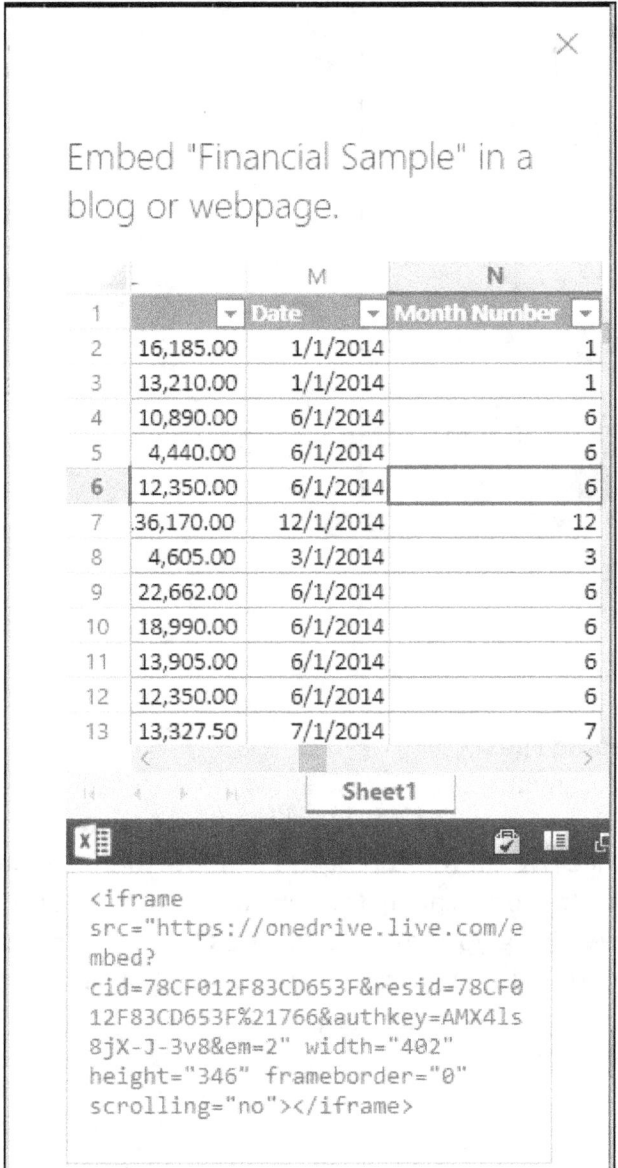
Figure 2.8

- **Version history** — If you have files that have been in your OneDrive account for some time, then you might have some older versions that you can restore or download to your computer. You can find out by selecting a file and then clicking on *Version history*. If you do have some older versions, you can view them by clicking on the specific date you want to look at before deciding if you want to restore or download them.

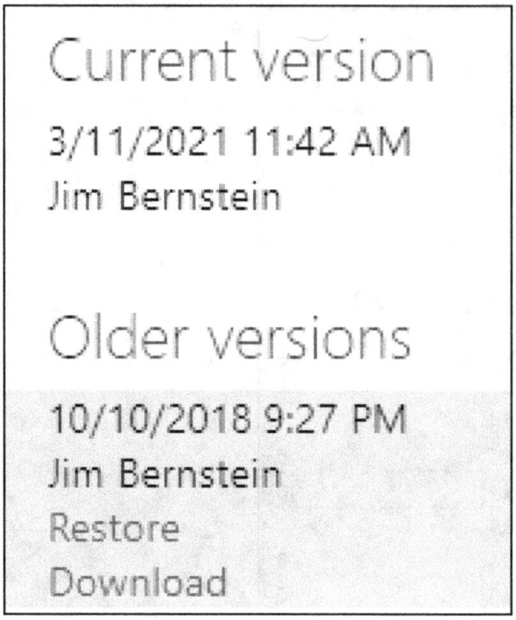

Chapter 2 – OneDrive

> Current version
> 3/11/2021 11:42 AM
> Jim Bernstein
>
> Older versions
> 10/10/2018 9:27 PM
> Jim Bernstein
> Restore
> Download

Figure 2.9

Creating Folders and Uploading Files

Cloud storage is no good to anyone unless you know how to upload files and create folders to put those files in, so now I want to discuss how to do exactly that. While in the Files area of OneDrive on the top of the window there should be an option called *New*, and another one called *Upload*. Next to New and Upload should be a drop down arrow giving your more choices as to what types of items you want to work with (figure 2.10). You can also right click a blank area and choose New or Upload from the menu that pops up.

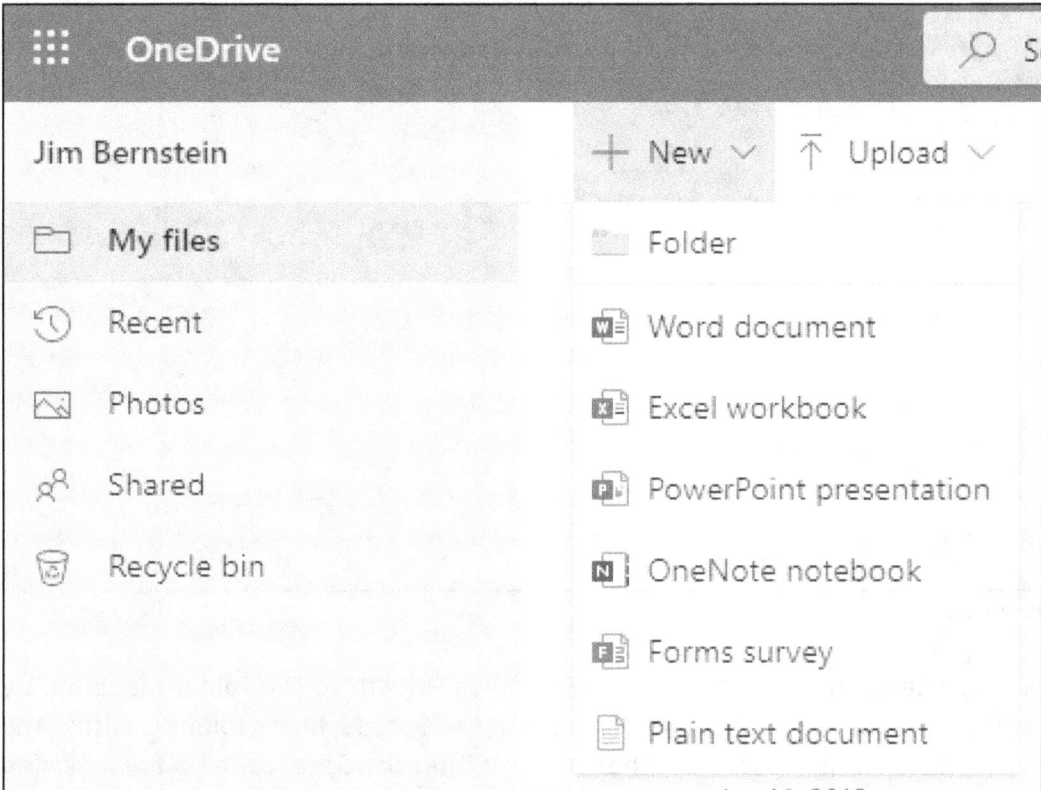

Figure 2.10

Since OneDrive is a Microsoft product, of course they will have choices such as Word document and Excel workbook under the New section. That way you can create a new Office file and work on it online directly from OneDrive. In my case I want to create a new folder, so I will click on the *Folder* option, enter the name *Spreadsheets*, and click the *Create* button. Then this new folder will appear with the other files and folders in the Files section. Next, I will click on the folder to open it and see that there is nothing inside of the folder since it is new (figure 2.11).

Chapter 2 – OneDrive

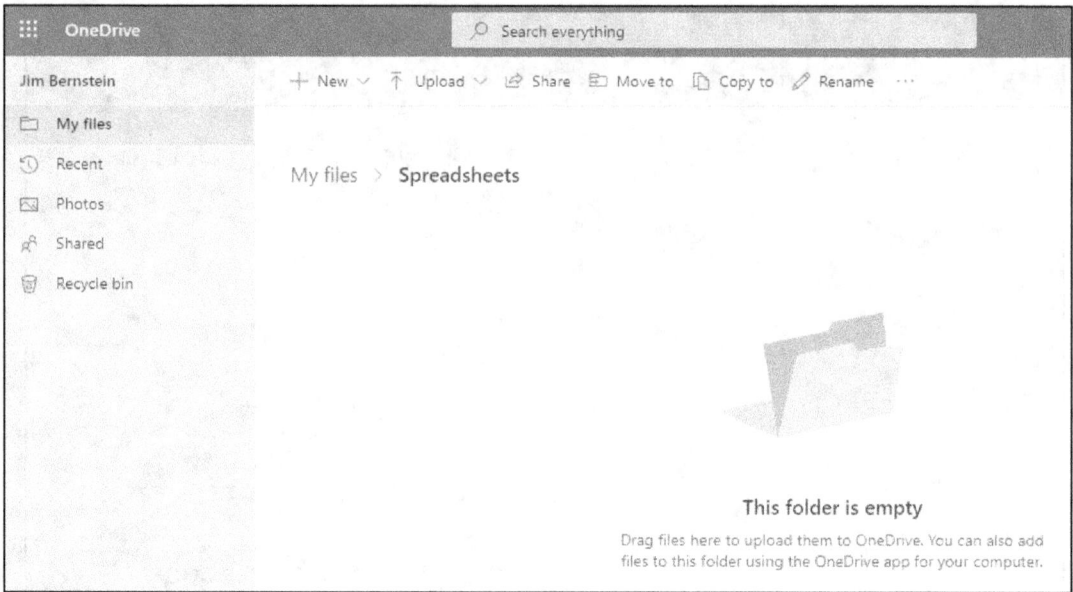

Figure 2.11

One important thing to note in figure 2.11 is the path to the folder indicated by *My Files > Spreadsheets*. This shows me that the Spreadsheets folder is within the My Files section. If I create another folder within the Spreadsheets folder called Sales, then the path would read as *Files > Spreadsheets > Sales*.

Now it's time to add a file to the new Spreadsheets folder. To do so click on *Upload* and choose *Files* since we want to upload a file rather than a folder. Then browse to the location of the file and click on *Open* to have it uploaded to your OneDrive folder. You will see it appear when the upload is complete (figure 2.12).

Chapter 2 – OneDrive

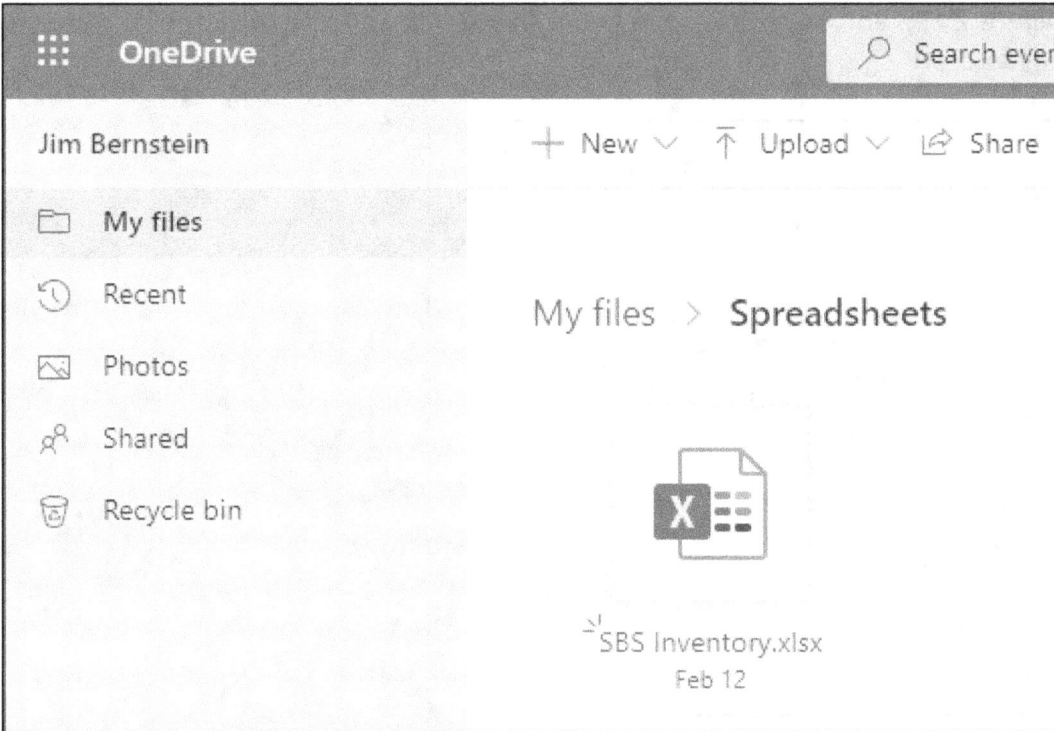

Figure 2.12

If you want to preview the file in your browser, all you need to do is click on it. In this example, it will open with the online version of Excel because it's an Excel spreadsheet that was uploaded.

OneDrive will also let you drag files to folders if you don't want to go through the process of using the *Move to* option from the toolbar. It's the same process as dragging and dropping a file in Windows or on a Mac. But if you want to move a file from a folder to another folder, then you will have to use the Move to option because you won't be able to see both folders at the same time to drag the file from one to the other.

To search for files and folders within OneDrive all you need to do is type in your search term in the search box at the top of the page and it will show you all the results that match your search criteria.

One thing to keep in mind when using OneDrive is how much space you are using and how much space you have left. Just like with your computer, it's always a good idea to do a periodic cleanup to remove files that you don't need to keep things clean and organized. If you look at the bottom left corner of the OneDrive window, it will tell you how much space you have used and how much space you have left (figure 2.13), and, of course, give you a link to upgrade to a higher level plan at a higher cost!

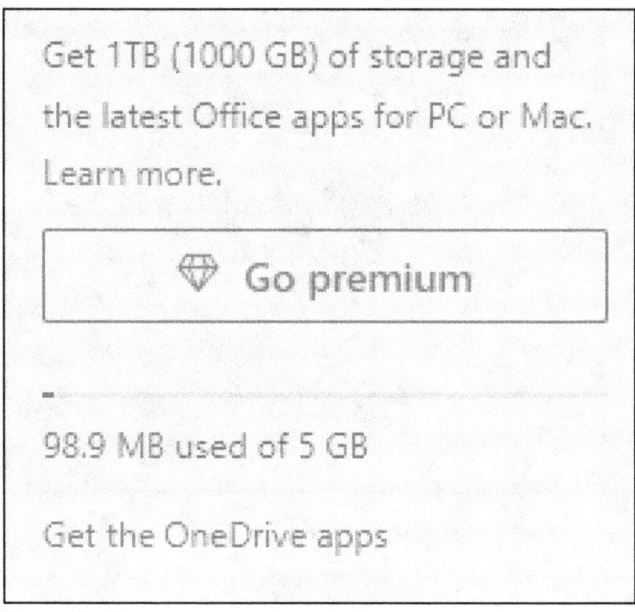

Figure 2.13

OneDrive Desktop App
If you decide to use OneDrive on a regular basis it's a good idea to install the OneDrive application on your local computer so you don't have to do everything from your web browser. Starting with Windows 8, Microsoft introduced Windows Apps, which work a little differently than Windows programs and are more like the apps you would install on your smartphone.

To get the OneDrive app for Windows you need to go to the Microsoft Store and search for it or click on the link shown at the bottom of figure 2.13. To use the Microsoft Store method in Windows, open the Microsoft Store on your computer and do a search for OneDrive (as shown in figure 2.14), follow the prompts to install it on your computer, and then open it from your Apps.

Chapter 2 – OneDrive

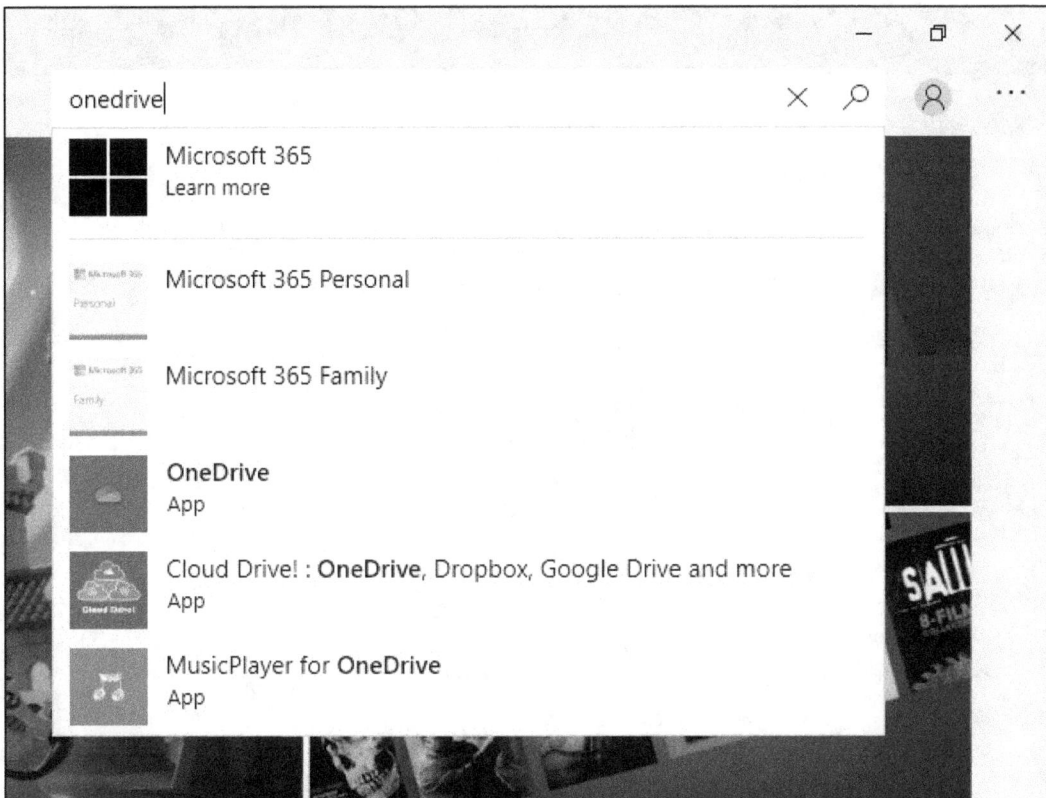

Figure 2.14

 If you are running Windows 10 there is a very good chance that the OneDrive app is already installed on your computer, so if you go to the Microsoft Store and search for OneDrive and it says Launch rather than Install, that means you already have it on your computer.

As you can see from figure 2.15, it looks very similar to the web browser version that we were working with previously and has identical categories on the left side of the window. So if you would rather use the locally installed OneDrive app over the website version, you can perform the same tasks in either one.

Chapter 2 – OneDrive

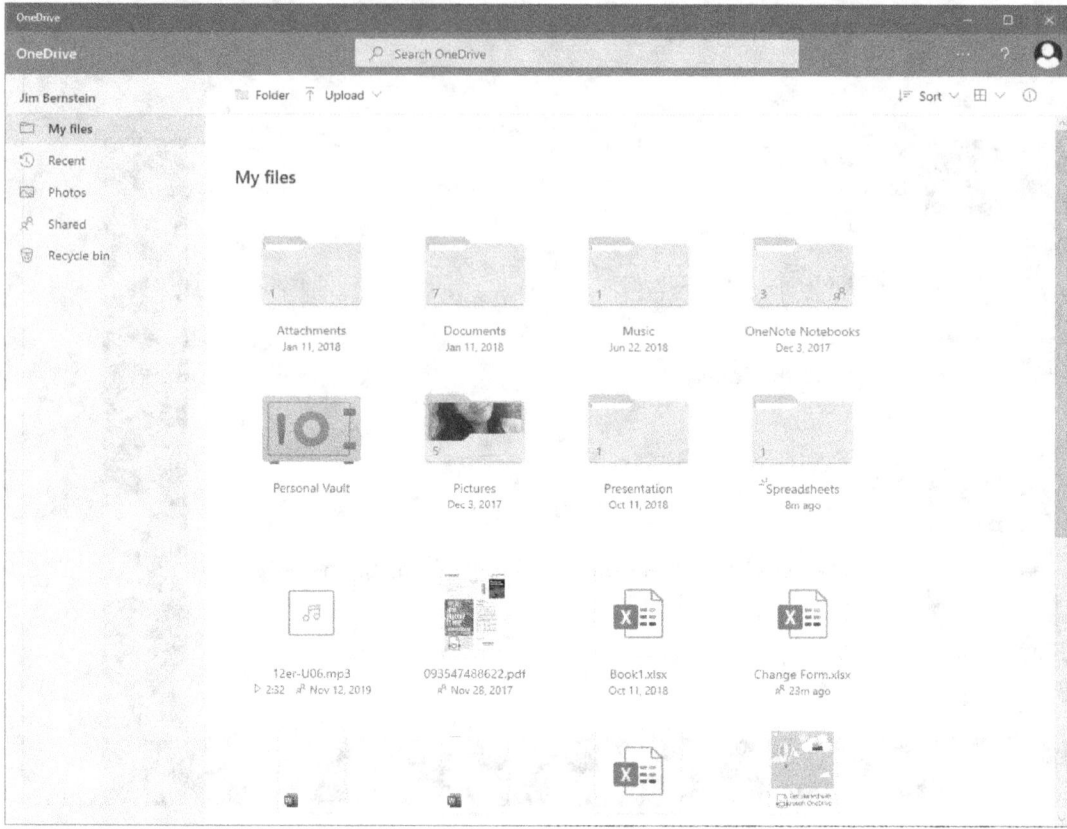

Figure 2.15

When you click on a file, the OneDrive app will open that file within the app itself and also give you an option to open the file in any other supported apps that you might have available to you. As you can see in figure 2.16, there is an option to open this presentation file in PowerPoint Online or the PowerPoint desktop program. There is also a *Download* option if you would like to download the file to your computer to work on it with the locally installed Office program assuming you have that available to you. You can also right click on a file to get the same options you have available to you when you right click on a file using the web version of OneDrive.

Chapter 2 – OneDrive

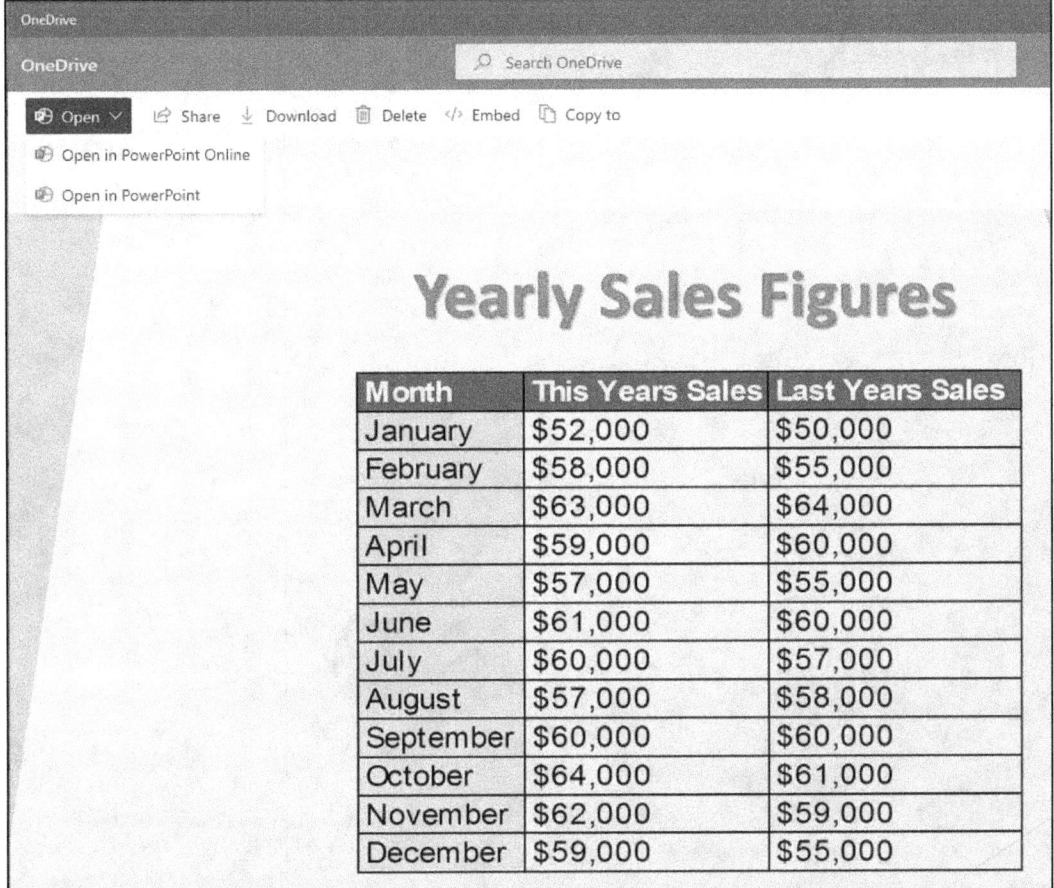

Figure 2.16

Sharing Files and Folders
One great thing about OneDrive is the ability to share your files so you don't have to email files back and forth. Plus, a lot of the time the files you want to share will be too large to email.

If you select a file and click on the *Share* option (in the web version of OneDrive), you will be prompted to enter the name or email address of the person or people you wish to share the file with. You can also add a personal message that will be sent along with the shared file link (figure 2.17).

If you would rather send an invitation yourself then you can click on the *Copy link* button and then paste the link into an email or instant message etc. and share your file that way.

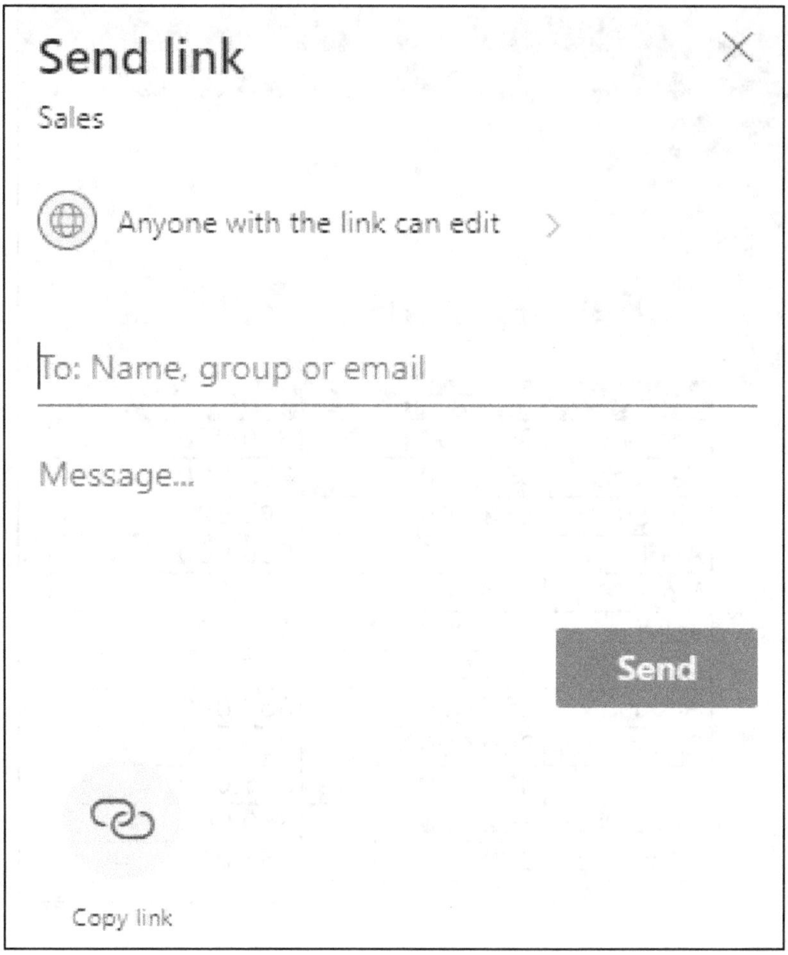

Chapter 2 – OneDrive

Figure 2.17

By default, the shared file setting is for anyone with the link can edit the file. If you click on this you will be able to fine tune your share options as seen in figure 2.18. For example, you can disable editing, set the link to expire or even set a password to open the shared file.

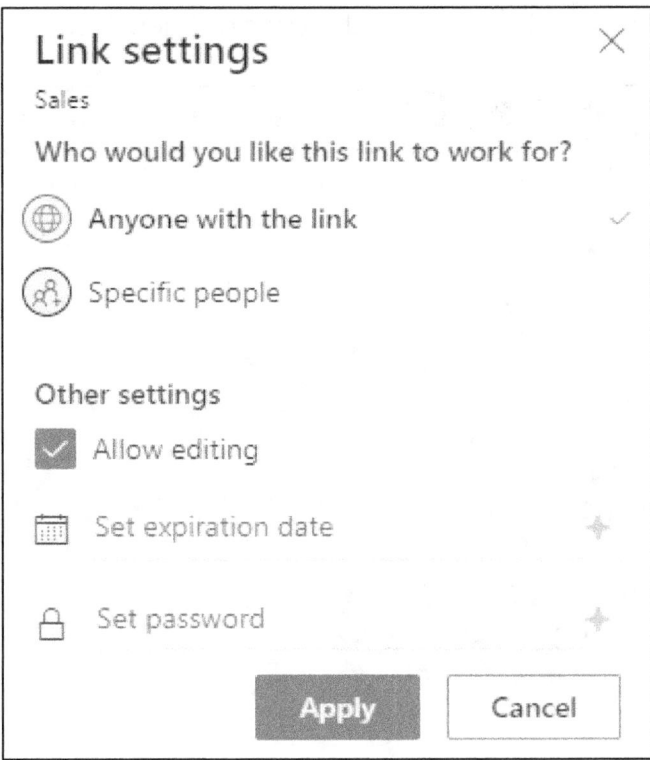
Figure 2.18

When OneDrive sends the shared link via an email, the recipient will see a message similar to figure 2.19. Then all they need to do is click on the *Open* button to view your file.

Figure 2.19

Chapter 2 – OneDrive

Once you share a file it will then be listed in the Shared section of OneDrive.

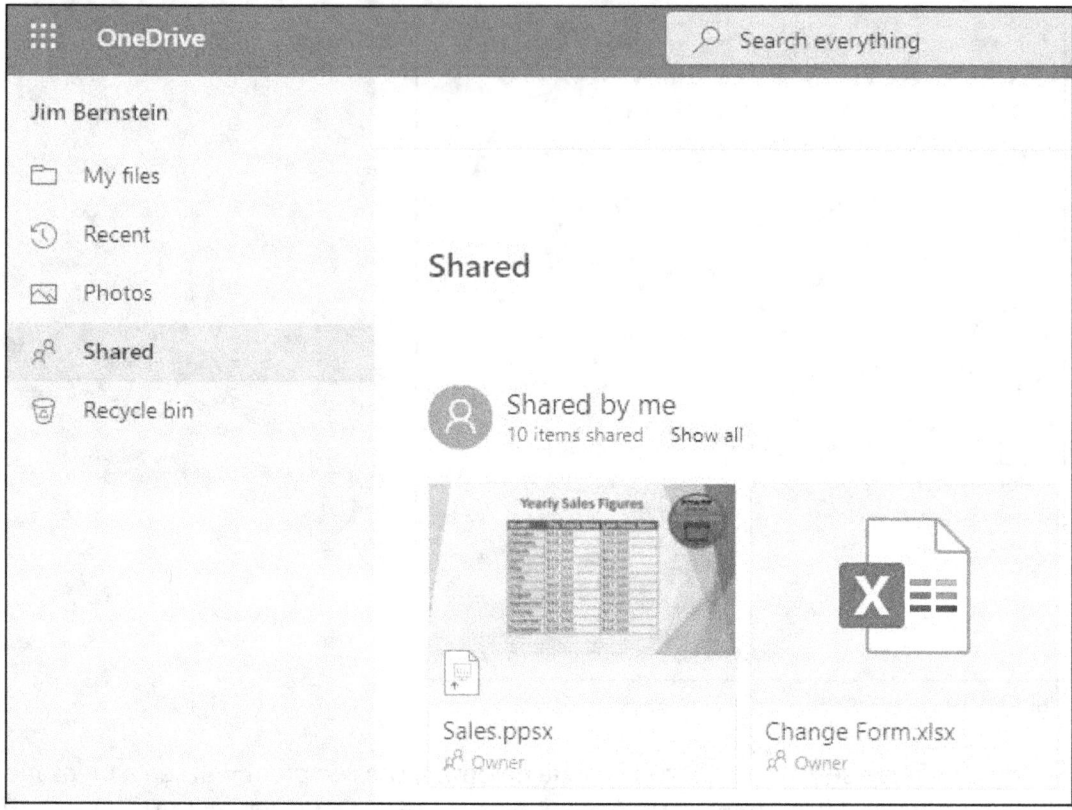

Figure 2.20

One last part of the OneDrive interface I want to discuss are the sort, view and details options which are located at the top right of the page.

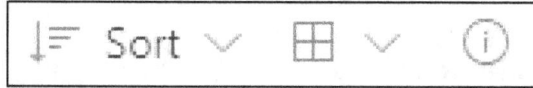

Figure 2.21

The *Sort* option will let you sort your files and folders by name, size and modified date, making it easier to find what you are looking for.

Then *View* option will let you view your files and folder in a list, tiles or photo view depending on which style works best for you.

The *Details* option will show you what changes you have made within your files.

Chapter 2 – OneDrive

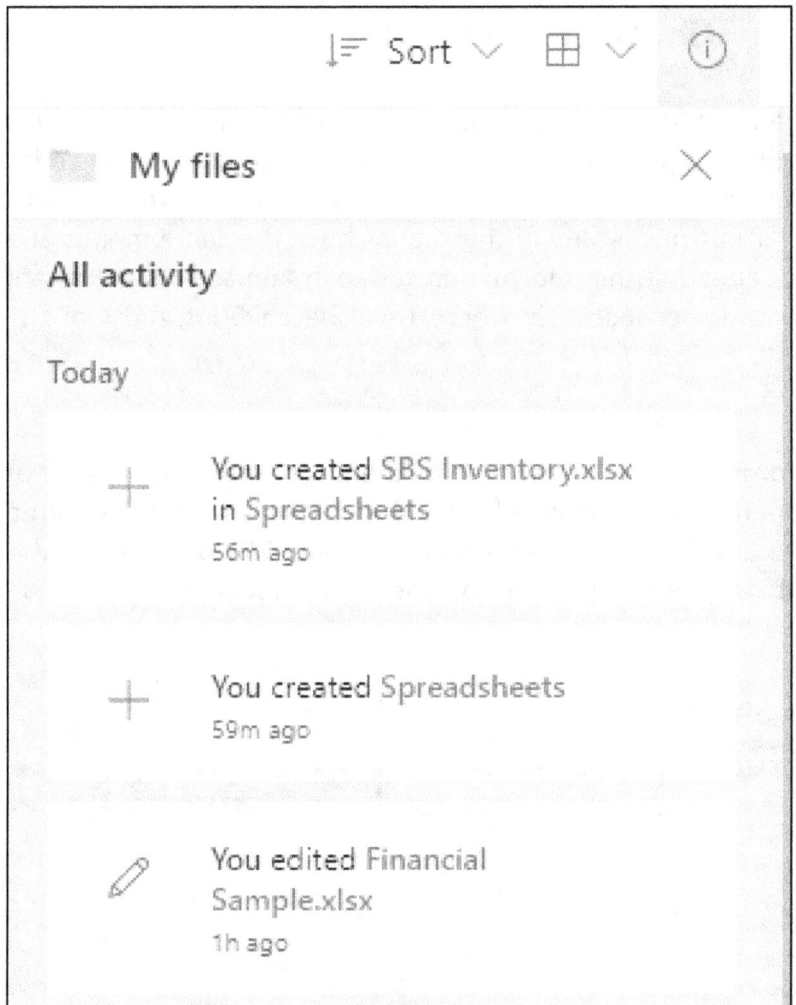

Figure 2.22

Chapter 3 – Word

Now that we have the introduction and OneDrive overview out of the way, it's time to start focusing on the apps that you have available to you within Office for the Web. I will be going over the main features of each app as well as their various menu items and toolbar buttons. Many of these apps have the same menus and buttons so I won't be repeating the information for each app so it is important that you read this chapter because it is where I will be covering most of the features.

The Word Interface

When you click on Word on the left hand side of the page where you see all of your app icons it will open up the main interface and show you any recently edited documents if you have any. Since I am working with a new Microsoft Account, I don't have any recent documents, pinned documents, or documents that have been shared with me.

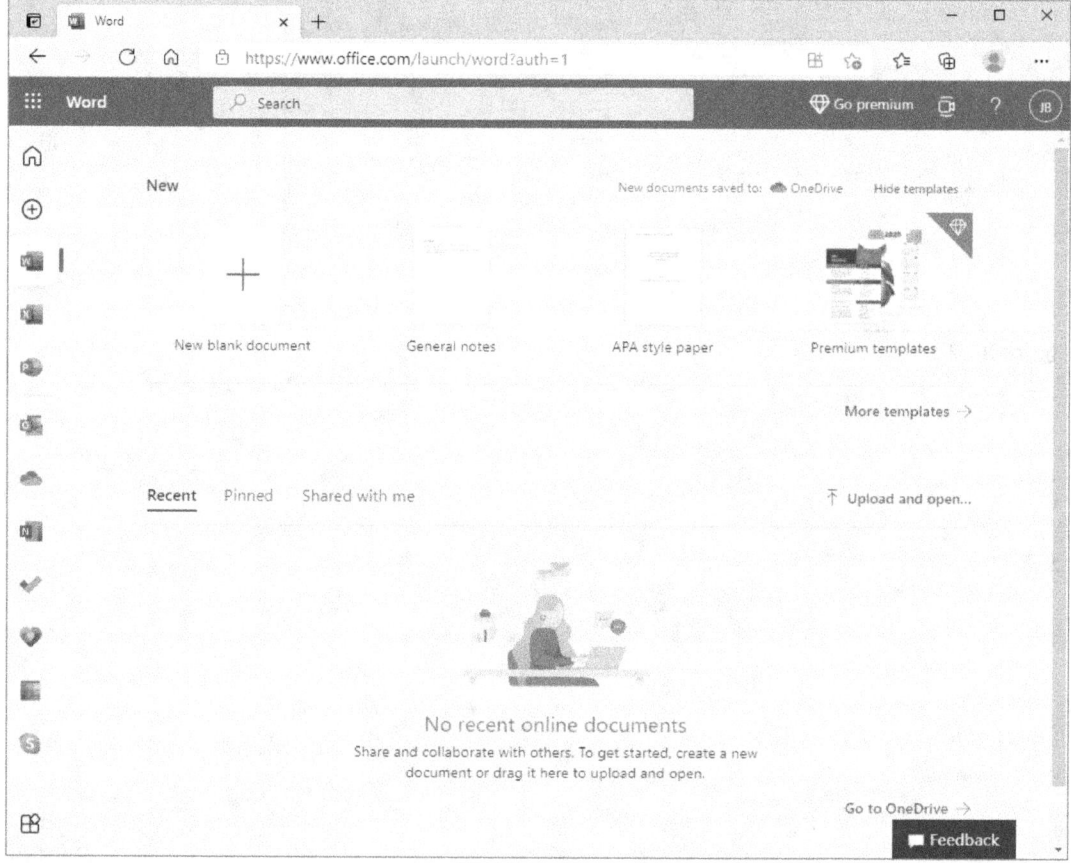

Figure 3.1

Chapter 3 – Word

To the right of the page I have an option that is named *Upload and open* which will allow me to upload a Word document from my computer to be used within Word on the web.

There is also a link that says *Go to OneDrive* that I can click on to open my OneDrive file storage repository and then open a Word document that I have saved there.

Other than that, there is not much to the main Word interface and not much you can do until you open a document or start a new document.

Using Templates
One thing you will find in any version of Office are templates that you can use to base your document on and save yourself some work at the same time. You can think of templates as documents that have already had the formatting applied so all you need to do is add your own text or images etc. You can find templates for many types of documents such as flyers, resumes and form letters.

If you look at the top of figure 3.1, you will see that there are a few templates displayed that you can choose from. If you click on Premium templates you will be taken to the Microsoft 365 subscription page meaning you will need to sign up for a plan in order to use them.

Figure 3.2

Chapter 3 – Word

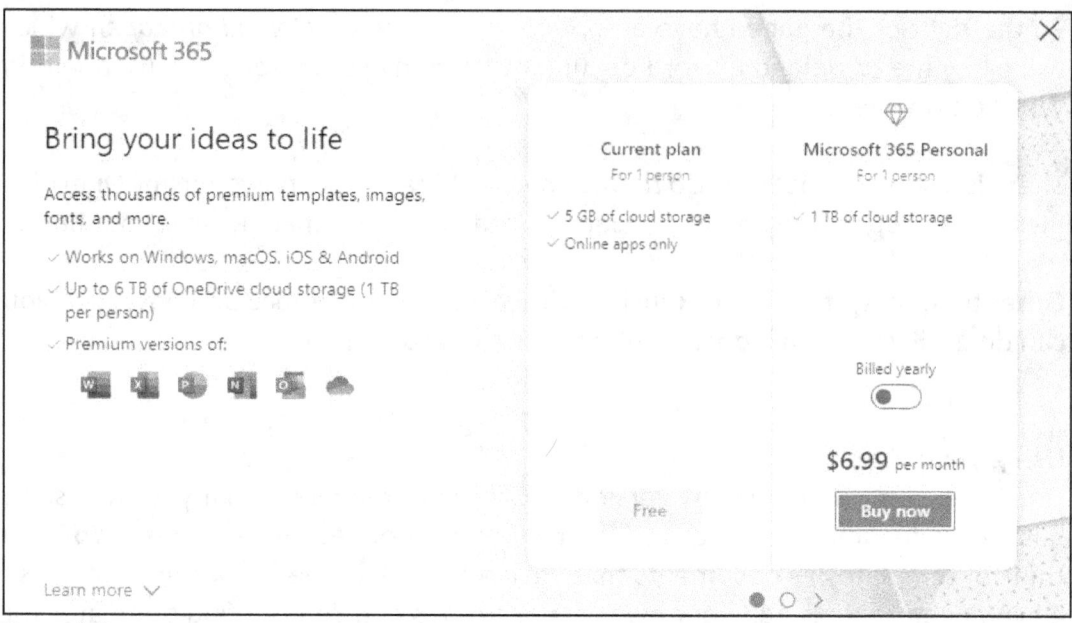

Figure 3.3

If you click on the *More templates* link, you will be shown additional templates that you can select to start your document. I will choose the template named *Chronological Resume* and it will open the template and name it *Document 1* since it's the first document I have worked on since going into Word. If you look at the top of figure 3.4 you will see the name Document 1 and also that it says it's saved to OneDrive.

If I wanted to rename the document from Document 1 or change its saved location within my OneDrive storage drive then all I would need to do is click on this section of the title bar and change the file name and\or its location as seen in figure 3.5.

Chapter 3 – Word

Figure 3.4

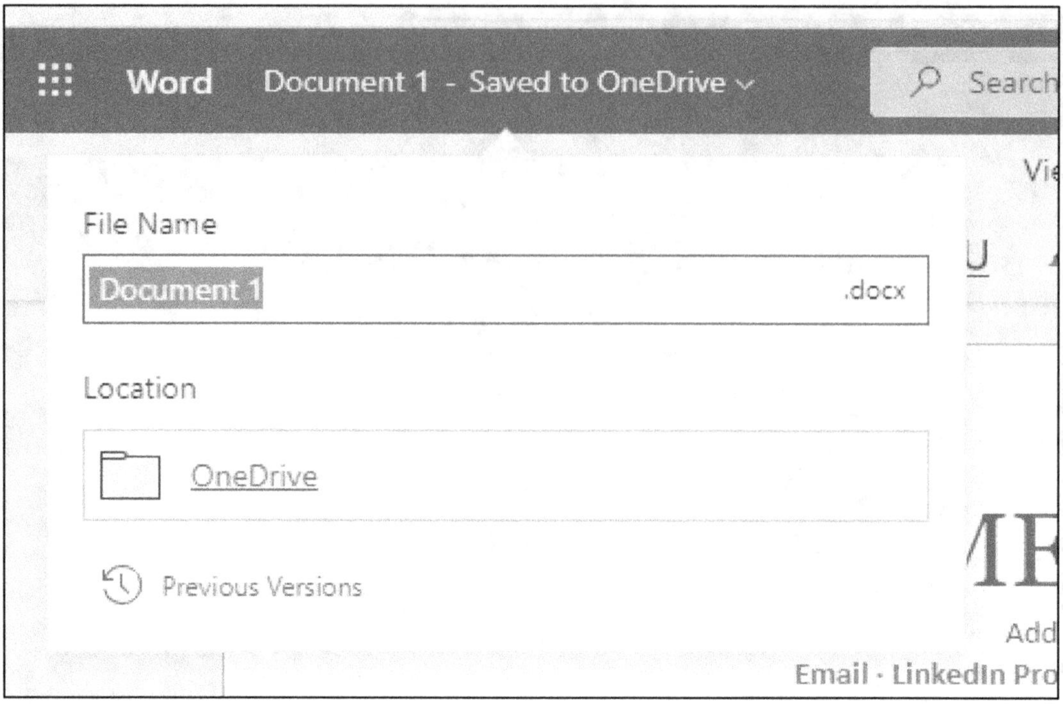

Chapter 3 – Word

Figure 3.5

If you take a closer look at figure 3.4, you can see that this resume template has all the formatting and text added and all I would need to do is change the text to match the information related to what would be on my resume. I can also change the font styles, sizes and colors if I want to change the overall look of the document.

If I don't want to use a template and simply create my own document from scratch then I can click on the *New blank document +* button within the main Word interface.

Chapter 3 – Word

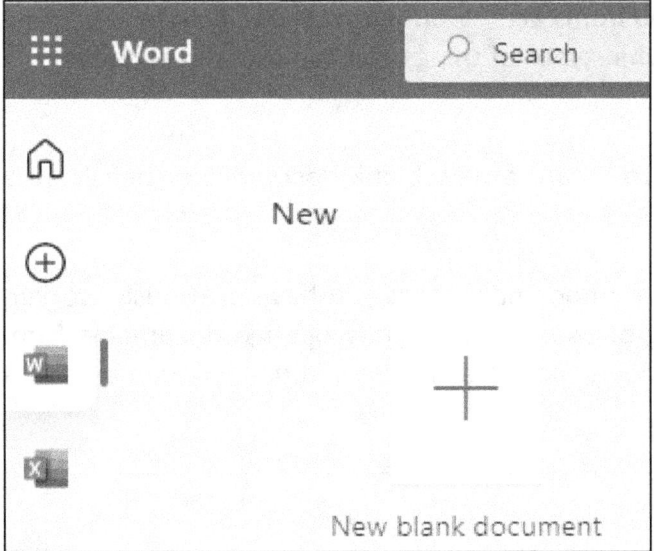

Figure 3.6

Tabs and Ribbon Items

All of the Office apps will have their own tabs (menus) and Ribbon items as well as items that are shared between the apps such as the File tab or Help tab. Figure 3.7 shows which part of the interface I am referring to when I say tab and Ribbon items. The Ribbon is a term used with Office programs referring to the icons\buttons below the text tab items as seen in figure 3.7.

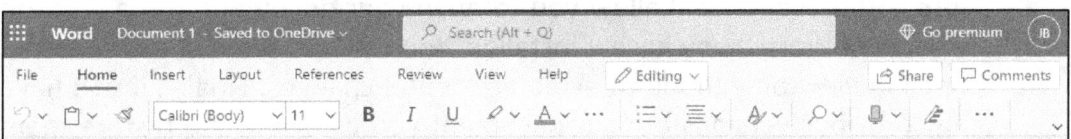

Figure 3.7

 One thing you will notice in figure 3.7 is that there is a tab item named **Table**. This is a special type of menu item that will only appear when you are working on a part of the document that would use this menu. So if I were to click on a table in my document, the Table menu item would appear with various editing options for my table.

45

Chapter 3 – Word

Now that you know what the tab items are, I would now like to go over each one of them to give you an idea of what types of things you can do from each tab.

File Tab

- **New** – This allows you to create a new blank document or one from a template

- **Open** – Here you can open documents that you have previously worked on. You will see a listing of your most recently opened documents from here or you can click on *View more files* to see additional documents that aren't in your Recent list.

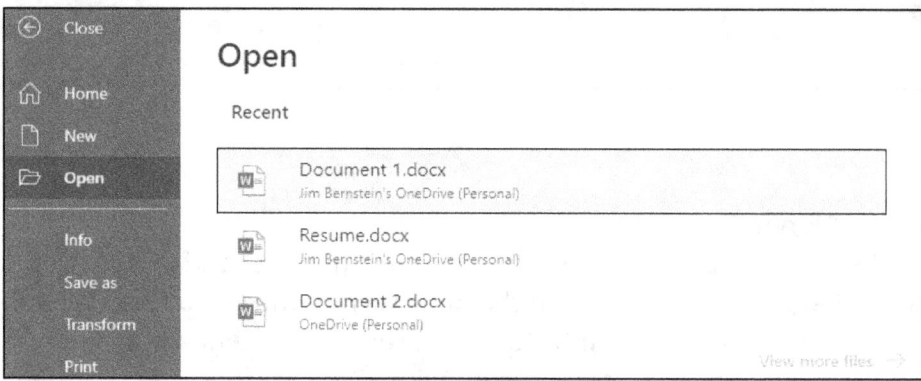
Figure 3.7

- **Info** – This section will allow you to open your document in the desktop version of Word if you have it installed. You can also set your document to open in view-only mode to avoid accidental changes. Finally, if you have any previous versions of your document you can view and restore them from here.

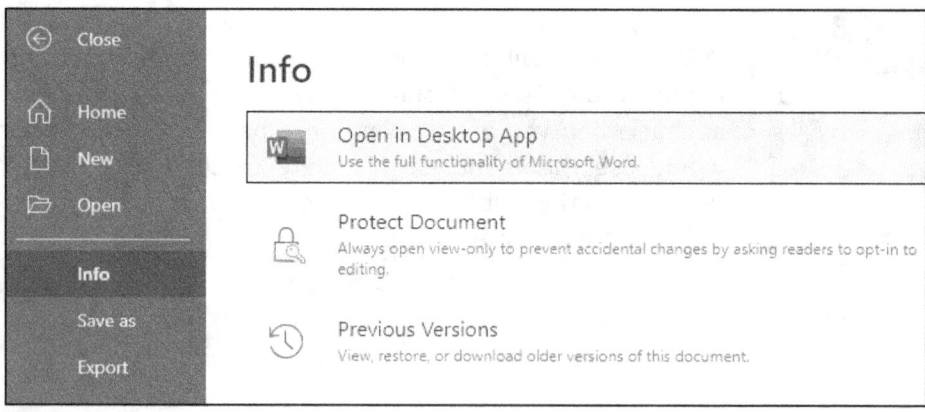
Figure 3.8

Chapter 3 – Word

- **Save As** – If you need to give your document a new name or want to download a copy to your computer you can do so from here. You can also have it converted to a PDF or ODT file and then have the option to download the converted file.

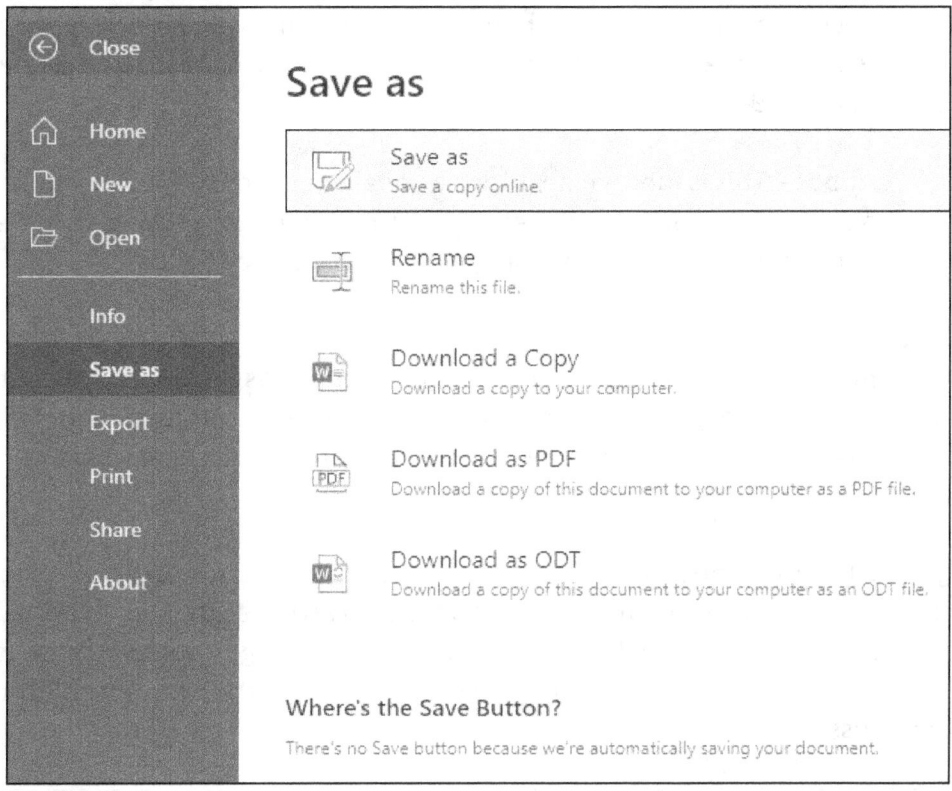

Figure 3.9

 You might have noticed at the bottom of figure 3.9 that it says there is no save button and that is because your changes are saved automatically to your online document as you make them so there is no need to manually click on Save. You can review and restore previously saved versions of your documents if you need to go back to an older version before you made a change.

- **Export** – You can use this option to export your document to a multi slide PowerPoint presentation. How well this works will depend on the document you are exporting.

- **Print** – You will most likely want to print your documents at some point and here is where you can go to configure your printing options and print your document. More on printing in Chapter 9.

- **Share** – One of the main reasons for using online applications for your documents is so you can share them with others or have others open and make changes to your documents as well. Sharing will also be covered in Chapter 9.

- **About** – This is more of an informational area and will give you information about things such as the version of the app you are using and the terms and conditions you are abiding by in order to use the app.

Home Tab

The Home tab is most likely where you will spend most of your time, hence the name Home. Here is where you will find most of your text and paragraph formatting tools. Figure 3.10 shows the buttons on the Ribbon that are part of the Home group.

Figure 3.11 shows the same tab but expanded to give you more of a graphical look. You can expand the Ribbon by clicking on the up arrow at the very right hand side of the Ribbon itself for any tab that you are in. I am going to stick with the compact view since it will be easier for you to see what buttons\icons I am referring to in our discussion.

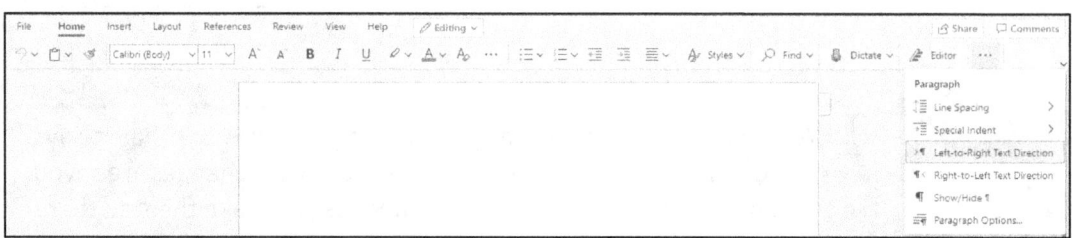
Figure 3.10

Figure 3.11

Now I will go over the items under the Home tab in groups since many of these items are related and in the same general category. I will be going from left to right in regards to the button order.

Chapter 3 – Word

Undo\Redo, Clipboard and Format Painter

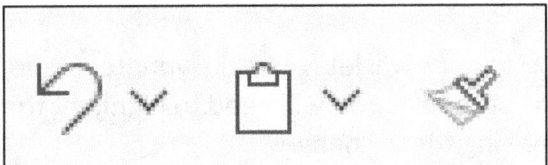

Figure 3.12

- **Undo\Redo** – If you make a change and then want to revert it you can click the Undo button. If you undo a change and then change your mind you can then click the Redo button.

- **Clipboard** – The clipboard is where text and images are temporarily stored when you copy them in a document. Here you can cut, copy or paste your items within your document.

- **Format Painter** – This tool can be used to apply formatting from existing text to some other text within your document. For example, if you have some text that uses a particular font and is also bold and red you can highlight that text, click the Format Painter button and then highlight some other text and it will apply that same formatting to your other text all at once.

Text Formatting

Figure 3.13

- **Font and size** – Here you can select one of the available fonts to use with your text and also choose or type in the size you want to text to be.

49

- **Increase and decrease font size** – Clicking the up or down **A** buttons will increase or decrease the font\text size incrementally.

- **Bold, italics and underline** – These options will let you make your text bold, italicized, or put an underline under the text. You will need to highlight the text you wish to change before making these changes.

- **Highlighter** – This tool acts just like a highlighter pen would if you were using it on a printed copy. You can change the highlighter color as well if you don't like the default yellow.

- **Text color** – The default text color is black but that can be changed from here. Once again, you need to highlight the text you wish to change before using this tool.

- **Clear formatting** – If you have made formatting changes to your text and want to revert it back to the default formatting then you can highlight that text and click on this button.

- **More font options** – Clicking the three horizontal dots (ellipsis) will give you some additional text formatting options such as adding a strikethrough effect, using subscript and superscript and giving you the ability to change the case of your text to all upper case, all lower case and so on.

<u>Lists and Alignment</u>

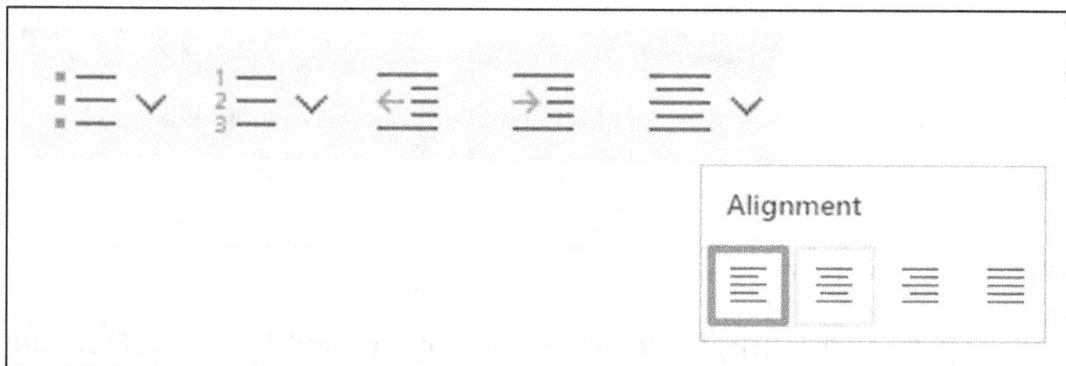

Figure 3.14

- **Bulleted list** – Bulleted lists are used to organize your text so it's easier to read and group lists together. I am using a bulleted list in this section of the chapter.

- **Numbered list** – This is similar to a bulleted list except you are using numbers or Roman numerals rather than bullet icons. Figure 3.15 shows that you can choose other styles of bullets and numbers for your lists besides the defaults by clicking the down arrow next to the type of list you wish to create.

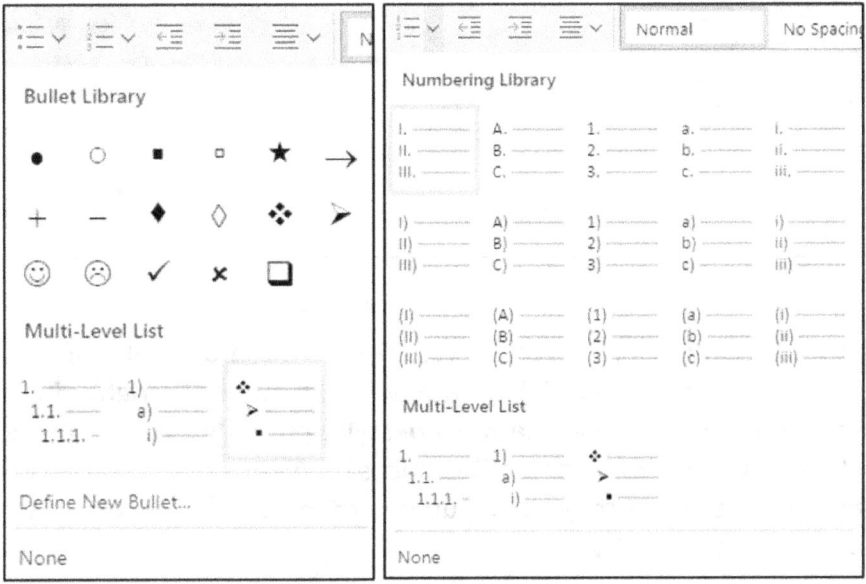

Figure 3.15

- **Indent left or right** – Use these options to indent a line or paragraph to the left or the right. Just be sure that either the paragraph you want to indent is highlighted or the cursor is in front of the paragraph itself.

- **Paragraph alignment** – Here you can adjust the text in your paragraphs to be left aligned, centered, right aligned or justified.

Text Styles

Figure 3.16

Figure 3.16 shows the available text styles that you can use with Office and you can see all of them when you click on the down arrow to the right of Heading 3. For the most part you will use the *Normal* style, but I always like to use the *No Spacing* style myself because I don't like spaces between my sentences. If you plan on creating an outline from your document then you should use the Heading styles, so it displays correctly.

Find, Dictate, Editor and Additional Options

Figure 3.17

- **Find** – This should be pretty self-explanatory but if you are looking for a certain word or phrase within your document you can search for it from here.

- **Replace** – Here you can search for words or phrases and then replace them with a different word or phrase. For example, if I want to change all instances of the name Joe to Joseph I would just type it in and then click

Chapter 3 – Word

on *Replace All* otherwise it will just replace the first one it finds rather than all 3.

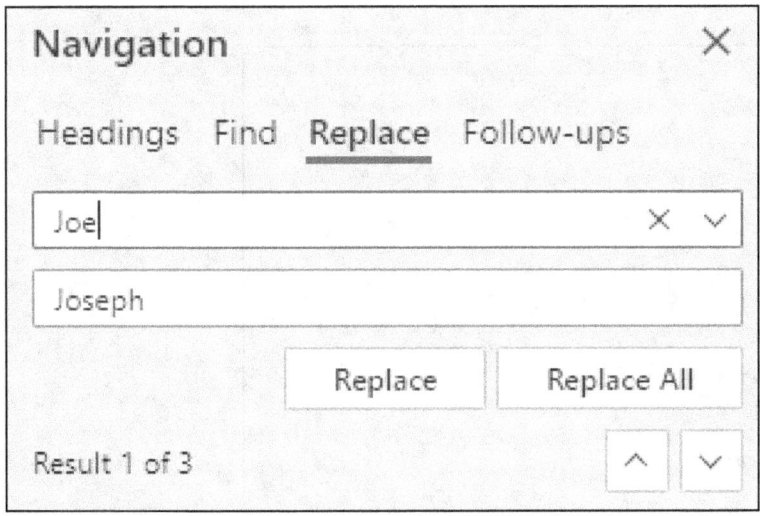
Figure 3.18

- **Dictate** – If you have a microphone attached to your computer then you can use this option to talk into it and have Word translate your speech into text. The first time you use this feature it will ask you for permission to use your microphone so you will need to click on *Allow*.

Figure 3.19

- **Transcribe** – Using this feature you can have Word convert speech to a text transcript with each speaker individually separated. As of this writing, the transcribe feature is only active if you use one of the paid versions of Office.

- **Editor** – Here is where you can check your document for spelling and grammar mistakes. By default, Word will underline spelling errors in red and grammar errors in blue so you can see them as you are working. But if you want a summary of your "mistakes" and want to have your entire document checked at once then you can use this option. Of course the paid-for versions have additional proofing features if you need them.

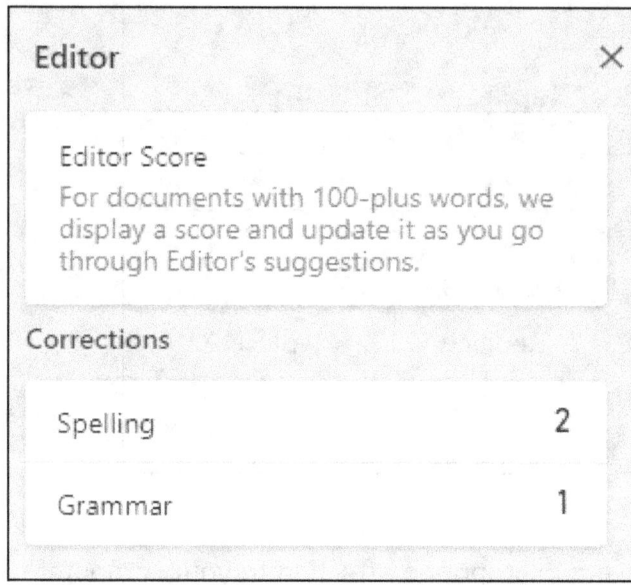

Figure 3.20

- **Additional options** – Figure 3.21 shows some additional options you have when you click on the ellipsis next to the Editor button. From here you can do things such as configure custom line spacing between your sentences as well as custom indents such as indent the first line only.

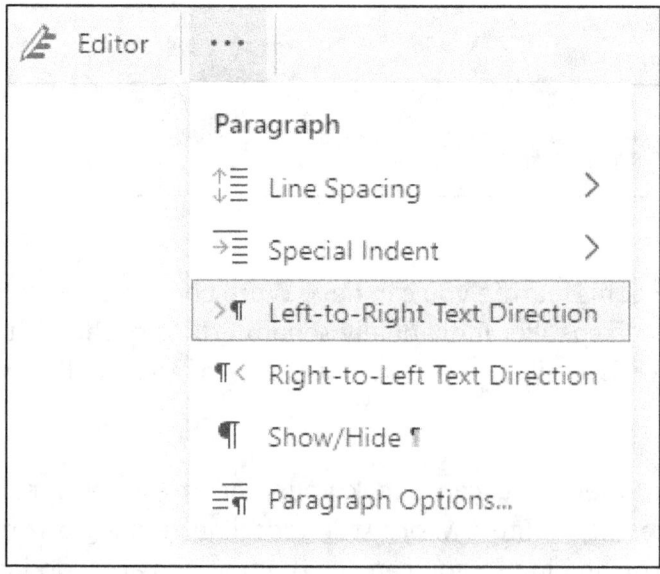

Figure 3.21

You can also change the text direction from the default left to right to right to left if you ever need to do so. The Paragraph Options settings might come in handy if you need to customize the way your paragraphs look in regards to alignment, indentation and spacing.

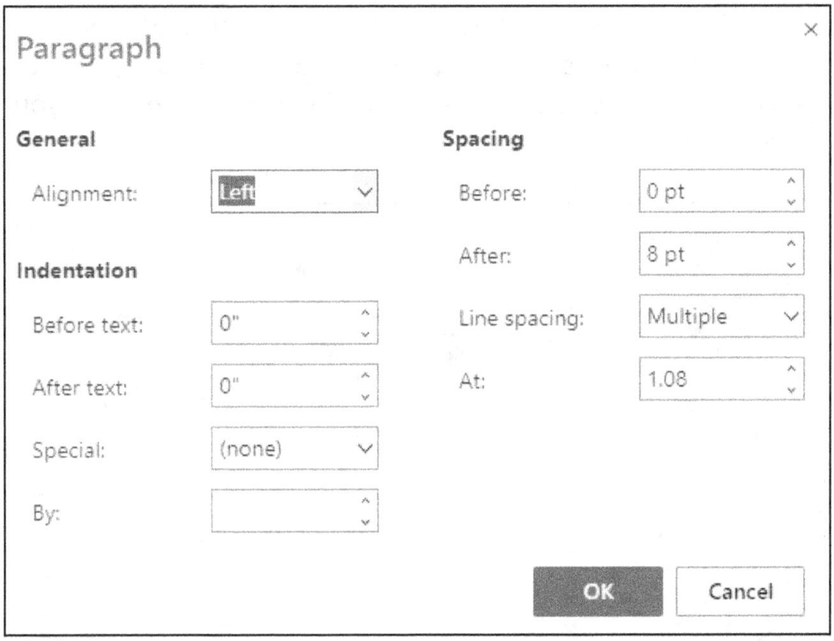

![Paragraph dialog box]

Figure 3.22

Insert Tab

The items from the Insert tab are meant to be… inserted into your document so if you are wondering where you would insert a particular object then you should look here first. It should be fairly easy to figure out what each item is used for, but I will now go over all of them individually

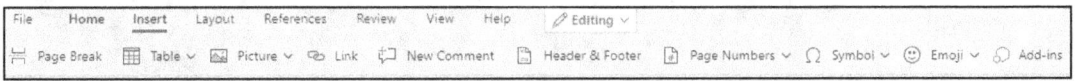

Figure 3.23

Page Break, Tables, Pictures and Links

Figure 3.24

Chapter 3 – Word

- **Page Break** – If you are at the end of a page of content then you can insert a page break to start a new page rather than pressing the enter key a bunch of times to make the cursor start down at a new page.

- **Table** – You can insert tables into your documents to help organize your information in a structured format. You can either choose your table size by dragging your mouse in the grid until you get your size, or you can click on Insert Table and enter the number of columns and rows you wish to have manually.

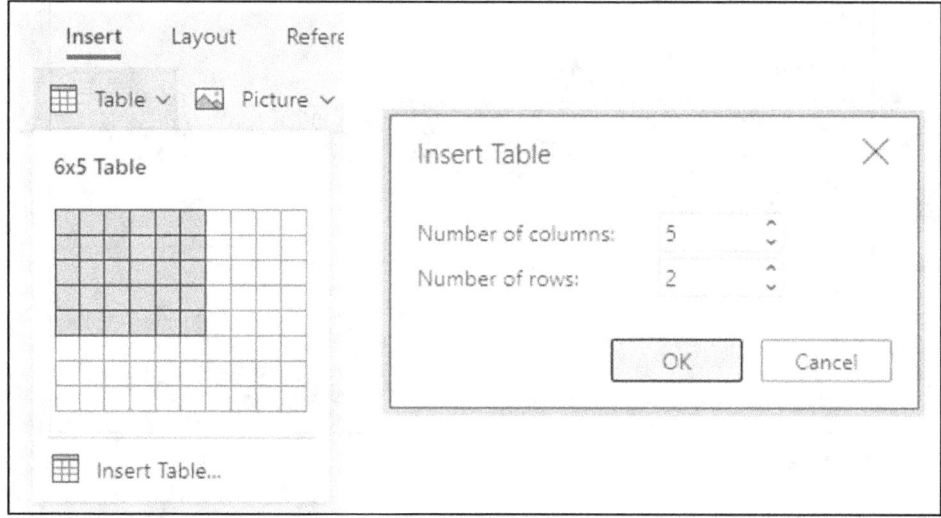

Figure 3.25

Once You have your table in place, you can then start entering information such as text and numbers. You can then format the text the same way you can any other text such as changing fonts, colors or making it bold etc. If you hold your mouse next to one of the edges of a cell until it makes a double-lined pointer, you can then drag your mouse to resize a row or column.

Product 1	Product 2	Product 3	Product 4	Product 5
25	75	23	8	75
12	47	33	5	80
22	48	42	3	68

Figure 3.26

Right clicking on the table will give you additional options such as the ability to add a color to a cell or cells plus insert and delete rows or columns.

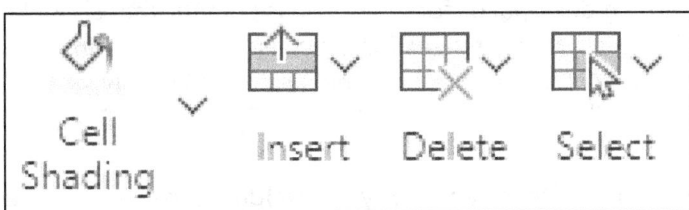

Figure 3.27

- **Picture** – It's common to insert images into your documents and you have a few choices as to where you can insert these images from. If you have a picture on your hard drive you want to add to your document then you would use the option named *This Device*. If you have images in your OneDrive storage repository then you can add those using the *OneDrive* option.

Figure 3.28

The *Stock Images* option will show you images provided by Microsoft that you can use royalty-free, but you will notice that if you are not using the paid-for version of Office, you won't have nearly as many pictures to choose from. Finally, you can search *Bing Pictures* to find images that are available on the internet.

Chapter 3 – Word

If you plan on using images you find on the internet, just be aware that they are most likely owned by other people and you might not have the rights to use them. If you are adding images for something personal or for a school assignment that should be ok. But if you are using images for advertising or marketing purposes then you might be using someone's pictures illegally.

- **Link** – If you would like to have a way to include a particular website in your document then you can add a link that will open a web browser and take you to that page when you click on it. All you need to do is enter the text you want to be displayed on the page in the *Display text* box and then enter the website address in the *Address* box. Figure 3.29 shows this process with the results displayed underneath.

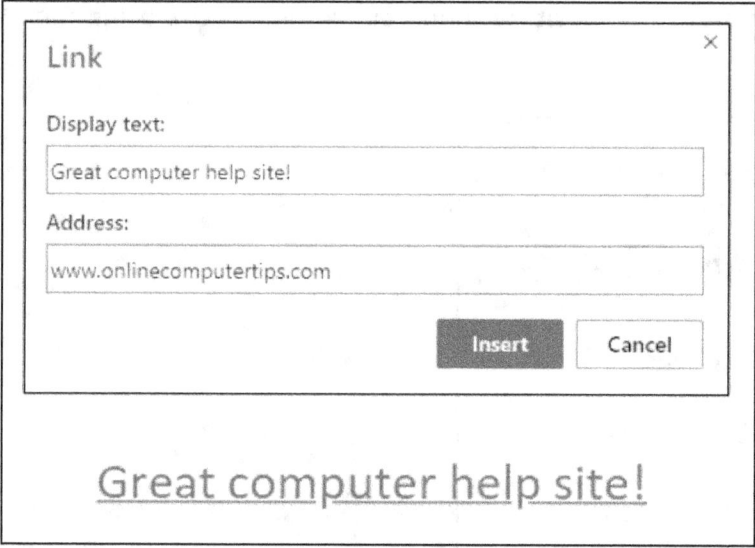

Figure 3.29

Comments

Figure 3.30

Chapter 3 – Word

Comments are used to add notes or changes to your documents so that other people who are accessing the document will be able to see and act on them if needed. To add a comment, highlight the area of the document you wish to comment on and then click on the *New Comment* button.

You will then be given a comment box with your name on it where you can type in some text pertaining to the highlighted area of your document. When you are finished with your comment simply click on the paper airplane send button to have your comment applied to the document.

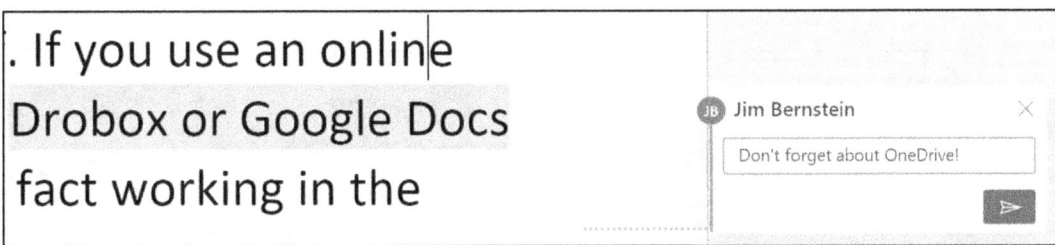
Figure 3.31

Now when your other collaborators open the document they will see a text buttle icon indicating that there is a comment. When they click on it the same area of the document will become highlighted and they will then see the comment. They can then reply to your comment or click the ellipsis to do things such as edit the comment, mark it as resolved or even delete it (depending on their permission level). You can even create a link to the comment that you can share with others that will take them to your document and right to that comment.

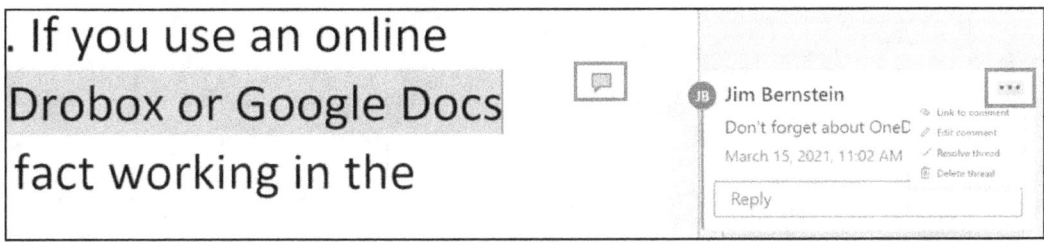
Figure 3.32

Headers, Footers and Page Numbers

Figure 3.33

- **Header & Footer** – You can use headers and footers to add text to the top or bottom of every page for things like chapter titles or document change dates etc.

- **Page Numbers** – If you would like to have your pages sequentially numbered then you can add page numbers and choose what location you would like them to be placed on your page. As you add pages, the page numbers will automatically increase and be added to new pages. The box that says *Include Page Count* checkbox is used if you want to show the total pages such as 5 of 20 and so on.

Figure 3.34

After you add page numbers, footers or headers, you will have an options section on the side of the page where you can adjust their settings.

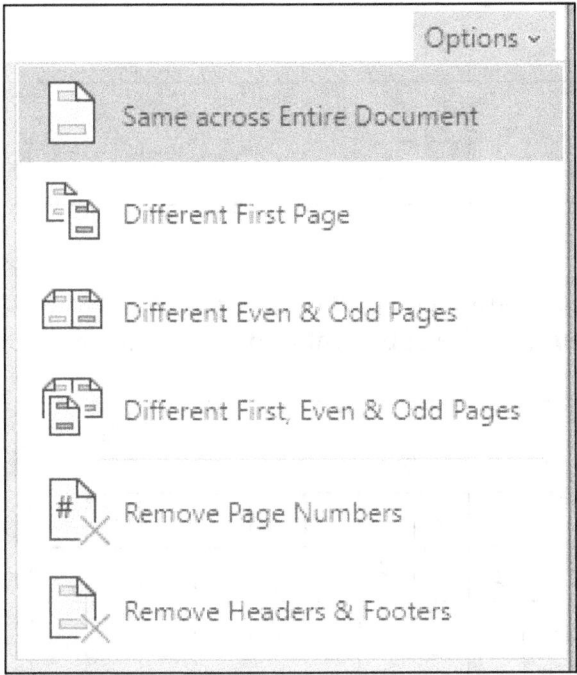

Figure 3.35

To get out of the header view and go back to the normal editing mode you will need to click on the Header & Footer button again. To see how your headers, footers or page numbers will look, you will need to go into *Viewing* mode.

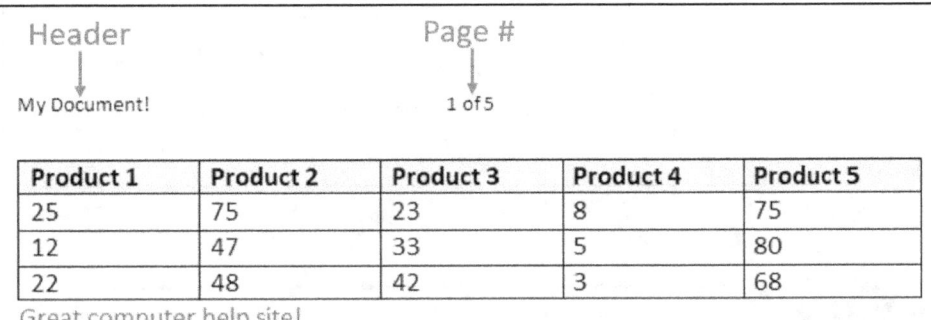

Figure 3.36

Chapter 3 – Word

Symbols, Emojis and Add-ins

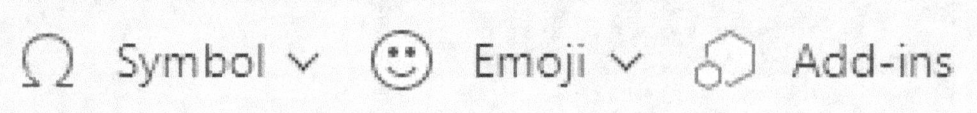

Figure 3.37

- **Symbol** – Symbols are text based characters that you can insert along with your text. Examples would be the copyright and trademark symbols.

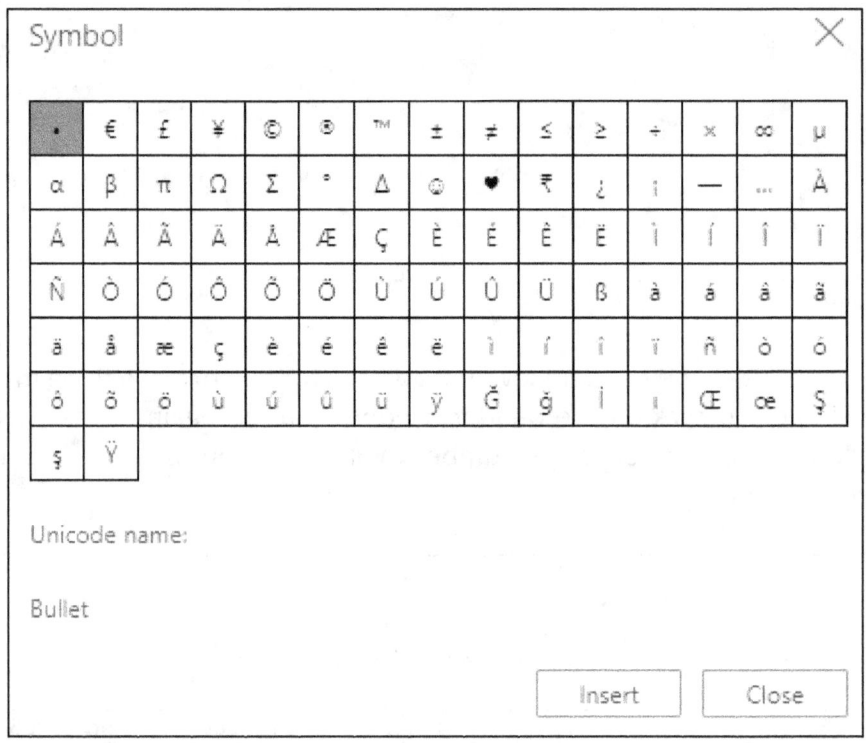

Figure 3.38

 If you are a Microsoft Windows user then you can also use the built in Character Map tool that comes included with Windows to add many more types of symbols to your document. Just type in **character map** in the search box after clicking on the Start button and it should appear in the results.

- **Emoji** – Anyone who has sent a text message knows what an emoji is and if you want to insert some of them into your document, then you can find

Chapter 3 – Word

them here. There are many categories such as smileys, animals and food for example.

- **Add-ins** – These are extra apps or additions to Office that you can install to add extra functionality such as additional proofreading tools or file converters. I will be discussing how to install these add-ins in Chapter 10.

Layout Tab
This tab is where you will find tools that will help you with page layout settings for your document. You always want to be sure you have your overall page appearance correct before sending out any final copies of your document as well as before you print it.

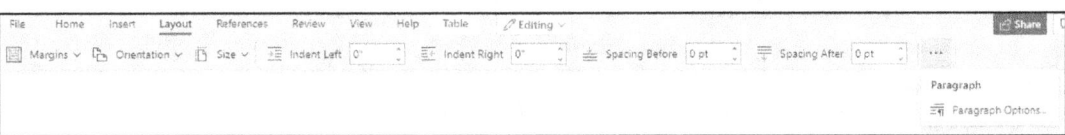
Figure 3.39

Margins, Orientation and Size

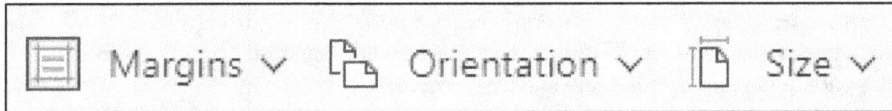
Figure 3.40

- **Margins** – Margins is the amount of unused blank space on the top, bottom, left and right hand side of the page where no text or images can go. By default, Word uses a 1 inch margin on all sides of the page, but you can choose one of the other preconfigured margins or type in your own custom margins if you like.

- **Orientation** – This refers to the positioning of your document page. You can either have it in portrait mode which is upright or vertical or you can use landscape mode which is horizontal. The default is portrait mode.

- **Size** – Word uses a default page size of 8.5" by 11", also referred to as letter size. You can change the paper size to one of the other built in sizes or create your own custom size if needed.

Chapter 3 – Word

Indents

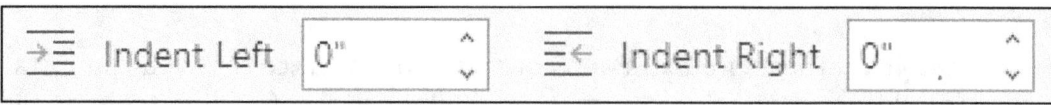
Figure 3.41

Indents are used to move a line or paragraph to the left or right and here you can place your cursor to the left of the paragraph you wish to indent and then either type in a number or click the up or down arrow next to *Indent Left* or *Indent Right* to have your paragraph repositioned. Keep in mind that indent left means starting from the left side of the page, not moving the paragraph to the left.

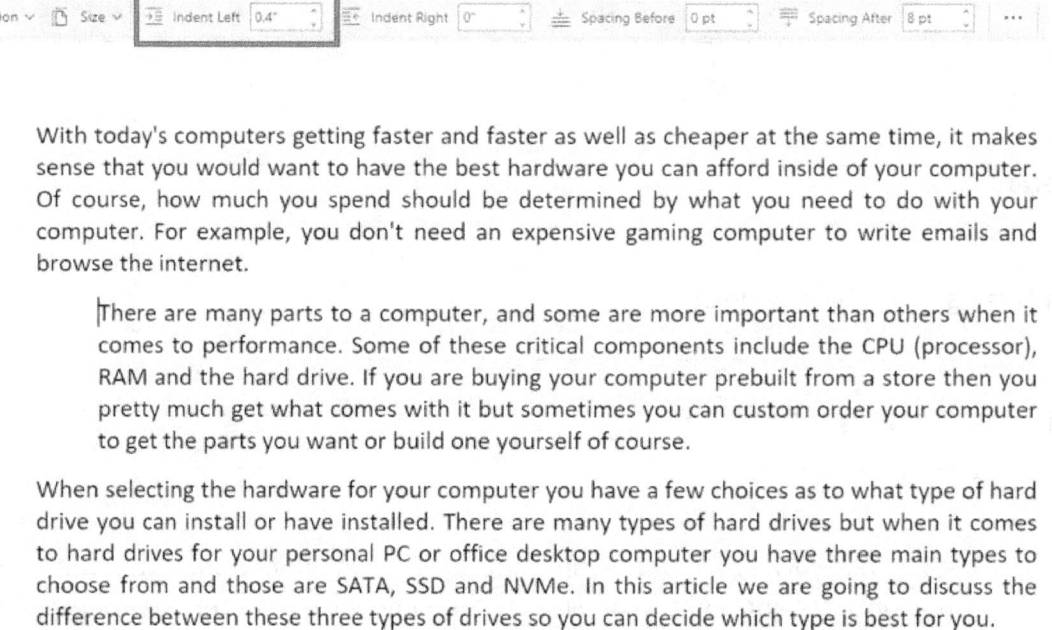
Figure 3.42

Spacing

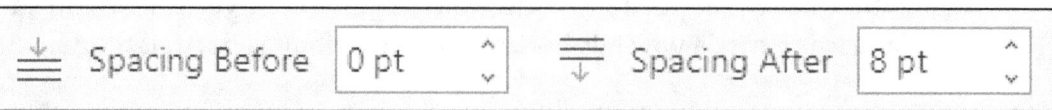
Figure 3.43

Chapter 3 – Word

Spacing determines how much space there is before and after a certain paragraph. If you want to have a paragraph stand out on its own then you can increase the spacing or if you want it closer to the text above or below it then you can decrease the number.

As an example, figure 3.44 shows the middle paragraph with the Spacing Before setting much higher than the Spacing After setting. You can see that there is much more space before the middle paragraph compared to after the paragraph.

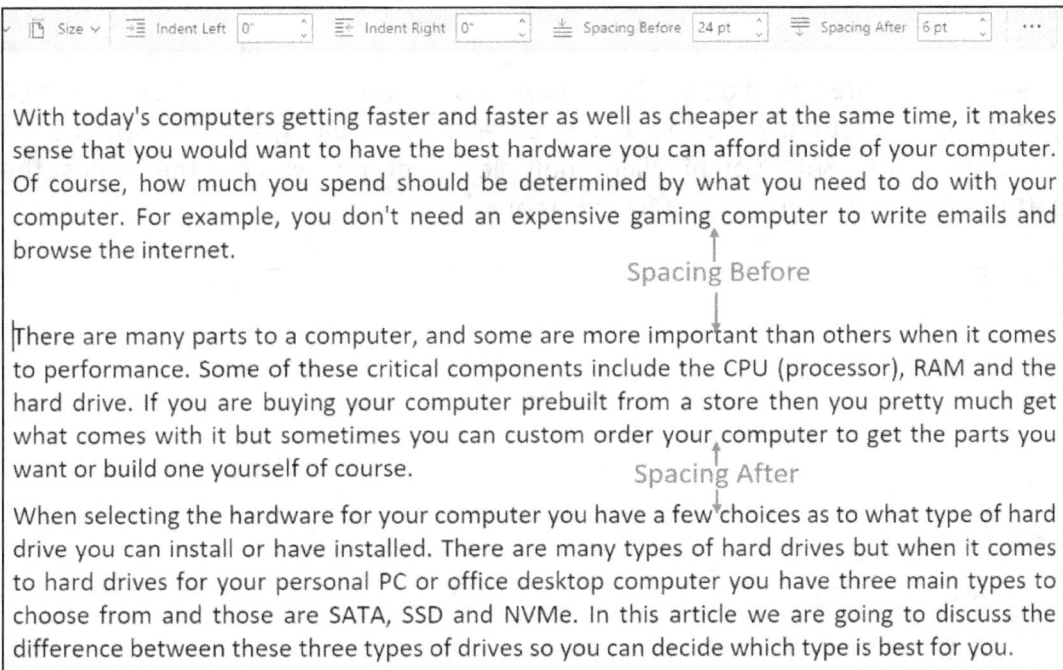

Figure 3.44

Paragraph Options

The last section of the Insert tab can be accessed by clicking on the ellipsis at the end of the Ribbon which will give you a place to edit your paragraph options all from one place as seen in figure 3.46.

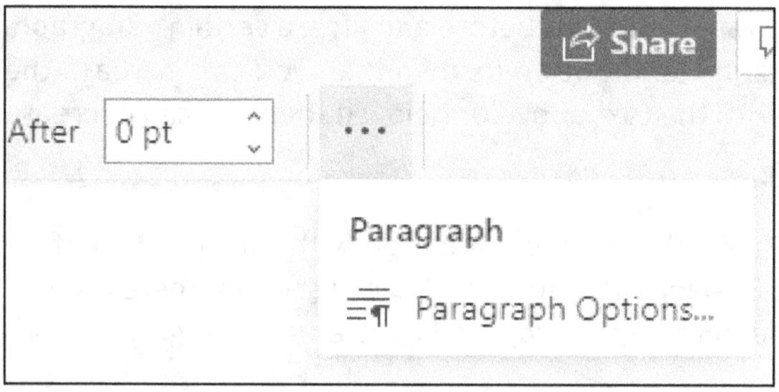

Figure 3.45

These settings are based on the paragraph your cursor is currently placed on so if you change something here and then select a different paragraph, the options will not be the same. But if you highlight multiple paragraphs, you can then adjust the settings for all of them at once from this area.

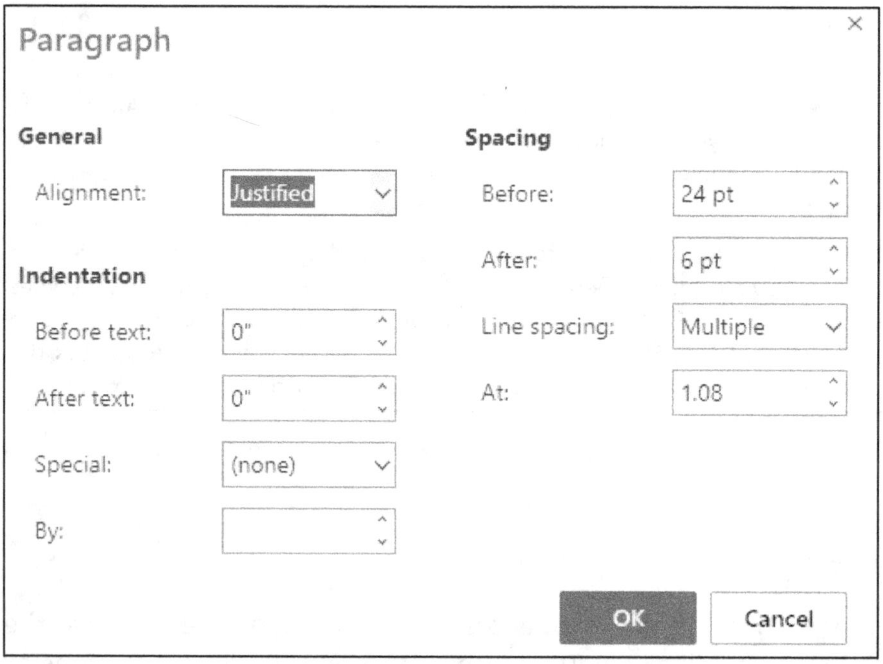

Figure 3.46

References Tab
Depending on the type of document you are creating, you might have the need to cite references or create a table of contents so your readers will be able to navigate to the sections they want to read. There are only a few choices with this tab, but they do come in handy.

Chapter 3 – Word

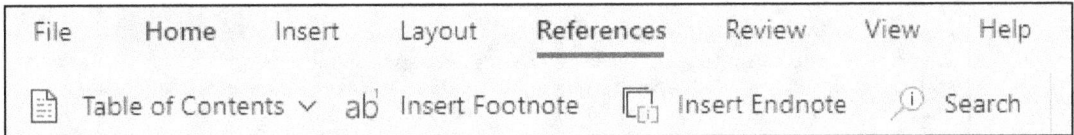

Figure 3.47

- **Table of Contents** – To create a table of contents, you will need to have your text formatted properly using the Heading style as I discussed earlier in the chapter from the Home tab. Word uses text formatted with the Heading style to build the table of contents so if you are not using this style you will get the error shown in figure 3.48.

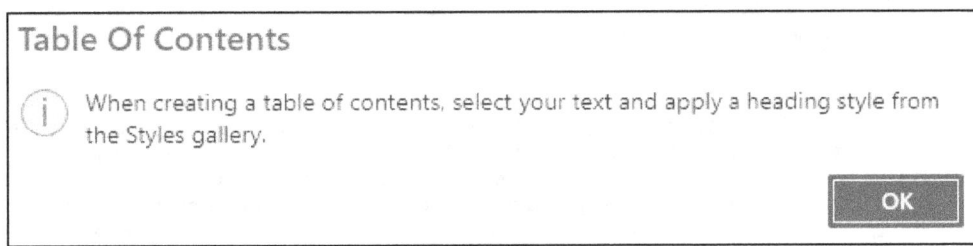

Figure 3.48

Figure 3.49 shows a sample document with some very basic text with the chapter names using the Heading text style.

Chapter 3 – Word

> Chapter 1 – The beginning
> With today's computers getting faster and faster as well as cheaper at the same time, it makes sense that you would want to have the best hardware you can afford inside of your computer. Of course, how much you spend should be determined by what you need to do with your computer. For example, you don't need an expensive gaming computer to write emails and browse the internet.
>
> Chapter 2 – The next part
> With today's computers getting faster and faster as well as cheaper at the same time, it makes sense that you would want to have the best hardware you can afford inside of your computer. Of course, how much you spend should be determined by what you need to do with your computer. For example, you don't need an expensive gaming computer to write emails and browse the internet.
>
> Chapter 3 – The part after that
> With today's computers getting faster and faster as well as cheaper at the same time, it makes sense that you would want to have the best hardware you can afford inside of your computer. Of course, how much you spend should be determined by what you need to do with your computer. For example, you don't need an expensive gaming computer to write emails and browse the internet.
>
> Chapter 4 – One more part
> With today's computers getting faster and faster as well as cheaper at the same time, it makes sense that you would want to have the best hardware you can afford inside of your computer. Of course, how much you spend should be determined by what you need to do with your computer. For example, you don't need an expensive gaming computer to write emails and browse the internet.
>
> Chapter 5 – The last part
> With today's computers getting faster and faster as well as cheaper at the same time, it makes sense that you would want to have the best hardware you can afford inside of your computer. Of course, how much you spend should be determined by what you need to do with your computer. For example, you don't need an expensive gaming computer to write emails and browse the internet.

Figure 3.49

Now I can place my cursor at the beginning of the document where I want my table of contents to be placed and when I click on the Table of Contents button, it will create the table of contents based on my Heading text. All the entries say page 1 because all of my Heading text is actually on page 1, so this won't happen when you try it yourself assuming all of your content is not on one page!

Figure 3.50

- **Insert Footnote** – Footnotes are used to add a note or comment to a particular part of your document as a reference. In figure 3.51 I have placed the cursor at the end of the first paragraph and then I clicked on the Insert Footnote button. Now I can type my comment and there will be a number 1 placed at the spot where my cursor was that matches the number on the footnote at the bottom of the page.

    The *Format Footnotes* button will allow you to change the type and its size in case you are having trouble reading your footnotes.

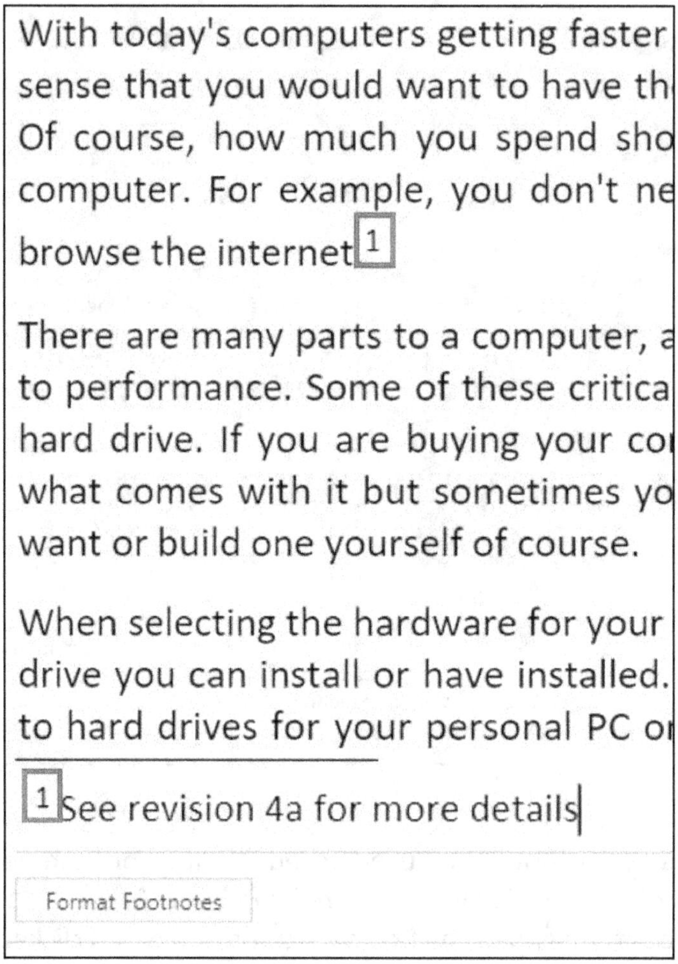

Chapter 3 – Word

> With today's computers getting faster
> sense that you would want to have th
> Of course, how much you spend sho
> computer. For example, you don't ne
> browse the internet[1]
>
> There are many parts to a computer, a
> to performance. Some of these critica
> hard drive. If you are buying your co
> what comes with it but sometimes yo
> want or build one yourself of course.
>
> When selecting the hardware for your
> drive you can install or have installed.
> to hard drives for your personal PC o
> _____
> [1] See revision 4a for more details
>
> Format Footnotes

Figure 3.51

- **Insert Endnote** – Endnotes are similar to footnotes except that footnotes are at the end of a page where endnotes are placed at the end of the document.

- **Search** – You might think that this search function is there to search your document but that is not the case. This is used to search the internet for whatever topic you might want to use in your document. You can then click on the ellipsis and then add the link as a reference in your document. Just be sure to highlight the word or text in your document that you want to be made into the link.

Chapter 3 – Word

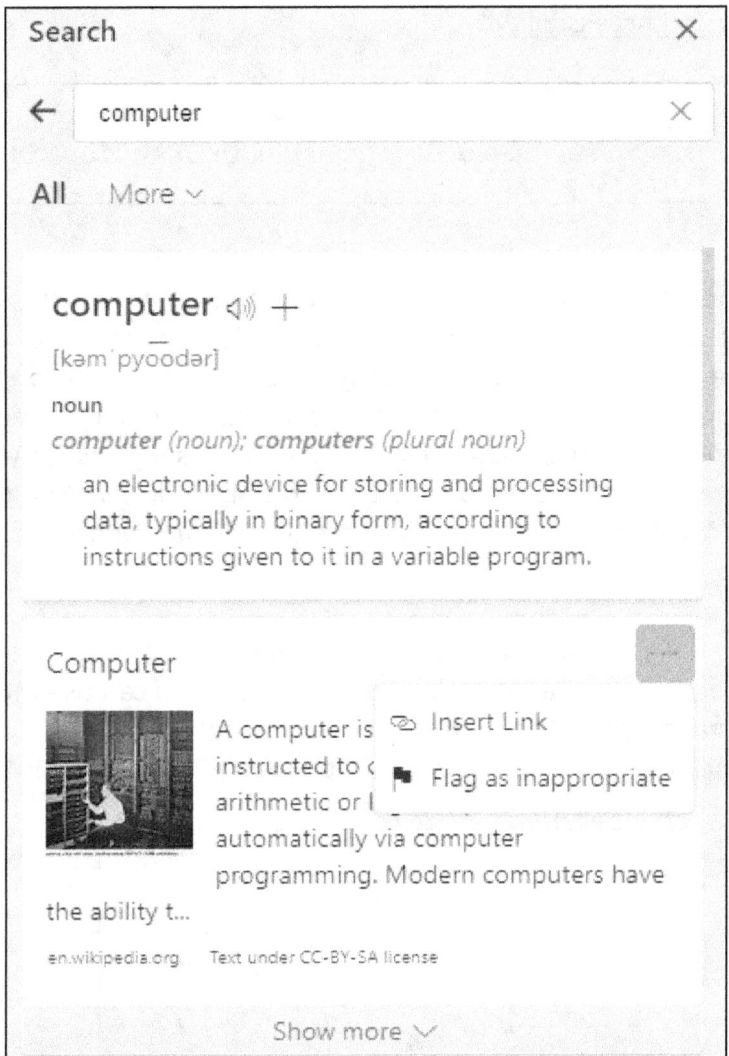
Figure 3.52

Review Tab

The purpose of the tools in this tab are to do things such as help you check your document for errors, keep track of your changes, translate your document to a different language and so on.

Figure 3.53

Chapter 3 – Word

Editor, Word Count and Accessibility

Figure 3.54

- **Editor** – When it comes time to check your document for errors, you will be using the Editor tool to do so. This tool will let you check for spelling and grammar errors and if you are using the paid-for version you will get additional proofreading tools. You can go through your document and accept or ignore any of the changes that the Editor suggests for you. You might remember that the Editor was also on the Home tab. You can also change the Word autocorrect settings from the Editor dropdown arrow on the Ribbon.

- **Word Count** – If you would like to see information such as the number of words, characters or paragraphs in your document you can use this too. If you look down at the bottom left of your document then you will also see a word count that you can review without needing to go into this tool.

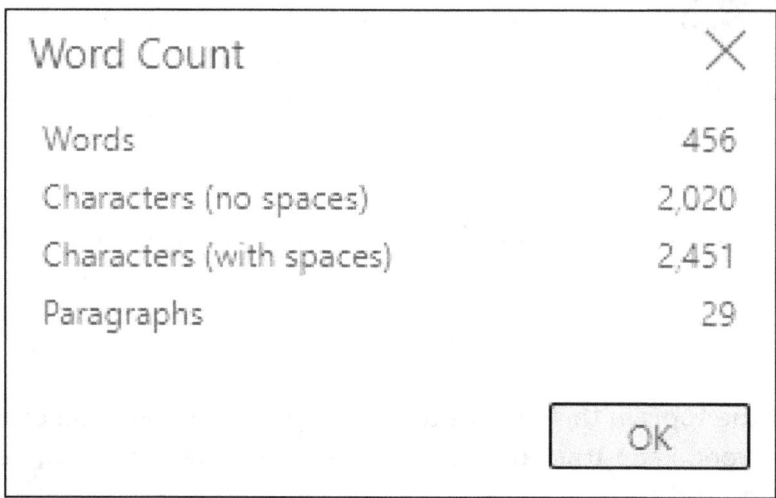
Figure 3.55

Chapter 3 – Word

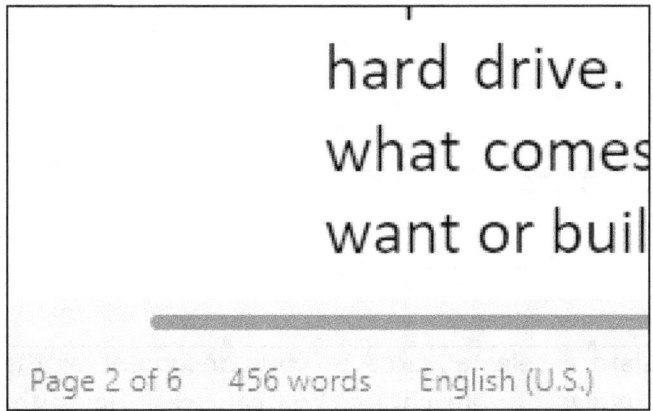
Figure 3.56

- **Check Accessibility** – This will check your document against a set of rules that identify possible issues for people who have disabilities and then offer suggestions on how to fix any potential problems.

Figure 3.57

Translate

Figure 3.58

The translator will translate a selected area of your document or the entire document to another language of your choice. You can scroll down the list of supported languages, choose the one you want, and Word will then do the translation and show you the results. You can then copy the translated text and paste it in wherever it is needed or click on the *Insert* button at the bottom of the translated text to have it inserted directly into your document.

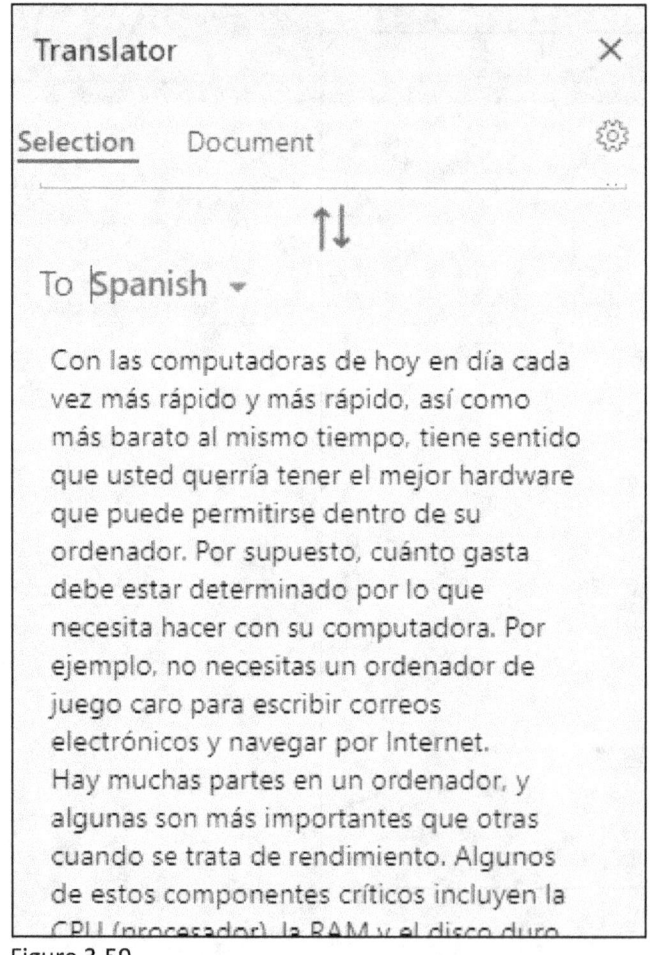

Figure 3.59

Chapter 3 – Word

Show Comments

Figure 3.60

I discussed comments earlier in the chapter but from this section of the Review tab, you can do things such as add a comment, delete a comment (after you select it), browse through the comments with the next and previous buttons or have all of the comments shown with the *Show Comments* button.

Track Changes

Figure 3.61

The *Track Changes* feature will let you keep a record of changes (amendments) that have been made to a document and is used when you have several people working on the same document. You can then choose to accept or reject these changes. You can use the previous and next buttons to cycle through all of the changes made to your document. You can also choose to track changes that only you make or track changes for everyone from the drop down menu next to the Track Changes button. More about tracking changes in Chapter 10.

View Tab

The View tab is where you can go to change how you view your document on your computer. You can also do perform some of the same functions here as with other tabs such as add headers & footers, footnotes and endnotes.

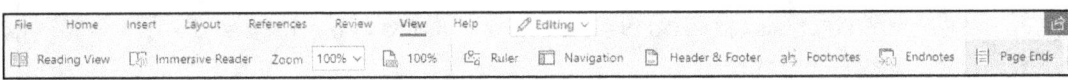
Figure 3.62

Chapter 3 – Word

Reading View and Immersive Reader

Figure 3.63

- **Reading View** – This will let you see your document in a view similar to how it would be printed or how someone who only has view permissions would see it. Once you click on this view, the Ribbon changes and you will have some additional options as seen in figure 3.64. To go back to editing mode you will need to click on the *Edit Document* button.

Figure 3.64

- **Immersive Reader** – This feature will allow you to have your document read to you by your computer. It will also highlight the text it is reading as it is reading it to you. You can click the speaker\gear icon by the play button to change the voice from female to male and also adjust the speed of how fast it reads your document back to you.

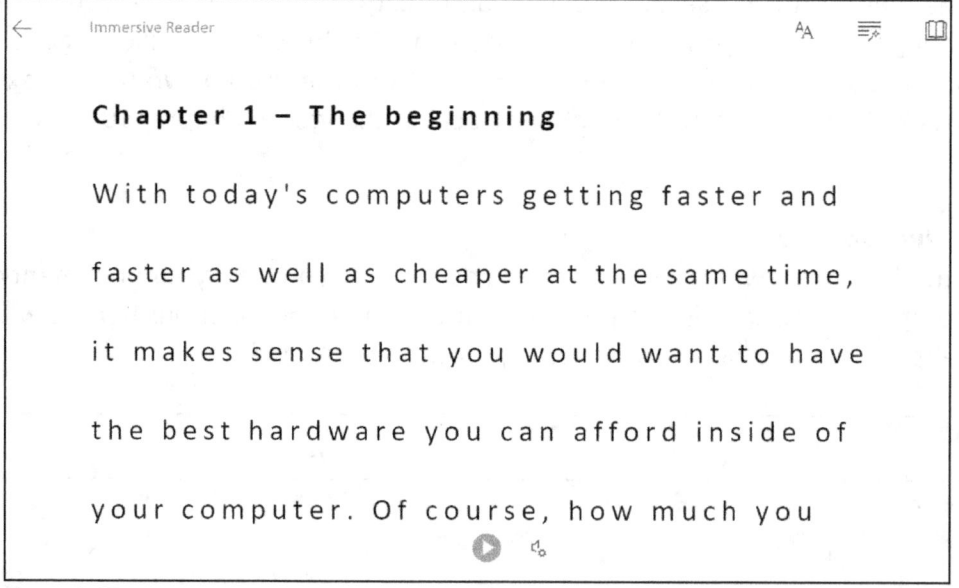
Figure 3.65

Chapter 3 – Word

You can also change things such as the text size, font and colors to make things easier to see as well as some additional options. To go back to edition mode, simply click on the left arrow at the top left of the screen.

Zoom

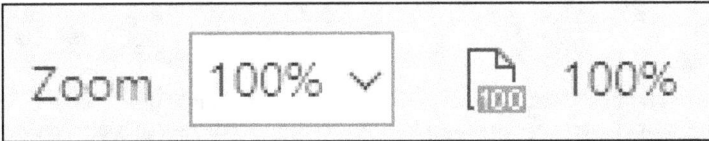
Figure 3.66

The Zoom section should be self-explanatory. You can choose a zoom level for your document on the screen by choosing one of the built in levels or type in a specific zoom level of your own. You can also click on the 100% button at any time to go back to the default zoom level.

At the bottom right corner of the screen there is also a zoom level where you can click on the + or – to adjust the size of the page on your screen.

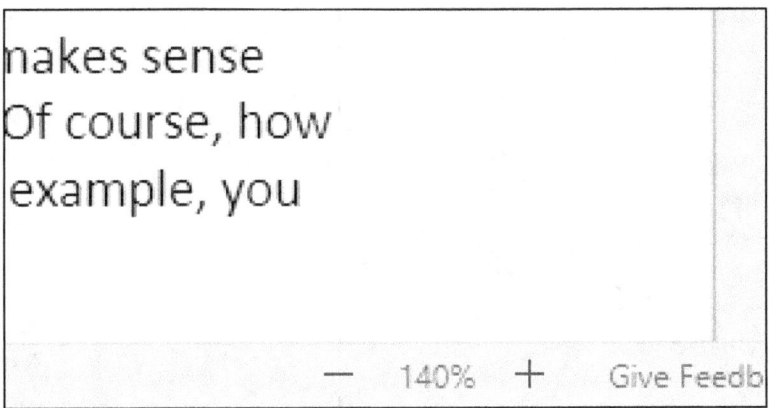
Figure 3.67

Ruler and Navigation

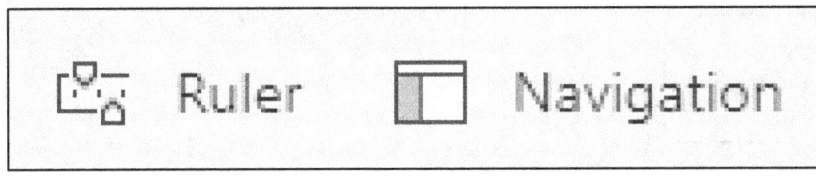
Figure 3.68

Chapter 3 – Word

- **Ruler** – If you need an on screen ruler to help you with the sizing of your text and images you can add one by clicking on this button. The ruler will then be placed at the top of your document and you will have markers for your margins and also for indents if you are using them.

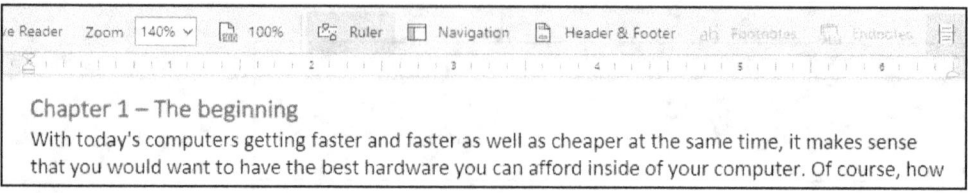

Figure 3.69

- **Navigation** – Clicking on this button will open up the Navigation pane where you can view any heading text you might have as well as allow you to search your document or perform find and replace tasks.

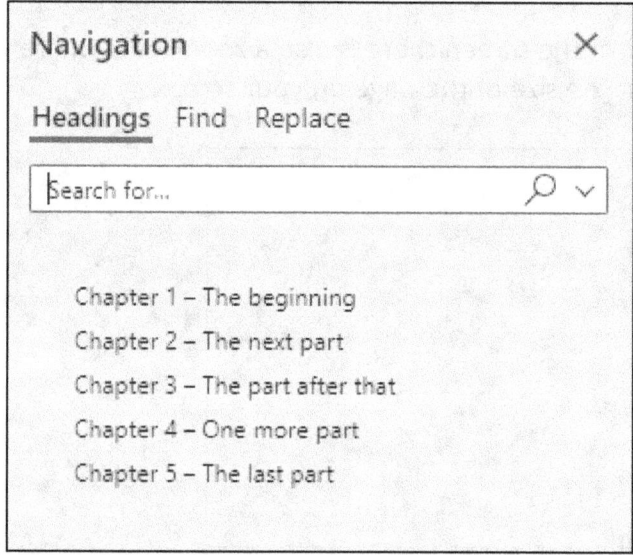

Figure 3.70

Page Ends

Figure 3.71

When in editing mode, it might not be that easy to see where your page breaks are, so you know what content is on what page. If you click on the Page Ends button it will show you where one page ends and the next begins by adding a line through the page at the page break. It will also show the page number and give you an option to adjust your headers or footers by clicking on the corresponding item. Figure 3.72 shows a document with Page Ends turned off and figure 3.73 shows the same document with Page Ends turned on.

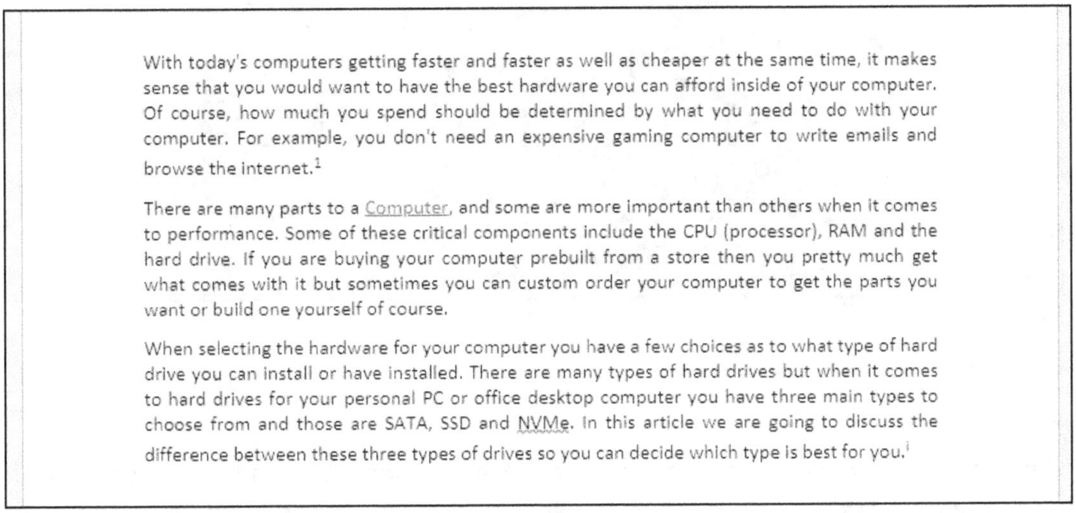
With today's computers getting faster and faster as well as cheaper at the same time, it makes sense that you would want to have the best hardware you can afford inside of your computer. Of course, how much you spend should be determined by what you need to do with your computer. For example, you don't need an expensive gaming computer to write emails and browse the internet.[1]

There are many parts to a Computer, and some are more important than others when it comes to performance. Some of these critical components include the CPU (processor), RAM and the hard drive. If you are buying your computer prebuilt from a store then you pretty much get what comes with it but sometimes you can custom order your computer to get the parts you want or build one yourself of course.

When selecting the hardware for your computer you have a few choices as to what type of hard drive you can install or have installed. There are many types of hard drives but when it comes to hard drives for your personal PC or office desktop computer you have three main types to choose from and those are SATA, SSD and NVMe. In this article we are going to discuss the difference between these three types of drives so you can decide which type is best for you.[i]

Figure 3.72

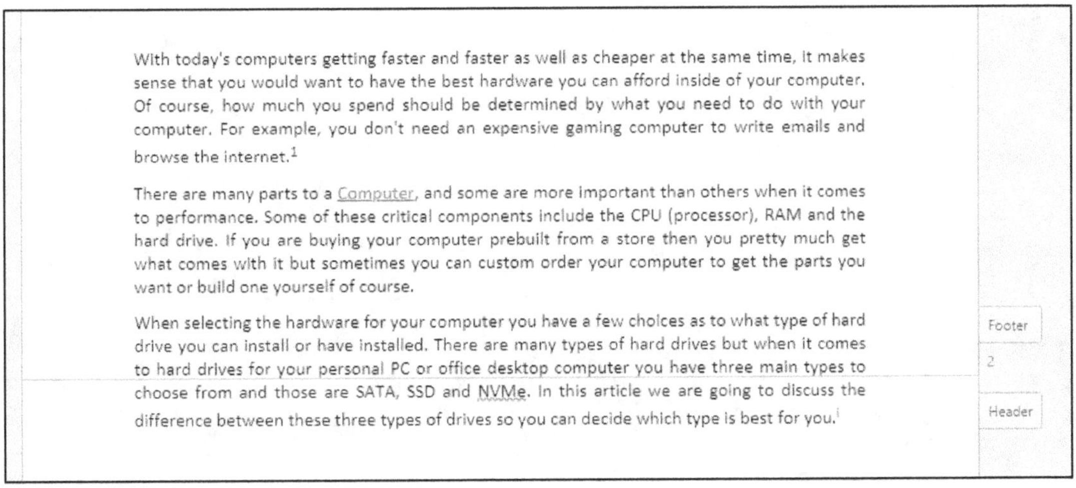
With today's computers getting faster and faster as well as cheaper at the same time, it makes sense that you would want to have the best hardware you can afford inside of your computer. Of course, how much you spend should be determined by what you need to do with your computer. For example, you don't need an expensive gaming computer to write emails and browse the internet.[1]

There are many parts to a Computer, and some are more important than others when it comes to performance. Some of these critical components include the CPU (processor), RAM and the hard drive. If you are buying your computer prebuilt from a store then you pretty much get what comes with it but sometimes you can custom order your computer to get the parts you want or build one yourself of course.

When selecting the hardware for your computer you have a few choices as to what type of hard drive you can install or have installed. There are many types of hard drives but when it comes to hard drives for your personal PC or office desktop computer you have three main types to choose from and those are SATA, SSD and NVMe. In this article we are going to discuss the difference between these three types of drives so you can decide which type is best for you.[i]

Figure 3.73

Chapter 3 – Word

Picture Tab

When you have images inserted into your document and then you select one of them you will then get a Picture tab that includes options to edit and format your picture.

Figure 3.74

Styles

Here you can choose from a variety of different styles that can be applied to your picture with just one click of your mouse button. If you choose one and don't like it simply undo your selection or click on another one.

Chapter 3 – Word

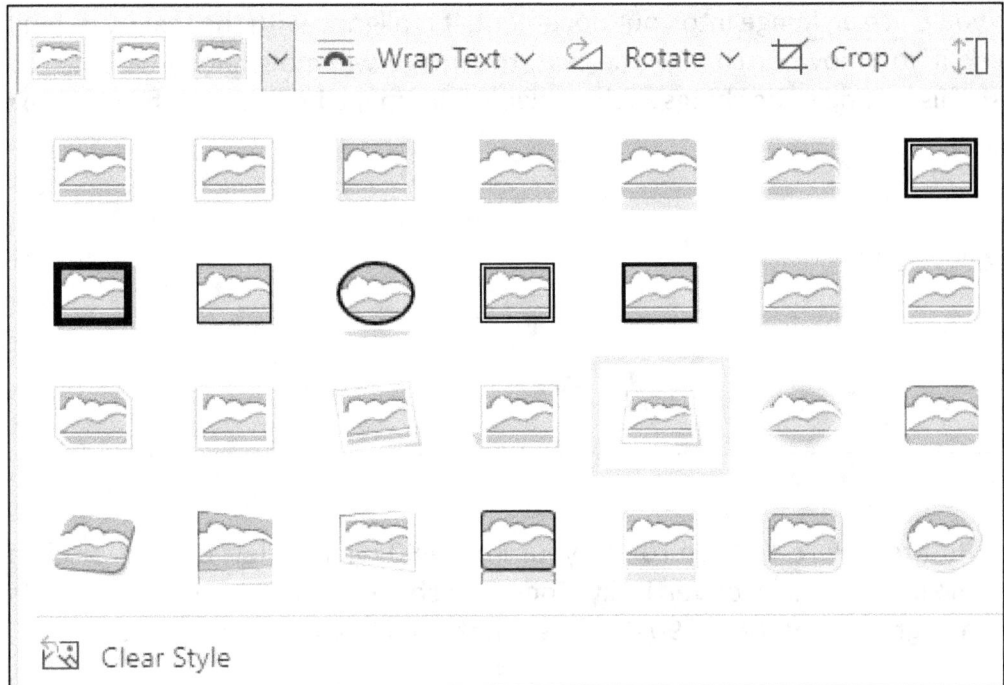

Figure 3.75

Wrap Text

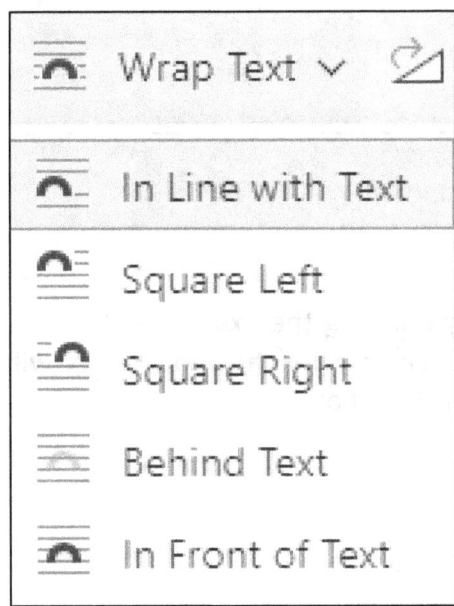

Figure 3.76

Chapter 3 – Word

When you place an image into your document, it is aligned with the text by default meaning if you move or change the text, the image will move along with it. You can use this setting to do things such as place your image behind or in front of text if desired.

Rotate and Crop

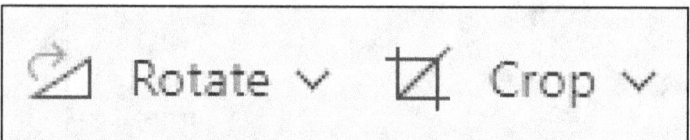
Figure 3.77

- **Rotate** – Here you can rotate your image 90 degrees left or right or even flip it horizontally or vertically. There is also an option to manually enter in a degree of rotation if 90 degrees is not what you are looking for.

- **Crop** – This will let you crop your image to remove any part of it that you don't want to be shown. Once you select crop, all you need to do is drag the black lines that appear to crop out the section of your image you don't need.

Height and Width

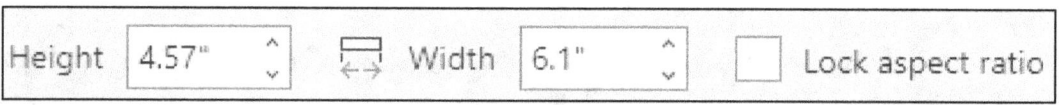
Figure 3.78

This setting allows you to resize your image by entering the exact size that you wish your image to be. If you check the *Lock aspect ratio* box then your image will be kept proportional, otherwise it might look stretched out.

Alt Text

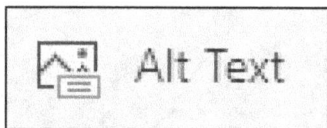
Figure 3.79

Chapter 3 – Word

Alt Text is used for people with visual impairments so they can get a better idea of what they are looking at in regards to images. When someone uses a screen reader to view documents, they will hear the Alt Text that you have added to your picture.

Basic Document Editing
Now that you have an understanding of what all the tabs and Ribbon items do, it's time to start a new document and get some text and images in place and see what we can come up with.

There isn't much to using Word when it comes to composing the types of documents that most of us will be creating. It's really just a matter of choosing your page size, margins, font and then typing in your text. Of course you can always adjust your formatting settings after you have already completed your document or any time in between.

Once you click on the *New Document* icon or go to the File tab and click on *New* you will be presented with a blank document with all of the default configuration settings in place. If you are planning on using different settings, you might want to change them first, especially if you plan on using a different font than the default.

Once you change the font, Word will keep using that font until you change it again. So if you work on your document and then decide you want to use a different font you will need to go back and change it for the entire document which isn't really a big deal if that's the case.

But if you decide that you want to change the style after the fact then you might be looking at a little extra work. For example, if you create a document using the default Normal style and then decide that you want to use the No Spacing style and highlight all your text and change it, it will wipe out some of your formatting settings such as font changes or bold text for example.

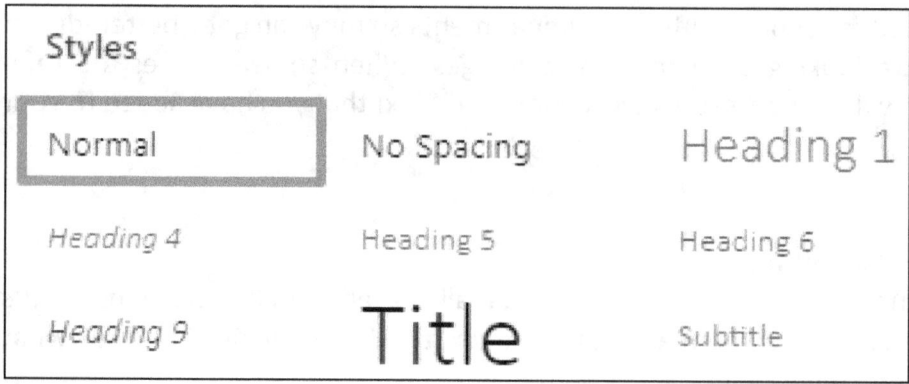
Figure 3.80

If you decide to change your margins after working on your document for a while then you should go back and see how it affected any of your paragraph alignment or if it moved text or images to a page that you don't want it to be on.

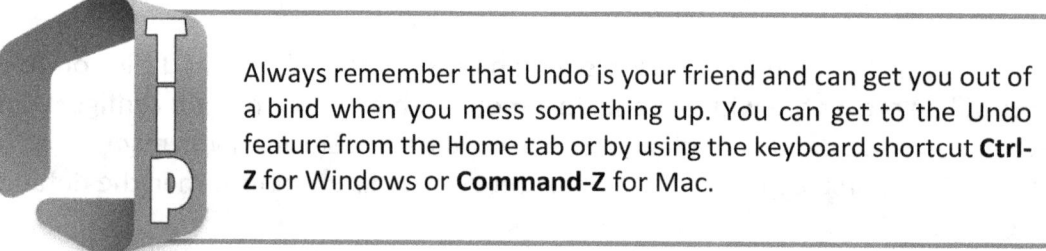

Always remember that Undo is your friend and can get you out of a bind when you mess something up. You can get to the Undo feature from the Home tab or by using the keyboard shortcut **Ctrl-Z** for Windows or **Command-Z** for Mac.

Also remember that if you want some text or an image to start on a new page you can insert a page break from the Insert tab because you don't want to press the enter key a bunch of times to move your objects down to the next page.

When you want to make changes to your text you will need to highlight the selected text first in most cases. So if you want to change the font, size, color or other attributes of some text then you will need to highlight just the text you wish to change. For other changes such as paragraph indentations, you can just place the cursor at the beginning of that paragraph to make the change. You can also highlight the paragraph to get the same results.

While working on your document you can always move text around by copying or cutting (moving) and then pasting it to a different location. Just be sure to put the cursor where you want the text (or image) needs to be before pasting. When you are pasting text, it will keep the formatting of that copied text but if you want to paste text without any formatting you can right click and choose *Paste Text Only*.

Speaking of right clicking, when you right click on things such as text or a picture, you will get different options for making changes and adjustments.

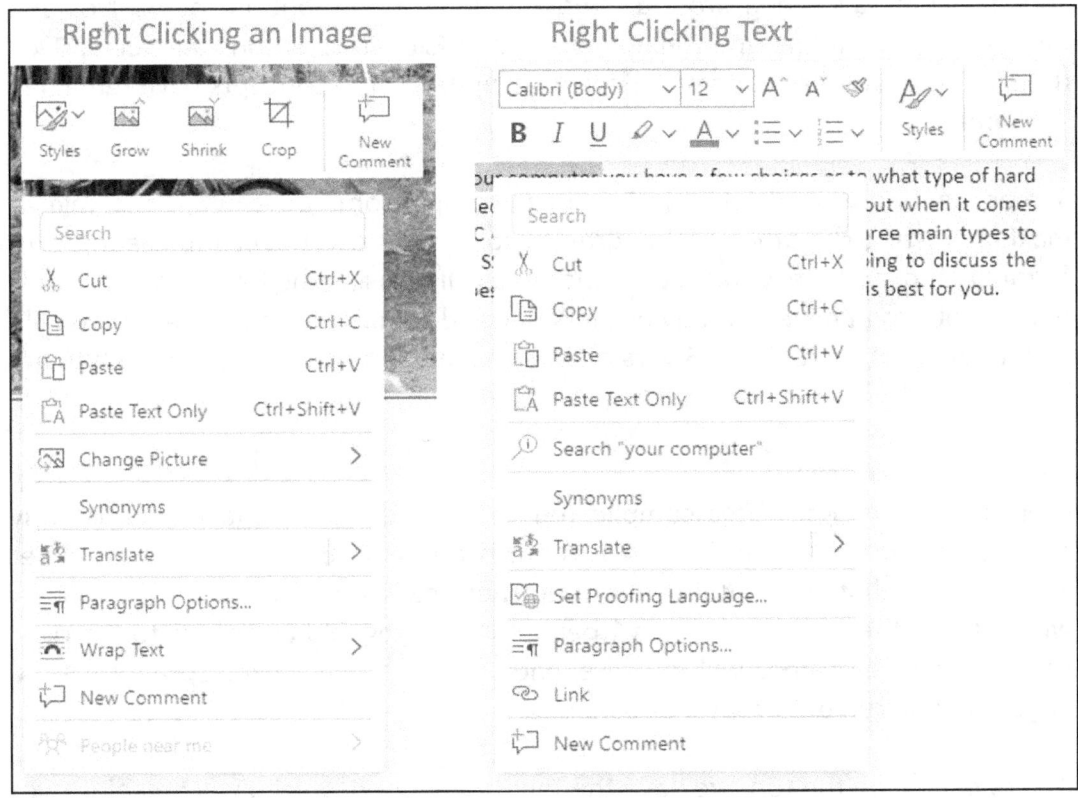

Figure 3.81

Many times you will find it faster to use the right click options when working in Word or any program for that matter so it's always a good idea to know what choices you have when using your right mouse button.

Chapter 4 – Excel

Spreadsheets have been around almost as long as computers themselves and there have been many upon many versions of Excel throughout the years. Even though there have been many versions and updates, the concepts have remained the same.

Spreadsheets are used for a variety of purposes from something as simple as making a listing of names and addresses to a complex budget forecasting with formulas and multiple worksheets. Since you will be using the free version of Excel online, you won't have as many of the fancy and sophisticated tools as you would with the Office\Microsoft 365 version but you most likely will have enough to get by.

The Excel Interface
Even though Excel can be a complicated app to use, the interface itself is fairly simple. As you can see in figure 4.1, there is the main body of the spreadsheet with the cells that will contain your data. These cells start with A1 at the top left with A being the first column and 1 being the first row. As you move to the right or down, the cell names will increase, and you will never have a spreadsheet so large that you run out of rows or columns.

And of course on the top, we have the tabs and Ribbon which I will be going over in the next section.

Chapter 4 – Excel

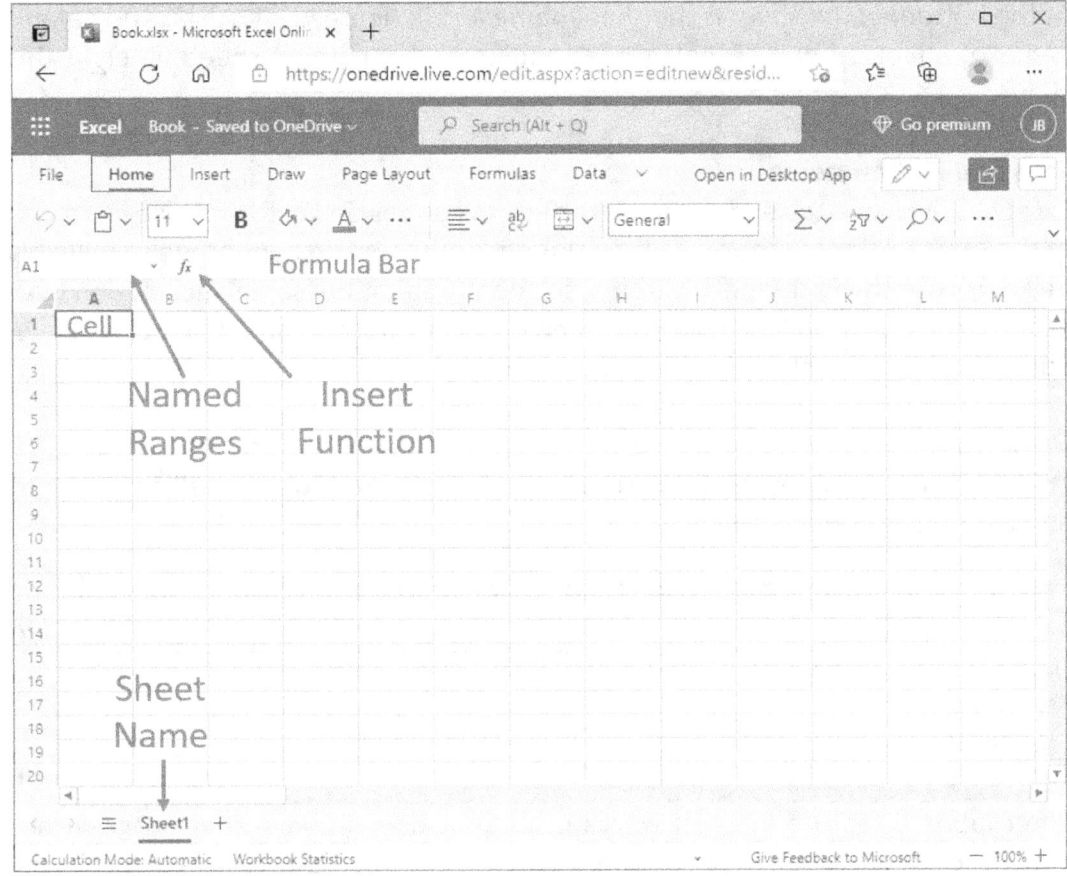

Figure 4.1

At the top left above cell A1, you have the *Named Ranges* box, and this is used to assign a name to a range of cells that you can later use to do things such as search on or use in formulas. Excel for the Web doesn't allow you to create named ranges but if you have an existing spreadsheet with named ranges then you can search and create formulas from those existing ranges.

Next to that you have the *Insert Function* button which is used to apply a preconfigured function or formula to your data. I will be going over functions and formulas later in the chapter.

Speaking of formulas, the *Formula Bar* is used to display a formula that is assigned to a specific cell. If you don't have a formula in that cell then it will simply show the data\text that is in that cell.

Chapter 4 – Excel

At the bottom of the sheet is the sheet name and in figure 4.1 it's using the default name of Sheet1. I will be going over adding and renaming sheets later in this chapter.

Tabs and Ribbon Items
Excel has the same tab and Ribbon interface as you saw in Word and also has many of the same options, and you will see this with other Office apps as well. I will only be going over the Excel specific items, so I don't repeat the same information over again. Once again I will be using the simple view rather than the full Ribbon view, but you can use whichever view works the best for you.

Home Tab
This tab contains many of the text and cell formatting tools as well as a way to apply formulas and filter your data.

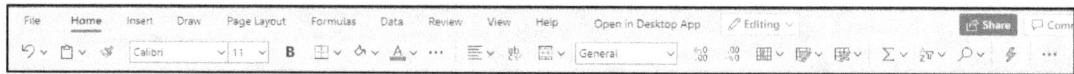
Figure 4.2

Clipboard

The clipboard feature in Excel works just like it does in any other program but when it comes to your paste options, you will have some Excel specific choices. The cut and copy features do the same thing but as you can see in figure 4.2, there are quite a few paste options.

Chapter 4 – Excel

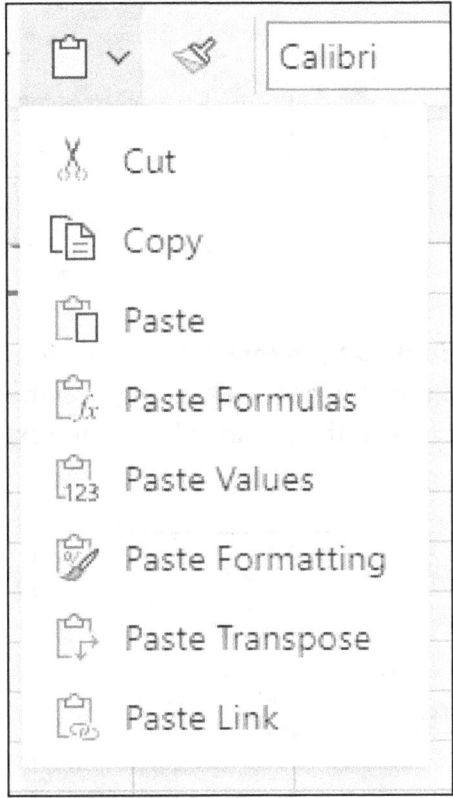

Figure 4.3

- **Paste** – This option will paste everything you have copied to the clipboard.

- **Paste Formulas** – If you copy a cell that contains a formula, this choice will paste that formula into another cell.

- **Paste Values** – This will only paste the value of a cell so if it has a formula, it will just paste the value of that formula.

- **Paste Formatting** – This will paste only the formatting applied that has been applied to the copied cell.

- **Paste Transpose** – This will reorient the content of copied cells and will put data that was in columns into rows and vice versa.

- **Paste Link** – Use this to paste a reference to the source cell rather than the copied cell contents itself.

Chapter 4 – Excel

Wrap and Merge

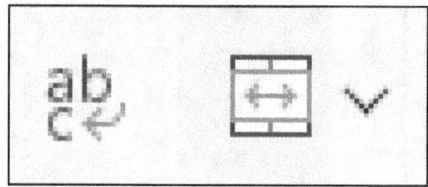

Figure 4.4

As you type text or numbers into a cell, you will find that the text "spills over" into the next cell as seen in figure 4.5. Technically, the text is not really going into the next cell but rather is being displayed over it. If I were to click in cell B1, the text in cell A1 would be cut off.

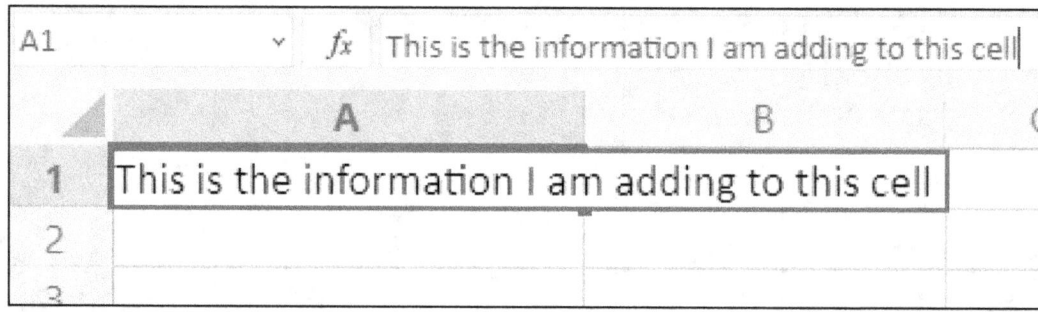

Figure 4.5

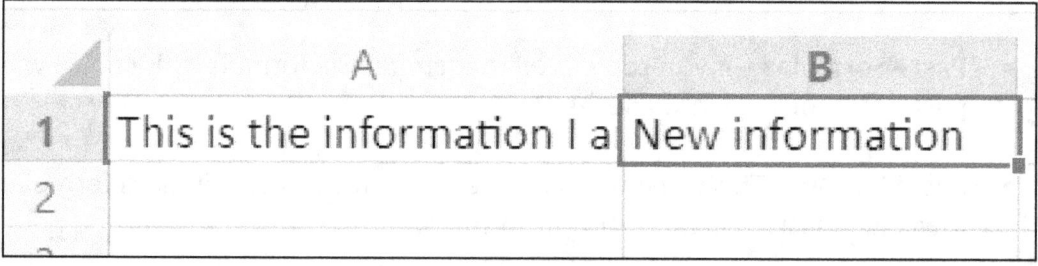

Figure 4.6

To fix this problem I can either extend the width of column A or use text wrapping, which is usually the better option, especially if you have a lot of text in a cell. To do this simply click in the cell and then click on the *Wrap* button. Excel will wrap the text and increase the row height to accommodate the wrapped text.

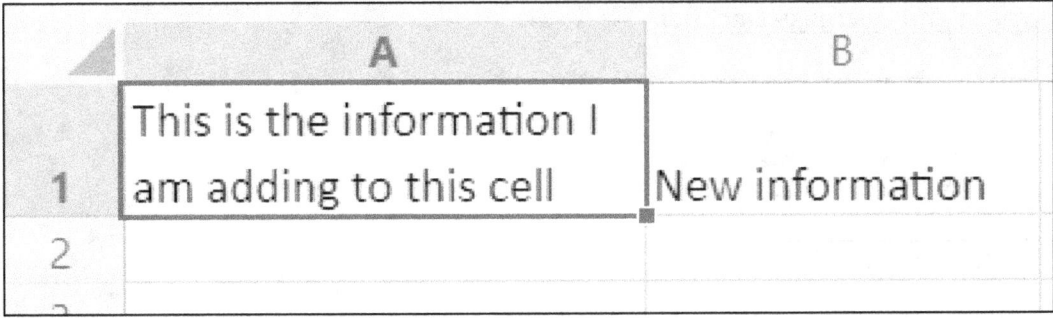

Figure 4.7

The *merge* feature can be used if you would like your longer text to take up multiple columns even though the data itself will only be in the one cell. Figure 4.8 shows my long text in cell A1 but if I were to highlight cells A1 through E1 and then choose the *Merge & Center* option then the cells would become merged, and my text would be centered in those cells as seen in figure 4.9. It might look like one giant cell, but the text is still only in cell A1 and if I were to add text to cell B1 then it would show over my merged text.

	A	B	C	D	E
1	This is the main title for my worksheet				
2	Date	Time	Name	Amount	Category
3	4/25/2021	11:30	Joe Smith	53.25	1
4	5/14/2021	1:45	Ana Gomez	85.62	8
5	8/7/2021	9:15	Dave Brown	24.87	10

Figure 4.8

	A	B	C	D	E
1	This is the main title for my worksheet				
2	Date	Time	Name	Amount	Category
3	4/25/2021	11:30	Joe Smith	53.25	1
4	5/14/2021	1:45	Ana Gomez	85.62	8
5	8/7/2021	9:15	Dave Brown	24.87	10

Figure 4.9

Chapter 4 – Excel

Increase and Decrease Decimal

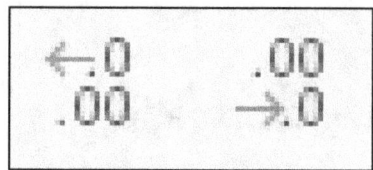

Figure 4.10

When you enter numbers into cells, you have the ability to tell Excel how many decimal places you want to be displayed. So if I have a long number such as **53.23658741** I can have Excel shorten it to let's say two decimal places and it will round the number accordingly by clicking the increase or decrease button as many times as needed.

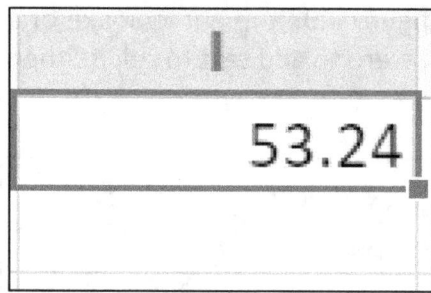

Figure 4.11

Conditional Formatting, Cell Styles and Format as Table

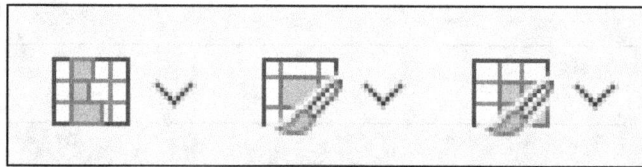

Figure 4.12

- **Conditional Formatting** – Even though I will be discussing formatting later in this chapter I will mention that you can use the Conditional Formatting option to add custom formatting to your data based on what type of data it is. Figure 4.13 shows the *Data Bars* option applied to some numbers and what this does is place colored bars behind the numbers and the bar width is determined by the number value in the cell. There are many other types of conditional formatting you can apply from this tool.

Chapter 4 – Excel

	A	B	C	D	E
1	This is the main title for my worksheet				
2	Date	Time	Name	Amount	Category
3	4/25/2021	11:30	Joe Smith	53.25	1
4	5/14/2021	1:45	Ana Gomez	85.62	8
5	8/7/2021	9:15	Dave Brown	24.87	10

Figure 4.13

- **Cell Styles** – These are preconfigured styles (or themes) that you can apply to a cell or range of cells that will help you express what type of data is in that cell. The choices on the bottom are meant to be used for numbers hence the name Number Format.

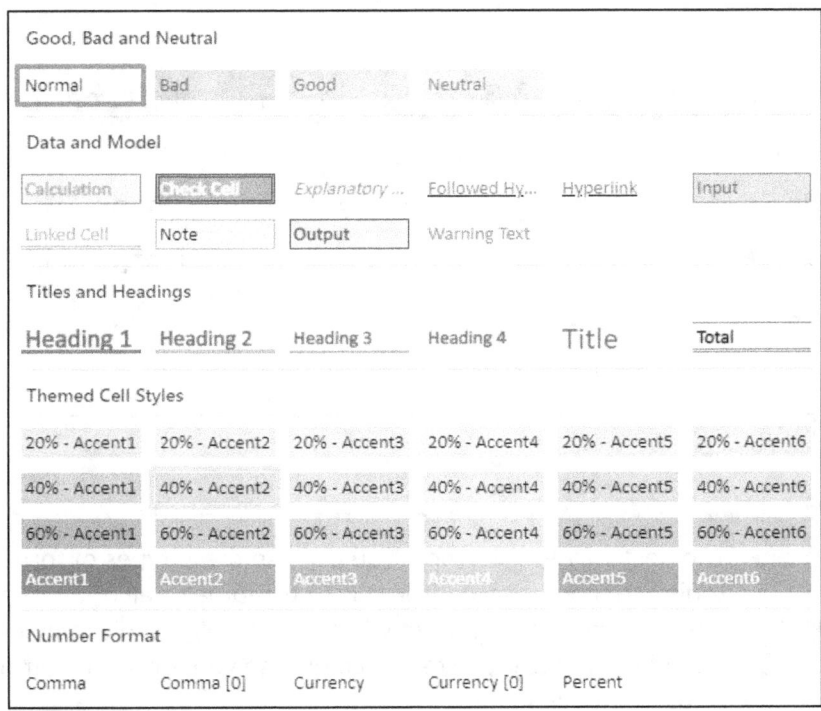

Figure 4.14

- **Format as Table** – If you have some data entered into a range of cells that you would like to use as a table then you can apply a table format to those cells rather than format them with lines and colors manually. Figure 4.15 shows my data before using the Format as Table option and figure 4.16 shows how it looks after only a couple of clicks of the mouse.

93

Chapter 4 – Excel

O	P	Q	R
Column 1	Column 2	Column 3	Column 4
Data	Data	Data	Data
Data	Data	Data	Data
Data	Data	Data	Data
Data	Data	Data	Data

Figure 4.15

The down arrows next to the column headings are using for filtering which I will be getting into later in this chapter.

O	P	Q	R
Column 1 ▼	Column 2 ▼	Column 3 ▼	Column 4 ▼
Data	Data	Data	Data
Data	Data	Data	Data
Data	Data	Data	Data
Data	Data	Data	Data

Figure 4.16

The best way to learn how you can use these types of formatting tools within your spreadsheet is to try some or all of them out on a test spreadsheet and see what they do. You can simply use the undo feature after you test each one, so you are starting from the same point each time.

Chapter 4 – Excel

Insert and Delete

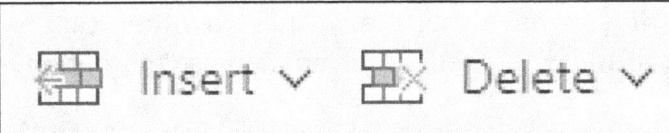
Figure 4.17

Even though there is an Insert tab, you have some additional insert items that can be found from the Home tab. Plus you also have a way to delete certain things that you no longer need.

Using these menu items you can do things such as insert new rows and columns as well as insert cells that you have copied. If you happen to have a cell that is part of a table selected then you can use this section to insert table rows or columns. And then anything that you can insert you can also delete from the Delete dropdown.

Format and Clear

Figure 4.18

I will be discussing formatting later in this chapter but for now I will tell you that you can do things such as automatically adjust row height and column width from here to fit your data and also hide rows, columns and sheets so they are not visible.

The Clear tool comes in handy when you want to "erase" some or all of the content of a cell or cells.

- **Clear All** – Use this to remove everything from a cell.

- **Clear Formats** – This will remove any formatting applied to a cell.

- **Clear Contents** – This will remove the contents of a cell but leave any formulas or comments in place.

Chapter 4 – Excel

- **Clear Comments** – Use this to remove any comments made on a cell.

- **Remove Hyperlinks** – If you have made any links to other cells or spreadsheets within a cell and want them removed then use this option.

AutoSum, Sort and Filter and Find and Select

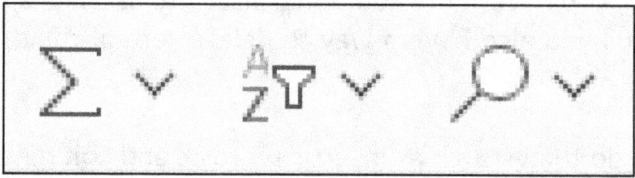

Figure 4.19

Even though the *AutoSum* will allow you to use the AutoSum function, there are other things you can do with this tool. If you click the drop down arrow next to the AutoSum symbol you will see that it gives you access to some of the more popular functions such as getting the average, minimum or maximum values of your data. I will be going over function and formulas later in this chapter so I will leave it at that for now.

Next to the AutoSum button is the *Sort & Filter* button which allows you to organize your data based on various criteria such as ascending and descending. It also allows you to filter out data you don't want to see to make your information easier to manage. Once again, I will be going over sorting and filtering later in this chapter.

Finally, the *Find & Select* feature will allow you to search for text and other values in your sheet so you can easily figure out where that data is located. If you need to replace some data with some other data then you can use the replace feature to tell Excel what to replace.

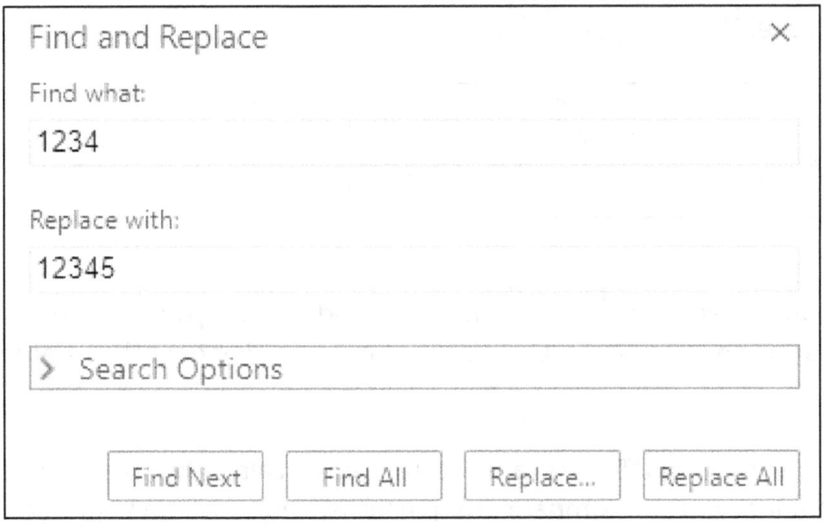

Chapter 4 – Excel

Figure 4.20

The *Go To* option will let you type in a range or cells or choose from a named range and then have Excel take you right to that range and then highlight the cell or range of cells. This is only really useful if you are working on a large spreadsheet, otherwise you can just scroll to where you need to go.

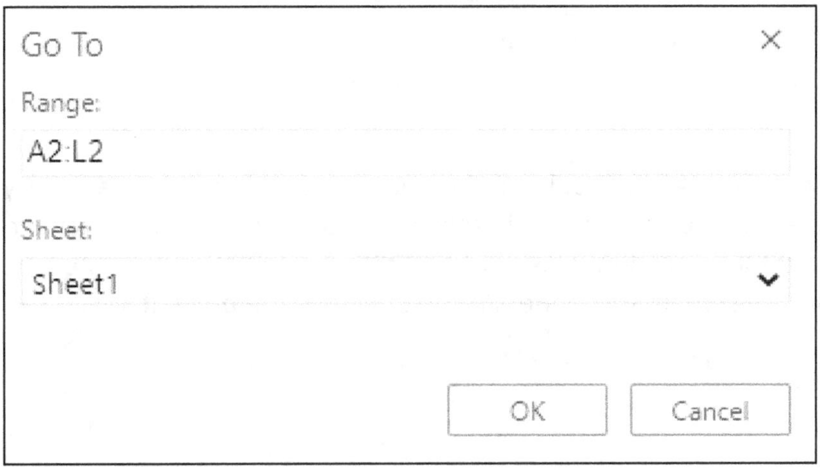

Figure 4.21

Insert Tab
By now you should know that the Insert tab is where you would go if you needed to insert a particular kind of object into your spreadsheet. We saw all of the things you are able to insert from the Word Insert tab and now I will be going over the Excel specific items that you can find here.

Chapter 4 – Excel

Functions and Pivot Tables

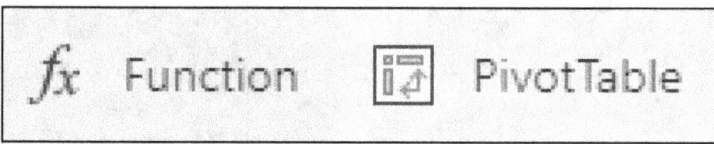
Figure 4.22

Functions are preconfigured formulas that Excel provides that you can use to quickly make calculations on your data. Once again, I will be going over these later in the chapter.

In the words of Microsoft, a *PivotTable* is a powerful tool to calculate, summarize, and analyze data that lets you see comparisons, patterns, and trends in your data. This is one of the more advanced features of Excel and beyond the scope of this book so feel free to play around with them and try not to get too frustrated!

Tables, Pictures and Shapes

Figure 4.23

- **Table** – Creating tables in Excel is a common practice and they are very easy to create. All you need to do is select the range of cells you want to use for your table and then click on the *Table* button. You will then be asked if your table will have headers or no so check the box if it will.

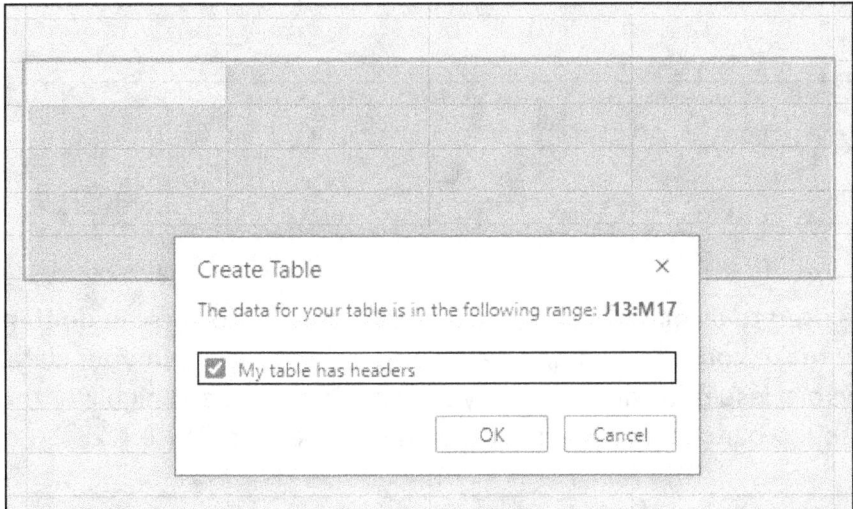

Figure 4.24

Once you click the OK button your able will be created with default column header names and filter drop down arrows.

Figure 4.25

- **Picture** – When inserting pictures into your spreadsheet you will only have the option to upload a picture from your local computer unlike Word where you can insert pictures from web searches or your OneDrive online storage.

- **Shapes** – Here you can insert the same types of common shapes that we saw with Word.

Chapter 4 – Excel

Charts

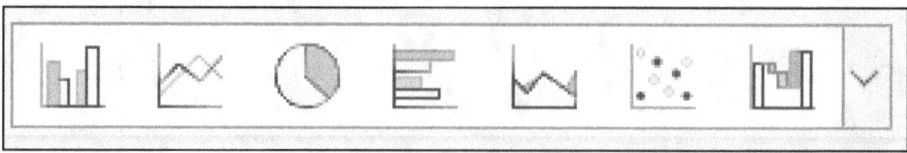

Figure 4.26

Charts are used to display your data in a graphical form so you can do things such as visually make comparisons and help show others trends in your data. Figure 4.27 shows a salesperson and quarterly sales table and when I highlight these cells and choose the bar chart option I get the chart as seen in figure 4.28

U	V	W	X	Y
Salesperson	Q1 Sales	Q2 Sales	Q3 Sales	Q4 Sales
Ana	25	21	35	21
Joe	33	42	42	38
Don	45	15	27	30
Lee	12	41	33	40
Sally	48	23	35	19

Figure 4.27

The chart shows each salesperson and their sales for each quarter and each person is assigned a different color for their bars making it easy to see who outsold whom.

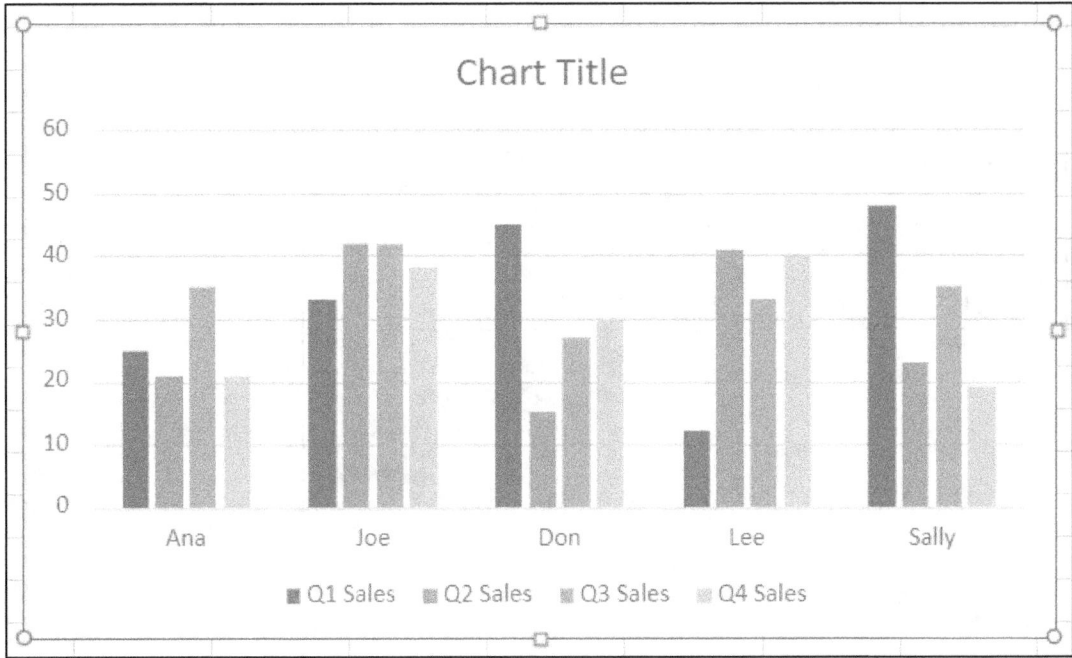

Figure 4.28

Links and Comments

Figure 4.29

You can create active (clickable) *links* on the data in your cells in case you want someone to be able to go to a website or send an email directly from your spreadsheet. More commonly, links are used to direct the person who is working with the file to another area of your spreadsheet such as a completely different worksheet itself.

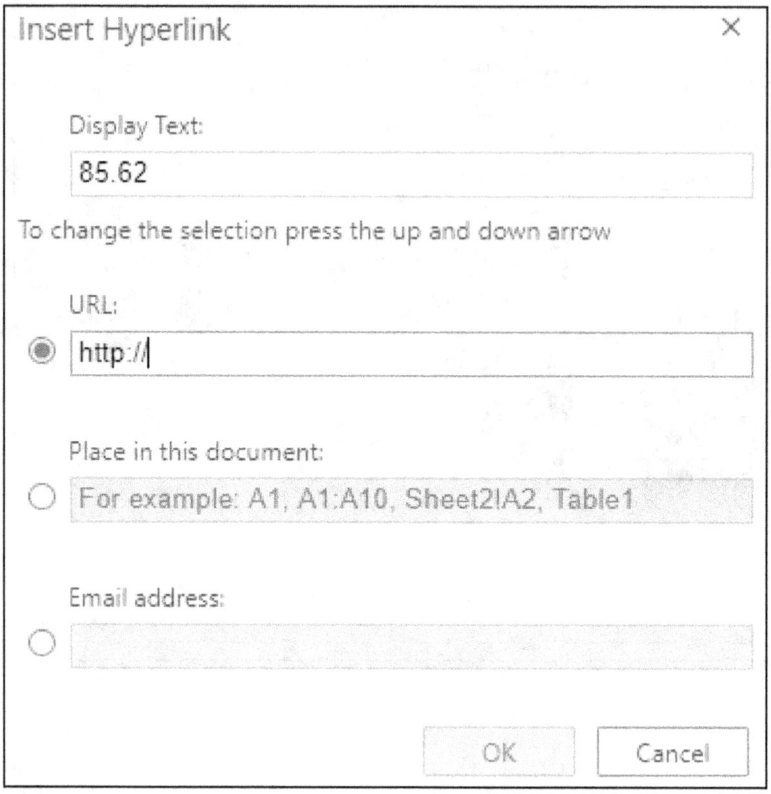

Chapter 4 – Excel

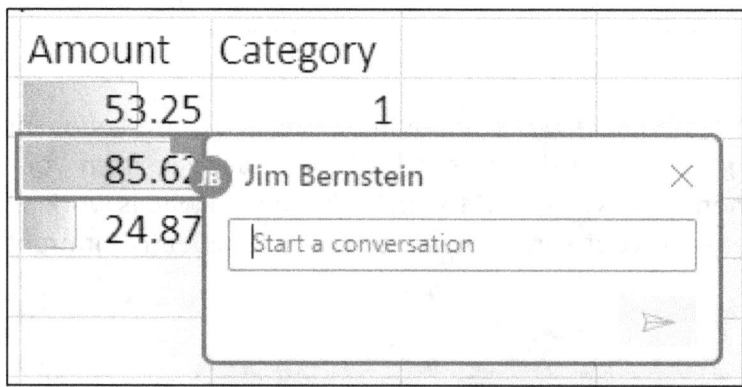

Figure 4.30

You can also add *comments* like you can with Word for others that are accessing your spreadsheet to see.

Figure 4.31

Draw Tab
There isn't much to the Draw tab, but it does have some useful tools to help you make your data stand out.

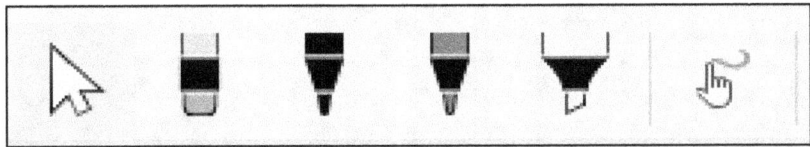
Figure 4.32

- **Select** – This allows you to select cells like you normally would with your mouse.

- **Eraser** – Use this to erase any drawings you have made on your sheet.

- **Pen** – This will let you free draw with your mouse in red or black "ink".

- **Highlighter** – This will highlight information in your cells like a highlighter marker would do.

- **Draw With Touch** – If you have a touchscreen you can use your finger or a stylus to draw on your sheets.

Page Layout Tab
If you plan on printing your spreadsheet then you will want to visit this tab to make sure things are laid out where they need to be.

There is only one button here and that is for Page Setup which I will be discussing in Chapter 9.

Figure 4.33

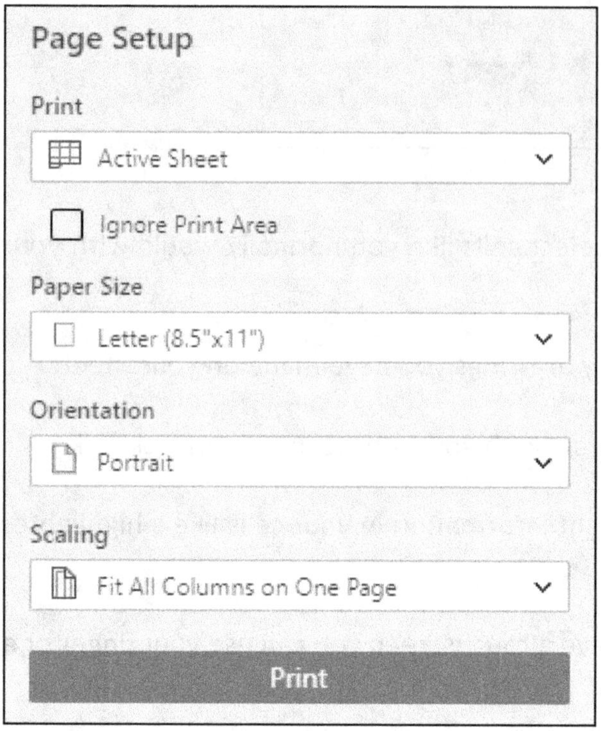

Chapter 4 – Excel

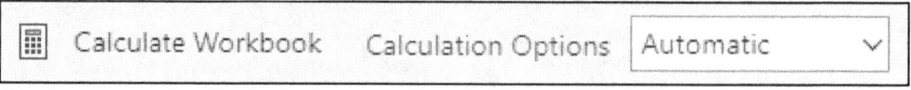

Figure 4.34

Formulas Tab

One of the most distinctive capabilities that Excel offers is the ability to use formulas to manipulate your data and perform calculations on it. You can use the built in functions that come with Excel or create your own custom made formulas. Since I will be having a section on formulas later in this chapter I will just go over the options in the Formulas tab.

Calculate Workbook and Calculation Options

Figure 4.35

These options are only really useful if you have a large spreadsheet with many sheets and linked formulas etc.

- **Calculate Workbook** – Use this to manually calculate your workbook.

Chapter 4 – Excel

- **Calculation Options** – This setting determines whether Excel will calculate formulas automatically or manually when cell values are changed. The *Automatic* setting will recalculate the workbook when a cell value changes or other actions. You can use the *Manual* setting if you have a lot of linked items in multiple sheets that might slow down your system every time it has to recalculate. Then you can perform a manual recalculation as you need it.

Show Formulas

Figure 4.36

You can use this button to have Excel display the formulas that you have applied to your worksheet. Figure 4.37 shows a column of numbers with the AutoSum formula applied to give it a total of $418.07. When I click on the Show Formulas button, Excel will show the formula that was applied to give me that total.

H	H
Sales	Sales
$53.25	$53.25
$85.62	$85.62
$24.87	$24.87
$85.21	$85.21
$65.87	$65.87
$103.25	$103.25
$418.07	=SUM(H2:H7)

Figure 4.37

Chapter 4 – Excel

Data Tab
The Data tab contains many powerful tools that you can use to manipulate your data such as sorting, filtering, grouping and so on.

Refresh All, Workbook Links, and Stocks & Geography

Figure 4.38

- **Refresh All** – If you have links to external data in your workbook and want to manually refresh the data then you can do so with the Refresh All button.

- **Workbook Links** – If you have data that is linked to another Excel workbook then you can view your links from here.

- **Stocks & Geography** – Excel has the capability to show real time data for stocks as well as information about geographic locations.

    If I were to type the Microsoft stock ticker symbol (MSFT) in a cell and then click on Stocks, it would change to what is shown in figure 4.39.

    Figure 4.39

    From there I could click on the icon to the left of Microsoft and be shown their current stock information.

Chapter 4 – Excel

Figure 4.40

You can do the same type of thing for geographic locations. If I were to type Seattle in a cell and then click on Geography I would then see information about the city of Seattle.

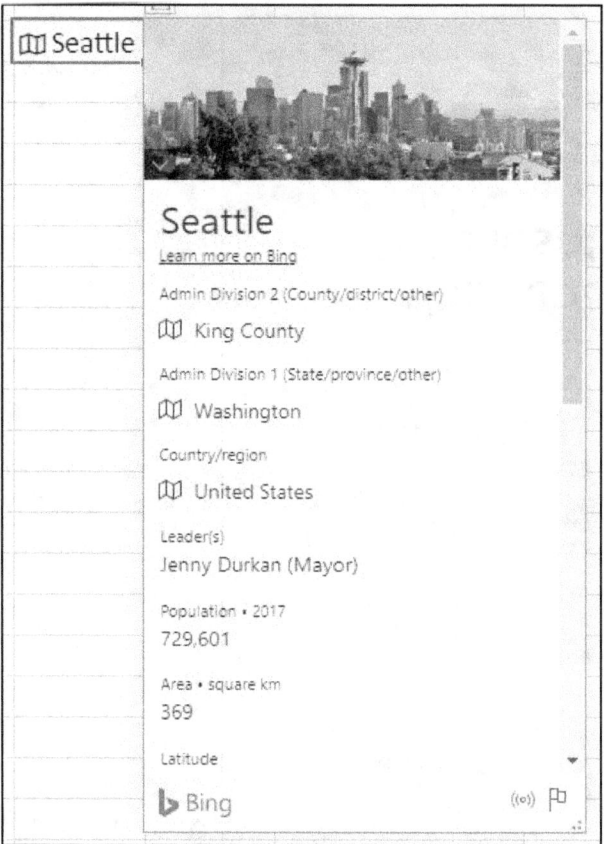
Figure 4.41

Sorting and Filtering

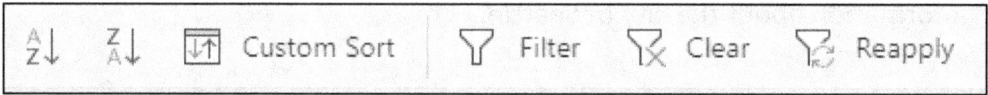
Figure 4.42

I will be going over sorting and filtering later in this chapter but for now just know that you can get to the related buttons and options from this section.

Text to Columns, Flash Fill, Remove Duplicates and Data Validation

Figure 4.43

Chapter 4 – Excel

- **Text to Columns** – If you have data in one column that you would like to separate into more than one column then you can do so by highlighting the data and then click on the Text to Columns button.

A	B
Smith, Joe	
Gomez, Ana	
Brown, Dave	
Adams, Sally	
KLee, Kelly	

Figure 4.44

Next you will choose your *delimiter*. In my case, it will be a comma since I have commas between the last and first names in my list.

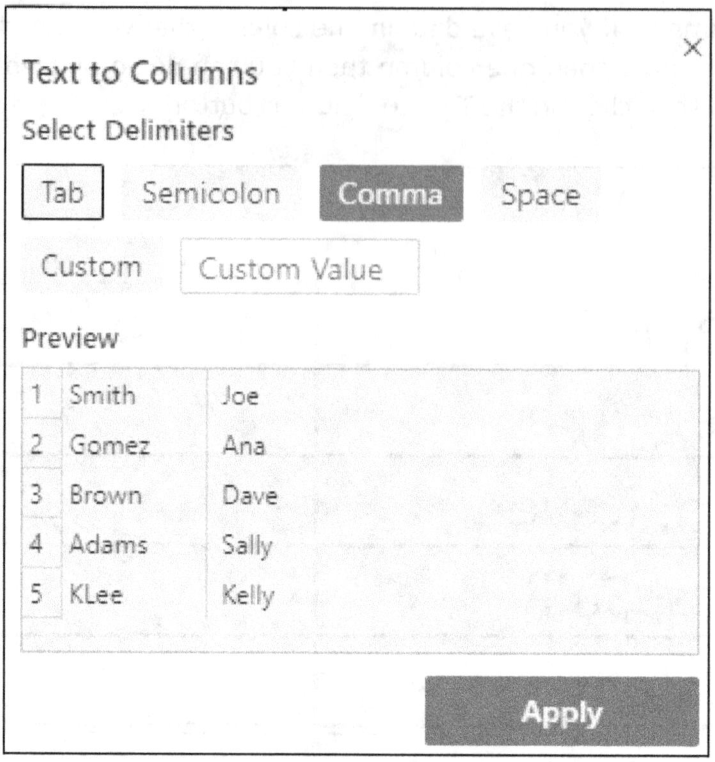

Chapter 4 – Excel

Text to Columns

Select Delimiters

[Tab] Semicolon **Comma** Space

Custom [Custom Value]

Preview

1	Smith	Joe
2	Gomez	Ana
3	Brown	Dave
4	Adams	Sally
5	KLee	Kelly

Apply

Figure 4.45

When you click on *Apply*, the data will then be split into two columns. If this were a large list of names then it would really be a time saver.

A	B
Smith	Joe
Gomez	Ana
Brown	Dave
Adams	Sally
KLee	Kelly

Figure 4.46

- **Flash Fill** – This feature can be used to help you complete typing tasks based on what you have already started working on.

    For example, I am taking a list of email addresses and making a new column with just the first part of the email address (the name).

F	G
Joe@google.com	Joe
Ana@google.com	Ana
Dave@google.com	
Sally@google.com	
Kelly@google.com	

    Figure 4.47

    Once Excel "senses" what you are doing, you can highlight the new column (G) and click on the Flash Fill button and Excel will finish the job for you.

F	G
Joe@google.com	Joe
Ana@google.com	Ana
Dave@google.com	Dave
Sally@google.com	Sally
Kelly@google.com	Kelly

    Figure 4.48

- **Remove Duplicates** – you might come across a situation where you have duplicate values in your spreadsheet and want to get rid of them. You can use this feature to find and remove these duplicates in just a few clicks. Simply highlight the data that contains the duplicates and then click on Remove Duplicates. It will then show you what column it will be removing the data from and list the column header name if it has one.

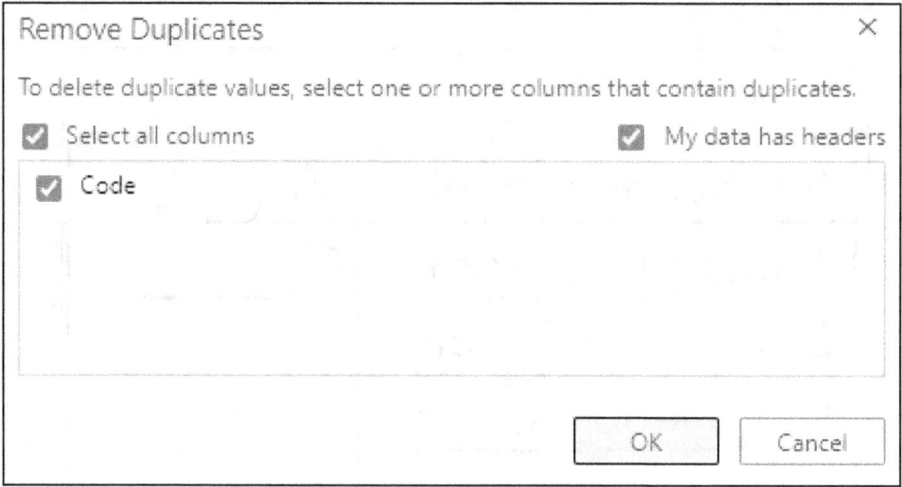
Figure 4.49

Then once you click the OK button it will remove the duplicates and show you a summary of what it did.

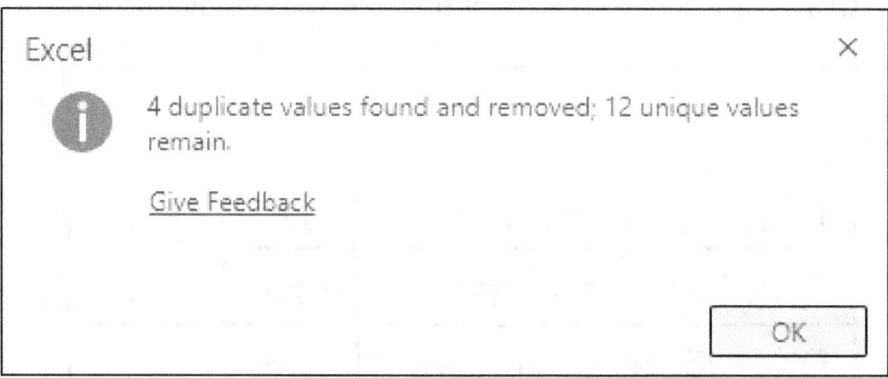
Figure 4.50

- **Data Validation** – This is used to make sure that the correct type of data is entered into cells and allows you to limit the type of data that people can enter. Let's say you had a column labeled Date and you only wanted date formatted text such as 5/25/21 entered into that column.

Chapter 4 – Excel

	AA	AB	AC
	Category	Date	Shift

Figure 4.51

To do this you would highlight all of the cells that you wanted this rule to apply to and then click on Data Validation. From there you would choose the *Date* setting under Allow and choose a setting such as between or less than under the *Data* setting (figure 4.52). When you choose a setting under the Data section, that will determine how the rest of the settings look. In my example since I chose the Between option, I will get *Start date* and *End date* choices where I can type in dates that I choose.

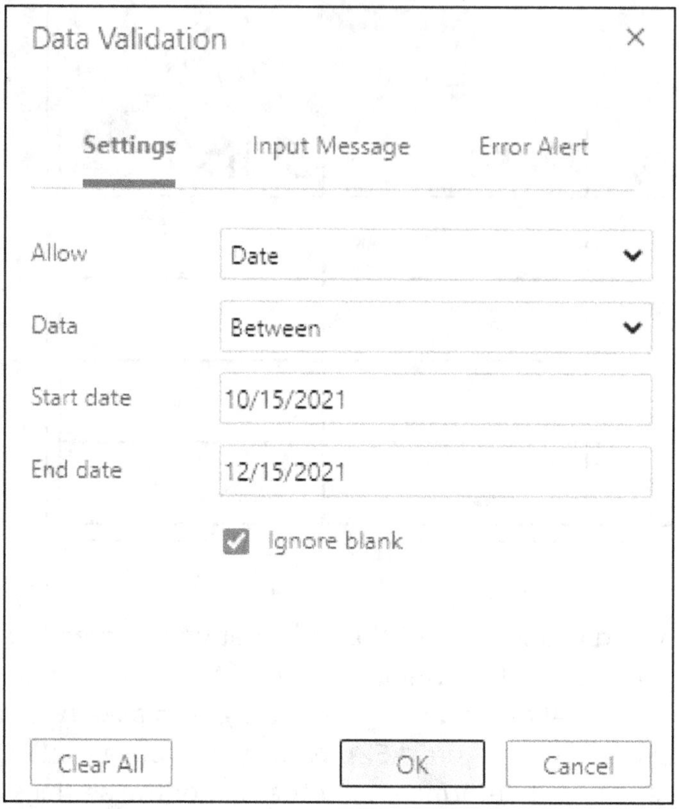

Figure 4.52

Now if someone tries to type in some non-date formatted text or a date that doesn't fall into that range they will get an error as seen in figure 4.53. You can even change the error message from the Error Alert choice to be something a little more personalized as seen in figure 4.54

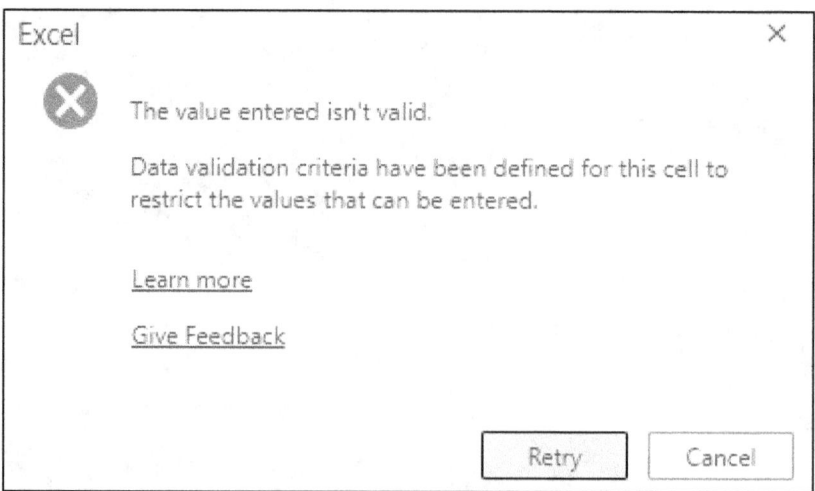

Figure 4.53

Chapter 4 – Excel

Figure 4.54

One advanced feature of Data Validation is the option to create a list of accepted entries which will make a drop down list of choices that the spreadsheet user can only choose from so keep that in mind if you ever need to create such a thing.

Group and Ungroup

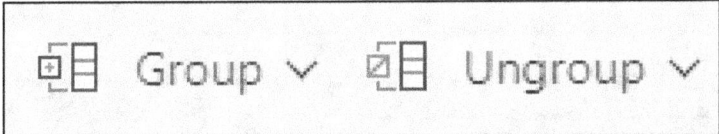

Figure 4.55

This feature is used when you want to group some rows or columns together so you can do things such as quickly hide them if needed. Figure 4.56 shows a larger spreadsheet and I want to group columns C, D, E and F so I can easily hide them if needed. To do this I will simply select those columns and click on *Group>Columns*.

Chapter 4 – Excel

	A	B	C	D	E	F	G	H
1	Segment	Country	Product	Discount	Units Sold	Manufacturing	Sale Price	Gross Sales
2	Government	Canada	Carretera	None	1618.5	$ 3.00	$ 20.00	$ 32,370.00
3	Government	Germany	Carretera	None	1321	$ 3.00	$ 20.00	$ 26,420.00
4	Midmarket	France	Carretera	None	2178	$ 3.00	$ 15.00	$ 32,670.00
5	Midmarket	Germany	Carretera	None	888	$ 3.00	$ 15.00	$ 13,320.00
6	Midmarket	Mexico	Carretera	None	2470	$ 3.00	$ 15.00	$ 37,050.00
7	Government	Germany	Carretera	None	1513	$ 3.00	$ 350.00	$ 529,550.00
8	Midmarket	Germany	Montana	None	921	$ 5.00	$ 15.00	$ 13,815.00
9	Channel Partners	Canada	Montana	None	2518	$ 5.00	$ 12.00	$ 30,216.00
10	Government	France	Montana	None	1899	$ 5.00	$ 20.00	$ 37,980.00
11	Channel Partners	Germany	Montana	None	1545	$ 5.00	$ 12.00	$ 18,540.00
12	Midmarket	Mexico	Montana	None	2470	$ 5.00	$ 15.00	$ 37,050.00
13	Enterprise	Canada	Montana	None	2665.5	$ 5.00	$ 125.00	$ 333,187.50
14	Small Business	Mexico	Montana	None	958	$ 5.00	$ 300.00	$ 287,400.00
15	Government	Germany	Montana	None	2146	$ 5.00	$ 7.00	$ 15,022.00
16	Enterprise	Canada	Montana	None	345	$ 5.00	$ 125.00	$ 43,125.00
17	Midmarket	United States of America	Montana	None	615	$ 5.00	$ 15.00	$ 9,225.00
18	Government	Canada	Paseo	None	292	$ 10.00	$ 20.00	$ 5,840.00
19	Midmarket	Mexico	Paseo	None	974	$ 10.00	$ 15.00	$ 14,610.00
20	Channel Partners	Canada	Paseo	None	2518	$ 10.00	$ 12.00	$ 30,216.00
21	Government	Germany	Paseo	None	1006	$ 10.00	$ 350.00	$ 352,100.00

Figure 4.56

Now I will have a – sign box with a line that kind of looks like a slider bar.

	C	D	E	F	G
	Product	Discount	Units Sold	Manufacturing	Sale Price
	Carretera	None	1618.5	$ 3.00	$ 20.00
	Carretera	None	1321	$ 3.00	$ 20.00
	Carretera	None	2178	$ 3.00	$ 15.00
	Carretera	None	888	$ 3.00	$ 15.00
	Carretera	None	2470	$ 3.00	$ 15.00
	Carretera	None	1513	$ 3.00	$ 350.00
	Montana	None	921	$ 5.00	$ 15.00
	Montana	None	2518	$ 5.00	$ 12.00
	Montana	None	1899	$ 5.00	$ 20.00
	Montana	None	1545	$ 5.00	$ 12.00
	Montana	None	2470	$ 5.00	$ 15.00
	Montana	None	2665.5	$ 5.00	$ 125.00

Figure 4.57

If I click on the – button, my columns will "collapse" and be hidden from view. Then I will have a + button that I can click on to expand them. I will also have a 1 and a 2 button off to the left showing I have 2 different levels to my grouping

Chapter 4 – Excel

(normal and collapsed), and I can click on either of these to show that particular level.

	Segment	Country	Sale Price	Gross Sales
1	Segment	Country	Sale Price	Gross Sales
2	Government	Canada	$ 20.00	$ 32,370.00
3	Government	Germany	$ 20.00	$ 26,420.00
4	Midmarket	France	$ 15.00	$ 32,670.00
5	Midmarket	Germany	$ 15.00	$ 13,320.00
6	Midmarket	Mexico	$ 15.00	$ 37,050.00
7	Government	Germany	$ 350.00	$ 529,550.00
8	Midmarket	Germany	$ 15.00	$ 13,815.00
9	Channel Partners	Canada	$ 12.00	$ 30,216.00
10	Government	France	$ 20.00	$ 37,980.00
11	Channel Partners	Germany	$ 12.00	$ 18,540.00
12	Midmarket	Mexico	$ 15.00	$ 37,050.00
13	Enterprise	Canada	$ 125.00	$ 333,187.50
14	Small Business	Mexico	$ 300.00	$ 287,400.00
15	Government	Germany	$ 7.00	$ 15,022.00
16	Enterprise	Canada	$ 125.00	$ 43,125.00
17	Midmarket	United States of America	$ 15.00	$ 9,225.00
18	Government	Canada	$ 20.00	$ 5,840.00
19	Midmarket	Mexico	$ 15.00	$ 14,610.00
20	Channel Partners	Canada	$ 12.00	$ 30,216.00
21	Government	Germany	$ 350.00	$ 352,100.00

Figure 4.58

Review Tab

Here is where you can come to ensure your spreadsheet is ready to share with others or check what others have to say about your work. Most of the items here have already been covered in the chapter on Word.

Chapter 4 – Excel

Spelling and Workbook Statistics

Figure 4.59

By now you should know about the spell check feature and how it works so there is no need to go over the Spelling button. The *Workbook Statistics* button will show you general information about your spreadsheet such as how many cells have data and how many formulas it has.

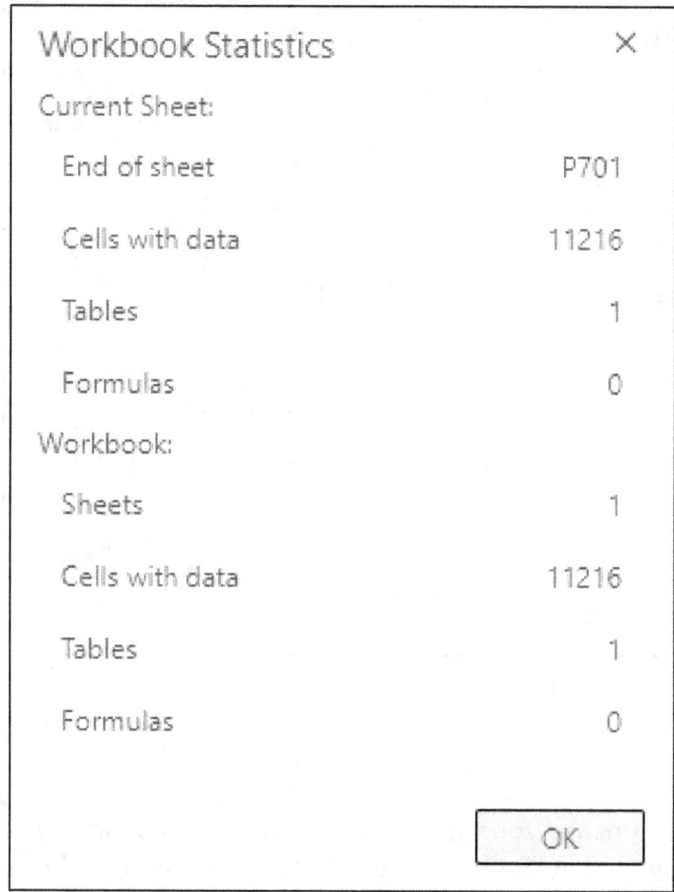

Figure 4.60

> You might have noticed that I use the word **workbook** when discussing Excel spreadsheets. If you haven't figured it out already, a workbook is the name used to describe the container for all of your individual sheets since you can have multiple sheets within Excel.

Convert All Notes

Figure 4.61

You can create notes in the Office 365 and desktop versions of Excel so if you are opening a file created in either one of those in Excel for the Web then you will be able to view the notes by hovering your mouse over the small red triangle at the top right of the cell. You can think of notes as sticky notes like you would paste on your monitor but when you open these notes in Excel for the Web they act more like comments.

Note as viewed in the Excel desktop app.

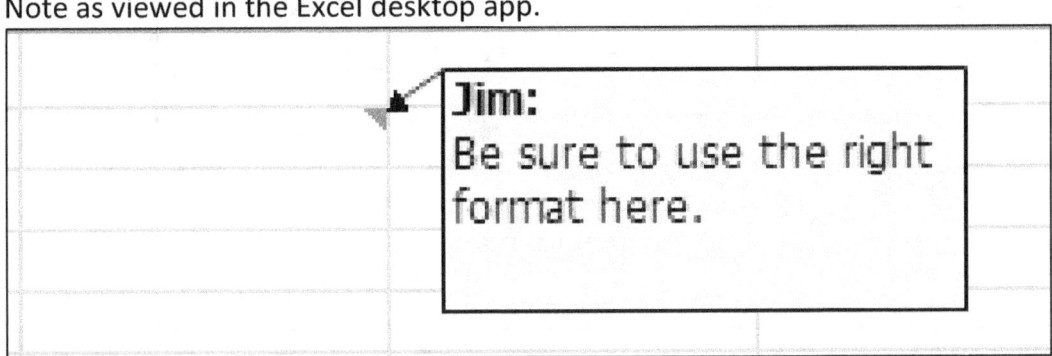

Figure 4.62

Chapter 4 – Excel

Note viewed in Excel for the Web.

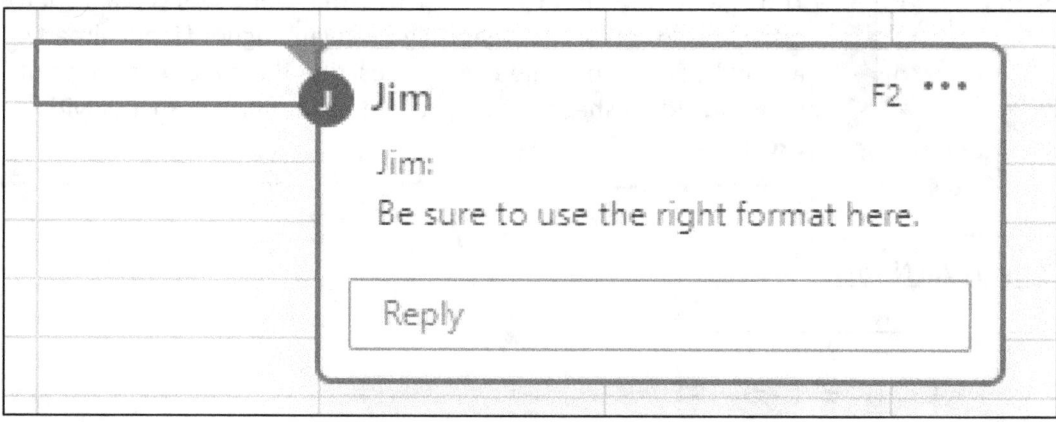

Figure 4.63

You can use the *Convert All Notes* button to convert these notes to comments that you can then reply to just like you would any other comment you or someone else has made.

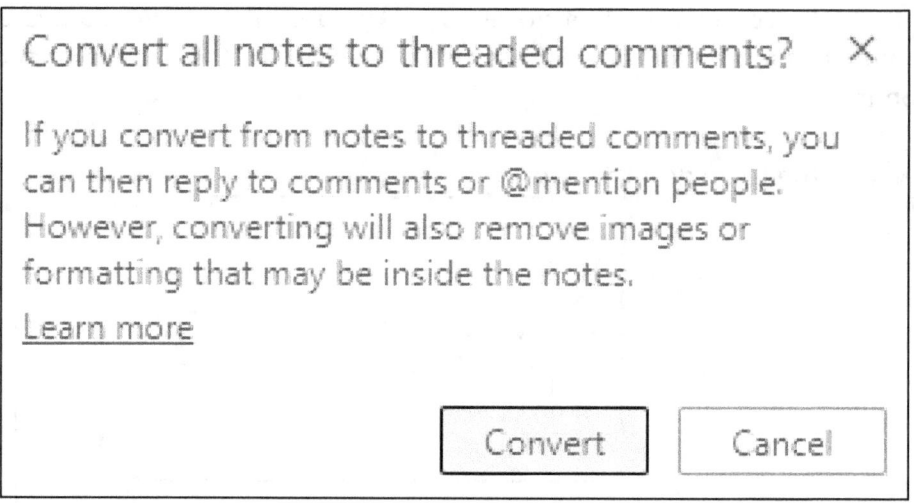

Figure 4.64

After doing so, they will look very similar to the way they did before the conversion.

Chapter 4 – Excel

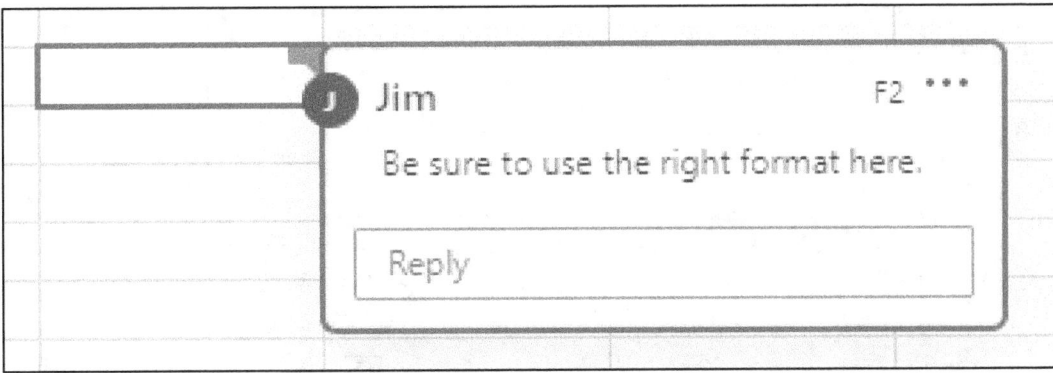

Figure 4.65

View Tab

This tab has settings that will allow you to change how your spreadsheet is viewed and you can use these settings to have Excel show only the data you wish to be displayed.

Sheet View

Figure 4.66

The Sheet View settings allow you to create custom views to display selected data so you can easily switch back and forth between them as needed. By default, the only view available is called Default but to add a new view you would click on the *New* button and then type in a name for your view.

Figure 4.67 shows the Default view with no changes made to my spreadsheet. Notice how the rows are in order from 1 to 21 and there are several different countries displayed.

Chapter 4 – Excel

	A	B	C
1	Segment	Country	Product
2	Government	Canada	Carretera
3	Government	Germany	Carretera
4	Midmarket	France	Carretera
5	Midmarket	Germany	Carretera
6	Midmarket	Mexico	Carretera
7	Government	Germany	Carretera
8	Midmarket	Germany	Montana
9	Channel Partners	Canada	Montana
10	Government	France	Montana
11	Channel Partners	Germany	Montana
12	Midmarket	Mexico	Montana
13	Enterprise	Canada	Montana
14	Small Business	Mexico	Montana
15	Government	Germany	Montana
16	Enterprise	Canada	Montana
17	Midmarket	United States of America	Montana
18	Government	Canada	Paseo
19	Midmarket	Mexico	Paseo
20	Channel Partners	Canada	Paseo
21	Government	Germany	Paseo

Figure 4.67

If I were to create a new view and name it *Jim's View*, I can then change the way my data looks such as adding a filter to only show Germany and United States of America in the Country column.

When you are in a custom view, the row numbers and column letter boxes will turn from grey to black to let you know that you are in a custom view. Figure 4.68 shows my custom view with the filter added and you can see the only countries listed are Germany and United States of America and the numbers are inconsistent meaning some data is not being displayed.

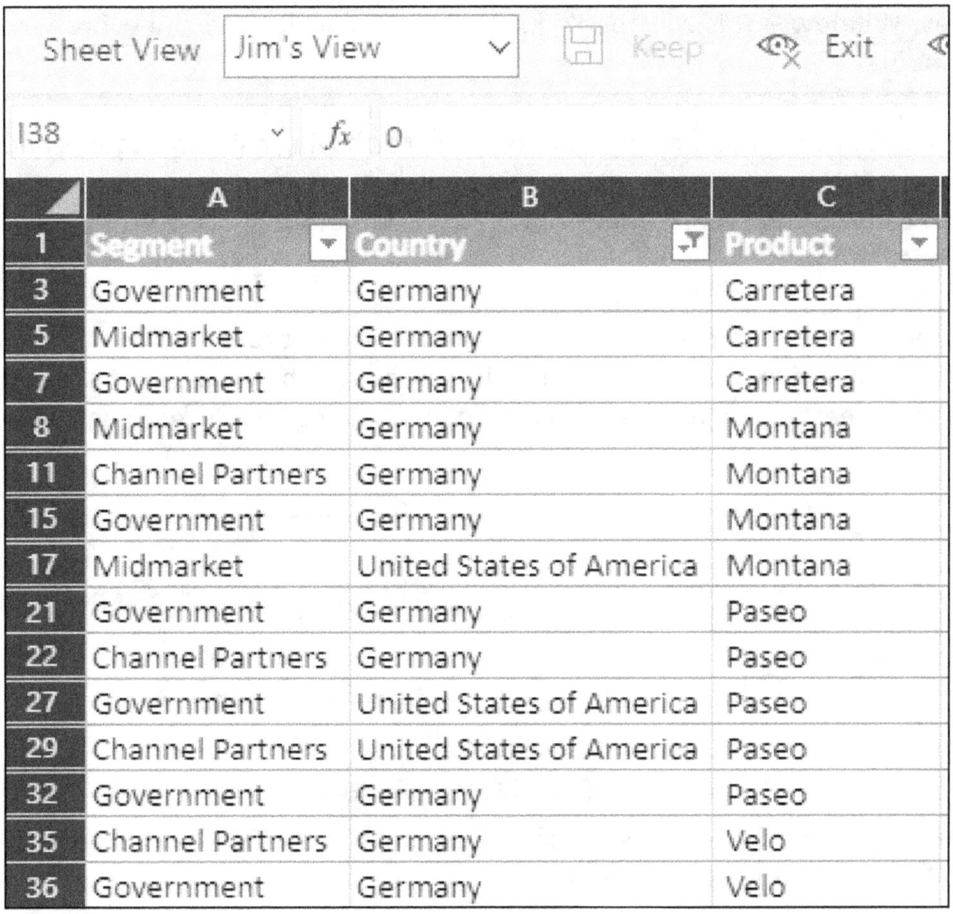

Chapter 4 – Excel

Figure 4.68

If I were to change the view back to Default then my spreadsheet would look like figure 4.67 once again. I can also click on the *Exit* button to go back to the default view.

Clicking on *Options* will let you do things such as switch to, rename, duplicate or delete your saved views.

New Window, Freeze Panes, Headings and Gridlines

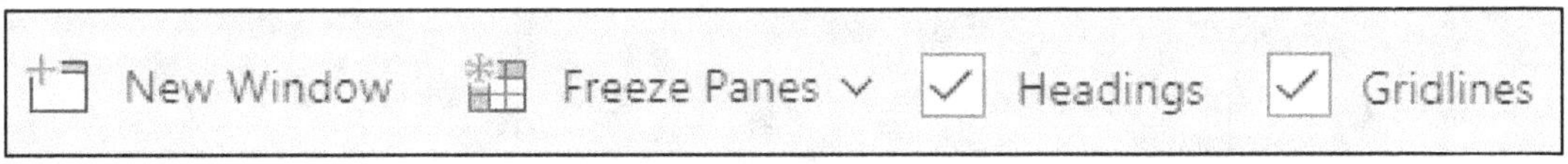

Figure 4.69

Chapter 4 – Excel

- **New Window** – This will open your current spreadsheet in a new browser window.

- **Freeze Panes** – If you have a situation such as having column headers and you want them to stay in place as you scroll down your spreadsheet then you can use the Freeze Panes option to lock them in place so they don't move.

    If I were to use the *Freeze First Row* option then that row would not move as I scrolled down my sheet. Notice in figure 4.70 that row 1 is at the top of the sheet and I was able to scroll down to row 26 while keeping row 1 in view.

	A	B	C
1	Segment	Country	Product
26	Midmarket	Mexico	Paseo
27	Government	United States of America	Paseo
28	Government	Canada	Paseo
29	Channel Partners	United States of America	Paseo
30	Midmarket	Canada	Paseo
31	Government	Canada	Paseo
32	Government	Germany	Paseo
33	Government	Mexico	Velo

    Figure 4.70

- **Headings** – You can use this checkbox to toggle the headings view on or off which will show or not show the column letters and row numbers.

    Headings on

    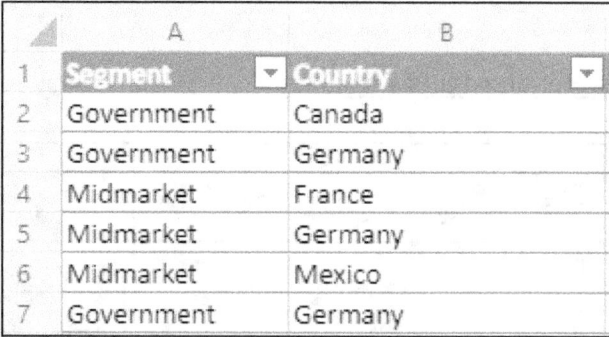

    Figure 4.71

Chapter 4 – Excel

Headings off

Segment	Country
Government	Canada
Government	Germany
Midmarket	France
Midmarket	Germany
Midmarket	Mexico
Government	Germany

Figure 4.72

- **Gridlines** – This will allow you to turn the gridlines that surround each cell on or off as needed.

Entering Data

Entering text and numbers into your spreadsheet is a pretty simple process and it is just a matter of clicking on the cell you want to add that data and typing it or pasting it in from another location.

When you enter information into a cell, it will also be shown in the formula bar in the same format. Anything you enter into a cell will look this way unless it's an actual formula itself, in which case it will show the formula in the bar rather than the cell contents.

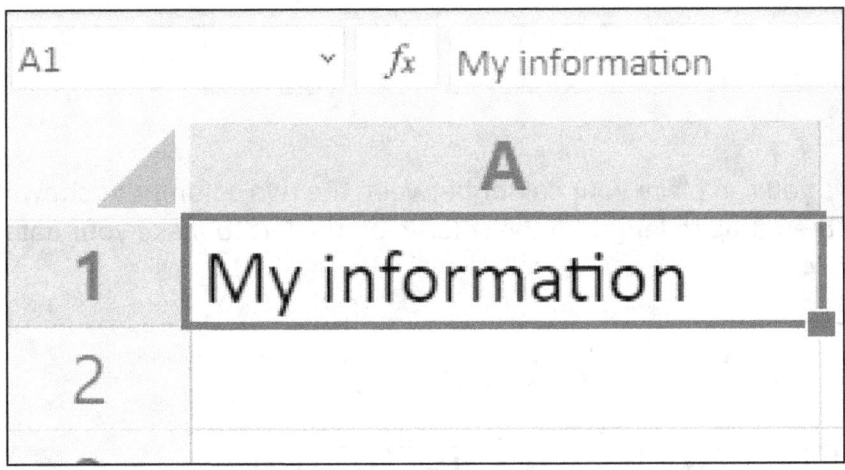

Figure 4.73

If you need to move the contents of one cell to another then you can simply cut and paste the information or you can place your mouse over the cell outline box

Chapter 4 – Excel

until it makes a four-sided pointer as shown in figure 4.72. Then you can drag the cell contents to another cell.

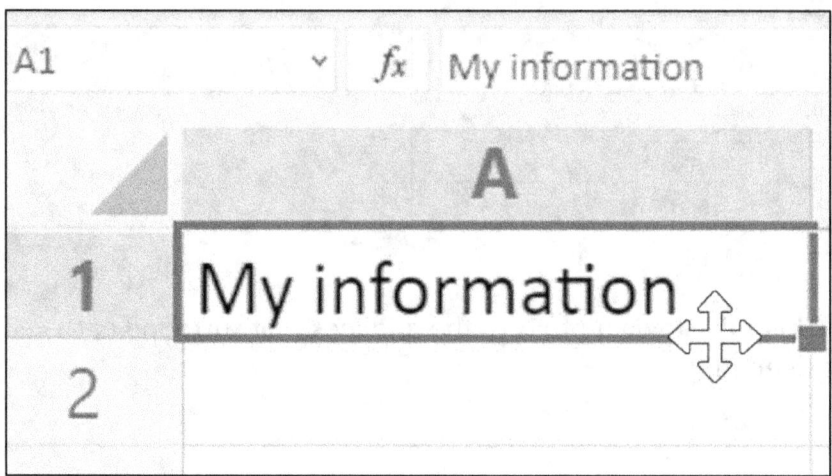
Figure 4.74

When entering data into your cells you will most likely run across a situation where the data is too long to fit into the space provided by the cell as seen in figure 4.75.

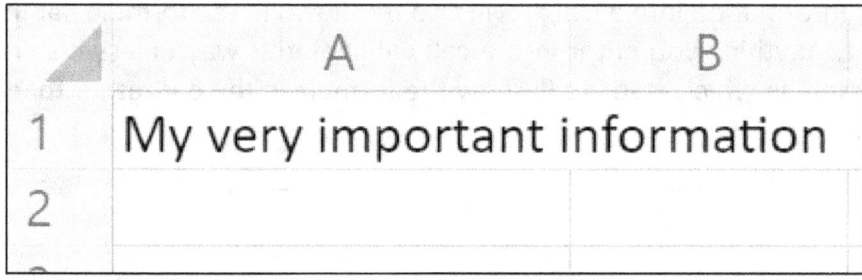
Figure 4.75

When this happens you can place your cursor between the two columns as shown in figure 4.76 and then drag to lengthen the column on the left to make your data fit as seen in figure 4.77.

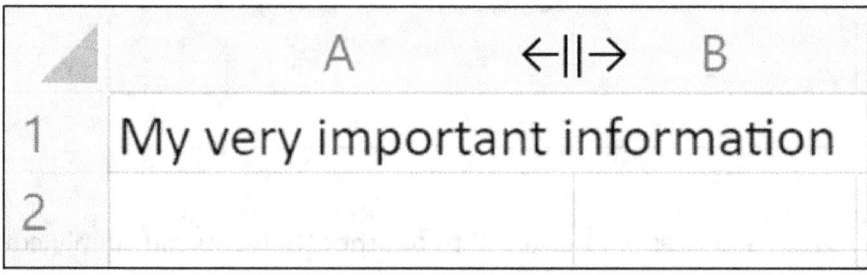
Figure 4.76

Chapter 4 – Excel

	A	B
1	My very important information	
2		

Figure 4.77

When expanding the length of columns and height of rows, be aware of how it will make your spreadsheet look over all. If you expand an entire row just to accommodate the size of the data in one cell, it might make the rest of the cells look off because there will be so much extra space after the data.

Another way to enter information is to simply click on the cell you wish to contain the data and then type in the data in the formula bar itself. I find if you are pasting in data from another source that this will work better because it won't paste any text formatting that might have been applied to the data.

There really isn't much to entering data into your spreadsheet but formatting your data is a little more involved but still fairly simple. I will have a section on spreadsheet formatting coming up later in this chapter.

Number Formatting
I was just mentioned how I will be discussing formatting later in the chapter but before I get to that I wanted to take a moment to discuss number formatting which is not the same thing.

Since Excel is more about numbers than text, it is important to be able to have your numbers displayed in the right format so they can relate to their purpose.

Figure 4.78 shows a column with four different numbers and no formatting applied. This might be fine for many cases but if you need to show that these numbers represent something like currency or a negative number then it might not be so obvious to convey this.

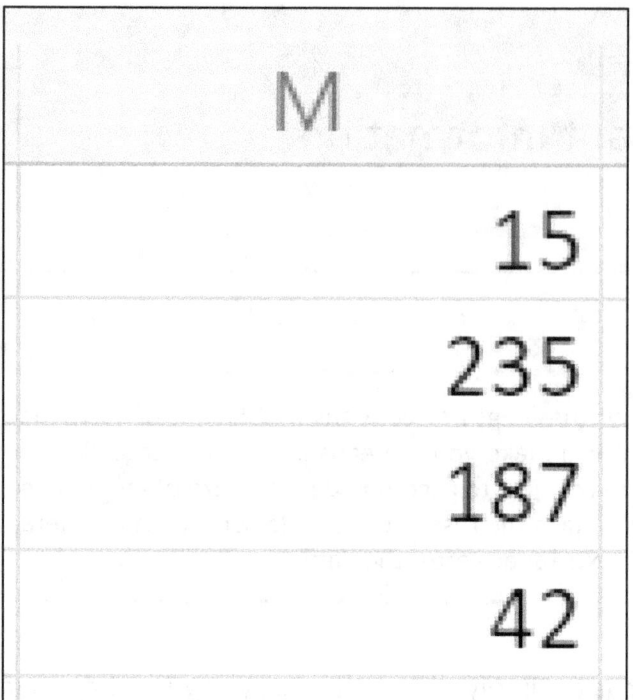
Figure 4.78

If I were to highlight the cells with the numbers, go to the *Home* tab and click on *Number Format* I would be able to choose how I want to display my numbers by selecting one of the categories such as *Currency*. Here you will also be shown a preview of how your numbers will look if you apply the selected number format.

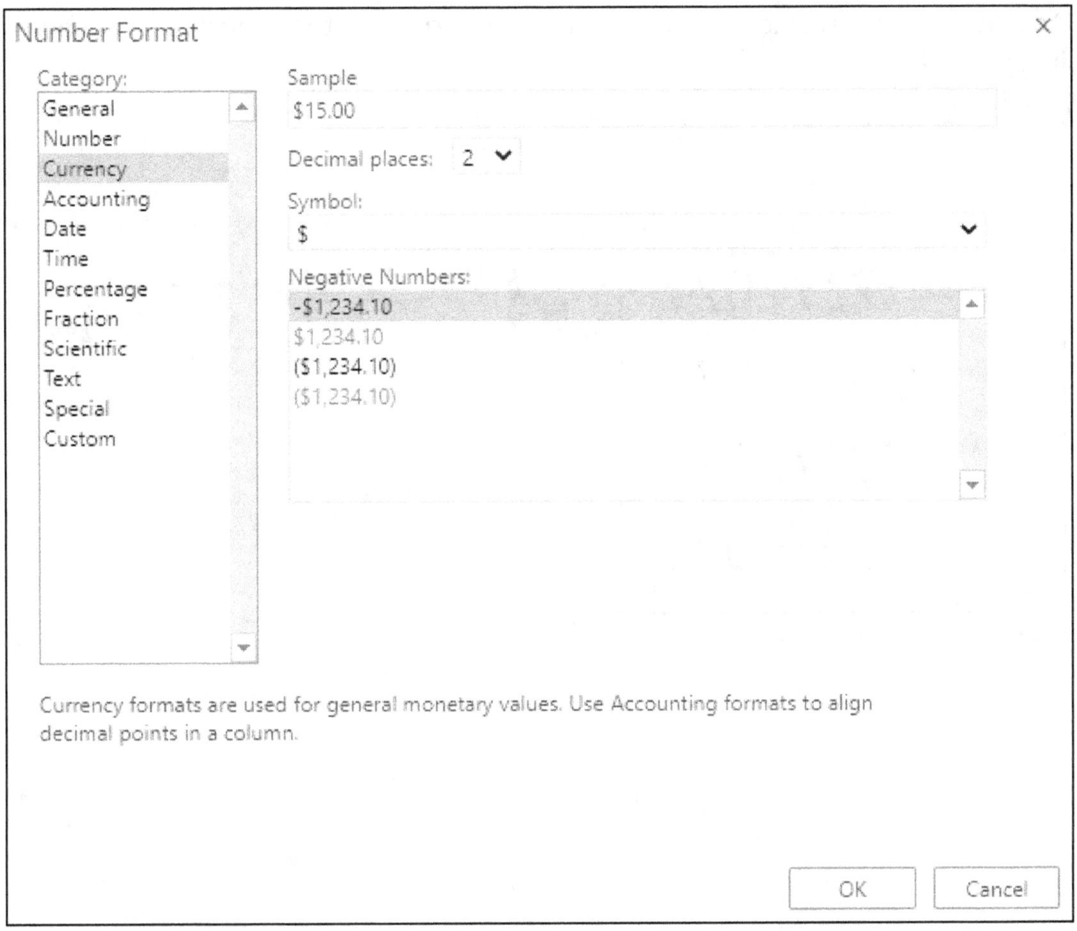

Chapter 4 – Excel

Figure 4.79

Here are how my numbers look after applying the currency format.

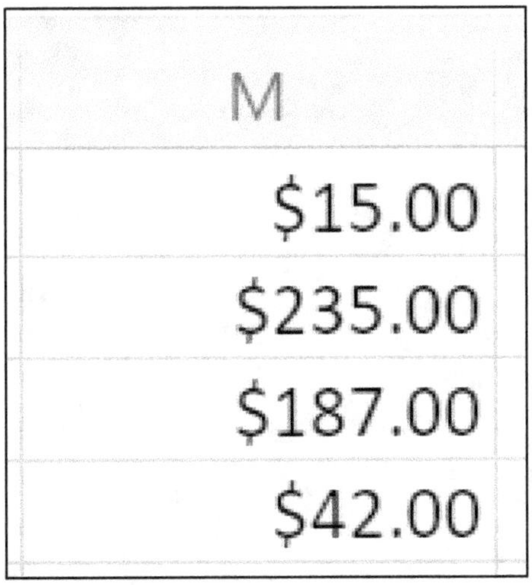

M
$15.00
$235.00
$187.00
$42.00

Figure 4.80

Chapter 4 – Excel

Another example would be changing the date format on the general text as shown in figure 4.81.

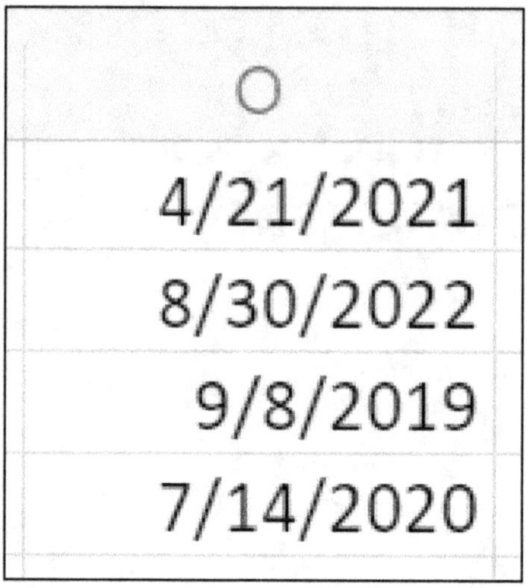

4/21/2021
8/30/2022
9/8/2019
7/14/2020

Figure 4.81

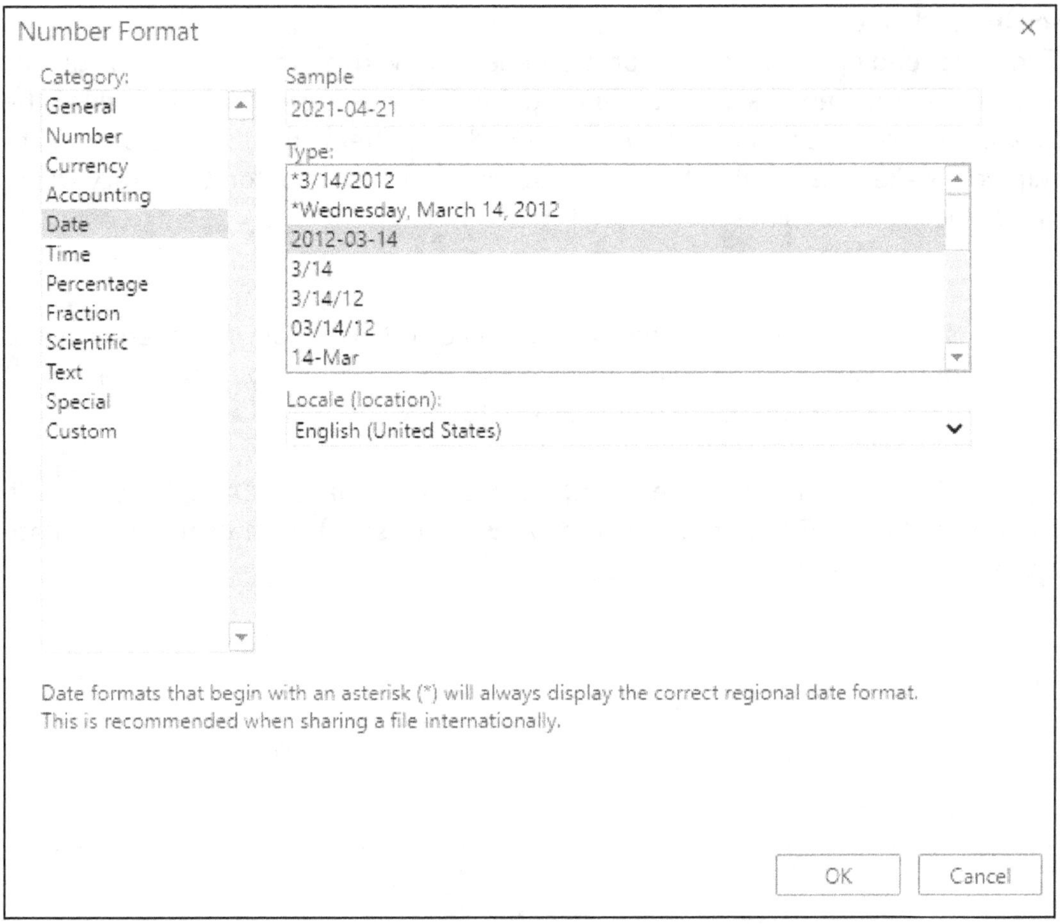

Chapter 4 – Excel

Figure 4.82

Figure 4.83 shows how my numbers look with the new date formatting applied.

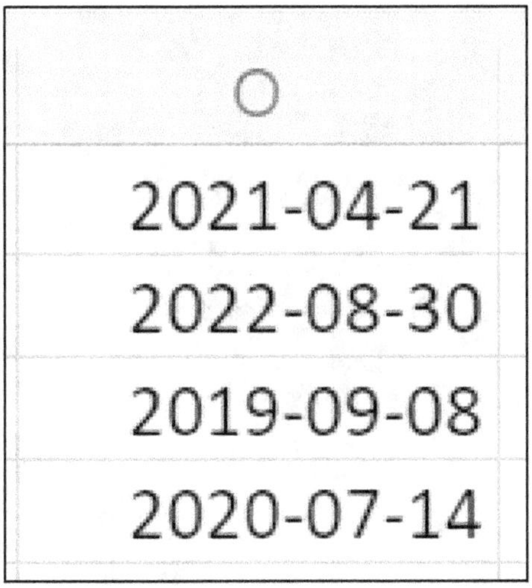

Figure 4.83

Sorting and Filtering

If you ever end up working on a large spreadsheet with a lot of data then you will most likely find it necessary to organize the data so it's easier to read or filter the data, so you only see what you need to see. Excel offers you a couple of ways to help you make sense of what is in your spreadsheet, so you don't go crazy trying to read between the lines... of the cells that is.

Sorting

Sorting is the process of organizing your data according to specific criteria such as by date or alphabetically. It's very easy to sort your data and you can even sort it by more than one value depending on the situation.

Figure 4.84 shows a spreadsheet with four columns named Date, Reference #, Amount and Code. For my first example I want to sort this information by date with the latest date being on the top.

Chapter 4 – Excel

	A	B	C	D
1	Date	Reference #	Amount	Code
2	11/12/19	32567	25.52	AC-25
3	11/15/19	32654	62.24	AC-52
4	10/4/19	15756	15.25	AC-65
5	9/25/19	54521	45.21	AC-85
6	12/15/19	55698	52.51	BR-52
7	10/7/19	78921	96.25	BR-63
8	5/15/19	45985	45.21	BR-63
9	8/21/19	37521	52.47	BR-74
10	3/8/19	79521	89.25	BR-85
11	3/12/19	78952	23.54	TR-98
12	5/15/19	37521	15.87	TR-96
13	7/14/19	96585	62.87	TR-85
14	10/9/19	22147	86.25	TR-42
15	7/7/19	62987	35.24	TR-21
16	12/19/19	25632	15.25	TR-45
17	9/25/19	78912	63.25	TR-53
18	1/12/19	36758	45.12	TR-85
19	2/21/20	15892	16.89	TR-85
20	9/25/20	97621	18.75	GB-45
21	9/15/20	75136	65.32	GB-65
22	7/18/20	12685	56.52	GB-45
23	6/4/20	39521	14.25	GB-74
24	8/23/20	45236	63.52	GB-56
25	6/14/20	97235	78.52	GB-75
26	9/14/20	56514	51.25	FR-65
27	5/15/20	37521	96.62	FR-51
28	8/14/20	96325	78.85	FR-45
29	3/14/20	45214	25.24	FR-63
30	7/18/20	58752	62.24	FR-75
31	6/4/20	14521	51.36	FR-56
32	3/14/20	69354	74.52	WS-56
33	5/12/20	98652	51.36	WS-45
34	5/18/20	21564	42.23	WS-63
35	2/24/21	88524	45.52	WS-12
36	8/26/21	66871	35.62	WS-65
37	9/14/21	23564	82.52	WS-78
38	3/17/21	15475	15.23	WS-45
39	6/21/21	16547	75.96	WS-62

Figure 4.84

To begin the sorting process I will highlight the cells that contain the information and then click on the *Sort & Filter* button. If I just highlight the cells that contain dates, Excel will ask me if I want to expand my selection, so the other columns get sorted at the same time, otherwise my information won't line up if I just sort the date column.

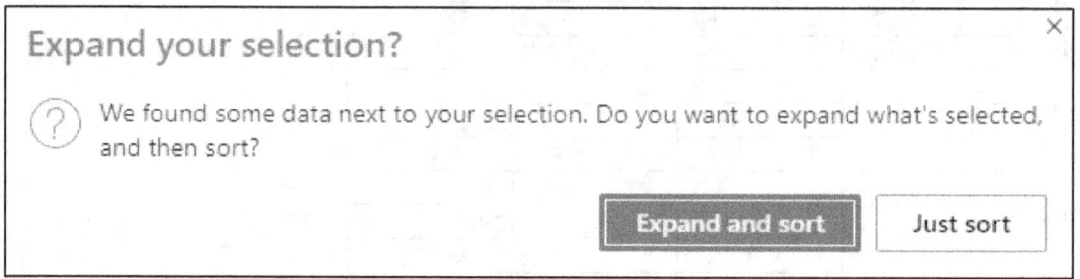

Figure 4.85

Since I want the newest dates to be on the top I will choose the Sort Descending option and the results are shown in figure 4.86.

Chapter 4 – Excel

	A	B	C	D
1	Date	Reference #	Amount	Code
2	9/14/21	23564	82.52	WS-78
3	8/26/21	66871	35.62	WS-65
4	6/21/21	16547	75.96	WS-62
5	3/17/21	15475	15.23	WS-45
6	2/24/21	88524	45.52	WS-12
7	9/25/20	97621	18.75	GB-45
8	9/15/20	75136	65.32	GB-65
9	9/14/20	56514	51.25	FR-65
10	8/23/20	45236	63.52	GB-56
11	8/14/20	96325	78.85	FR-45
12	7/18/20	12685	56.52	GB-45
13	7/18/20	58752	62.24	FR-75
14	6/14/20	97235	78.52	GB-75
15	6/4/20	39521	14.25	GB-74
16	6/4/20	14521	51.36	FR-56
17	5/18/20	21564	42.23	WS-63
18	5/15/20	37521	96.62	FR-51
19	5/12/20	98652	51.36	WS-45
20	3/14/20	45214	25.24	FR-63
21	3/14/20	69354	74.52	WS-56
22	2/21/20	15892	16.89	TR-85
23	12/19/19	25632	15.25	TR-45
24	12/15/19	55698	52.51	BR-52
25	11/15/19	32654	62.24	AC-52
26	11/12/19	32567	25.52	AC-25
27	10/9/19	22147	86.25	TR-42
28	10/7/19	78921	96.25	BR-63
29	10/4/19	15756	15.25	AC-65
30	9/25/19	54521	45.21	AC-85
31	9/25/19	78912	63.25	TR-53
32	8/21/19	37521	52.47	BR-74
33	7/14/19	96585	62.87	TR-85
34	7/7/19	62987	35.24	TR-21
35	5/15/19	45985	45.21	BR-63
36	5/15/19	37521	15.87	TR-96
37	3/12/19	78952	23.54	TR-98
38	3/8/19	79521	89.25	BR-85
39	1/12/19	36758	45.12	TR-85

Figure 4.86

When you click on the *Sort & Filter* button you can then click on *Custom Sort* to choose from additional sorting options. Here you can choose which column you want to sort your data on as well as what values such as cell values (most common), cell color, font color or conditional formatting icons.

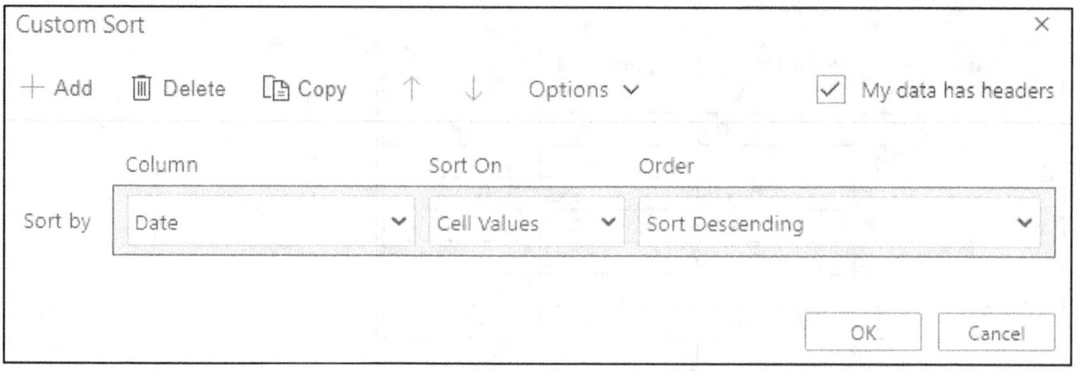

Chapter 4 – Excel

Figure 4.87

Many times you will want to sort on more than one value and to do this you will need to click on the *Add* button which will add another sort field to the list. Your data will be sorted by the first selection and then by the second selection. So in my case, I will be sorting by Amount and then by Reference #. If your spreadsheet has headers (column titles) you will want to check the box that says *My data has headers,* so they don't get sorted with the rest of your data.

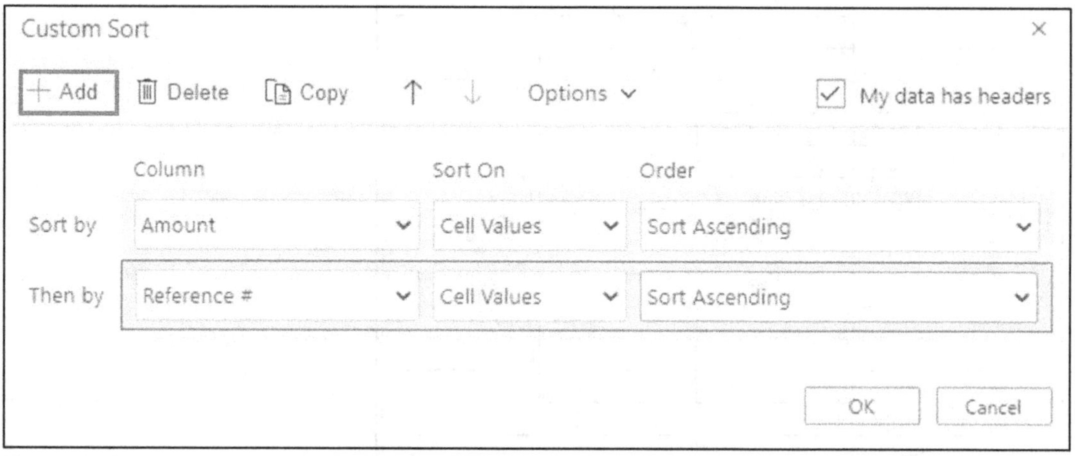

Figure 4.88

As you can see in figure 4.89, my list is sorted by Amount as the primary sort and then by Reference # as the secondary sort and for any cells with the same value in the Amount column will be sorted first and then the values in the Reference # columns will be sorted after that. I have highlighted a couple of examples of this.

Chapter 4 – Excel

	A	B	C	D
1	Date	Reference #	Amount	Code
2	6/4/20	39521	14.25	GB-74
3	3/17/21	15475	15.23	WS-45
4	10/4/19	15756	15.25	AC-65
5	12/19/19	25632	15.25	TR-45
6	5/15/19	37521	15.87	TR-96
7	2/21/20	15892	16.89	TR-85
8	9/25/20	97621	18.75	GB-45
9	3/12/19	78952	23.54	TR-98
10	3/14/20	45214	25.24	FR-63
11	11/12/19	32567	25.52	AC-25
12	7/7/19	62987	35.24	TR-21
13	8/26/21	66871	35.62	WS-65
14	5/18/20	21564	42.23	WS-63
15	1/12/19	36758	45.12	TR-85
16	5/15/19	45985	45.21	BR-63
17	9/25/19	54521	45.21	AC-85
18	2/24/21	88524	45.52	WS-12
19	9/14/20	56514	51.25	FR-65
20	6/4/20	14521	51.36	FR-56
21	5/12/20	98652	51.36	WS-45

Figure 4.89

The *Options* section shown in figure 4.88 will let you change your sorting to be case sensitive and also allow you to sort left to right rather than top to bottom even though this is not nearly as common.

Filtering
If you have a large spreadsheet with more data than you care to look at, you can use the filtering tool to have Excel only show you what you want to see. The filtering process will not delete the data you don't want to see but rather filter it out or hide it, so it is not displayed.

The filtering process works in a similar fashion as the sorting process where you highlight the data you wish to filter and then click on the *Sort and Filter* button

Chapter 4 – Excel

and then click on *Filter*. You will then see the cells in the top row change and have a dropdown arrow next to them. These arrows are used to choose your filtering options and different types of data will have different types of filtering choices.

	A	B	C	D	E	F
1	Date	Reference	Amount	Code		
2	6/4/20	39521	14.25	GB-74	Sort Ascending	
3	3/17/21	15475	15.23	WS-45		
4	10/4/19	15756	15.25	AC-65	Sort Descending	
5	12/19/19	25632	15.25	TR-45	Custom Sort	
6	5/15/19	37521	15.87	TR-96		
7	2/21/20	15892	16.89	TR-85	Sheet View	>
8	9/25/20	97621	18.75	GB-45		
9	3/12/19	78952	23.54	TR-98	Clear Filter from 'Code'	
10	3/14/20	45214	25.24	FR-63	Text Filters	>
11	11/12/19	32567	25.52	AC-25		
12	7/7/19	62987	35.24	TR-21	Filter...	
13	8/26/21	66871	35.62	WS-65		

Figure 4.90

Figure 4.91 shows the filtering options for text, numbers and dates and as you can see, you get a variety of different choices based on the data type.

Chapter 4 – Excel

Text	Number	Date
Equals...	Equals...	Equals...
Does Not Equal...	Does Not Equal...	Before...
Begins With...	Greater Than...	After...
Ends With...	Less Than...	Between...
Contains...	Between...	Tomorrow
Does Not Contain...	Top 10...	Today
Custom Filter...	Above Average	Yesterday
	Below Average	Next Week
	Custom Filter...	This Week
		Last Week
		Next Month
		This Month
		Last Month
		Next Quarter
		This Quarter
		Last Quarter
		Next Year
		This Year
		Last Year
		Year To Date
		All Dates in the Period >
		Custom Filter...

Figure 4.91

For my example, I want to filter out my data so only dates between 10/15/19 and 3/15/20 are shown. To do this I will click the down arrow on the Date column and choose the Between option and type in my dates and then click the OK button.

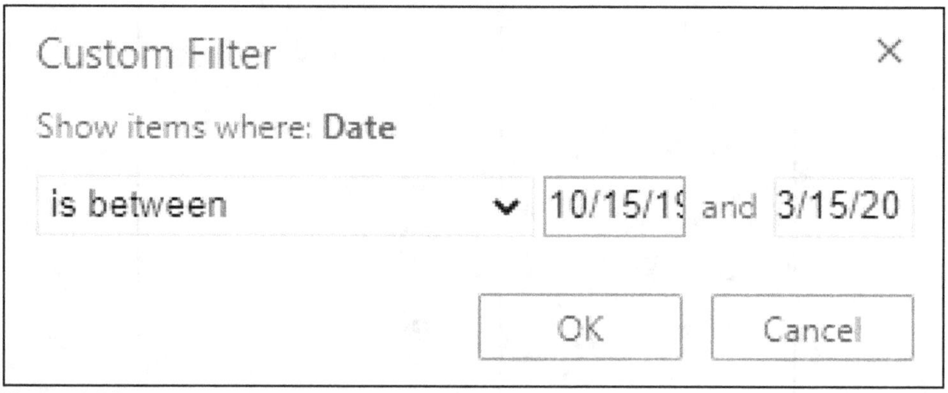

Figure 4.92

My sheet now only shows the data that match the date range I used for the filter and you can see a filter icon on the button next to the word Date. You might also notice that it keeps the row numbers for these filtered items the same as when they were not filtered. That is why there are missing numbers for some of the rows.

	A	B	C	D
1	Date	Reference	Amount	Code
5	12/19/19	25632	15.25	TR-45
7	2/21/20	15892	16.89	TR-85
10	3/14/20	45214	25.24	FR-63
11	11/12/19	32567	25.52	AC-25
23	12/15/19	55698	52.51	BR-52
25	11/15/19	32654	62.24	AC-52
31	3/14/20	69354	74.52	WS-56

Figure 4.93

To remove a filter you can go back to the Sort & Filter button and click on *Clear*. If you click on the *Filter* button again it will clear the filter and also remove the filter drop down selection arrows from your column headings.

Another way to filter is to just click on the word *Filter* as seen at the bottom of figure 4.90 and then choose the items you want to be displayed.

Chapter 4 – Excel

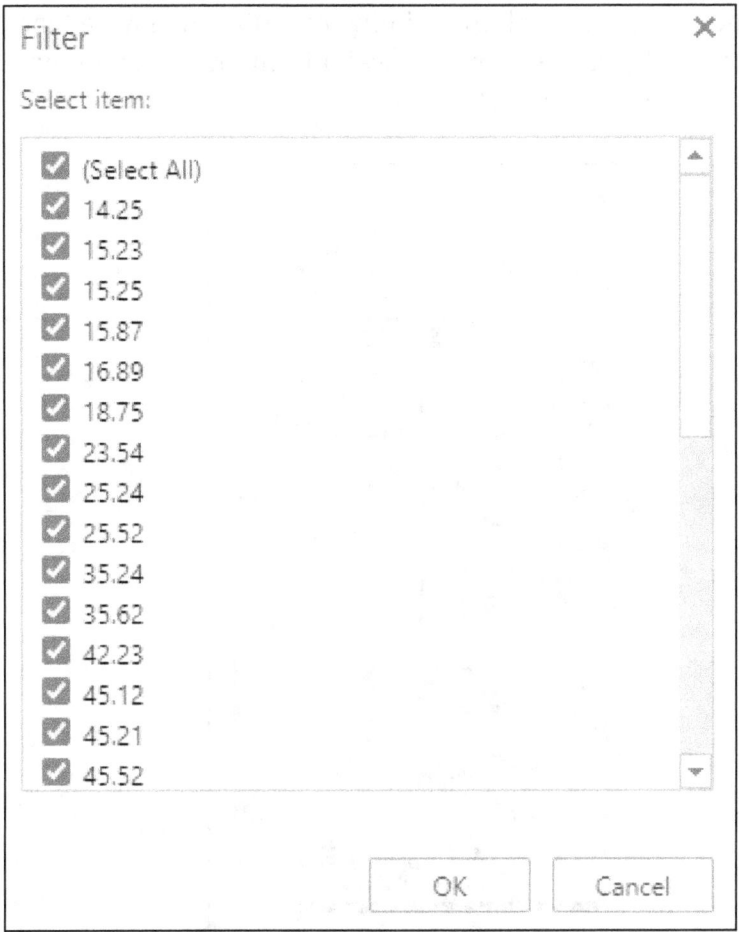

Figure 4.94

Functions and Formulas

One of the main reasons for using Excel is to have it manipulate your data for you and perform calculations, so you don't have to break out the old calculator and remember how to do math!

Functions are preconfigured formulas that you can have Excel apply to your data while formulas are expressions you create that then act on values in a cell or a range of cells.

One of the most basic and commonly used functions in Excel is the *AutoSum* function. This function will take a list of numbers and add them up and give you a total at the end of the row or bottom of the column. If you change any of the numbers or add more to the list then the total will automatically update itself.

Chapter 4 – Excel

If I were to highlight the numbers from column B in figure 4.95 and leave a blank spot at the bottom for the total, I can then have Excel add them up for me with one click of the AutoSum button (Σ) on the Home tab.

	A	B
1		**Sales**
2		$53.25
3		$85.62
4		$24.87
5		$85.21
6		$65.87
7		$103.25
8	Total	

Figure 4.95

Figure 4.96 shows the results of applying the AutoSum function to cell B8 and you can also see the actual formula for that cell in the formula bar (**=SUM(B2:B7)**). This tells me it is taking the sum of cells B2 through B7.

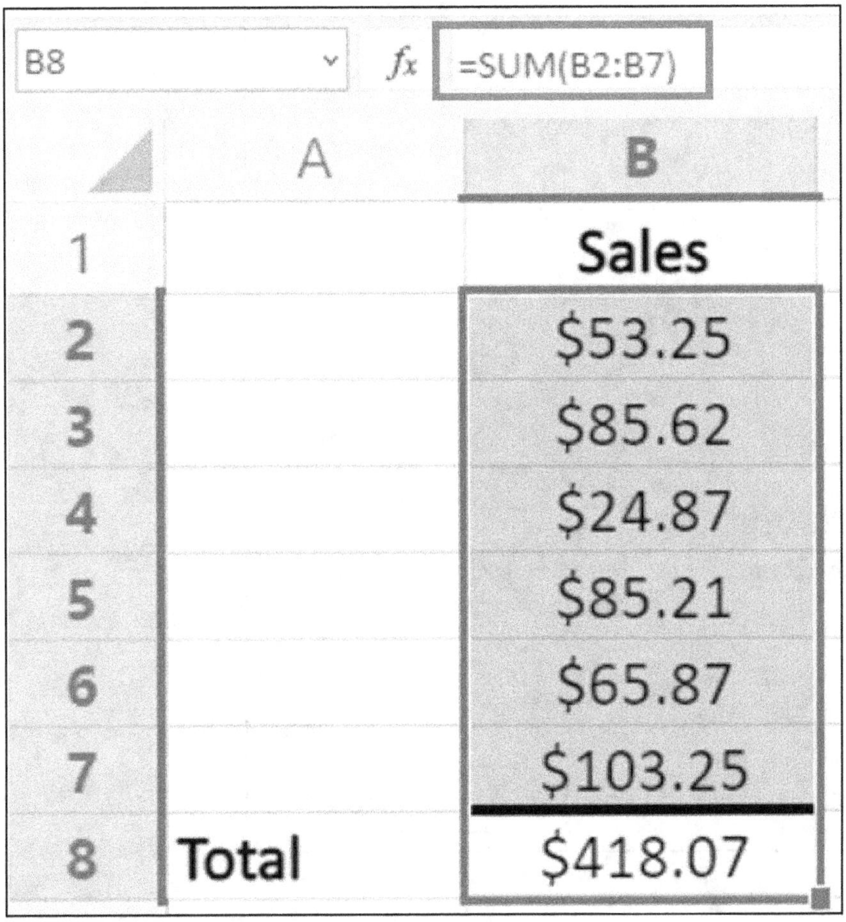

Chapter 4 – Excel

	A	B
1		Sales
2		$53.25
3		$85.62
4		$24.87
5		$85.21
6		$65.87
7		$103.25
8	Total	$418.07

B8   fx   =SUM(B2:B7)

Figure 4.96

If I were to click on More Functions from the AutoSum menu or by clicking on the **fx** function button to the left of the address bar I would see what other functions I have available to use. They are grouped by category or you can also have it show all of the functions. As you click on each one, you will be given a description of what that function does as well as the context that is used for that function.

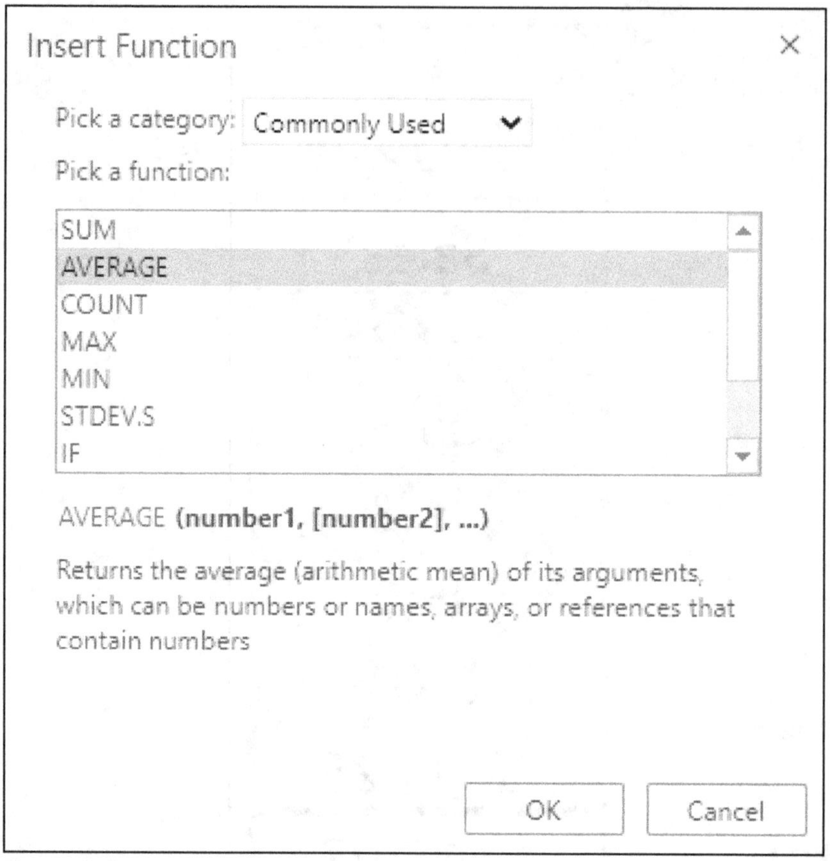

Chapter 4 – Excel

Figure 4.97

If the preconfigured functions don't work for you then you can create your own formulas to accomplish your goals. Formulas can be very simple like the AutoSum example or be very complex and span data covering multiple worksheets.

All formulas begin with an equal sign (=) and this tells Excel that the data that follows the equal sign is part of a calculation. Of course you can also use = within your formulas if needed.

Going back to my previous example, if I wanted to add up cells B2, B3 and B7 and then multiply the results by 2 and have the results in cell A1, I would create a formula that looks like **=(B2+B3+B7)*2** and type that in cell A1.

To begin I would select cell A1 and then type my formula in that cell or in the address bar itself.

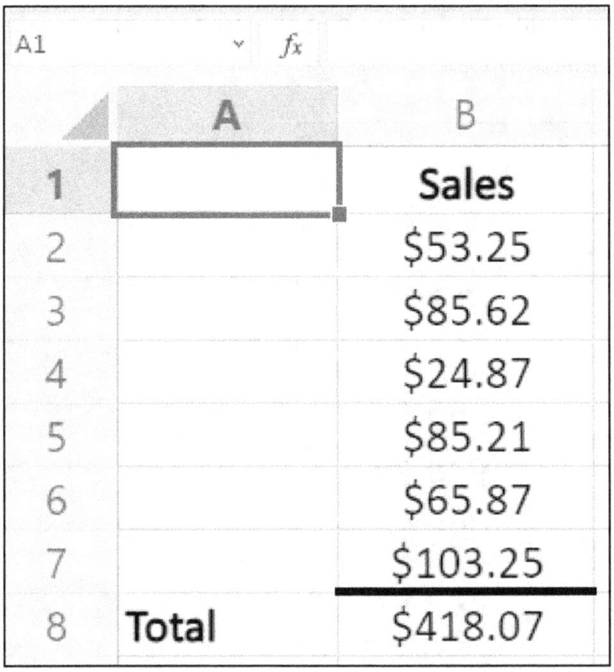

Chapter 4 – Excel

	A	B
1		Sales
2		$53.25
3		$85.62
4		$24.87
5		$85.21
6		$65.87
7		$103.25
8	Total	$418.07

Figure 4.98

As you can see in figure 4.99, Excel will highlight the cells that apply to my formula as I'm typing it in and if I wanted to add cell B5 to my formula, I could just click on it to have it added.

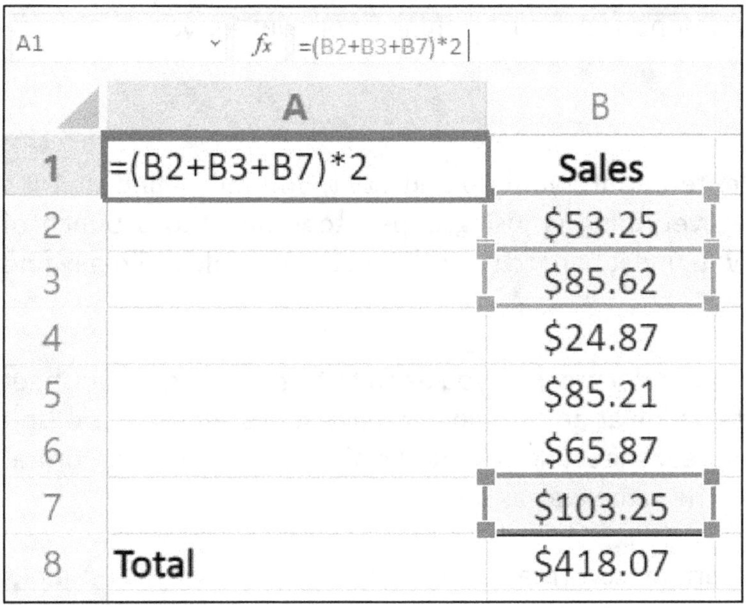

A1   fx =(B2+B3+B7)*2

	A	B
1	=(B2+B3+B7)*2	Sales
2		$53.25
3		$85.62
4		$24.87
5		$85.21
6		$65.87
7		$103.25
8	Total	$418.07

Figure 4.99

Chapter 4 – Excel

Now you can see that I have my results in cell A1 and the formula bar shows me the actual formula that has been applied to that cell.

	A	B
	A1 fx =(B2+B3+B7)*2	
1	$484.24	Sales
2		$53.25
3		$85.62
4		$24.87
5		$85.21
6		$65.87
7		$103.25
8	Total	$418.07

Figure 4.100

Formulas can be very complex and there are books written just on this subject so if you want to learn more then that is your best bet. Or you can just play around with some of your own creations and see how things work out for you.

Spreadsheet Formatting
Once you get your data entered into your spreadsheet, you might find that it's difficult to read because everything is just grouped together into a bunch of numbers and text. And if you find it hard to read, then other people will really find it hard to read.

Just like you do with your Word documents, you need to format your spreadsheet to make it more pleasant to look at and to have it make more sense. There isn't too much to formatting a spreadsheet and you should already know how to format your text because it works the same way as it did in Word.

Figure 4.101 shows an unformatted spreadsheet and as you can see, it just looks like a bunch of data thrown together with no real thought put into it.

	A	B	C	D	E	F	G	H	I	J	K	L	M	N	O	P
1	Segment	Country	Product	Discount Band	Units Sold	Manufacturing Price	Sale Price	Gross Sales	Discounts	Sales	COGS	Profit	Date	Month Number	Month Name	Year
2	Government	Canada	Carretera	None	1618.5	3	20	32370	0	32370	16185	16185	41640	1	January	2014
3	Government	Germany	Carretera	None	1321	3	20	26420	0	26420	13210	13210	41640	1	January	2014
4	Midmarket	France	Carretera	None	2178	3	15	32670	0	32670	21780	10890	41791	6	June	2014
5	Midmarket	Germany	Carretera	None	888	3	15	13320	0	13320	8880	4440	41791	6	June	2014
6	Midmarket	Mexico	Carretera	None	2470	3	15	37050	0	37050	24700	12350	41791	6	June	2014
7	Government	Germany	Carretera	None	1513	3	350	529550	0	529550	393380	136170	41974	10	December	2014
8	Midmarket	Germany	Montana	None	921	5	15	13815	0	13815	9210	4605	41699	3	March	2014
9	Channel Partners	Canada	Montana	None	2518	5	12	30216	0	30216	7554	22662	41791	6	June	2014
10	Government	France	Montana	None	1899	5	20	37980	0	37980	18990	18990	41791	6	June	2014
11	Channel Partners	Germany	Montana	None	1545	5	12	18540	0	18540	4635	13905	41791	6	June	2014
12	Midmarket	Mexico	Montana	None	2470	5	15	37050	0	37050	24700	12350	41791	6	June	2014
13	Enterprise	Canada	Montana	None	2665.5	5	125	333187.5	0	333187.5	319860	13327.5	41821	7	July	2014
14	Small Business	Mexico	Montana	None	958	5	300	287400	0	287400	239500	47900	41852	8	August	2014
15	Government	Germany	Montana	None	2146	5	7	15022	0	15022	10730	4292	41883	9	September	2014
16	Enterprise	Canada	Montana	None	345	5	125	43125	0	43125	41400	1725	41548	10	October	2013
17	Midmarket	United States of America	Montana	None	615	5	15	9225	0	9225	6150	3075	41974	12	December	2014
18	Government	Canada	Paseo	None	292	10	20	5840	0	5840	2920	2920	41671	2	February	2014
19	Midmarket	Mexico	Paseo	None	974	10	15	14610	0	14610	9740	4870	41671	2	February	2014
20	Channel Partners	Canada	Paseo	None	2518	10	12	30216	0	30216	7554	22662	41791	6	June	2014
21	Government	Germany	Paseo	None	1006	10	350	352100	0	352100	261560	90540	41791	6	June	2014
22	Channel Partners	Germany	Paseo	None	367	10	12	4404	0	4404	1101	3303	41821	7	July	2014
23	Government	Mexico	Paseo	None	883	10	7	6181	0	6181	4415	1766	41852	8	August	2014
24	Midmarket	France	Paseo	None	549	10	15	8235	0	8235	5490	2745	41518	9	September	2013
25	Small Business	Mexico	Paseo	None	788	10	300	236400	0	236400	197000	39400	41518	9	September	2013
26	Midmarket	Mexico	Paseo	None	2472	10	15	37080	0	37080	24720	12360	41883	9	September	2014
27	Government	United States of America	Paseo	None	1143	10	7	8001	0	8001	5715	2286	41913	10	October	2014
28	Government	Canada	Paseo	None	1725	10	350	603750	0	603750	448500	155250	41579	11	November	2013
29	Channel Partners	United States of America	Paseo	None	912	10	12	10944	0	10944	2736	8208	41579	11	November	2013
30	Midmarket	Canada	Paseo	None	2152	10	15	32280	0	32280	21520	10760	41609	12	December	2013
31	Government	Canada	Paseo	None	1817	10	20	36340	0	36340	18170	18170	41974	12	December	2014
32	Government	Germany	Paseo	None	1513	10	350	529550	0	529550	393380	136170	41974	12	December	2014
33	Government	Mexico	Velo	None	1493	120	7	10451	0	10451	7465	2986	41640	1	January	2014
34	Enterprise	France	Velo	None	1804	120	125	225500	0	225500	216480	9020	41671	2	February	2014

Figure 4.101

As you can see, many of the columns have extra space because the text or numbers in the cells are much smaller than the column headings. You can also see that it's hard to differentiate the column headings from the rest of the data in the cells.

The first thing I want to do is utilize the Word Wrap feature in some of the cells to get rid of some of the extra space and this will also shrink down the overall width of my spreadsheet which will help it fit on the screen and also help when it comes time to print it.

To do this, I will highlight the cells that I want this to apply to which in this case is the first cell of each column.

Chapter 4 – Excel

Discount Band	Units Sold	Manufacturing Price	Sale Price
None	1618.5	3	20
None	1321	3	20
None	2178	3	15
None	888	3	15
None	2470	3	15
None	1513	3	350
None	921	5	15
None	2518	5	12
None	1899	5	20
None	1545	5	12
None	2470	5	15
None	2665.5	5	125
None	958	5	300

Figure 4.102

Then I will go to the *Home* tab and click on *Wrap*. You won't see much happen except for the height of the row will increase.

Discount Band	Units Sold	Manufacturing Price	Sale Price
None	1618.5	3	20
None	1321	3	20
None	2178	3	15

Figure 4.103

Now when I shrink the row size down, the text will move to the next line down and I can adjust it the way I like. I can even center the text in the header if I like. And if I want to make the rest of the data match I can center that as well by highlighting the text and clicking the center option from the *Align* section on the Home tab.

Chapter 4 – Excel

D	E	F	G	H
Discount Band	Units Sold	Manufacturing Price	Sale Price	Gross Sales
None	1618.5	3	20	32370
None	1321	3	20	26420
None	2178	3	15	32670
None	888	3	15	13320
None	2470	3	15	37050
None	1513	3	350	529550
None	921	5	15	13815
None	2518	5	12	30216
None	1899	5	20	37980
None	1545	5	12	18540
None	2470	5	15	37050
None	2665.5	5	125	333187.5
None	958	5	300	287400

Figure 4.104

Next, I want to make my header text stand out a little better by increasing the font size, making it bold and also adding a yellow fill color to the cells. All I need to do is highlight the cells in row 1 and click on the bold button for the text and then increase its size. To add a fill color I will click on the paint bucket icon on the Home tab and choose my color. If I click on *More Colors* I can then create my own custom color if I don't like any of the default colors. Figure 4.106 shows the results of my formatting.

Chapter 4 – Excel

Figure 4.105

Chapter 4 – Excel

	A	B	C	D	E	F	G	H
1	Segment	Country	Product	Discount Band	Units Sold	Manufacturing Price	Sale Price	Gross Sales
2	Government	Canada	Carretera	None	1618.5	3	20	32370
3	Government	Germany	Carretera	None	1321	3	20	26420
4	Midmarket	France	Carretera	None	2178	3	15	32670
5	Midmarket	Germany	Carretera	None	888	3	15	13320
6	Midmarket	Mexico	Carretera	None	2470	3	15	37050
7	Government	Germany	Carretera	None	1513	3	350	529550
8	Midmarket	Germany	Montana	None	921	5	15	13815
9	Channel Partners	Canada	Montana	None	2518	5	12	30216
10	Government	France	Montana	None	1899	5	20	37980
11	Channel Partners	Germany	Montana	None	1545	5	12	18540
12	Midmarket	Mexico	Montana	None	2470	5	15	37050
13	Enterprise	Canada	Montana	None	2665.5	5	125	333187.5
14	Small Business	Mexico	Montana	None	958	5	300	287400

Figure 4.106

Now that I have my changes made, I still think I need to add some cell borders to make the rows and columns stand out a little better. To do this I will highlight all of the cells with data in the sheet and then click on the *All Borders* selection to add a border to all four sides of each cell. I will also add the *Thick Bottom Border* to the cells in the first row to make the headers stand out a bit more. You can also change the border color from the default black as well as change the style to something like a dotted line if that better suits your needs. The results are shown in figure 4.108.

Chapter 4 – Excel

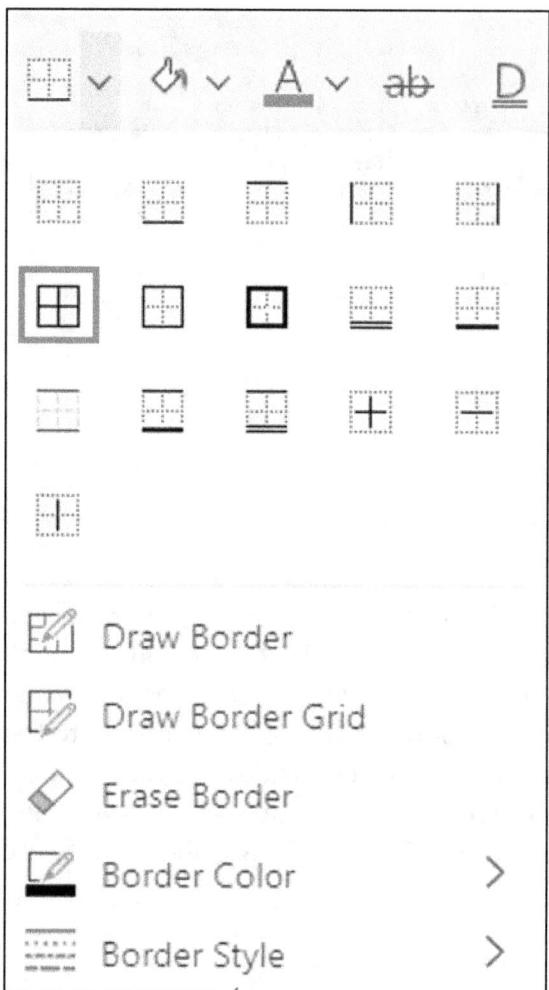

Figure 4.107

	A	B	C	D	E	F	G	H
1	Segment	Country	Product	Discount Band	Units Sold	Manufacturing Price	Sale Price	Gross Sales
2	Government	Canada	Carretera	None	1618.5	3	20	32370
3	Government	Germany	Carretera	None	1321	3	20	26420
4	Midmarket	France	Carretera	None	2178	3	15	32670
5	Midmarket	Germany	Carretera	None	888	3	15	13320
6	Midmarket	Mexico	Carretera	None	2470	3	15	37050
7	Government	Germany	Carretera	None	1513	3	350	529550
8	Midmarket	Germany	Montana	None	921	5	15	13815
9	Channel Partners	Canada	Montana	None	2518	5	12	30216
10	Government	France	Montana	None	1899	5	20	37980
11	Channel Partners	Germany	Montana	None	1545	5	12	18540
12	Midmarket	Mexico	Montana	None	2470	5	15	37050
13	Enterprise	Canada	Montana	None	2665.5	5	125	333187.5
14	Small Business	Mexico	Montana	None	958	5	300	287400

Figure 4.108

 When adding cell borders to your spreadsheet, keep in mind that if you have some borders in place and change them to another type then their neighboring borders might be changed as well on their touching and you will need to make some adjustments to get things looking uniform.

Adding, Renaming and Hiding Sheets

When you start a new Excel spreadsheet, it will have one sheet by default named Sheet1 This doesn't mean you are stuck with just this one sheet or the name for that matter. You might want to add additional sheets to help keep your data organized and you might also want to rename the default sheet to something that makes a little more sense.

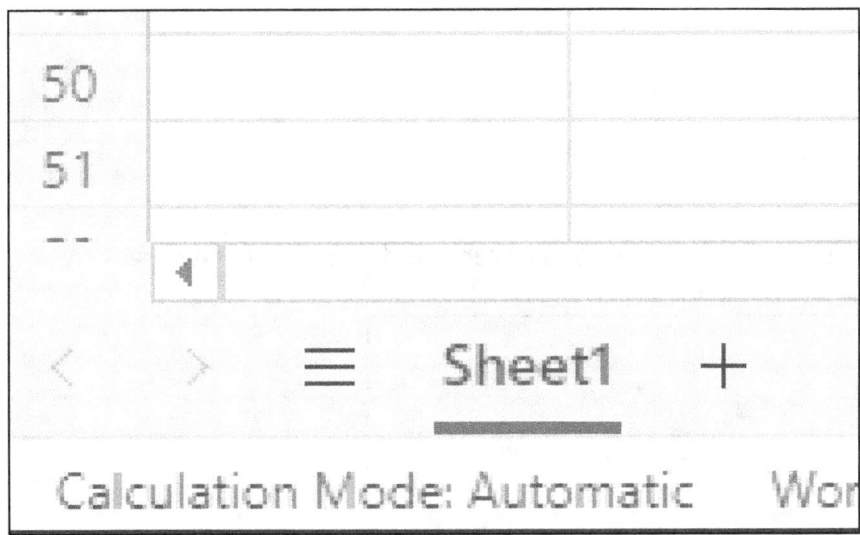

Figure 4.109

If you were to right click on Sheet1, you would be given many options to do things such as rename the sheet, insert a new sheet, delete the sheet and so on. You might have noticed in figure 4.110 that the delete option is greyed out and that is because you can delete a sheet if it's the only one in your workbook.

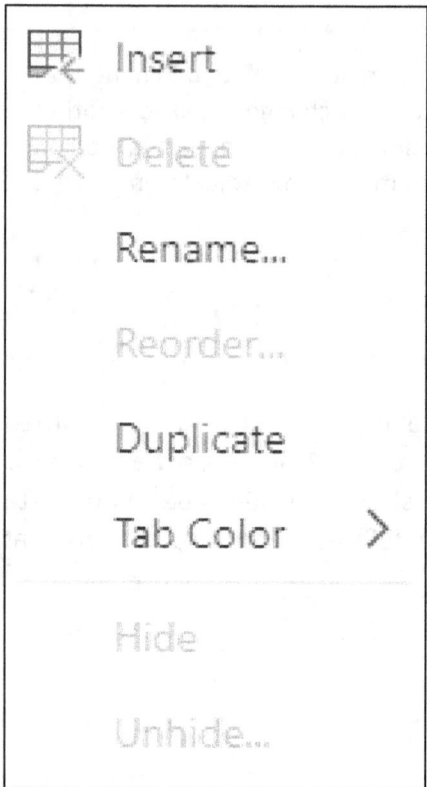
Figure 4.110

Figure 4.111 shows my Sheet1 sheet after I renamed it to **Sales Data**.

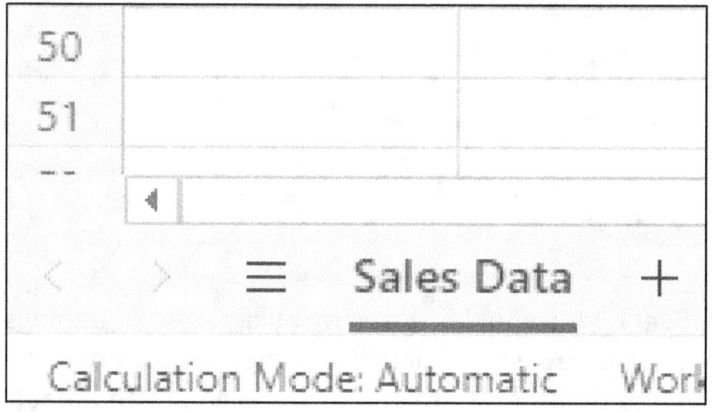
Figure 4.111

I will now create another sheet named **Marketing Data** and change its tab color to yellow.

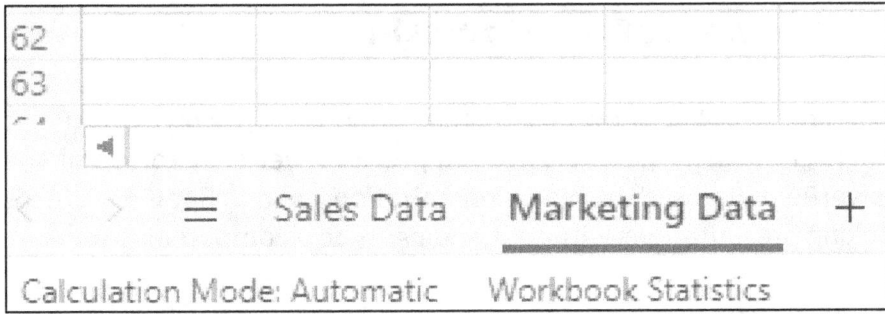

Figure 4.112

Now I can switch between sheets by clicking on the sheet name or by clicking on the three vertical line icon to bring up my sheet list. If I want to hide a particular sheet (but not delete it), I can right click on it and choose the *Hide* option. This will hide the sheet and there will be nothing indicating that you have a hidden sheet so to unhide it, you will need to right click on an unhidden sheet and choose the *Unhide* option. Then you will be shown a list of your hidden sheets and can unhide them from there.

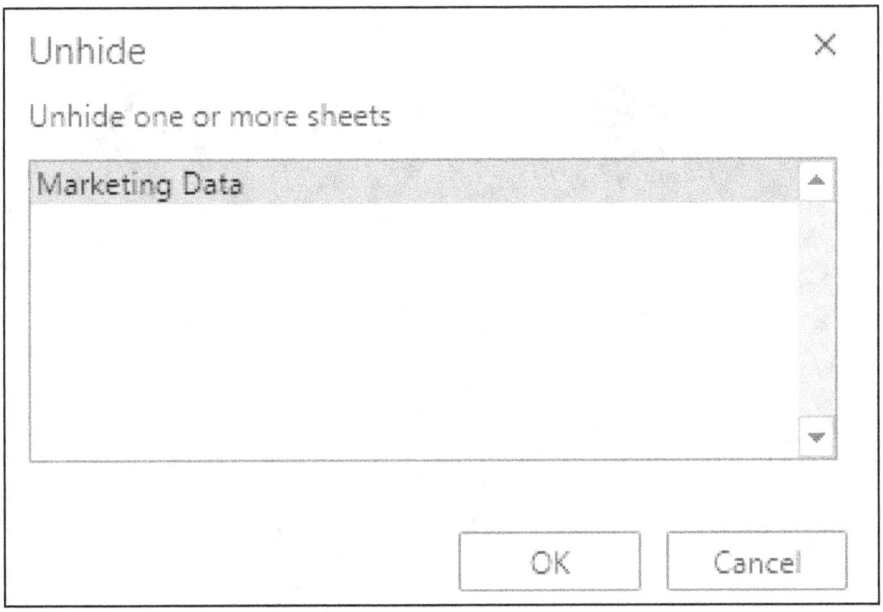

Figure 4.113

Chapter 5 – PowerPoint

When it comes to creating slide show based presentations, Microsoft PowerPoint is the go to program for most people since it's powerful yet easy to use at the same time. PowerPoint is used in many organizations and schools to create professional looking presentations without needing to be a computer guru.

The PowerPoint Interface
Just like with all of the other Office apps, when you open PowerPoint for the first time you will be presented with a listing of any recent, pinned or shared files unless it's your first time using the app with this user account. Then you will see a screen similar to figure 5.1. And from here you can start a new blank presentation or open a template or theme to get yourself started. I will be discussing templates and themes in the next section.

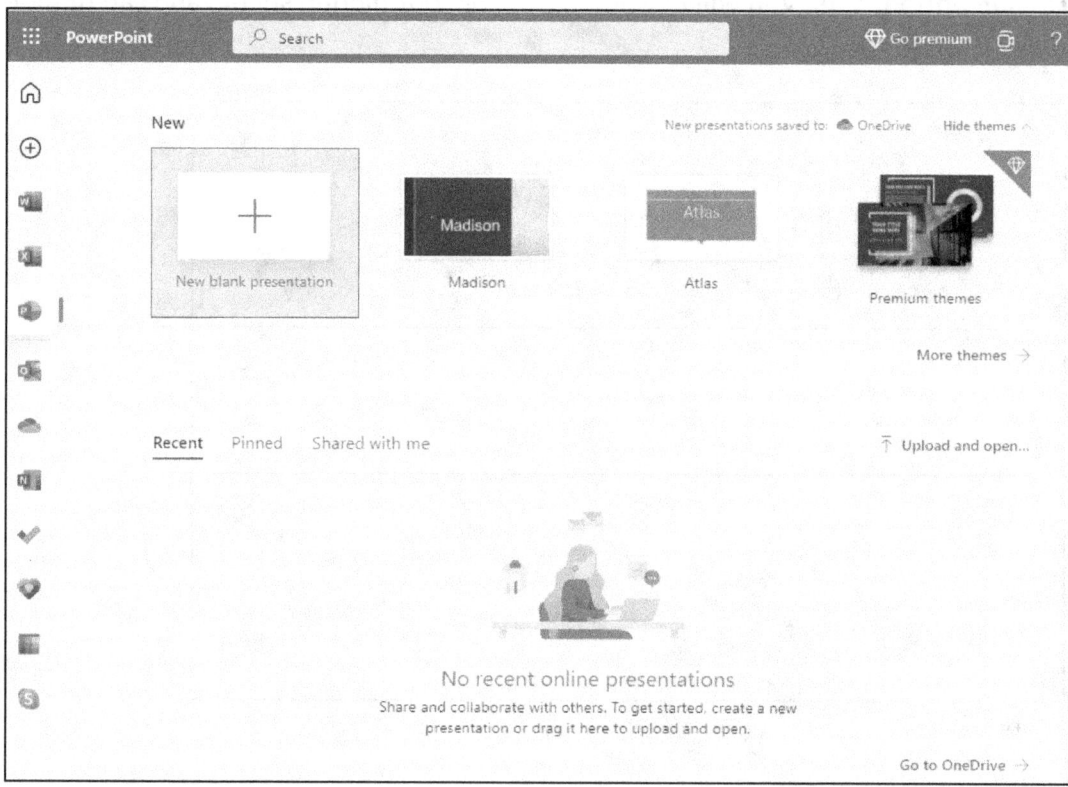

Figure 5.1

If you were to click on *New blank presentation* you would then be given a new file with one slide and two text boxes. You can then either start with what you have here and edit the existing text boxes or you can click on the box itself to highlight

Chapter 5 – PowerPoint

it and then delete it. If you click on the text and then press the delete key it will just delete the text itself and leave the text box there.

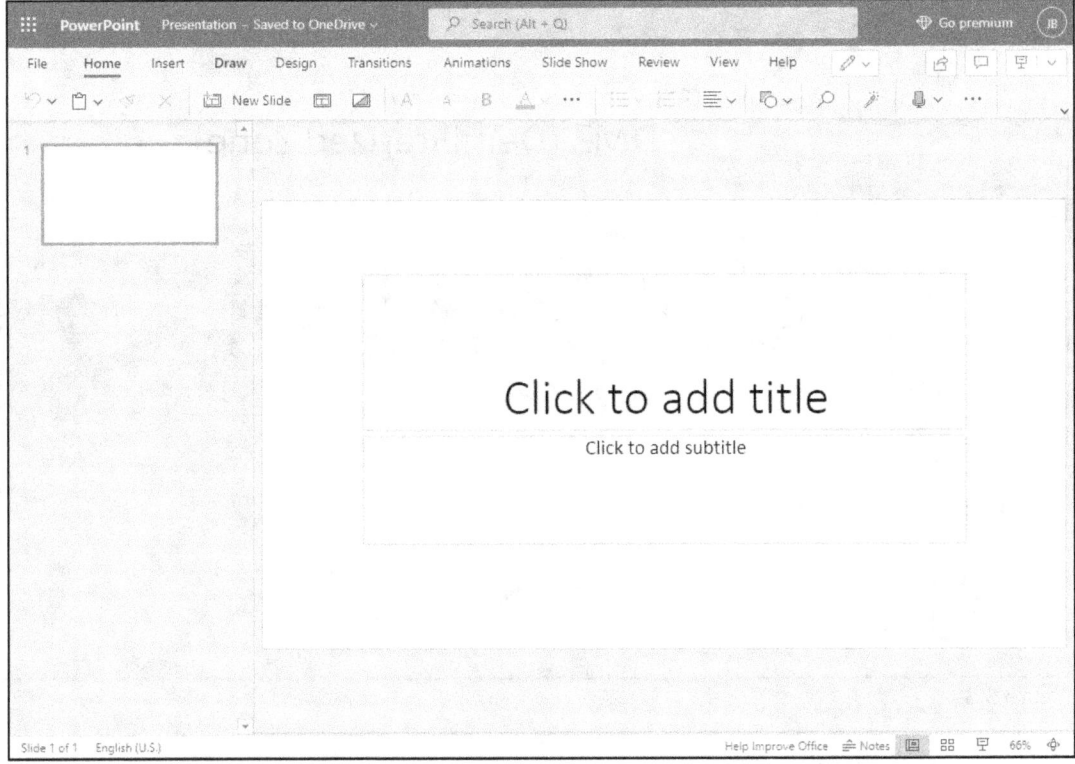

Figure 5.2

On the left side of the window you will see your slide deck which will show you a thumbnail type of view of your slides in the order that they are arranged in. Then you can click on any slide in the deck to make it your active slide. You can also click and drag slides around to rearrange their order.

Figure 5.3 shows you a better idea of how the slide thumbnail will look in your slide deck once you actually have some content on the slide.

Chapter 5 – PowerPoint

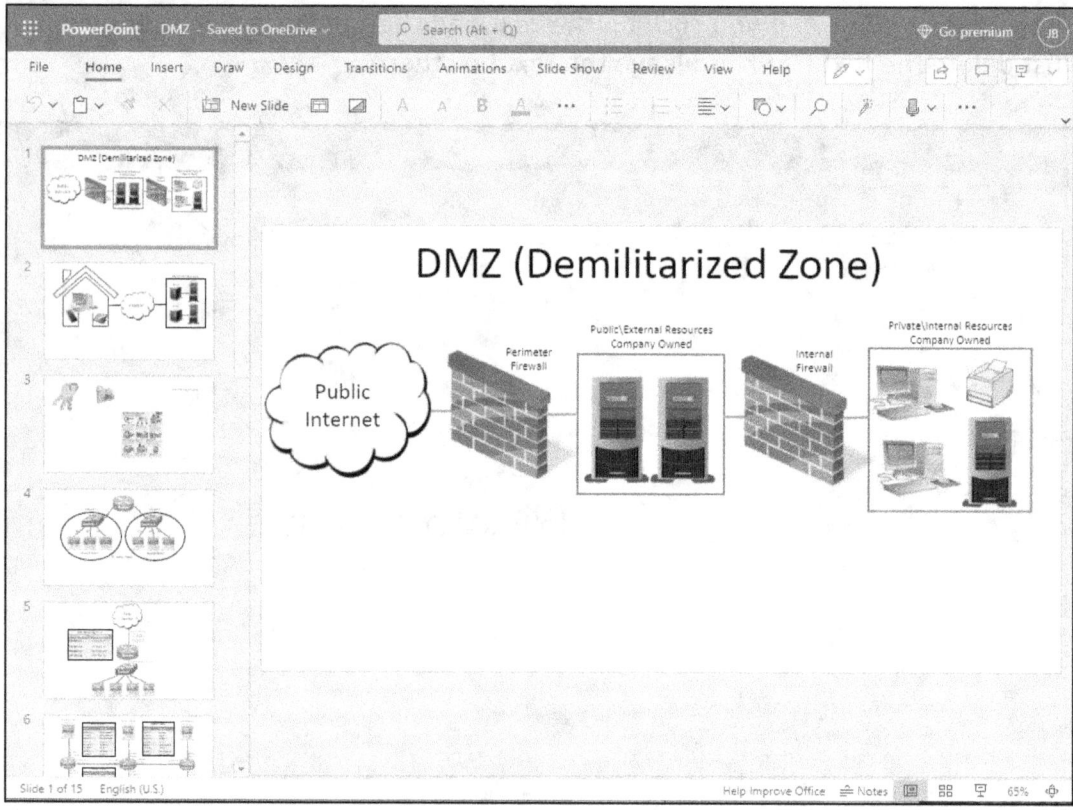

Figure 5.3

At the bottom right corner of the screen, there are some other utilities that you can access as needed.

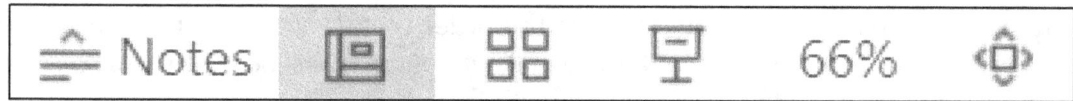

Figure 5.4

- **Notes** – This is used to add notes to your slides for your own reference when running your presentations. I will be discussing this in more detail later in the chapter.

- **Editing View** – This is the default view that you use when working on your presentation. If you change to Notes or another view you can click on this to get back to your working view.

- **Slide Sorter** – Here you can manage the slides in your presentation and rearrange them if needed by dragging them around to change their order. You can also right click on a side to do things such as duplicate or delete the slide. Another nice feature is the ability to add sections to help organize your slides and I will be going over that later in this chapter.

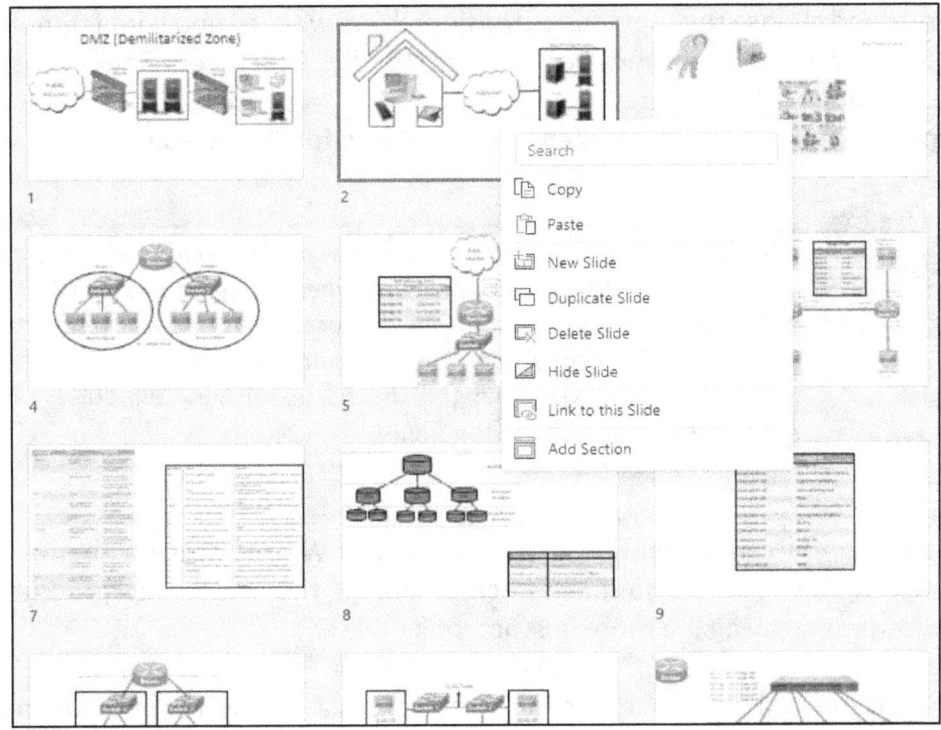
Figure 5.5

- **Slide Show** – When you are ready to run a full screen slide show of your presentation or to preview what your slide show will look like, you can use this option.

- **Zoom Level** – This will let you zoom in and out of your presentation to help you see your content more clearly.

- **Fit slide to current window** – Clicking on this will either zoom in or zoom out on your slide to make it fit the size of the window.

Themes and Templates
By now you should know what templates are and how to use them since I discussed them in the chapter on Microsoft Word. When it comes to using templates for PowerPoint for the Web, you can't just open one up from the File menu like you can for Word.

Chapter 5 – PowerPoint

PowerPoint template files come with the **.potx** file extension which can't be opened with PowerPoint for the Web. So what you need to do is have someone who has the regular PowerPoint software open a template file for you and do a save as and choose the **.pptx** file extension. If you want to find some template files that you can then convert you can go to the Office template website and download them from there.
https://templates.office.com/en-US/templates-for-PowerPoint

 File extensions are the letters (or numbers) after the period such as in a Word file called *Resume.docx* where **.docx** is the file extension. File extensions are used by Windows (and Macs) to make sure they open the program that corresponds to that file type. So if you changed the file extension, Windows wouldn't know how to open the file.

One thing you can do with PowerPoint for the Web is apply a theme to your presentation which will do things such as change the colors, background images and fonts etc., giving it a more custom look.

You can apply a theme to an existing presentation as shown in the before and after images in figures 5.6 and 5.7 or when you create a new presentation as seen in figure 5.8.

Figure 5.6

Chapter 5 – PowerPoint

Figure 5.7

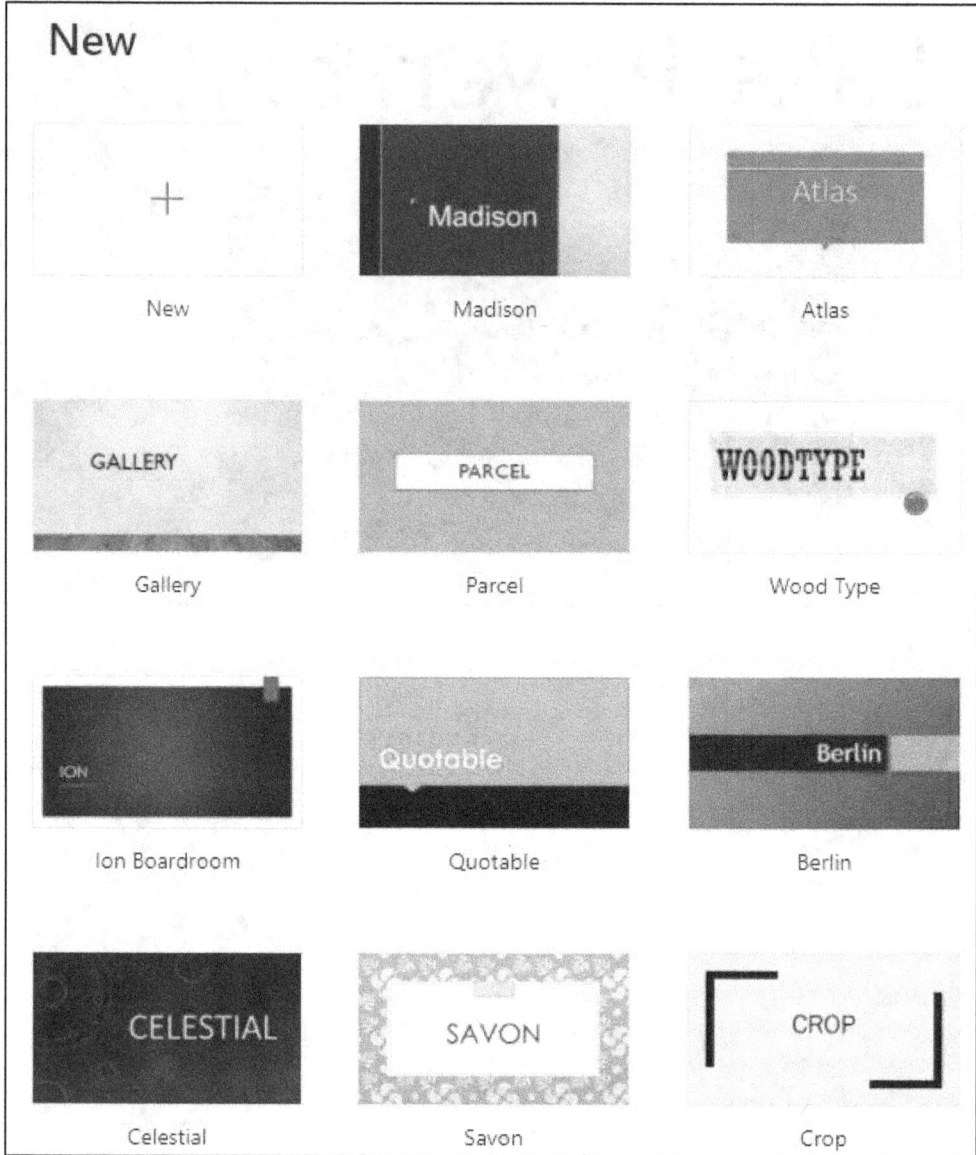

Figure 5.8

You can access the built in themes from the *Design* tab which I will show you in the next section.

Tabs and Ribbon Items
Once again we are at that part of the chapter where I will be discussing PowerPoint specific tabs and Ribbon items and once again I will only be covering the items that I have not discussed already.

Chapter 5 – PowerPoint

Home Tab

Here you will find your typical text formatting options as well as tools to help you arrange your slides and add some fancy design elements to your presentation.

New Slide, Layout and Hide Slide

Figure 5.9

- **New Slide** – There is a very good chance that your slide show will contain more than one slide so you can add additional slides from here. You can pick one of the built in layouts or choose a blank slide to start from scratch. If you have a theme applied to your presentation then that theme will be carried over to any new slides that you add.

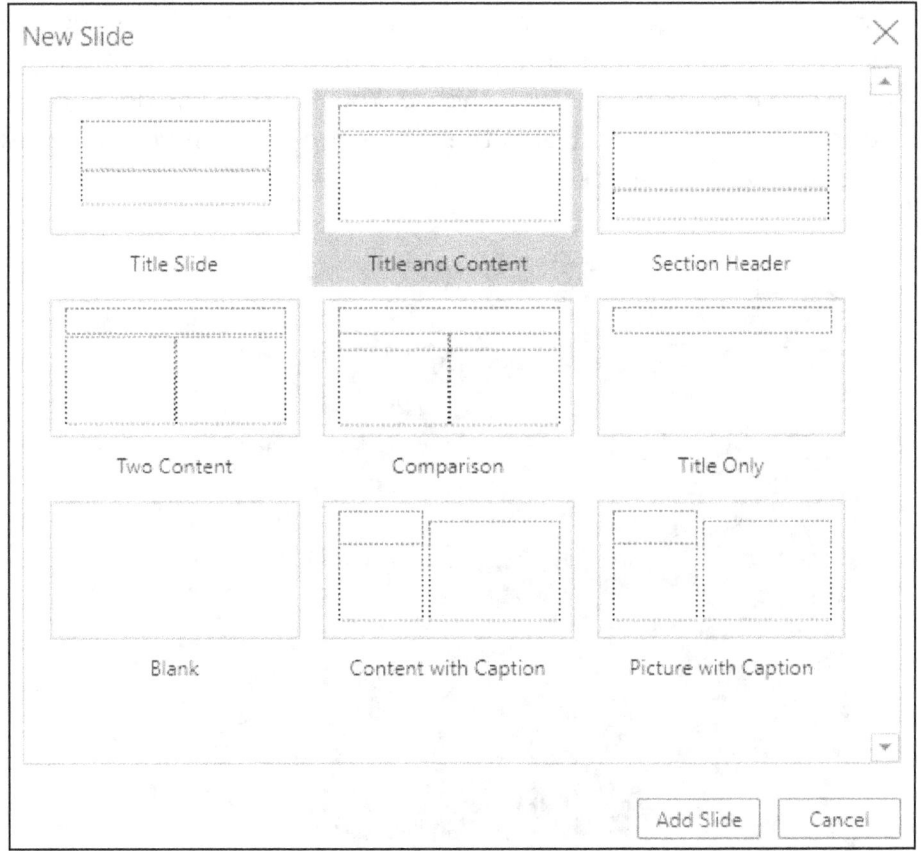

Figure 5.10

- **Layout** – Clicking this button will let you apply a new layout to your existing slide(s).

- **Hide Slide** – This will let you hide a slide, so it doesn't show during your slideshow. It will not delete the slide so you can bring it back later if you choose to do so. When a slide is hidden, it will appear greyed out in your slide deck.

Shapes and Shape Options

Figure 5.11

- **Shapes** – You can add a variety of shapes to your presentation such as squares, circles, arrows, stars, callouts and so on. Once you select the shape you want to add simply use your mouse to draw that shape on your side and make it any size you choose. You can click and drag on the corner or sides to enlarge or stretch the shape or click on the round arrow at the top to rotate the shape.

Figure 5.12

- **Shape Fill** – When you add a shape, it will be filled with a color (usually blue) by default as seen in figure 5.12. You can use the fill option to either change the color or remove the color which will make the interior of the shape transparent as seen in figure 5.13.

Figure 5.13

- **Shape Outline** – You can use this option to change the color of the shape outline or remove it completely. Just keep in mind if you don't have a fill or an outline applied then you won't be able to see your shape on the slide.

- **Shape Styles** – PowerPoint comes with some built in shape styles that you can apply to your shapes with one click.

Chapter 5 – PowerPoint

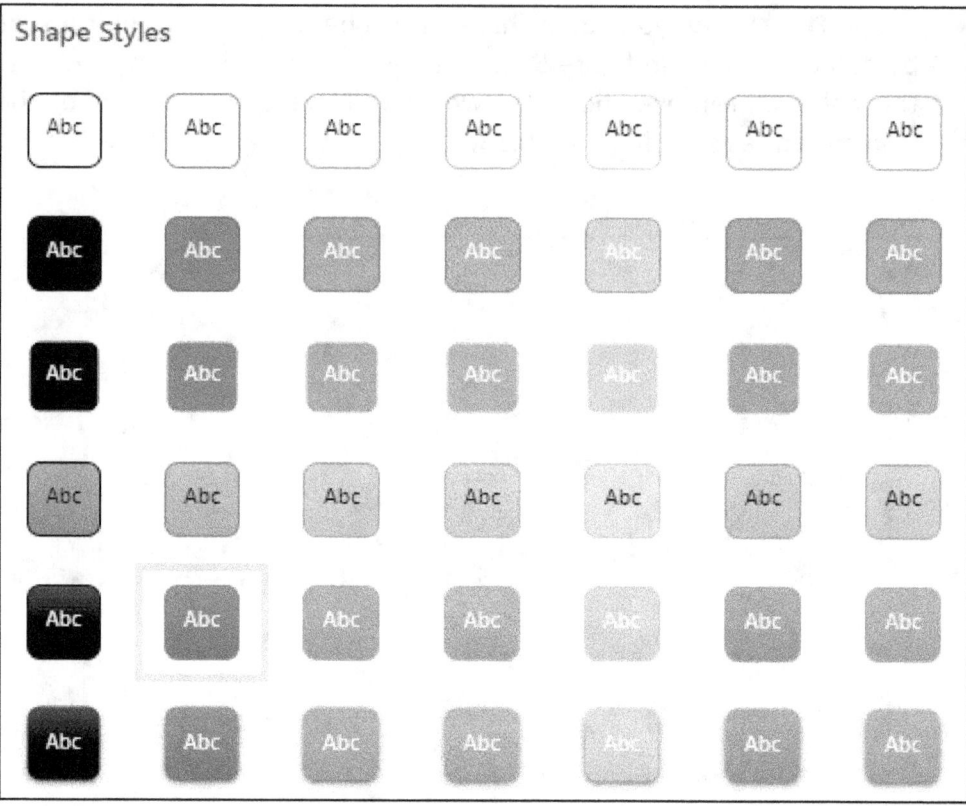

Figure 5.14

Chapter 5 – PowerPoint

Order Objects

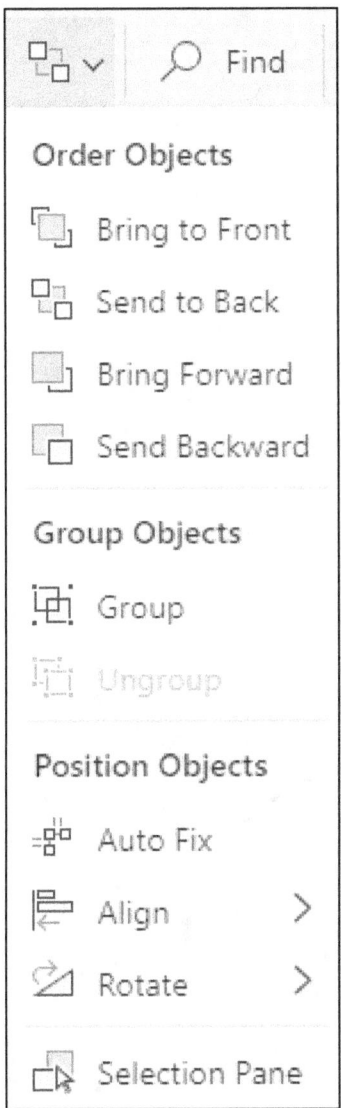

Figure 5.15

Once you start adding things such as shapes, pictures, text and so on to your slides you will most likely need to change their order so certain objects are not overlapping other objects and affecting the look of your presentation.

Figure 5.16 shows a box that is overlapping a smiley face shape and I want the smiley face to actually be in front of the box. To do this, I can either select the box and choose *Send Backward* or select the smiley and choose *Bring Forward* to change their order on the slide. The results are shown in figure 5.17.

Chapter 5 – PowerPoint

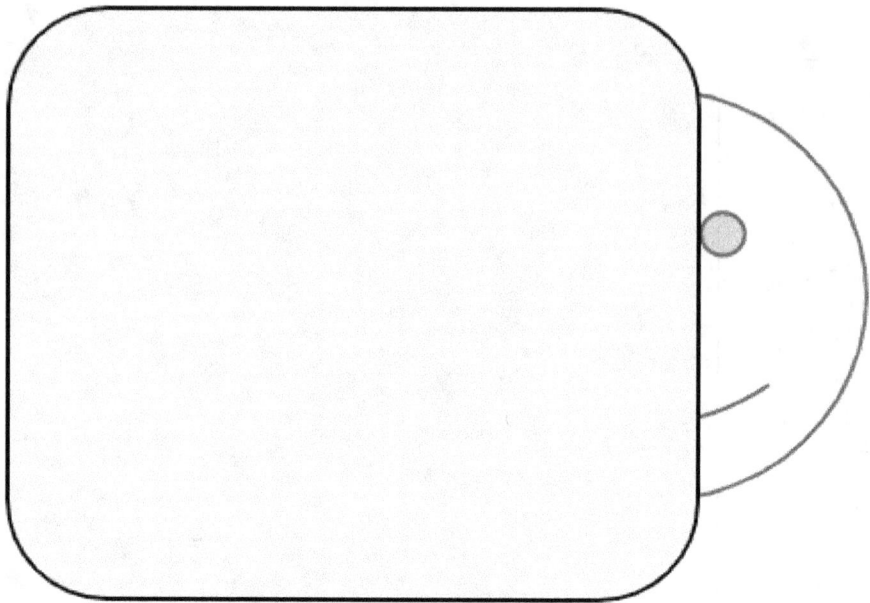

Figure 5.16

Figure 5.17

Send Backward and Bring Forward will move the selected item one step in the direction you choose. So if you have 4 objects stacked on each other and send the

Chapter 5 – PowerPoint

top one back one step, it will then be the second object from the top of the stacked objects.

The *Bring to Front* and *Send to Back* choices will bring the selected object all the way to the front or send it all the way to the back all in one step.

The *Group Objects* option can be used to group multiple objects together into one object allowing you to resize, move or rotate them all at once without having to select each one individually. If you need to move one of the grouped objects separately then you will need to ungroup the objects first.

The *Position Objects* settings can be used to do things such as change your alignment settings such as left, right, center and so on. You can also use the rotation objects to set custom rotation amounts or flip your objects vertically or horizontally.

The *Selection Pane* will show you your objects and let you do things such as change their order or hide them.

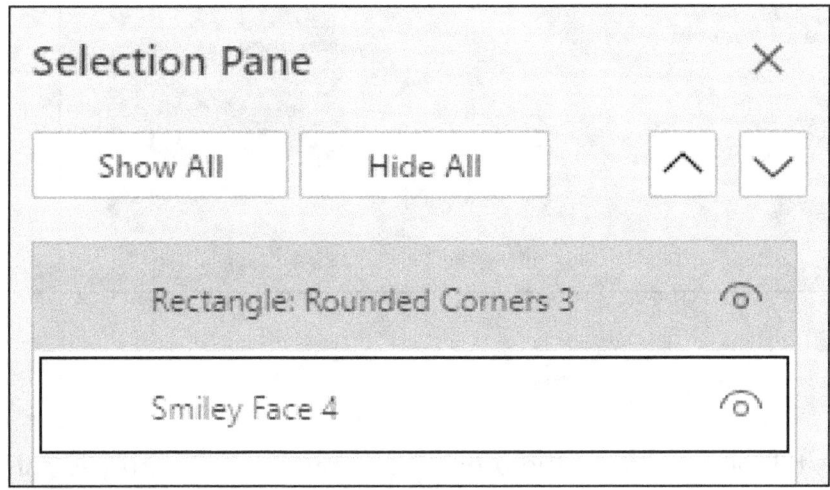

Figure 5.18

Designer

Figure 5.19

Chapter 5 – PowerPoint

The Designer can be used to have PowerPoint apply its own design ideas to your slides to save you time rather than having to pretend to be a designer yourself. The catch is that this feature is for premium members (Office 365\Microsoft 365).

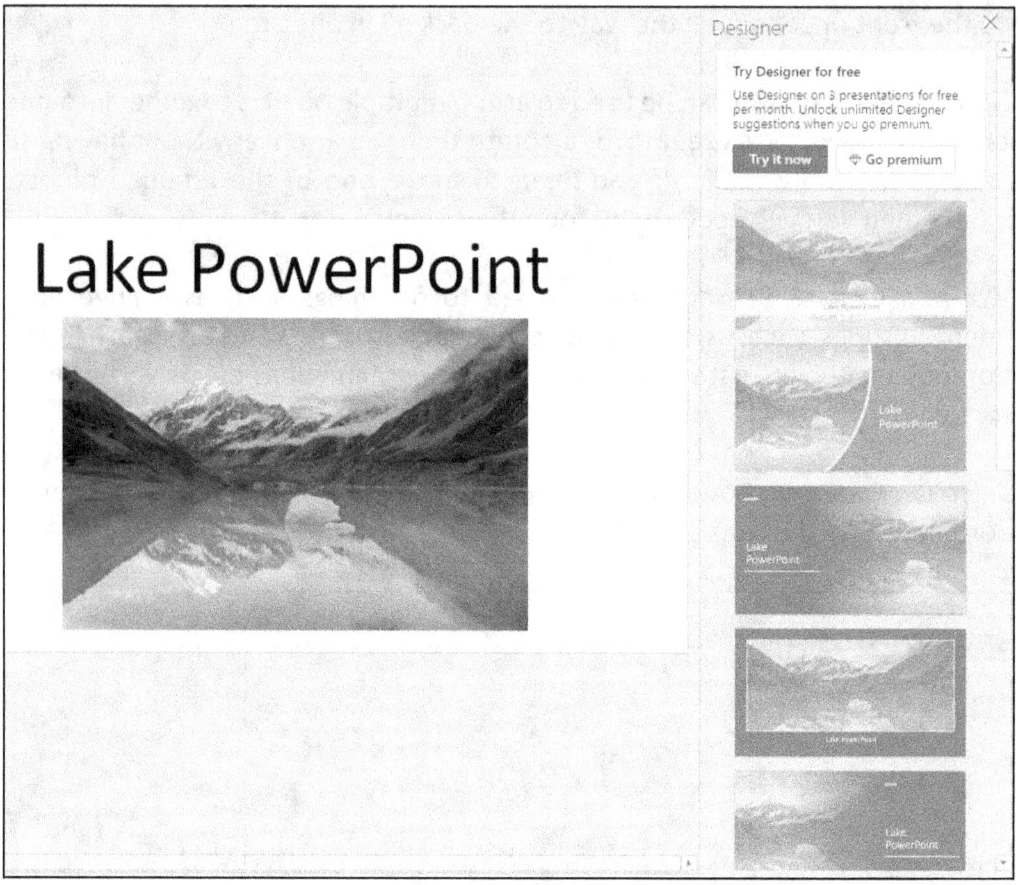

Figure 5.20

Insert Tab

The options on this tab are similar to the other Office programs where you can insert things such as pictures, shapes, videos and so on. There are some PowerPoint specific items you can insert though.

<u>New Slide and Table</u>

Figure 5.21

Chapter 5 – PowerPoint

I have already discussed how to add a new slide to your presentation but just wanted to show you that you can do the same thing from the Insert tab as well. You will get the exact same choices when inserting a slide from here.

The insert table option works exactly the same way it does in Word where you can drag your mouse to add as many rows and columns as you need (up to 10x8) for your table. You can't customize the table the same way you can with Word in regards to being able to type in the number of columns and rows.

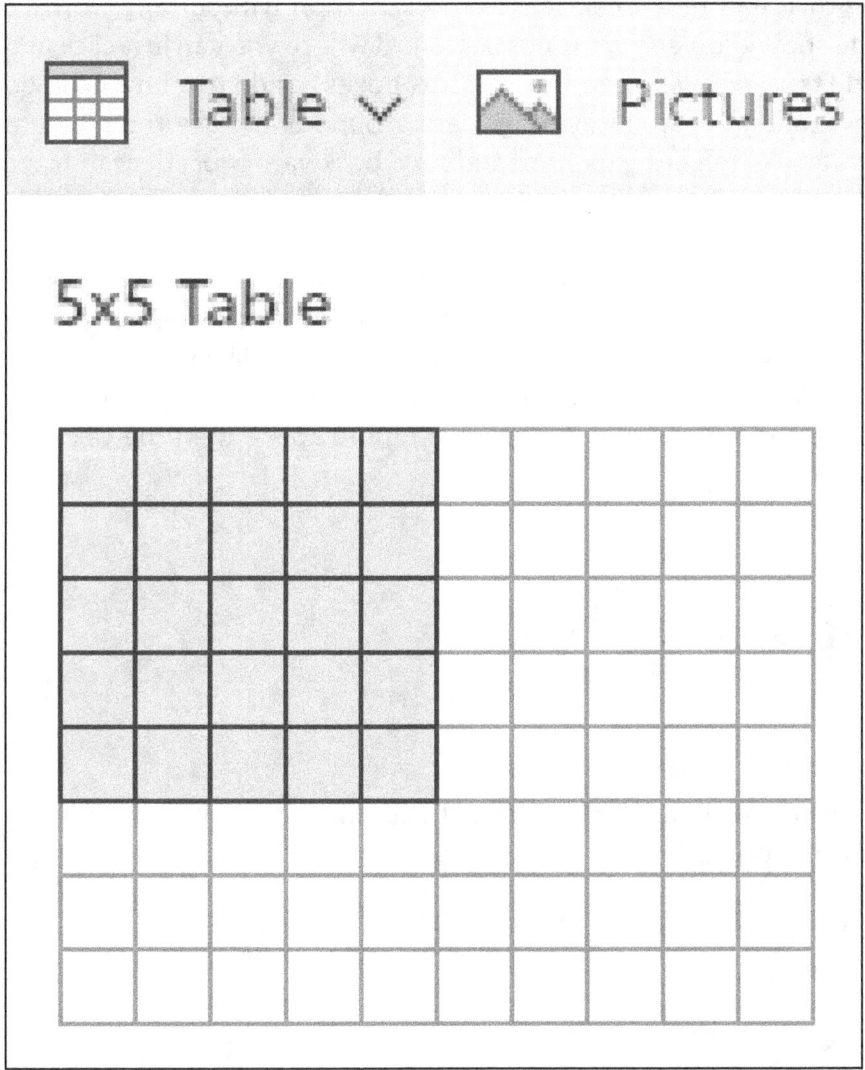

Figure 5.22

Text Box

Figure 5.23

You will be using this feature a lot because a presentation without any words is just a picture slide show! PowerPoint is not like Word where you can just click and get a cursor to add text. You will need to insert text boxes to add text but the good thing about this is that you can easily drag them around and place them where you like. Plus you can use the bring forward and send backward procedure to place your text in on top of your images or shapes.

When you add a text box it will automatically add some text that you can click on to change to whatever you like. The text will also be left justified by default so you can change that along with the font, size, color and so on just like with any other text. You can also resize or rotate your text box the same way you do with shapes and you will need to do this if your text takes up more space than the text box itself.

Figure 5.24

By default, the text box won't have a border, but you can add one just like you can with shapes and other objects.

Audio and Online Video

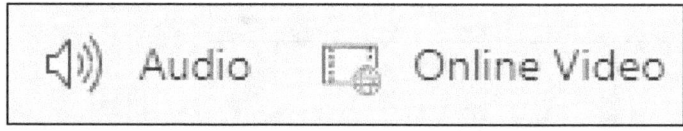

Figure 5.25

If you have an audio file such as an MP3 file that you want to insert into your presentation you can use the Audio option. This will actually import the file into your presentation and give you a speaker icon that you can click on to play the file during your slideshow.

Figure 5.26

If you would like to insert a video from a site such as YouTube then you can copy and paste its URL\address into the address bar as seen in figure 5.27 and then click on the Insert button to have it placed within your slide (figure 5.28). Then you can play that video right from your slideshow assuming you have an internet connection.

Chapter 5 – PowerPoint

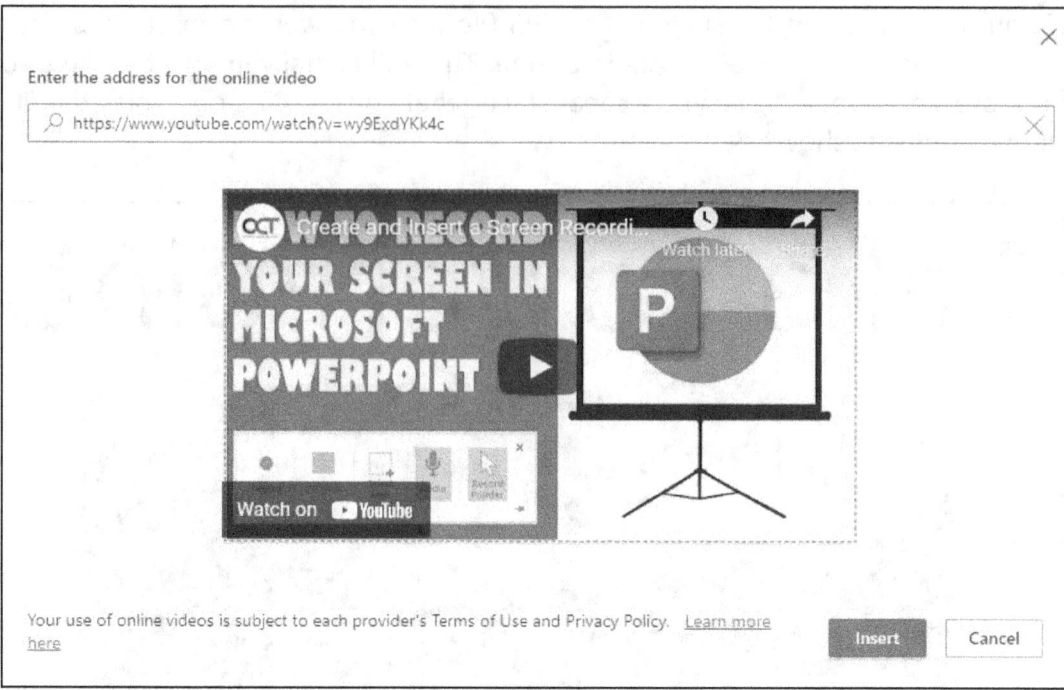

Figure 5.27

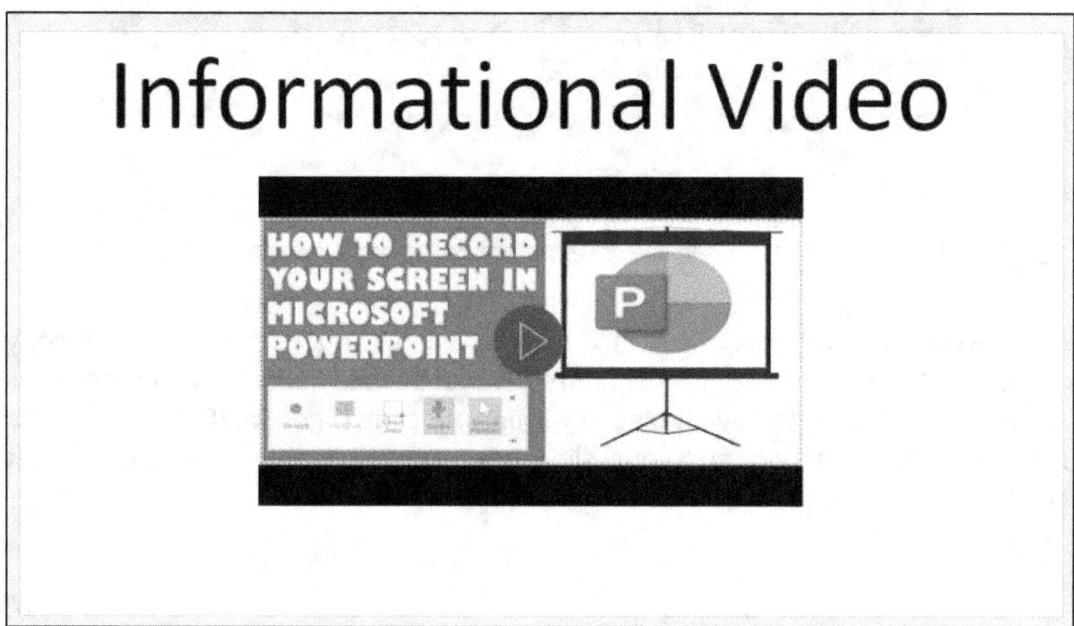

Figure 5.28

Chapter 5 – **PowerPoint**

A URL (Uniform Resource Locator) is another term for website address such as **www.microsoft.com**. When you are on a webpage you can copy the address from the address bar and paste it into an email or instant message so your recipient can easily go to the website or shared file that you are trying to get them to.

Draw Tab

The choices on the Draw tab are the same as they are for Excel with the exception of the *Lasso Select* tool. You can use this tool to select all or parts of objects that you have drawn using the other tools from this tab. You can't use it on objects such as pictures, text boxes or shapes.

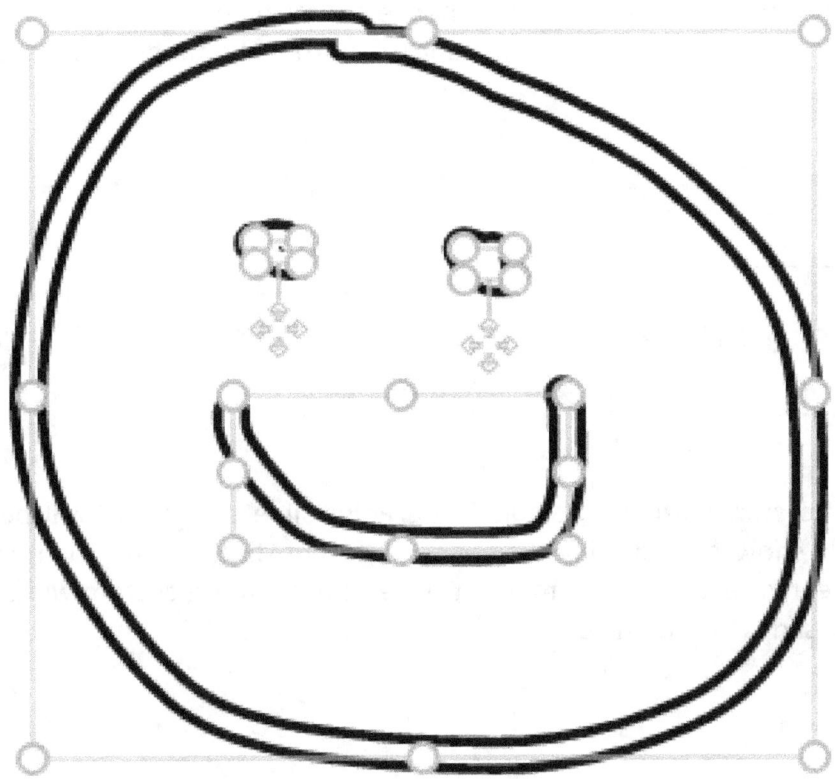

Figure 5.29

Chapter 5 – PowerPoint

Design Tab
Since having an eye catching design is important to keep your audience interested in your presentation and also to keep them paying attention, it makes sense that PowerPoint would have a design tab to help you to get your presentation looking great.

Themes and Variants

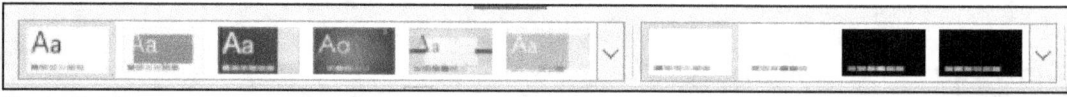
Figure 5.30

I have already discussed themes and when you are ready to apply one to your presentation you can do so from here. When you use one of the themes you will then be able to choose a variant of that theme which you can think of as a different version of the same thing with some minor changes. Just remember that every time you apply a theme you can easily change it to another theme or remove it completely.

Slide Size

Figure 5.31

You do not have to stick with the default PowerPoint slide size if you will be showing your slide show on a display that has a different display ratio such as standard, widescreen or even portrait mode. You can even enter a custom width and height to your slides based on your needs.

Chapter 5 – PowerPoint

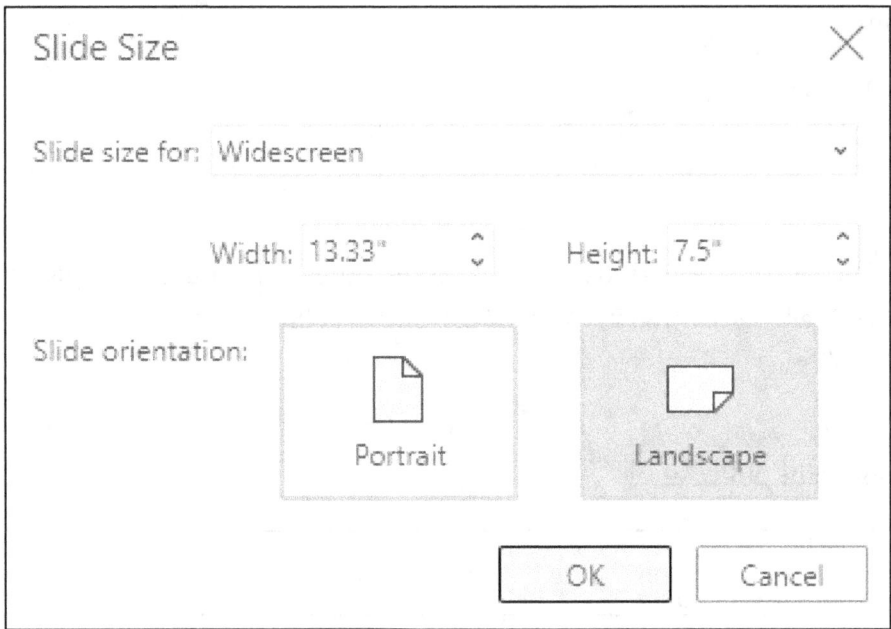

Figure 5.32

Background

Figure 5.33

By default, all of your slides will have a white background unless you apply a theme to them. Fortunately, this is easy to change, and you have the option to apply either a solid color as a background or use a picture for your background.

The *Apply to All* option will add the background from the slide you are currently on to all of your other slides. As you add new slides, the same background will be applied to them as well.

Transitions Tab
Transitions and animations are what make PowerPoint stand out for presentations compared to just using something like Word and adding a bunch of different pages. I will be going over transitions and animations later in this chapter so for now I will just be showing you what tools you have available from these tabs.

Transition Types

Figure 5.34

Here you will find all of the various types of transitions that you can apply to objects within your slides. They are broken down into categories including subtle, dynamic and exciting.

Options, Duration and Apply to All

Figure 5.35

- **Options** – Different transitions will have different effects options so your choices here will change depending on what transition you are using.

- **Duration** – This setting determines how long the transition takes to complete its motion.

- **Apply to All** – This will apply the same transition to all of your slides.

Animations Tab
Animations are similar to transitions except they take place on individual objects rather than the slide itself. Animations can add a bit of flair to your presentation to help keep your audience… well, awake!

Animation Types

Figure 5.36

There are many types of animations to choose from and you can access all of them from the drop down arrow at the right side of the initial choices.

Effect Options

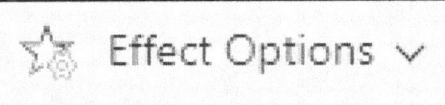
Figure 5.37

Certain animations will have configurable effects while others will not. If the Effect Options button is greyed out that means that there are no options for that particular animation.

Move Earlier and Move Later

Figure 5.38

You can use the Move Earlier and Move Later options to change the order of your animations. So if you would like your smiley face shape to appear before your text then you can change the order with these buttons.

Slide Show Tab
Once you are finished creating your slides you can then "play" them as a slide show for your audience. I will have a section on slide shows later in this chapter but for now, I will just show you what options are under the Slide Show tab.

From Beginning and From Current Slide

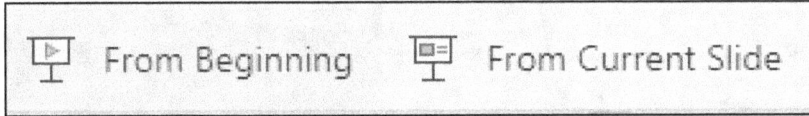
Figure 5.39

- **From Beginning** – This will start your slide show from your first slide no matter what slide you happen to be currently working on.

- **From Current Slide** – This will start your slide show from the slide that you have selected.

Rehearse with Coach

Figure 5.40

You can use this option to do a test run of your presentation with your microphone and then PowerPoint will make suggestions and give you a summary of what it finds when you are finished.

Review Tab
Just like with the other Office apps, PowerPoint has a tab that lets you do things such as check spelling, add comments and check your accessibility settings.

Check Slide and Check Accessibility

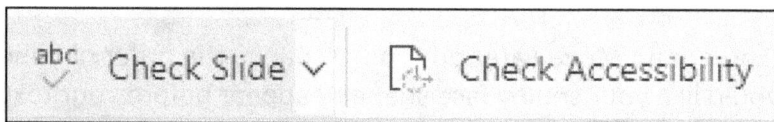
Figure 5.41

These two tools work in a similar way and regardless of which you click on, you will be able to see spelling and accessibility errors\suggestions from the same place.

Figure 5.38 shows the accessibility errors for my presentation and on the right side of the results you will see an **abc** icon with a checkmark underneath it. And if you click that you will then be able to see your spelling errors.

Chapter 5 – PowerPoint

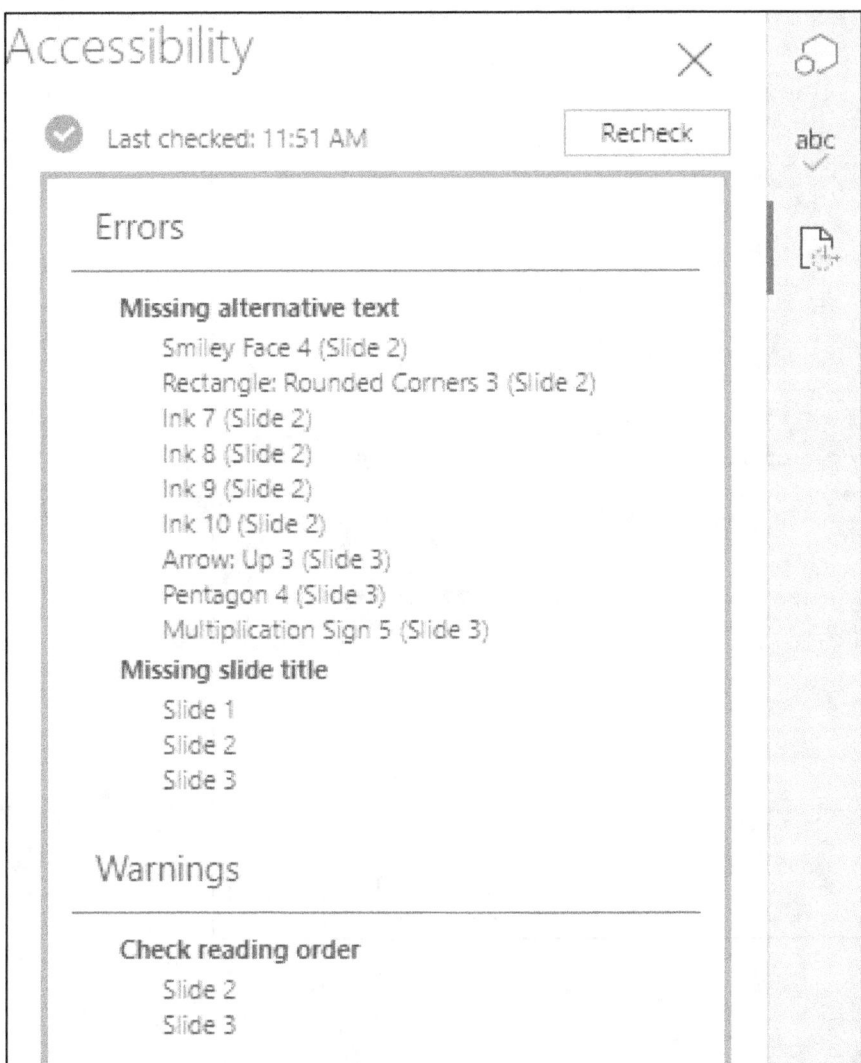

Figure 5.42

If you click *Editor Settings* under the Check Slide button you will then be able to change any proofing options that are available here.

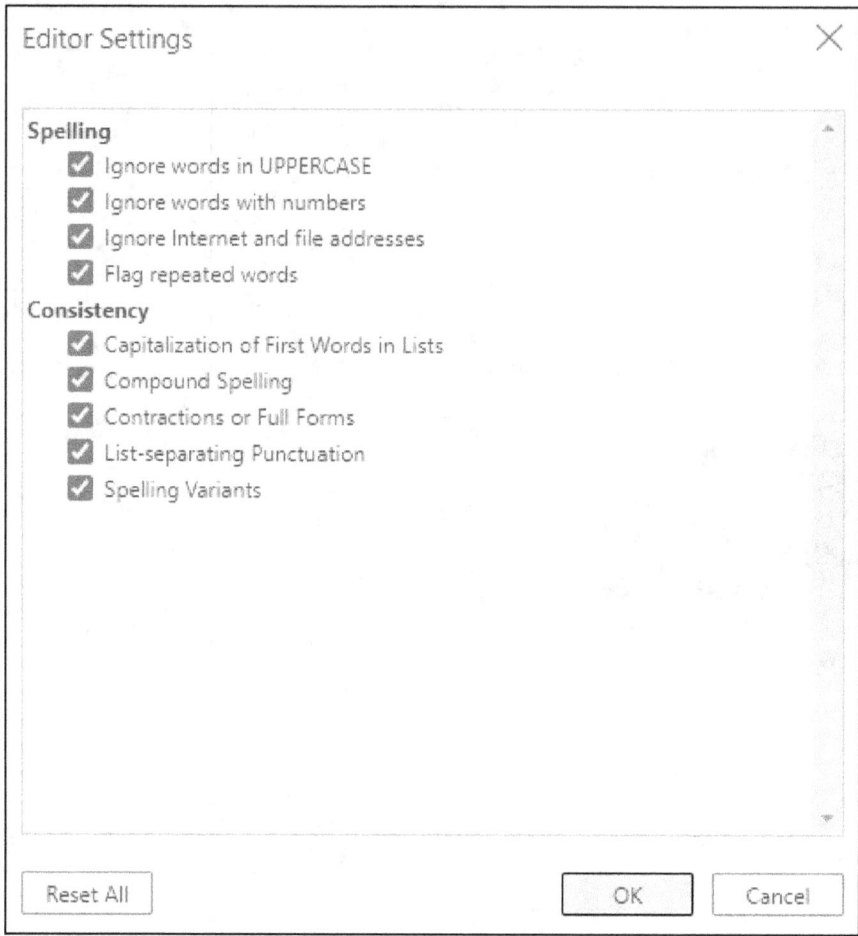

Figure 5.43

View Tab
The View tab is pretty basic and has a few settings for how you view your presentation on your screen.

Notes, Slide Sorter and Normal

Figure 5.44

I mentioned how you can add notes to your slides earlier in the chapter and here is where you can come to view them. I will be discussing Notes in more detail later in this chapter.

Chapter 5 – PowerPoint

I also mentioned how the *Slide Sorter* view will let you do things such as arrange your slides as well as copy and paste them. Once again you can also get to the slide sorter at any time from the buttons at the bottom right corner of the app.

The *Normal* button will allow you to toggle between the Slide Sorter and the standard view that you are used to working in. So if you are using the Slide Sorter feature and want to exit out and go back to the default view, you can click on the Normal button.

Zoom and Fit to Window

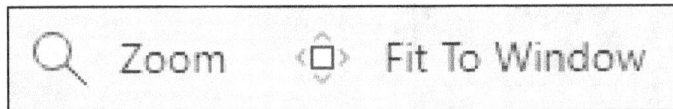

Figure 5.45

Clicking on the *Zoom* button will let you choose from one of the default zoom levels that PowerPoint has to offer. You can use the *Fit* option to have your slide be resized to fill your screen.

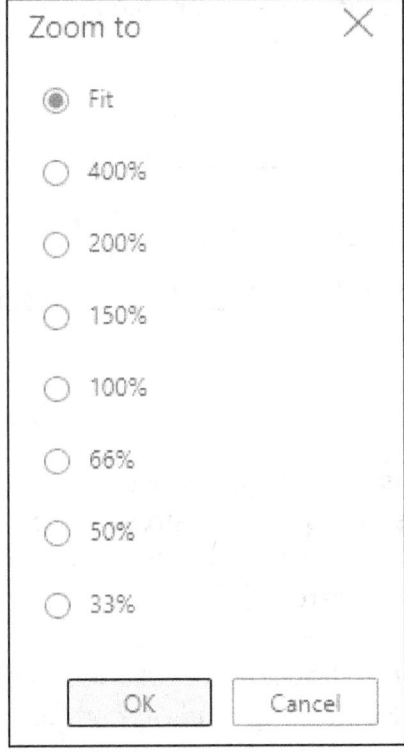

Figure 5.46

183

The *Fit to Window* button will do the same thing as choosing the Fit option under the Zoom button.

Shape and Picture Tabs

When you select either a shape or picture on your slide, you will see that you get a new tab item that looks a little different than the others. This is because it's specific to the object you selected and includes tools that only apply to that type of object.

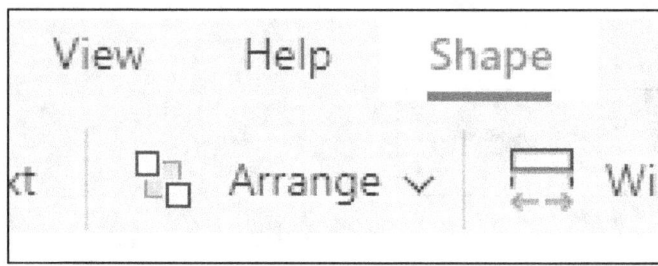
Figure 5.47

I will not be going over the options from these special tabs because they are the same options for the most part that I have already discussed but are all located on these special tabs rather than spread out on all the other tabs. Figure 5.45 shows the *Shape* tab options while figure 5.46 shows the *Picture* tab options.

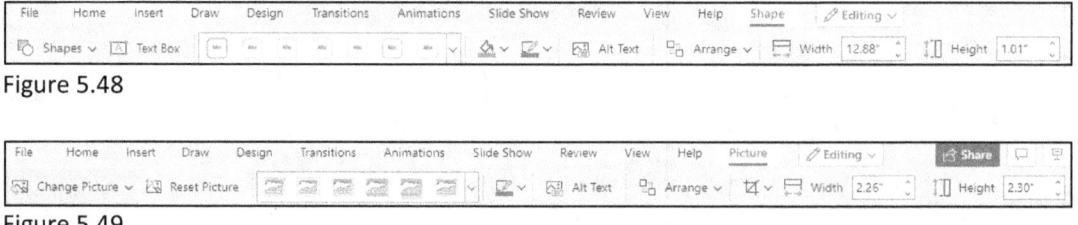
Figure 5.48

Figure 5.49

Adding New Slides and Slide Layouts

A PowerPoint presentation with just one slide is pretty much just a Word document so you will most likely be adding more slides to your presentation. When you add more slides you will need to decide which layout you want to use or if you just want a blank slide so you can start from scratch.

There are a few ways to add a slide and either way you choose will work the same way so it's completely up to you. You can go to the Home menu and click on New

Chapter 5 – PowerPoint

Slide, go to the Insert menu and click on New Slide or even right click on an existing slide in your slide deck and choose New Slide as seen in figure 5.50.

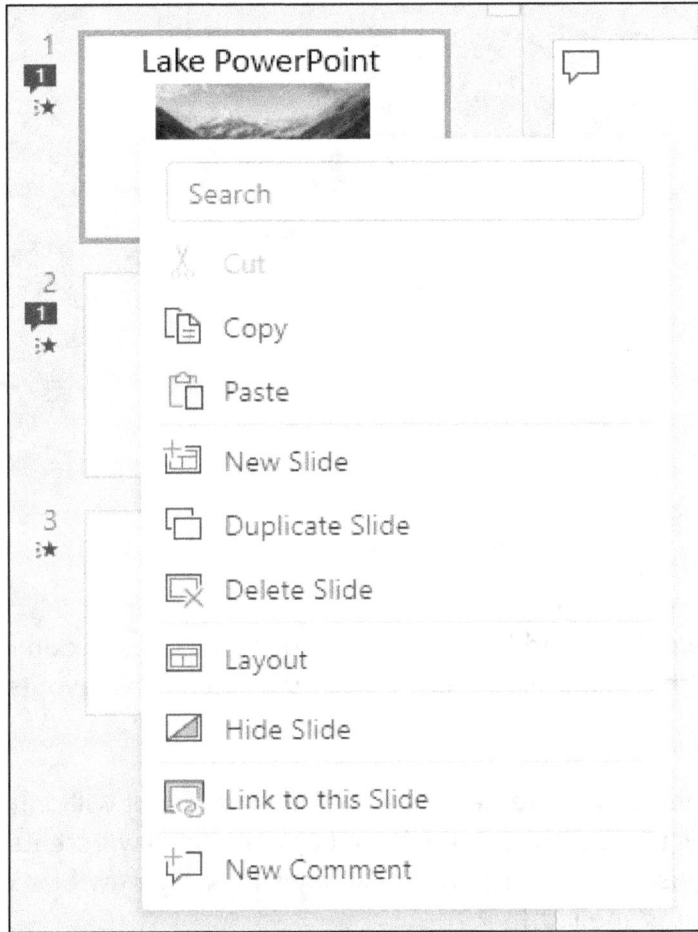

Figure 5.50

As you can see from figure 5.50 you have some additional options when you right click on an existing slide. You can do things such as duplicate the slide and its contents, delete the slide or even hide it.

The *Link to this Slide* option will let you create a link that you can send out to others so that they can view this slide and any others you have in this presentation. So no, I don't know why they call it link to this SLIDE. You can then decide if you want the people who have the link to be able to edit the slide or only view it. You can even set an expiration date and give it a password that they will need to know to be able to open the slide. You will find these options when you click on *Anyone with the link can edit*.

185

Chapter 5 – PowerPoint

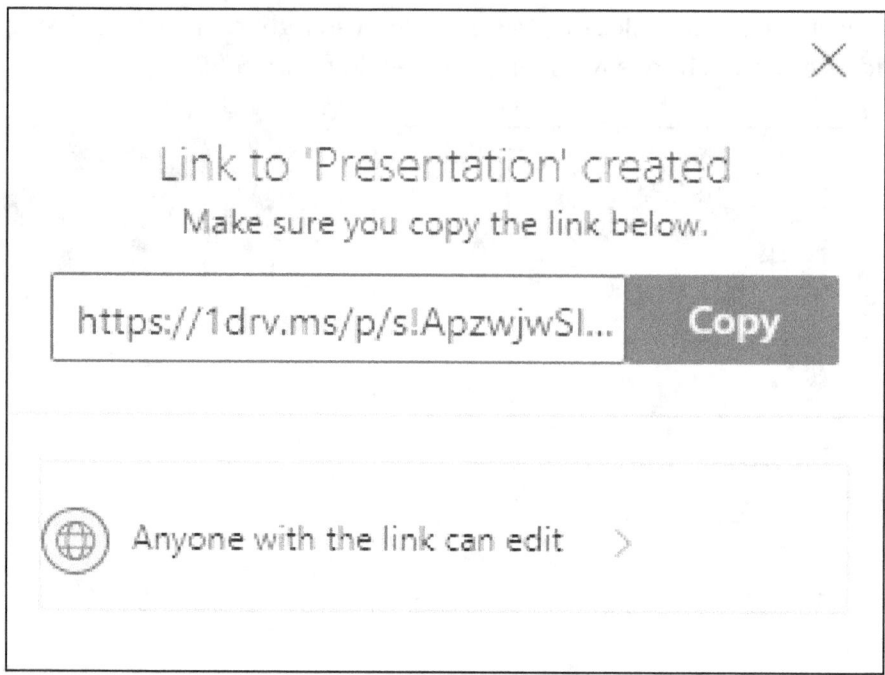

Figure 5.51

Layouts are used as a starting point for adding content to your slides. If you don't want to start from scratch with a blank slide then you can use one of the layouts that come with PowerPoint.

You can apply a layout to a slide as you create a new one and the layout will only be applied to your new slide. Figure 5.52 shows the layout options, and I will create a new slide using the *Comparison* layout. Figure 5.53 shows how my new blank slide will look when this layout is applied.

Chapter 5 – PowerPoint

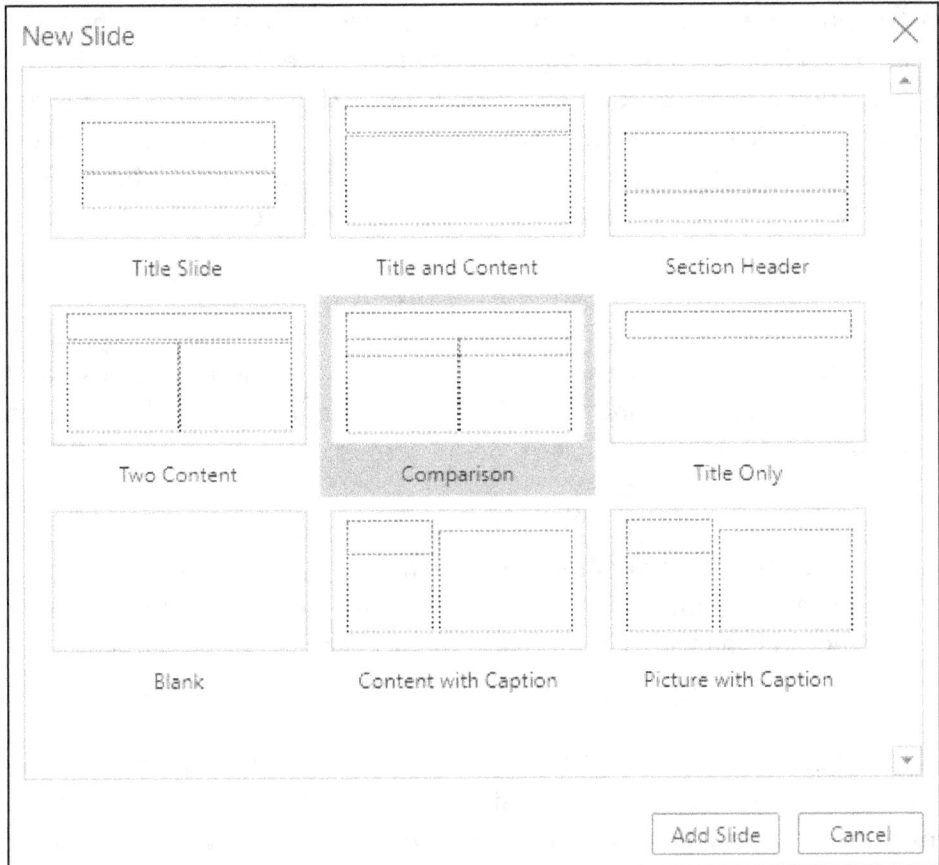

Figure 5.52

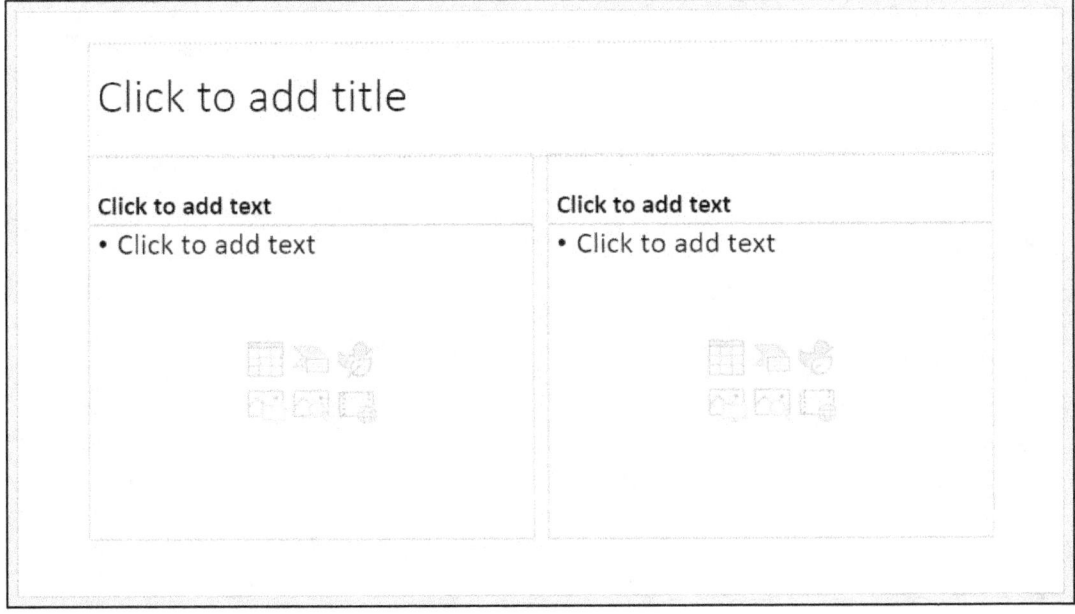

Figure 5.53

Chapter 5 – PowerPoint

If you want to apply the same layout to all of your slides then you will need to select them all by clicking on the first one, holding down the *Shift* key and clicking on the last one. You can also click on any slide in your slide deck and then press *Ctrl-A* (*Command-A* for Mac) to select all the slides. Then you can right click on any slide and then click Layout and choose your layout. When you click on the *Change Layout* button, the new layout will be applied to all of your slides.

Transitions and Animations
One of the best ways to make your presentations "pop" is to add transitions and animations to your slides. By adding these features you bring your slide shows to life and they make it easier to get your point across and will also keep your audience a little more entertained.

There is a difference between transitions and animations with transitions being a type of movement effect that happens between slides and animations being a movement or effect that happens on individual objects on a particular slide. You can have one transition between slides and many animations within a slide.

To apply a transition you will need to go to the *Transitions* tab where you can select from a variety of transition types that are organized into categories. There will be a small thumbnail image next to each one that is meant to give you an idea of how the transition will look.

Chapter 5 – PowerPoint

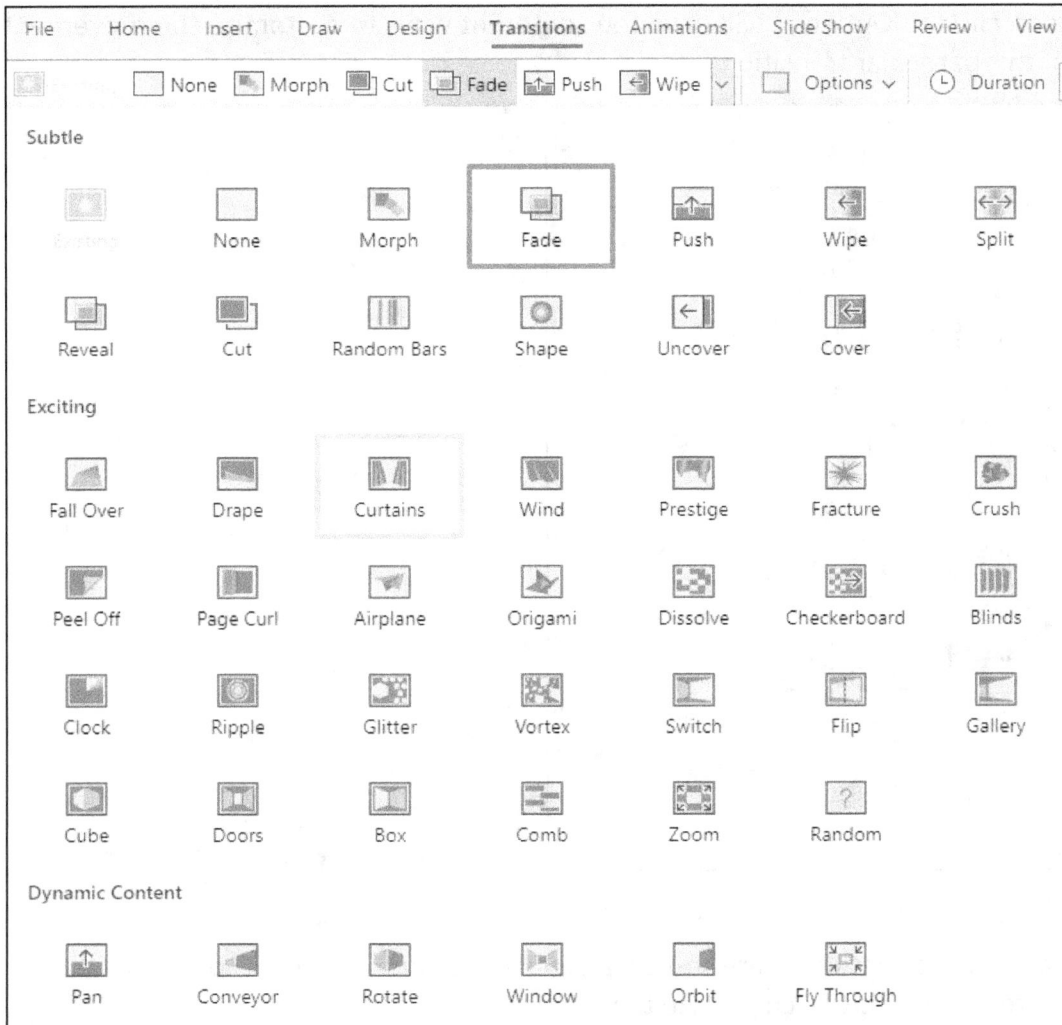

Figure 5.54

The transition you choose will only apply to the slide that you are on so if you want the same one for all of your slides you can click on the *Apply to All* button to make that happen.

To the left of the Apply to All button you will see an option for duration, and this is used to determine how long the transition between the slides will run. Be careful when using this because you don't want to have the transition take too long otherwise it might come across as looking strange.

You will have different options for different transitions that will allow you to customize how they work. For example if I choose the Page Curl transition and

Chapter 5 – PowerPoint

then click on Options I will have four different ways to customize the movement of this particular transition.

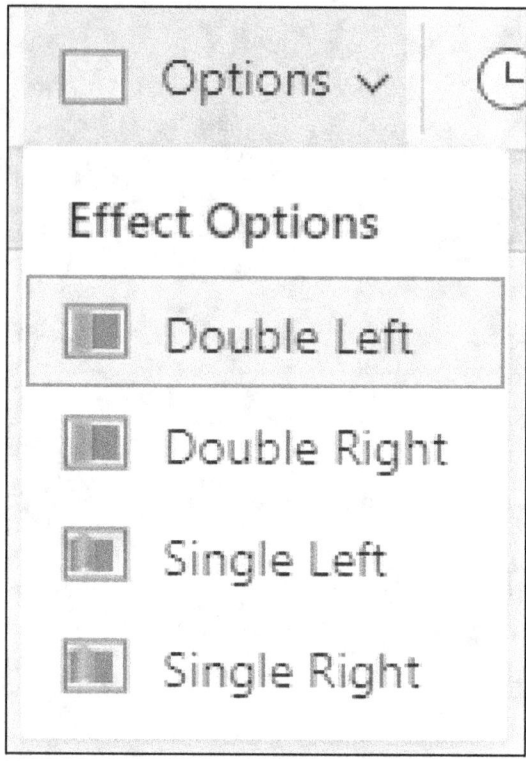

Figure 5.55

You will find that there are some transitions that don't have any options meaning there is not a way to customize them.

To test out your transition to see how it looks you can run your slide show from that page rather than run the slide show from the beginning. To do so simply go to the *Slide Show* tab and choose *From Current Slide*. Keep in mind that you don't need to use transitions between slides if you just want them to quickly change from one to the next.

Animations require a little more work than transitions because you can apply them to multiple objects (pictures, shapes, text) within a slide and also change the order of how the animations occur.

Figure 5.56 shows a slide that I have, and I want to make the *Come Visit* and *Fun for the Whole Family* graphics move into place separately after the lake picture is shown when I get to this slide.

190

Figure 5.56

First I will click on my Come Visit text which is actually an image I made in another program so I could add a custom style to it. Then I will go to the *Animations* tab and choose the *Fly In* effect and under *Effect Options* I will choose *From Left*.

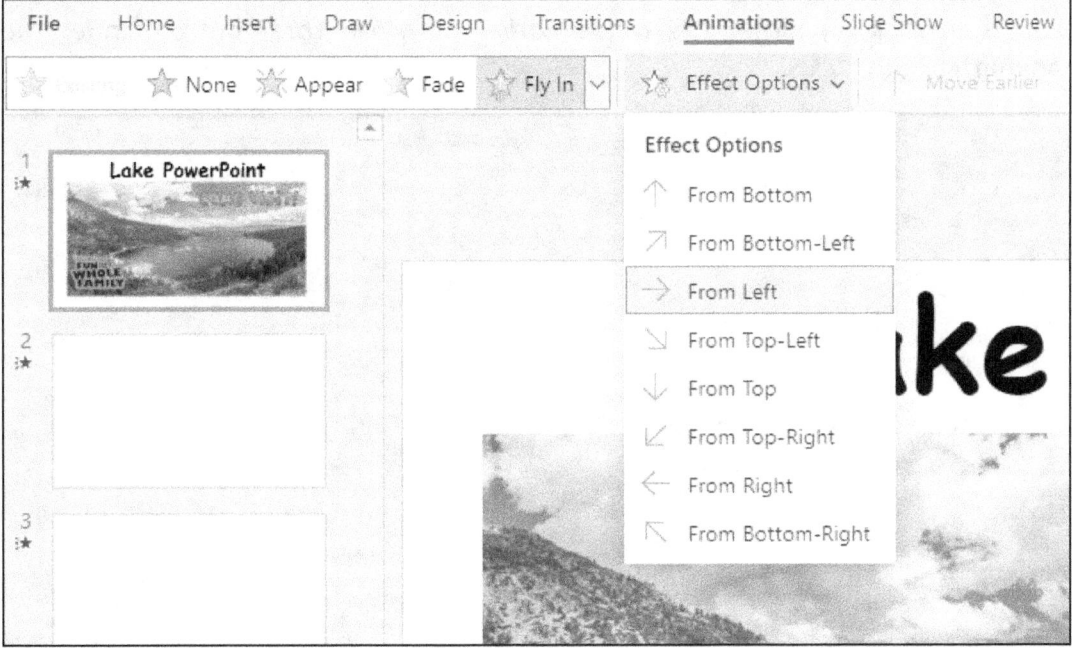

Figure 5.57

Chapter 5 – PowerPoint

Next, I will select my Fun for the Whole Family image and use the *Random Bars* animation with the *Horizontal* effect.

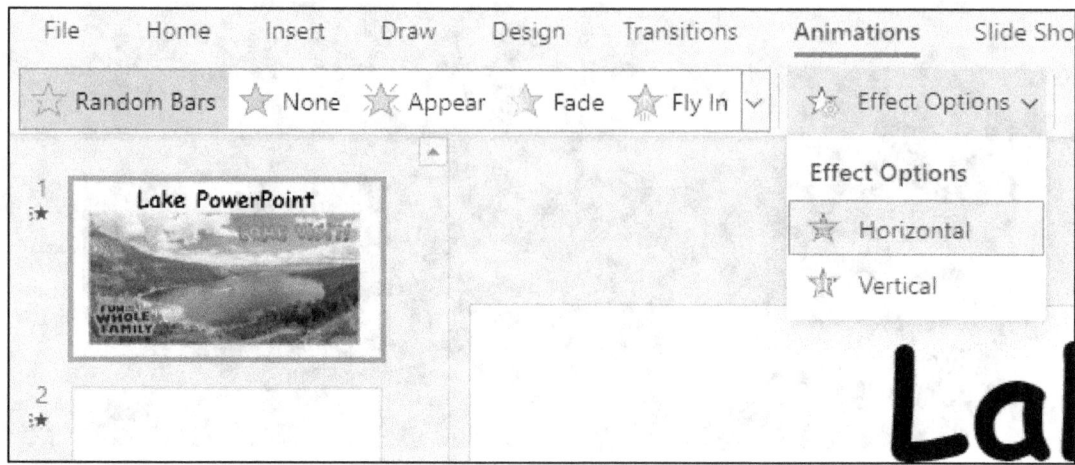

Figure 5.58

Now that I have my animations applied to my two objects, I can click on either one of them to see the order of how the animations will play out. So as you can see in figure 5.59, the Come Visit animation will happen first since it has a 1 next to it and then the Fun for the Whole Family animation will happen second since it has a 2 next to it. To change the order you can select the object you want to reorder and then click on either the *Move Earlier* or *Move Later* button under the Animations tab.

Chapter 5 – PowerPoint

Figure 5.59

To see how my animations will look I can run my slide show and what will happen is my Lake PowerPoint text and lake image will be in place since there are no animations applied to them and when I click my mouse, my Come Visit graphic will move in from the left of the screen into place. Then on the next mouse click my Fun for the Whole Family graphic will appear with its Random Bars animation.

Be sure not to go too crazy with your animations and apply them to too many objects. You will find that your presentation will look more like a cartoon and take twice as long because you will be clicking so often for each animation and it will make it look less professional.

Notes and Sections
After you have your presentation looking good and ready to go you will most likely want to show it to other people in the form of a slide show. When running your presentation you might need to have some information handy to talk about that

Chapter 5 – PowerPoint

you don't necessarily want to be shown on your slides. This is where Notes can help you out but not in PowerPoint for the Web unfortunately.

In order to use Notes the way they are meant to be used you will need to be able to show your slides using *Presenter View* which at the time of this writing is not available for PowerPoint for the Web. How Presenter View works is when you attach your computer to a projector or other monitor you can play your slide show on that screen and see your notes on your main screen without your audience being able to see them.

You can add notes to a slide by clicking on the Notes button at the bottom right of the screen while on that slide. You can also see your notes from the Notes button on the View tab.

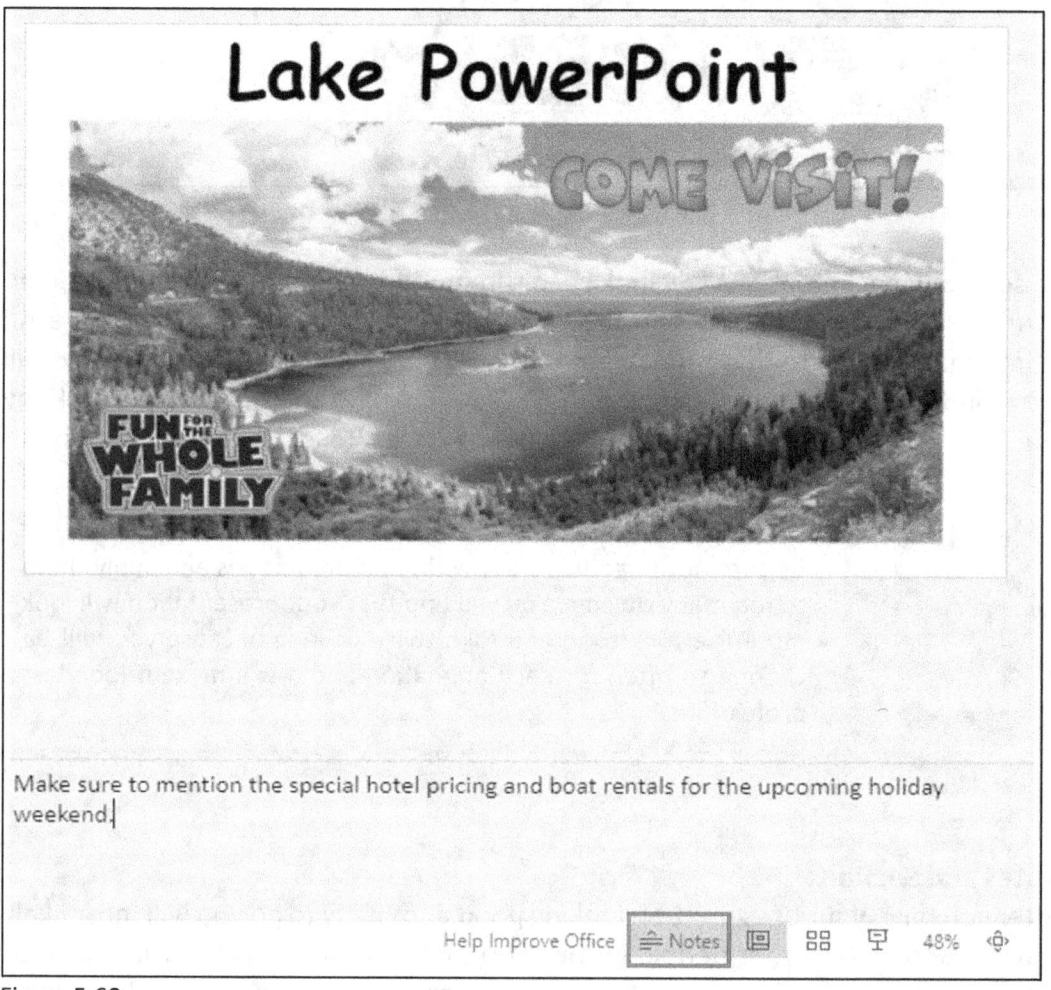

Figure 5.60

Chapter 5 – PowerPoint

You can always add notes to a presentation that you plan on showing with a version of PowerPoint that does support Presenter View so you can take advantage of this feature later on.

Sections

If you want to organize your slides into groups so that they are easier to manage or to assign certain slides to other people so they can work on them then you can use sections to accomplish this.

Sections are used for organizational purposes only and don't have any effect on how your slide show will be presented. To add a section you will need to go to the *View* tab and then click on *Slide Sorter*. Next, you will right click where you want to add your section and then click on *Add Section*.

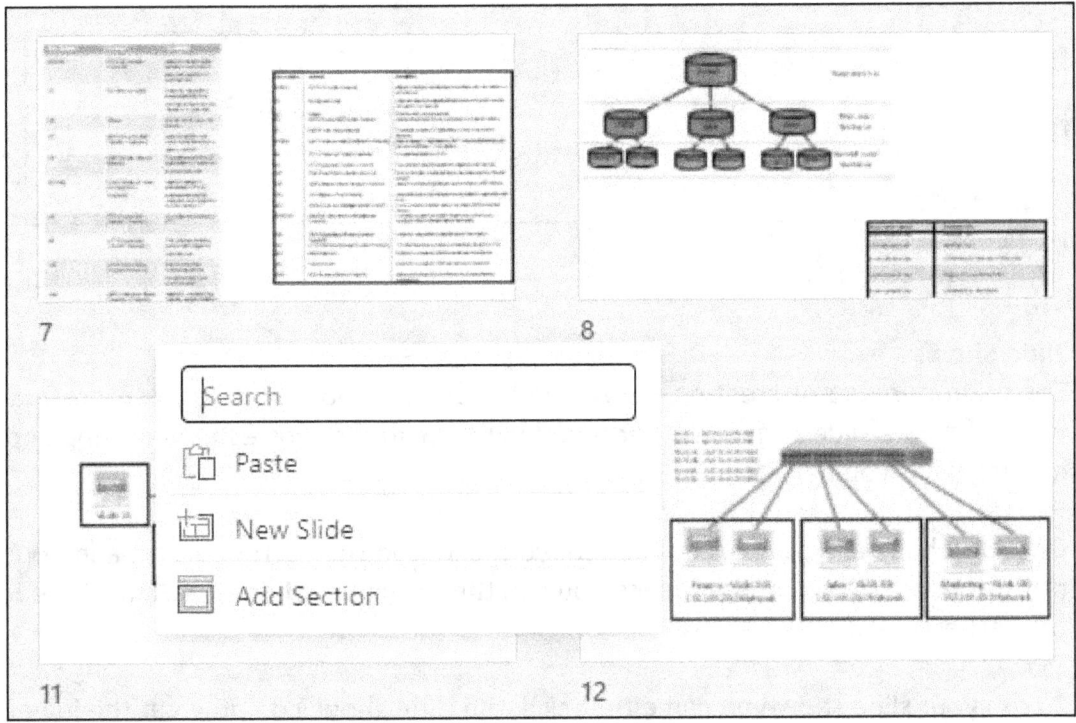

Figure 5.61

Then you can type in a name for that section, and it will appear as a new section whenever you go to the Slide Sorter view.

Chapter 5 – PowerPoint

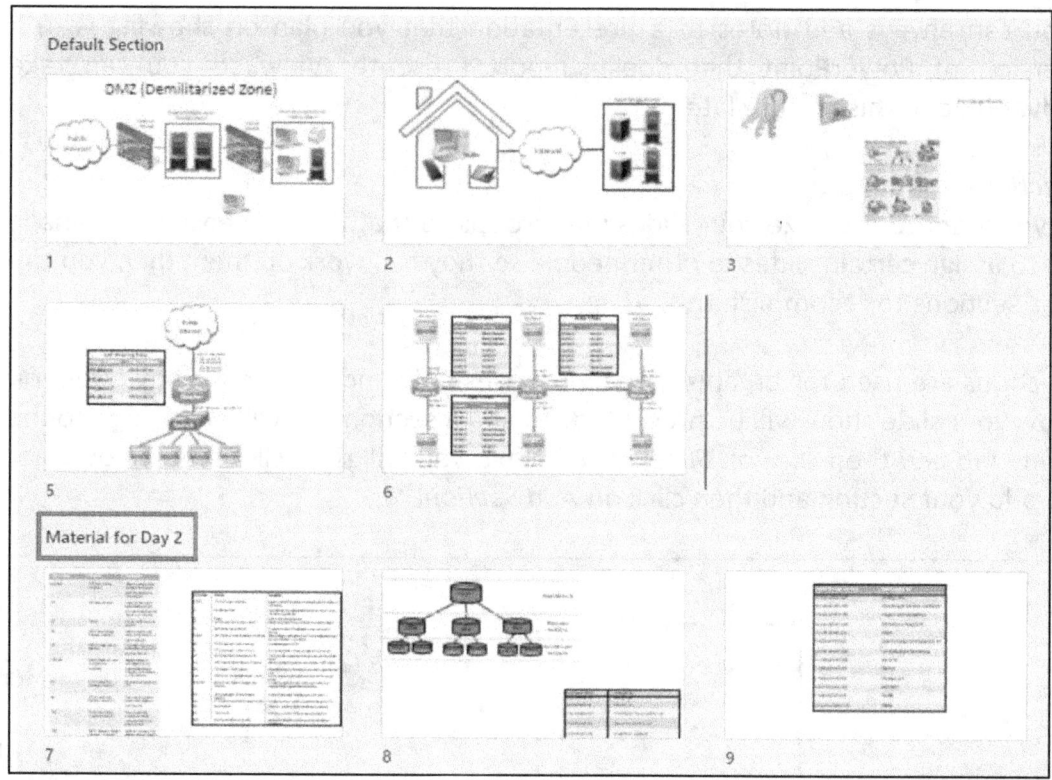

Figure 5.62

Slide Shows

The main purpose of creating a PowerPoint presentation is so you can present your work as a slide show to other people who might be interested in seeing and hearing what you have to say.

Once you have all your content added, your slides in the correct order, and your transitions and animations in place you can then run your slide show and share it with others.

To run your slide show you can either click the slide show icon down at the lower right corner of the screen or from the Slide Show tab. If you start your slide show from the *Slide Show* tab then you will be able to choose if it starts from the first slide or from the slide that you are currently on.

You can then use your mouse button or arrow keys on your keyboard to navigate from slide to slide. If you need to go back a slide then you can use the left arrow key to do so. You can also use the space bar to move forward and the Page Up and

Page Down keys to move forward and backward. To exit your slide show you can also use the Esc key.

While you are showing your slide show you will see some tools at the lower left corner of the screen that you can use to help you navigate around your presentation.

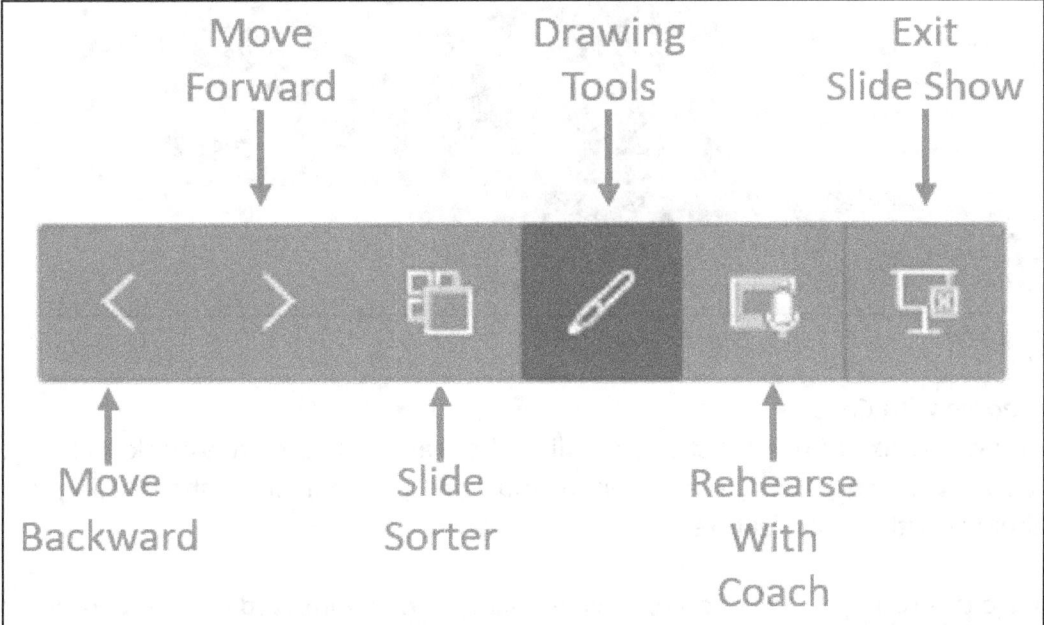

Figure 5.63

You can use the arrows to move forward and backward, open the Slide sorter, use some markup pens with the drawing tools (figure 5.64), open the Rehearse with Coach tool (discussed next), or exit your slide show.

Chapter 5 – PowerPoint

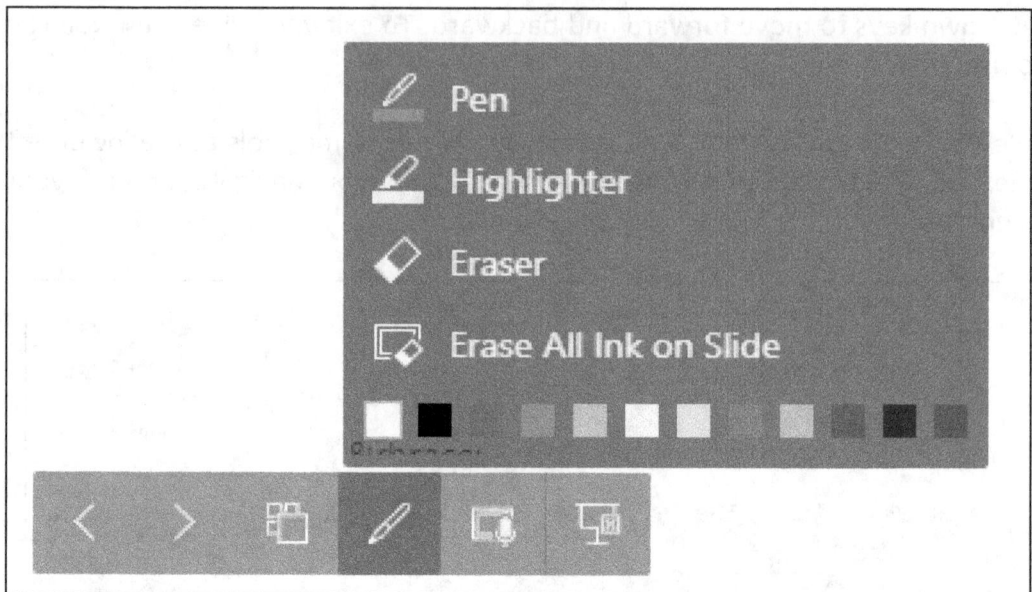

Figure 5.64

Rehearse with Coach

If you would like to run a test of your slide show and get some feedback on things such as your speaking pace or pitch you can run your slide show using the Rehearse with Coach feature.

To use this tool, you will need to have a microphone connected to your computer and also give your web browser access to your microphone which you should be prompted to do the first time you run the tool.

Once you click on *Start Rehearsing*, PowerPoint will run your slide show and analyze your speaking patterns and give you suggestions as you go along like shown in figure 5.66.

Chapter 5 – PowerPoint

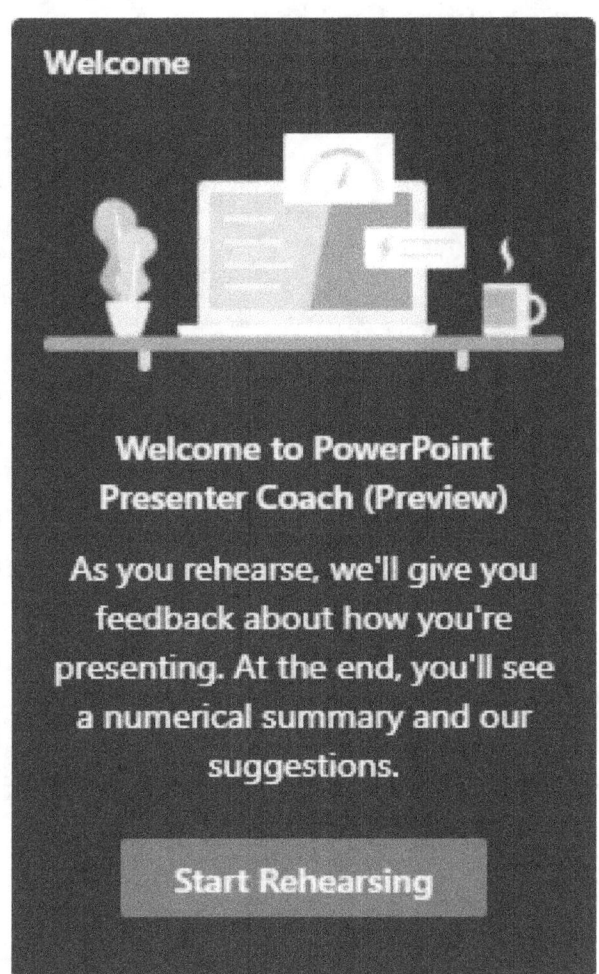
Figure 5.65

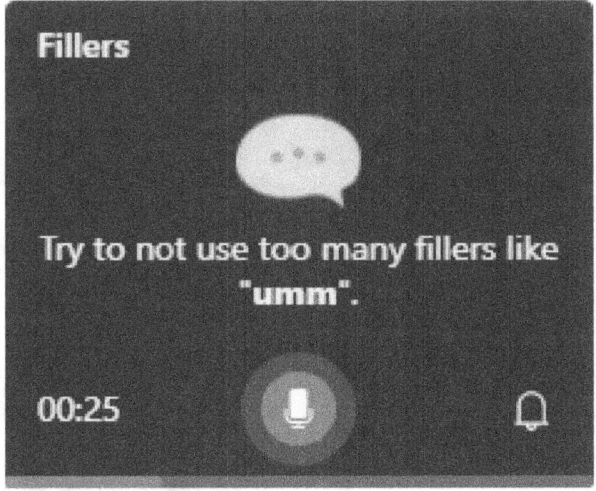
Figure 5.66

Chapter 5 – PowerPoint

When you are finished with the slide show, the Presenter Coach will show you a summary of your performance so you can make adjustments as needed.

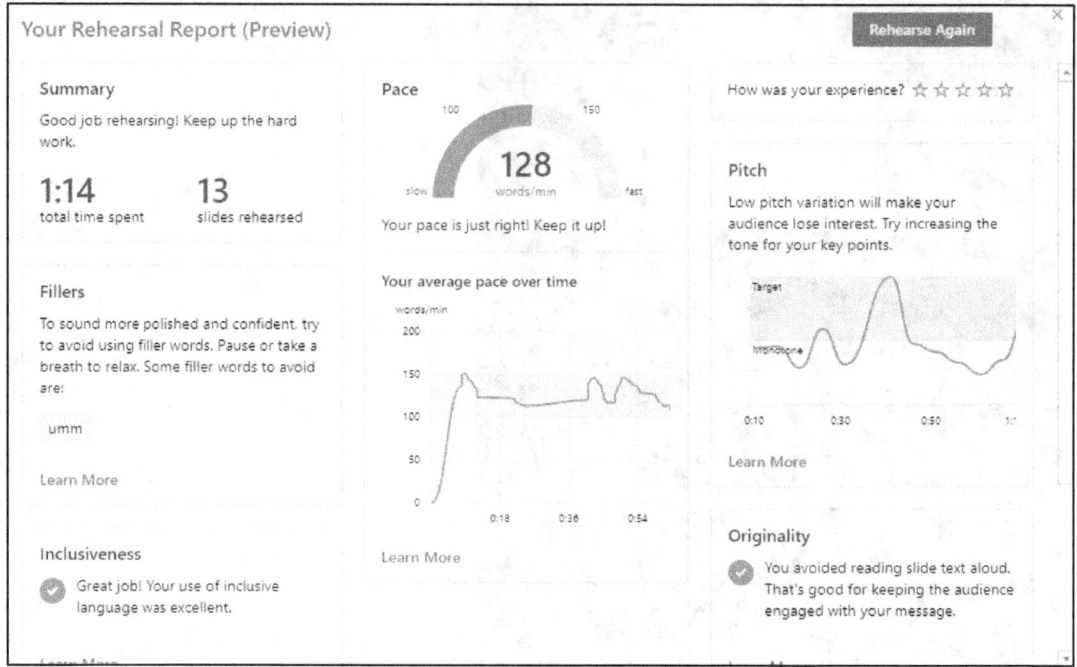

Figure 5.67

Chapter 6 – Outlook, Calendar and People

Most people know that Microsoft is the biggest player when it comes to office productivity software and almost everyone who has used a computer has most likely used Word or Excel etc. at some point. When it comes to email applications, Microsoft Outlook has the largest share of users compared to any other email application out there.

Overview
Besides being an email client, Outlook also comes with a built in calendar to help you schedule meetings and track your appointments. Plus there is a contacts area called *People* where you can keep track of all of your contacts and use it to help you compose emails and schedule meetings, so you don't need to remember anyone's email addresses.

The web version of Outlook looks very similar to the version you would install on your computer but just like with all the other apps, the web version will not have as many features as the pay-for versions. But for many people, including myself, the web version works just fine, especially if just need something to use for basic email and calendar events.

Since Outlook for the Web is accessed via a web browser, you can get your email and see your calendar events from any device that has an internet connection. If you were to use the installed Outlook client on your computer then you might only be able to see your email from that computer depending on the type of email account you are using on it. When you use Outlook for the Web, it will be configured with the email address you use for your Microsoft account so if you want to use a different email address, you will need to create a new Microsoft account with that address.

The Outlook Interface
When you open Outlook for the first time it might want you to go through some steps to complete your configuration as seen in figure 6.1 where it says *Get started*. Here you can do things such as choose a look or theme for Outlook if you don't like the default and also change your time zone if needed or import contacts from another source. You will also notice some advertisements that will pop up periodically but that's what you get when you use free software it these days.

Chapter 6 – Outlook, Calendar and People

You may also be prompted to enter your phone number to get a link sent to your phone that you can click on to install the Outlook app. I would just search the Play Store (Android) or App Store (iPhone) rather than give your phone number to Microsoft if you are interested in installing the mobile version on your phone.

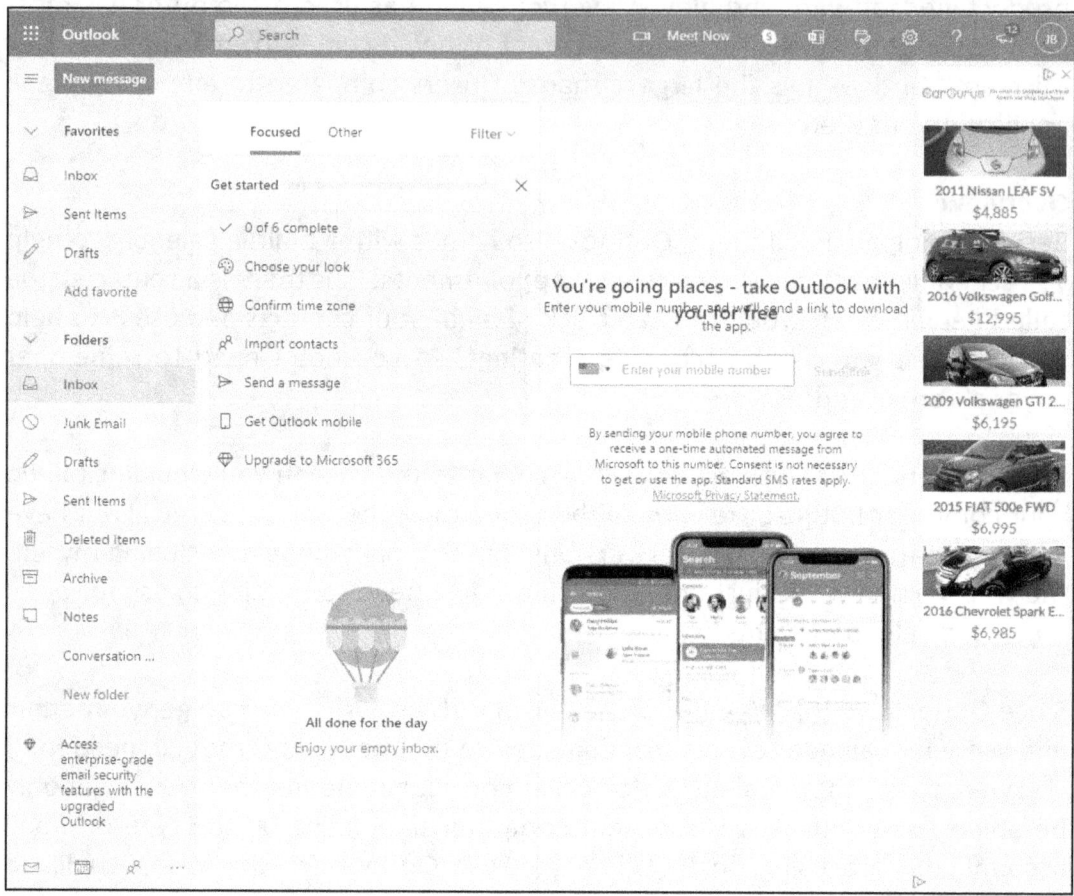

Figure 6.1

If you decide to change the look then you will have some color and layout options to choose from. If you pick one of these layouts and don't like it then you can always change it later.

Chapter 6 – Outlook, Calendar and People

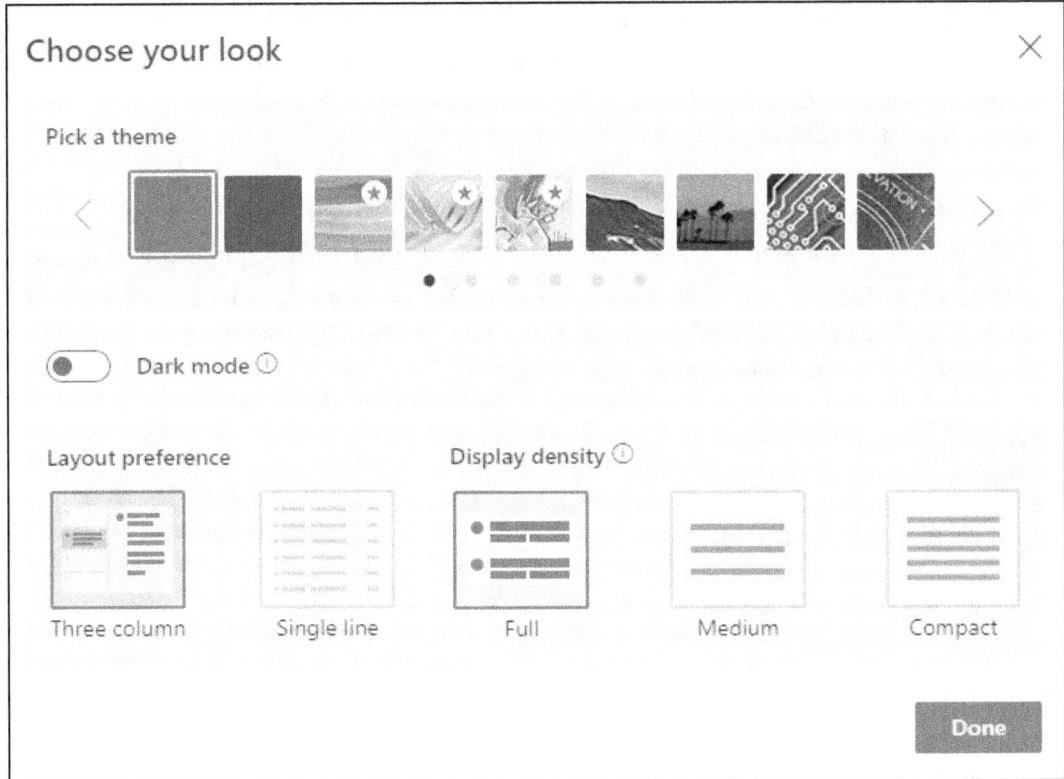

Figure 6.2

If you have contacts in another email program and that program has the capability to export your contacts in a CSV format then you can import them into Outlook to save you some time.

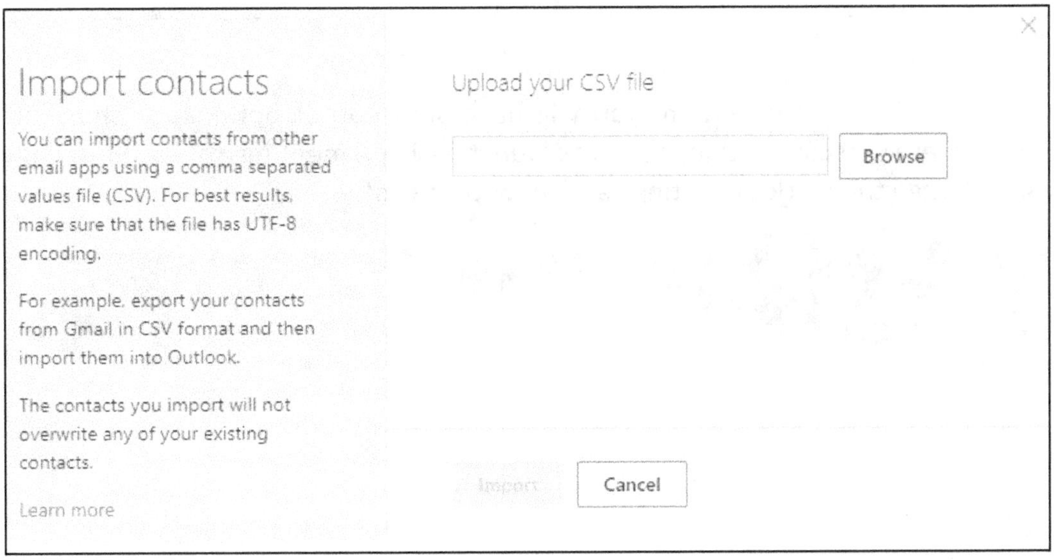

Figure 6.3

Chapter 6 – Outlook, Calendar and People

On the left side of the screen you will see your folders, and this is where your email is stored. You can create folders and also subfolders and then move specific emails into those folders to keep things organized. I will be discussing folders in more detail in the next section.

At the bottom left corner OR the left hand side of the Outlook window you will see some icons that will let you switch between your email, calendar, contacts (People), files and to do list. For some reason, these items might be found at either location. If it's at the bottom you will need to click on the three dots (ellipsis) to get to your Files and To Do sections.

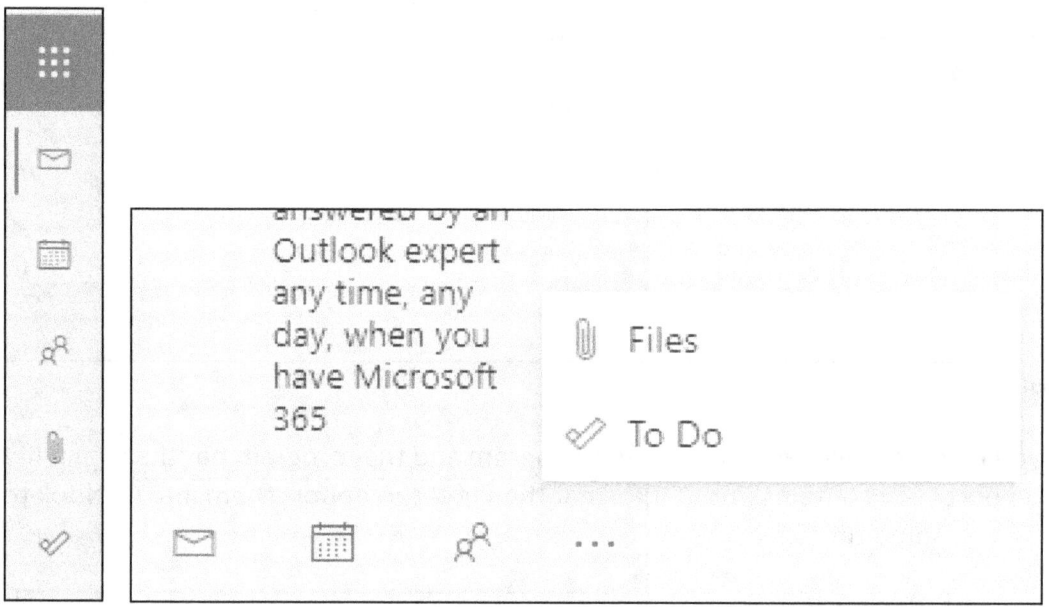

Figure 6.4

At the top right of the screen, you will have some other options, or shortcuts rather where you can do things such as launch a Skype meeting, review your daily tasks, change the Outlook settings and view your profile.

Figure 6.5

Chapter 6 – Outlook, Calendar and People

Folders
On the left side of the Outlook window you will see your folder list even though they don't really look like folders. Folders are where your emails will be stored, and you can add additional folders as needed. At the top of the list you will see a section called *Favorites*. You can think of this sort of like bookmarks or favorites that you have in your web browser. It's here so you have quick access to your commonly used folders. You can add specific folders to your favorites as needed.

Figure 6.6

If you take a closer look at figure 6.6 you will see that the Inbox is listed under Favorites and also under Folders. This doesn't mean that there are two separate

Inboxes because anything in the Favorites section is just a shortcut to its location in the Folders section. So if you removed a folder from your Favorites it wouldn't really be removing that folder but rather only the shortcut.

The *Inbox* is your mail Outlook folder and it's where all of your new emails will be placed as they arrive unless you create a rule telling Outlook to put certain types of emails in a different folder. Rules will be discussed later in this chapter.

The *Sent Items* folder is where you will be able to see emails that you have sent out to other people. So if you are not sure if you have sent an email or not, you can go into this folder to confirm that you did.

As you work on an email, Outlook will automatically save it in your *Drafts* folder until you send it. So if you started an email and never finished it or sent it out, you will most likely find it in your Drafts folder and can continue working on it from there.

Anyone who uses email knows about spam or junk email and Outlook provides a folder called *Junk Email* where it will place email that it thinks is spam or that you have marked as spam. If you get an email that is spam, and you want Outlook to mark it as junk then you can right click on it and select *Security Options>Mark as Junk* to have it moved to that folder. Then the next time an email comes in from that address, Outlook should automatically put it in the Junk Email folder.

When you delete an email, it will be moved into your *Deleted Items* folder just like files get moved to the Recycle Bin in Windows when you delete them. If you change your mind and don't want the email to be deleted, you can go into the Deleted Items folder, right click on it and choose the *Move* option to move it to a different folder or back to the Inbox.

To create a new folder, all you need to do is click on the *New Folder* link and type in the name for that folder. Then you can drag that folder to your Favorites section if it's a folder you are going to be accessing on a regular basis as I did for my *Project Emails* folder.

Chapter 6 – Outlook, Calendar and People

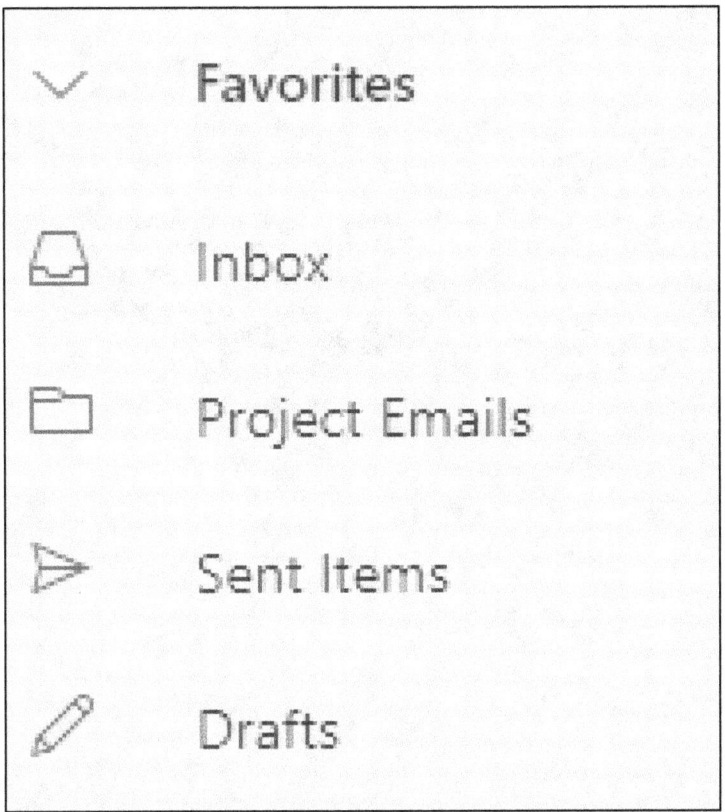

Figure 6.7

The *Notes* section is a place where you can create things such as reminder notes and go back and view them later on. You can also change the color of the notes and add pictures if needed. When you are finished with a note you can click on the trash can icon and delete it.

Chapter 6 – Outlook, Calendar and People

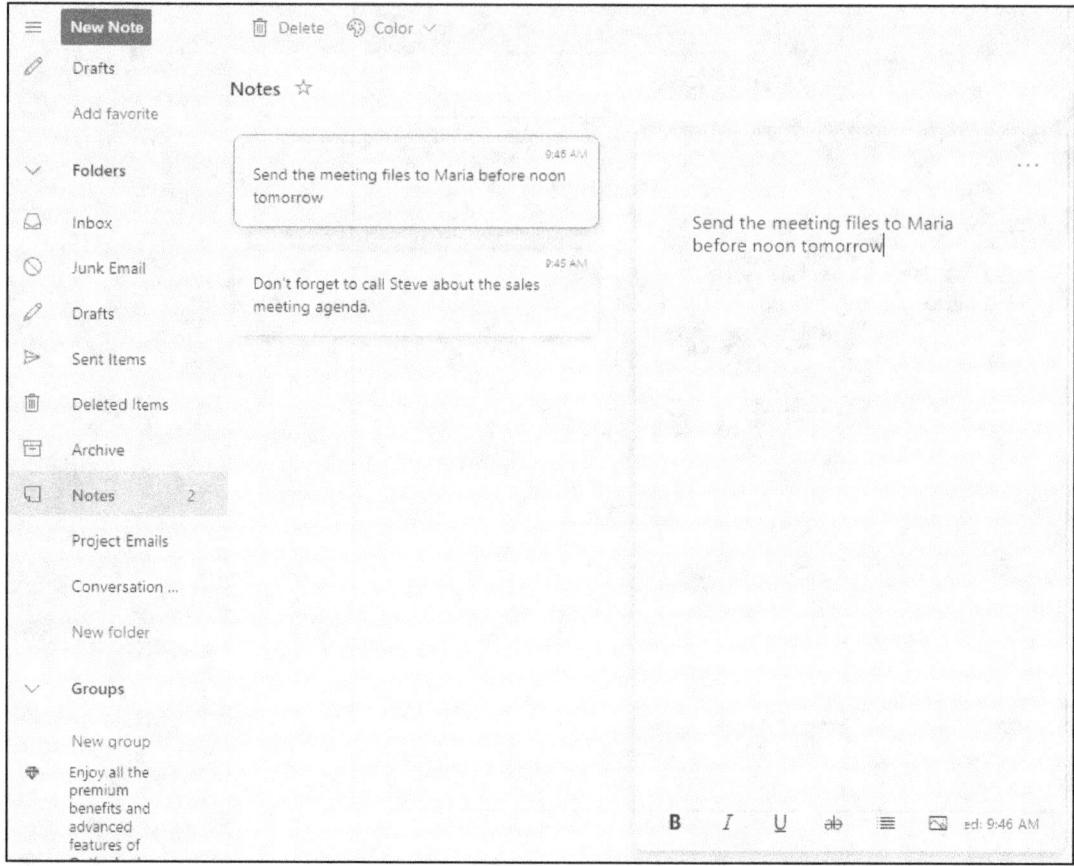

Figure 6.8

The *Conversation History* folder is used to keep track of your Skype messages if you ever decide to use it. I will be covering Skype in Chapter 8.

Groups
If you have several people that are in the same department or working on the same project etc. then you might want to add them to a group to make it easier to manage your emails and meetings with those people. That way you can do things such as send an email to that group rather than having to add all the individual people one at a time. This comes in handy when you are emailing a large number of people.

To create a group, go to the *Groups* section in your folder list and click on *New group*. Then you will name your group and add a description if desired.

Chapter 6 – Outlook, Calendar and People

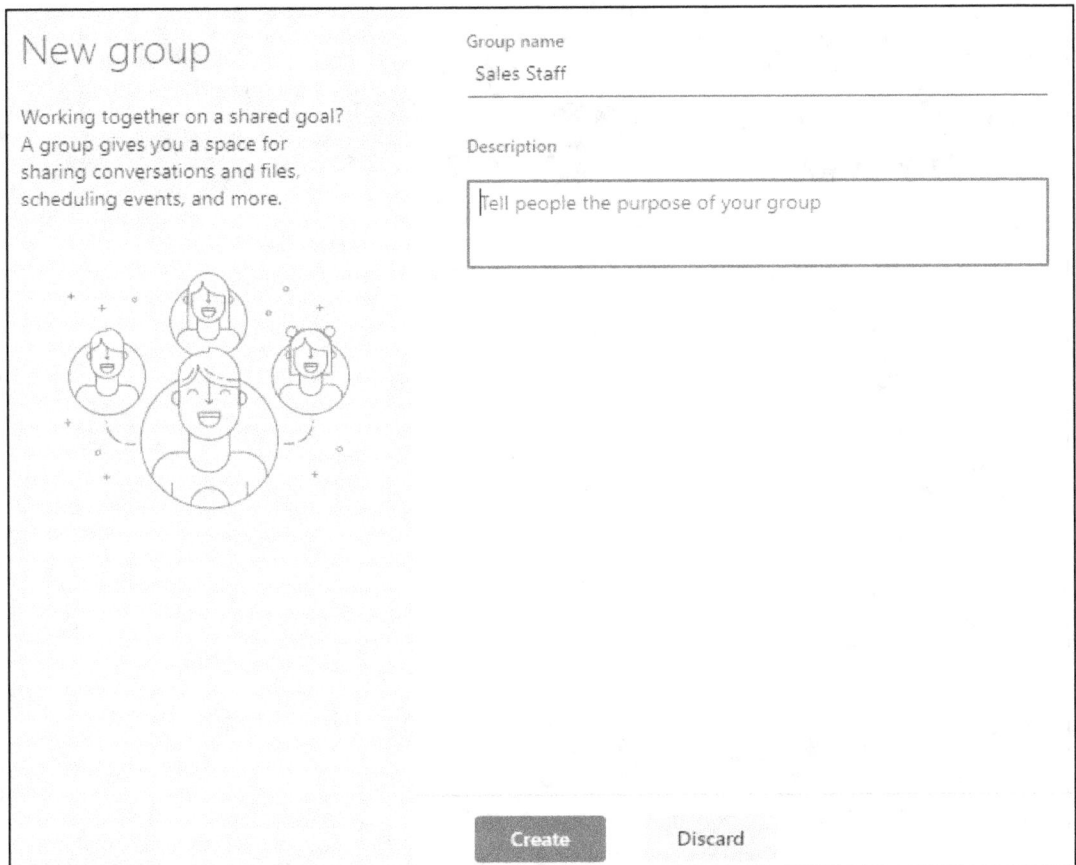

Figure 6.9

Next, you will be prompted to enter the email addresses of everyone you will want in your group.

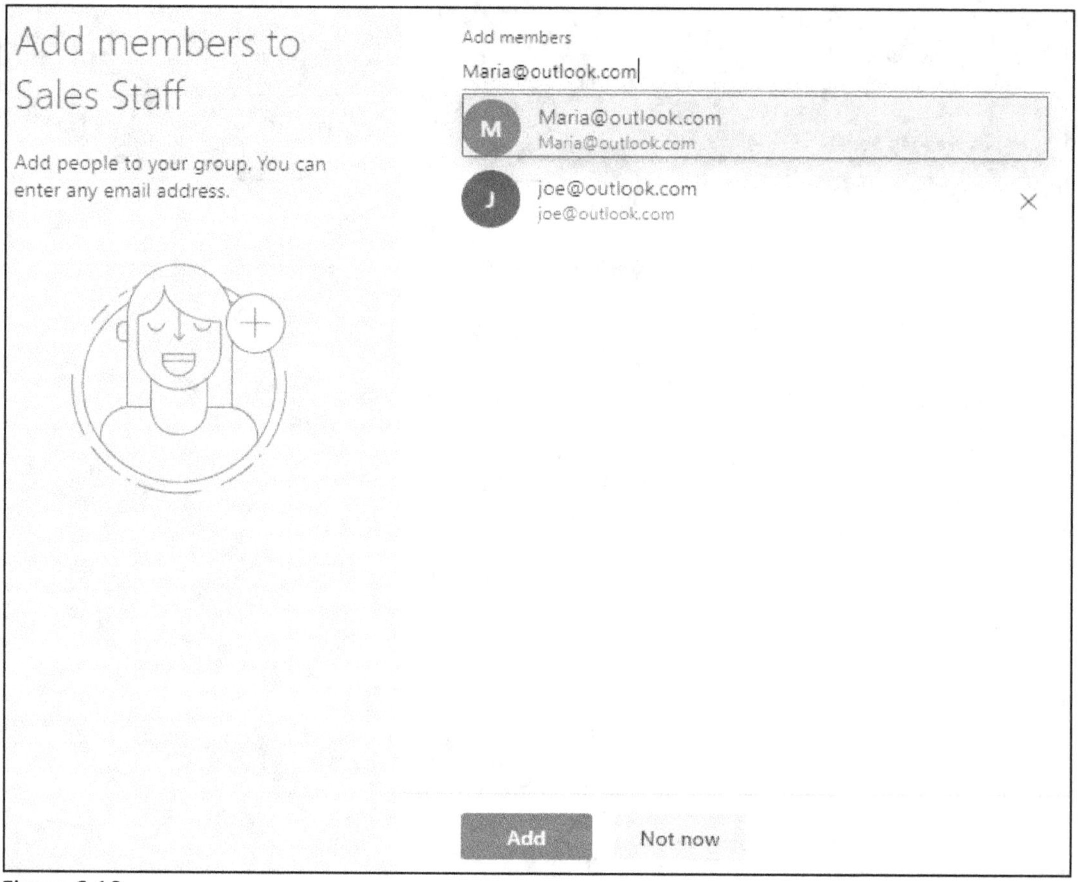

Add members to Sales Staff
Add people to your group. You can enter any email address.
Add members
Maria@outlook.com
M
Maria@outlook.com
Maria@outlook.com
J
joe@outlook.com
joe@outlook.com
Add
Not now

Figure 6.10

When you are finished, you will have that group listed under your Groups section and when you click on it you will be able to do things such as send an email or schedule a meeting with that group on the group calendar that will also be created.

SS
Sales Staff
4 members
Send email

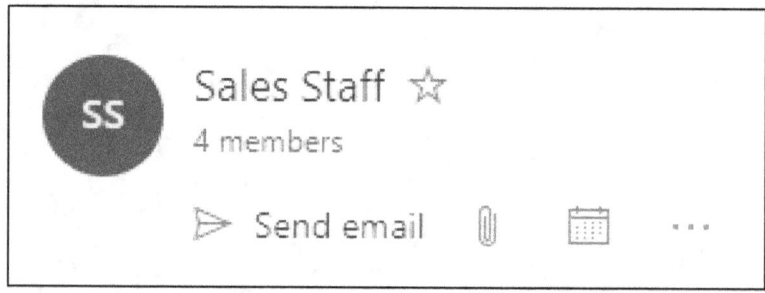

Figure 6.11

If I were to send an email to that group, the *To* section would show the group name itself and I wouldn't have to enter all the email addresses individually.

Chapter 6 – Outlook, Calendar and People

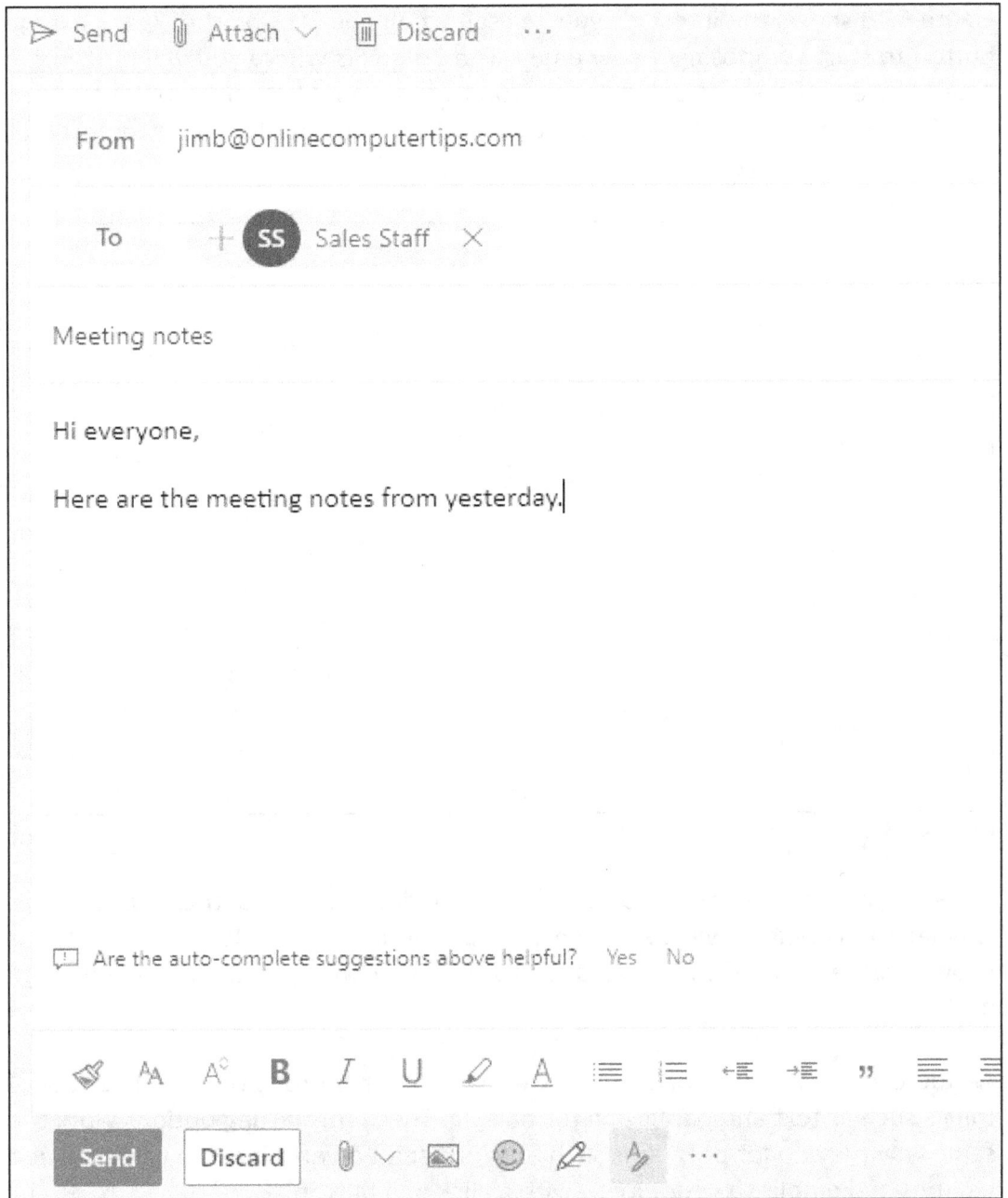

Figure 6.12

Composing, Reading, Replying to and Forwarding Emails
Since the main reason for using Outlook is to send and receive emails, I would now like to go over how you do this. The process for sending emails is fairly universal between email apps so if you are currently using another app for your email then it should be easy to get the hang of this in Outlook.

Chapter 6 – Outlook, Calendar and People

Figure 6.13 shows the interface you will see when you click on the *New message* button to start composing a new email. The *To* box is where you will type in the email address of the person or people you want to send the email to. If you want to add someone from your contacts then you can click on the To button itself to bring up your contacts.

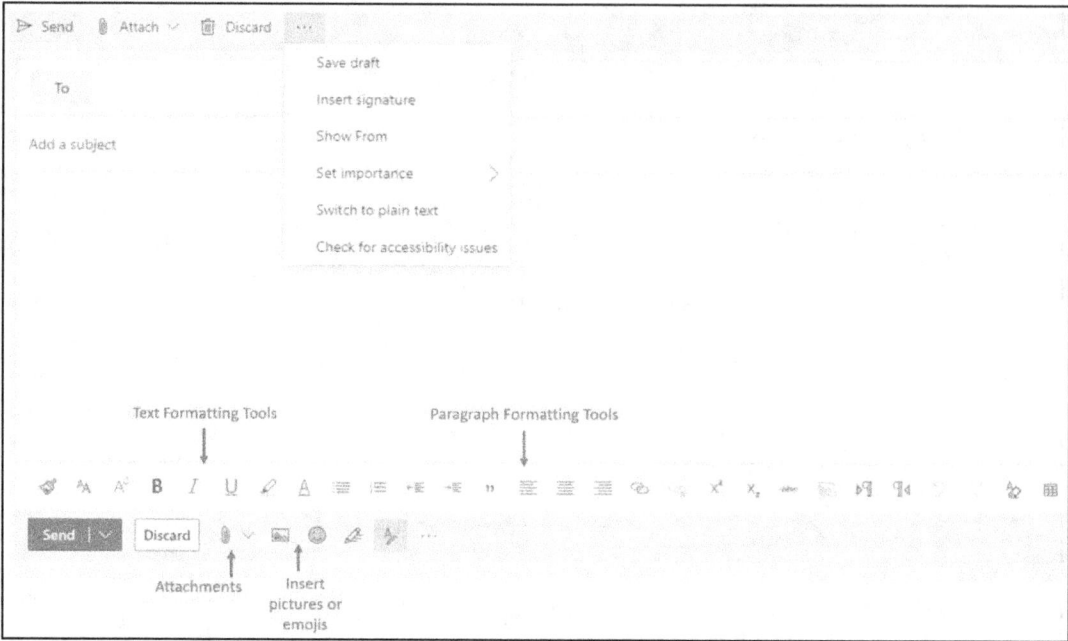

Figure 6.13

The section that says *Add a subject* is used to add the subject of the email and this is what the recipient will see when they get your email. Below that is what is known as the body of the email and is where you will type the actual message itself.

As you can see in figure 6.13 there are many other buttons that do a variety of things such as text and paragraph formatting. These formatting options work the same way they do for programs such as Word and PowerPoint. You can even add pictures and emojis to your emails with a click of a button.

If you were to click the down arrow next to the Send button you would see an option called *Send later* where you could enter a date and time in the future and Outlook would send your email at the time you specify.

Chapter 6 – Outlook, Calendar and People

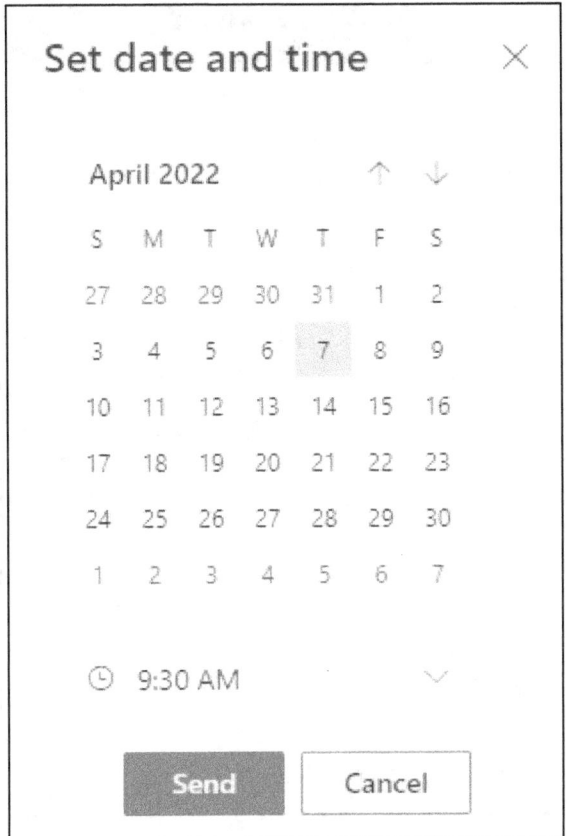

Figure 6.14

Once you have your recipient(s), subject and message typed in you can click on the *Send* button to send your email on its way. You should then be able to see it in the Sent Items folder to confirm it was sent.

Once you give out your email address and start receiving emails you will be able to find them in your Inbox. When the word Inbox is bold that means that you have unread emails. It will also show the number of unread emails next to it. In figure 6.15 you can see that there are three emails in the Inbox and two of them are unread because the subject line is bold and there is also a 2 next to the word Inbox. The middle email that has the subject of *The files for the meeting* has been read because it's not bold anymore.

If you would like to mark an email as unread as a reminder that you need to read it again etc. you can hover your mouse over that email and get some additional options as seen in figure 6.16. You can then click on the envelope icon to mark it as unread which will make the subject line bold again.

Chapter 6 – Outlook, Calendar and People

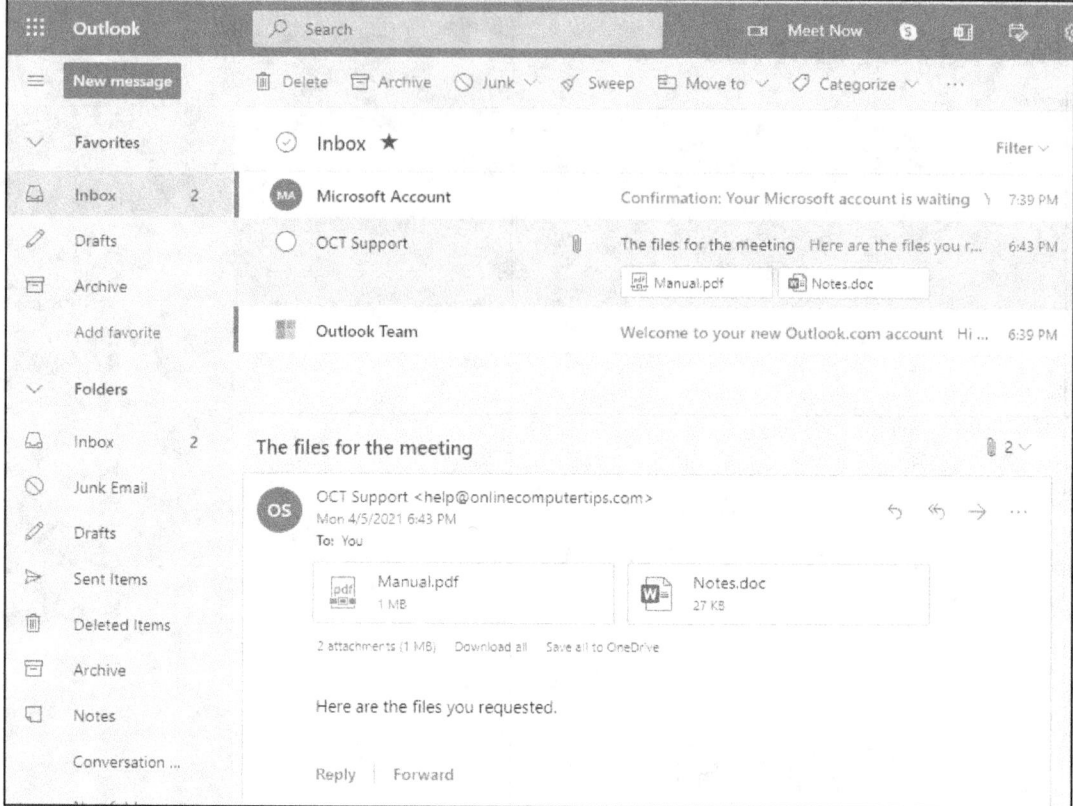

Figure 6.15

Figure 6.16

Another thing you will notice from figure 6.15 is that the body of the email that is selected shows in the *reading pane* underneath the main listing of emails. This way you don't need to double click the email to open it in a new window unless that's what you prefer of course. You can turn the reading pane off if you don't want to use it or change it, so it's displayed to the right of the emails instead of under them. I will be going over how to change your Outlook settings later in this chapter.

Chapter 6 – Outlook, Calendar and People

If you need to move an email to a different folder then you can simply select it with your mouse and then drag it to the new folder. Or you can go to the *Move to* menu and select your folder from there.

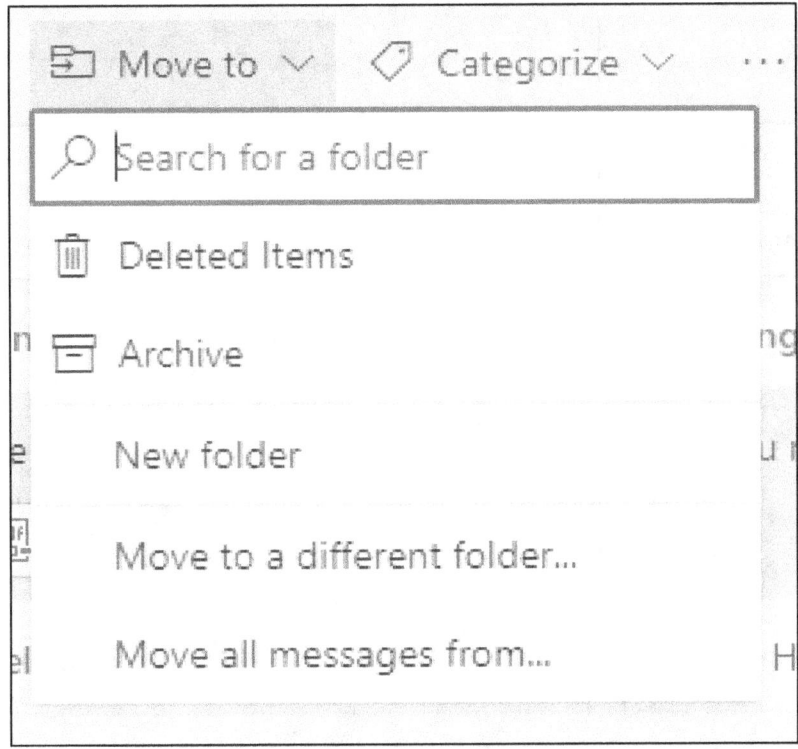

Figure 6.17

After you read an email you might have the need to reply to it or forward it off to someone else so they can read it. To do so simply select the message and click on one of the options at the top right of the message window as seen in figure 6.18. The single arrow will replay to the original sender. The double arrow will reply to everyone that is listed as a recipient of the email. The right arrow will allow you to forward the email to other people. Clicking on the ellipsis will bring up additional options such as delete, print and mark as unread.

Chapter 6 – Outlook, Calendar and People

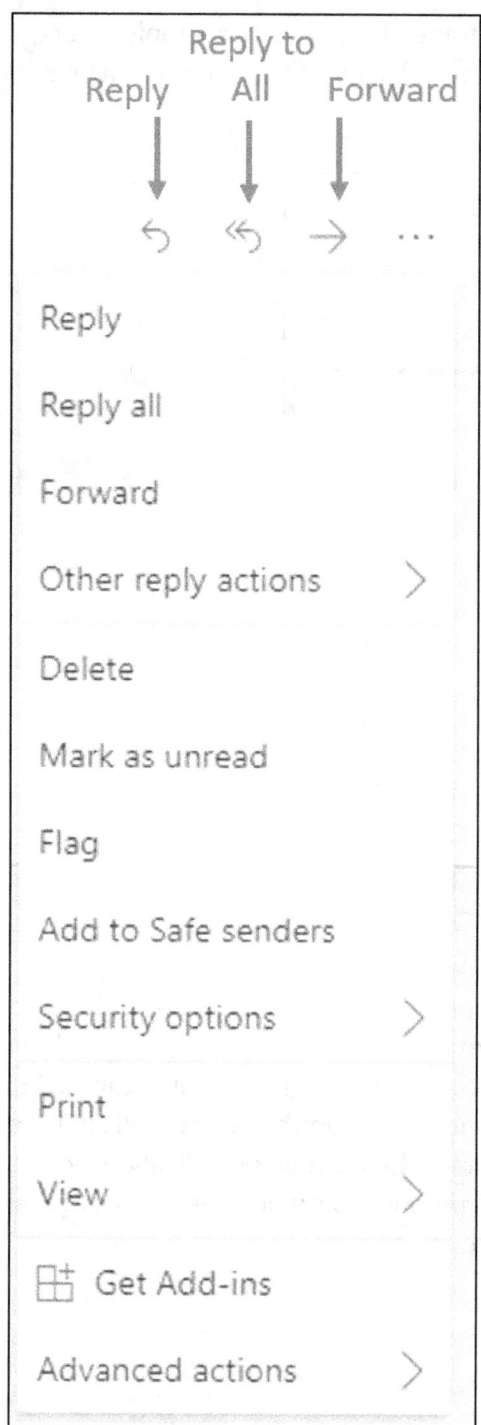

Figure 6.18

When you reply to or forward an email it will have the same look as it did when you composed a new email.

Chapter 6 – Outlook, Calendar and People

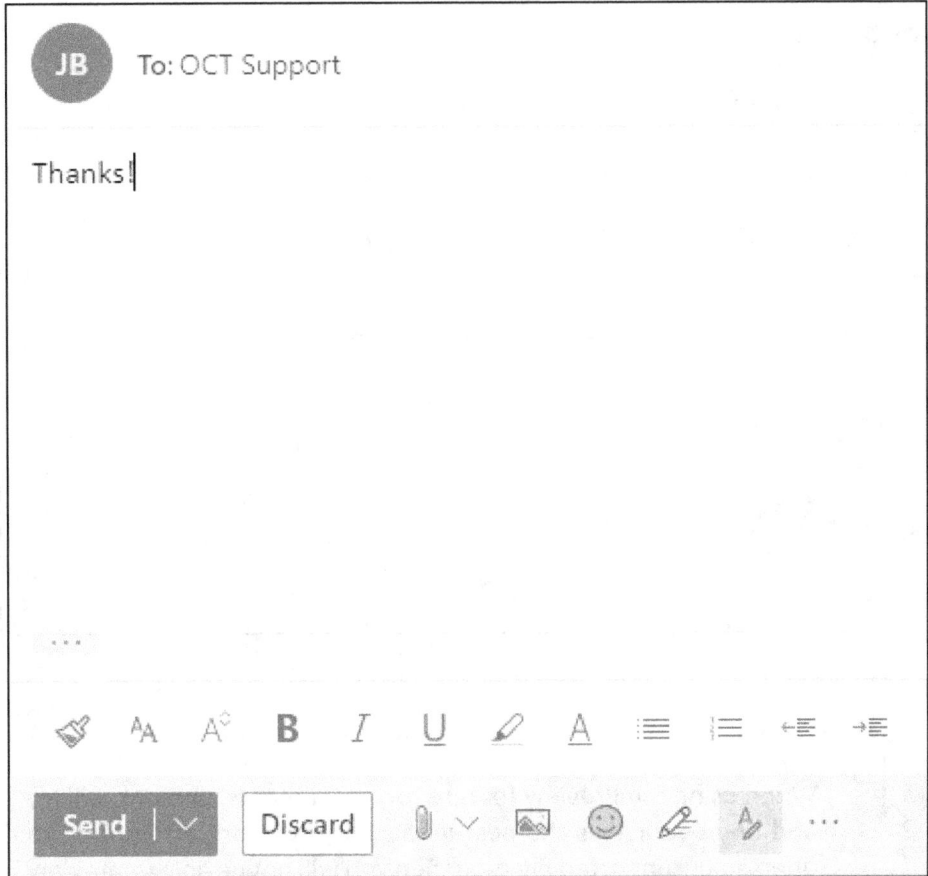

Figure 6.19

Attachments

If you look back at figure 6.15 you will see that there are two files attached to the email named **Manual.pdf** and **Notes.doc**. When you see these attachments in an email, that means the person you sent you the email attached the files on their end so you can have a copy on your end. You can either open the attachment right from the email itself or save them to your computer and then open them.

Underneath the attachments themselves you will have an option to download them or to save them to your OneDrive online storage account. If you click on the down arrow next to one of the attachments you will have options to preview or open the file, save to OneDrive or download the file. The *preview* option will attempt to open the file within your web browser and the *edit in* option will open the file with its corresponding app.

Chapter 6 – Outlook, Calendar and People

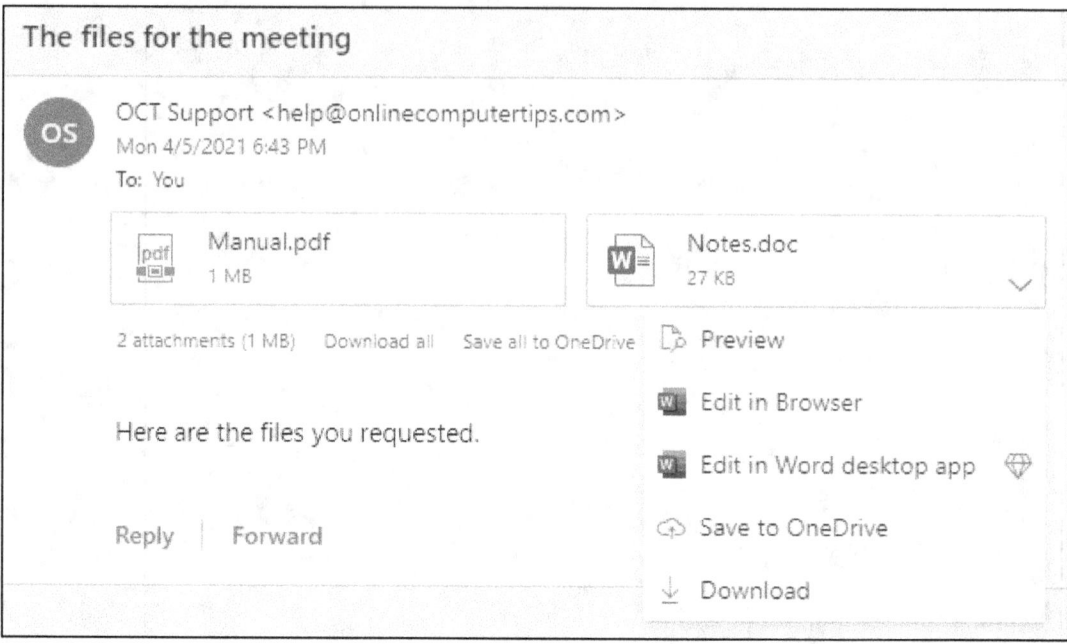

Figure 6.20

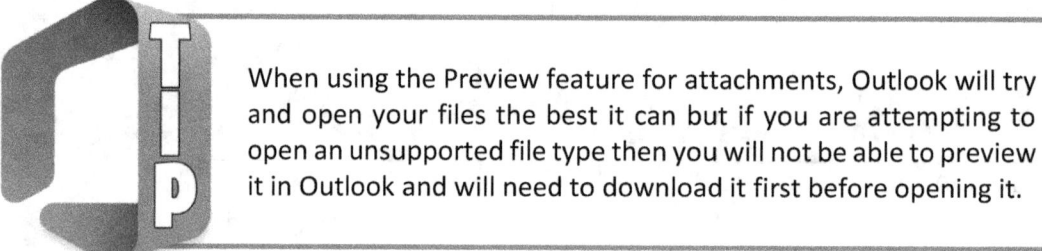

When using the Preview feature for attachments, Outlook will try and open your files the best it can but if you are attempting to open an unsupported file type then you will not be able to preview it in Outlook and will need to download it first before opening it.

When adding your own attachments to an email that you are sending, you have a few options as to how to accomplish this.

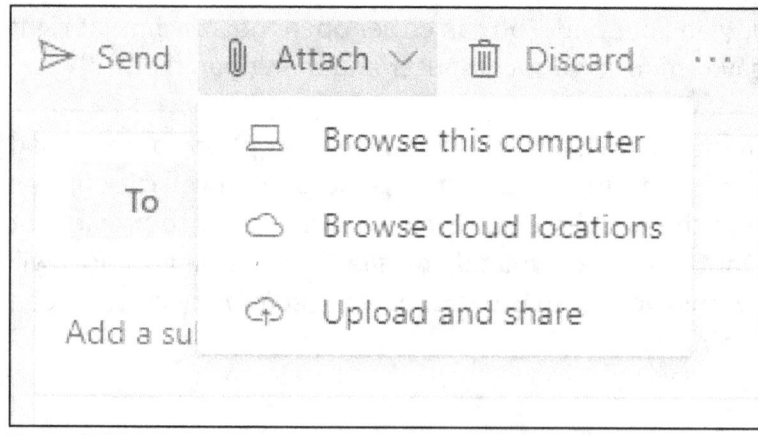

Figure 6.21

- **Browse this computer** – This is still probably the most common way to add attachments and the option you will use if the files you want to attach are stored on your computer's hard drive. All you need to do is browse to the folder on your computer where the file is located and attach it from there.

- **Browse cloud locations** – If you have files stored in your OneDrive repository then you can attach them using this method. You can also attach other online storage services that you may have from this method.

- **Upload and share** – This is a newer option that will let you upload a file to your OneDrive account and then share it at the same time. When using this option you will browse to your file location on your local hard drive like you do when adding an attachment from your computer. Then you will be prompted to choose a folder within your OneDrive account to upload to file to.

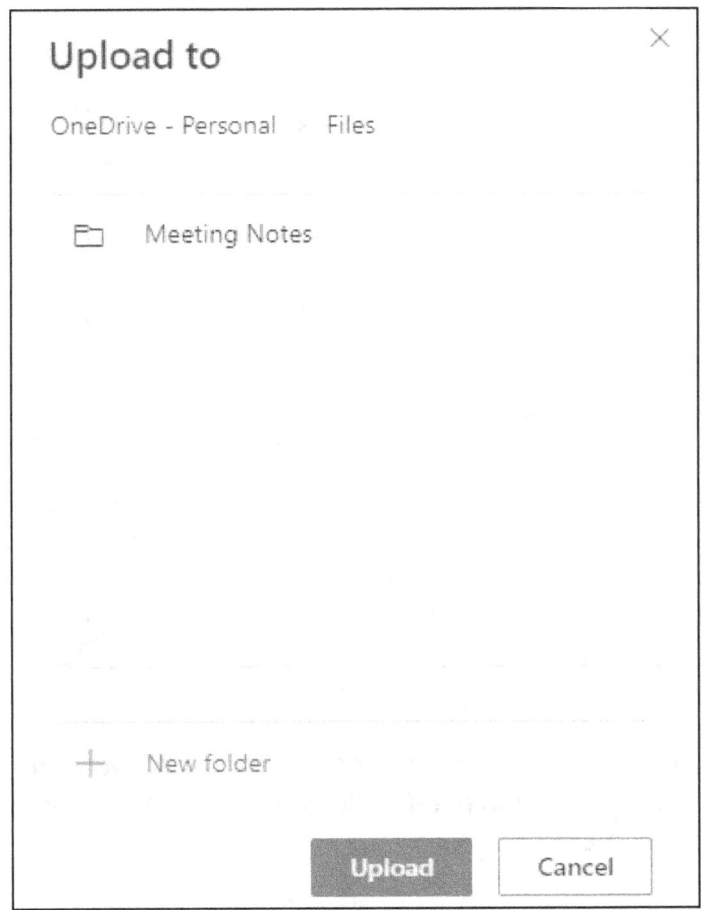

Figure 6.22

Once the file is uploaded to your OneDrive account you will see it as an attachment in your email, but it will have a cloud icon next to the attachment. If you click on the down arrow next to the attachment you will see additional options such as the ability to change the access permission for the file or to create a link to that file.

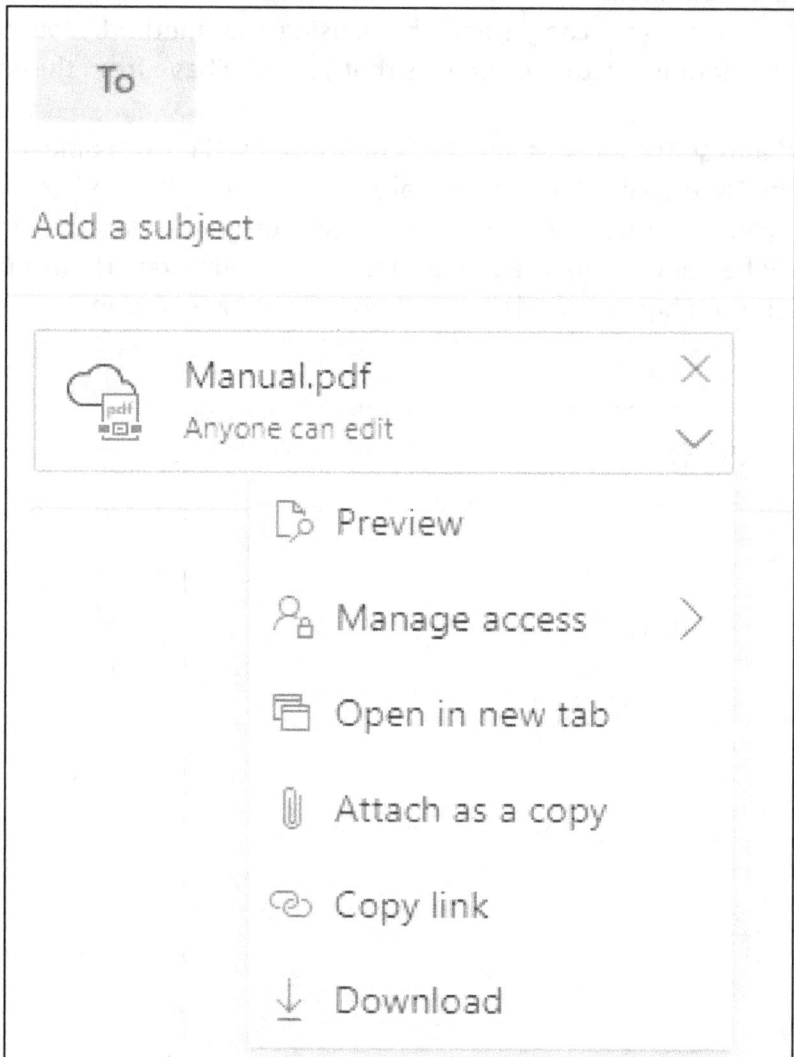

Figure 6.23

If you change your mind and want to remove an attachment from an email before you send it then all you need to do is click on the X at the top right corner of the attachment itself.

Chapter 6 – Outlook, Calendar and People

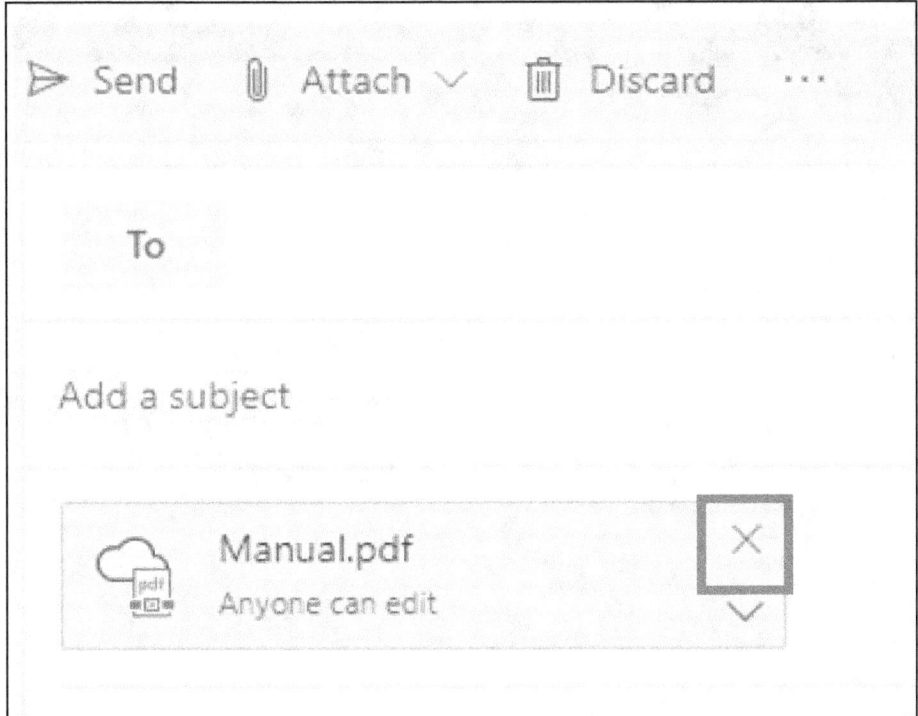

Figure 6.24

Outlook Calendar
If you click on the calendar icon at the lower left corner of the window you will then see your calendar any meetings or appointments you might have created. Your calendar will have one calendar by default, but you can add additional calendars for different purposes such as work, school and so on. That way you can keep everything separate and organized. Then if you want to share your calendar you can simply share the one you want and keep your other calendars private.

Chapter 6 – Outlook, Calendar and People

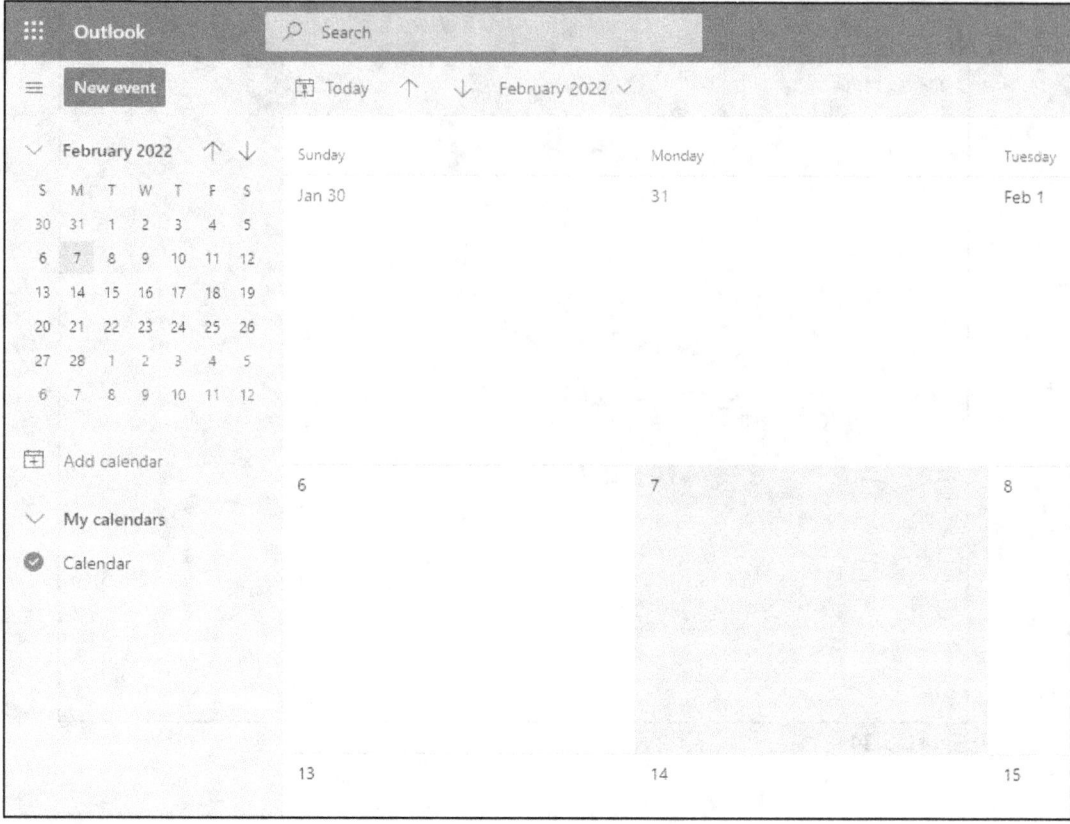

Figure 6.25

To schedule a meeting or other event you can click on the day you want to schedule it and you will get a popup box where you can add things such as the title, date, time, location, reminder time and a description. If you want to see additional options then you can click on the link that says *More options* and you will then be taken to a screen that looks like figure 6.27.

Chapter 6 – Outlook, Calendar and People

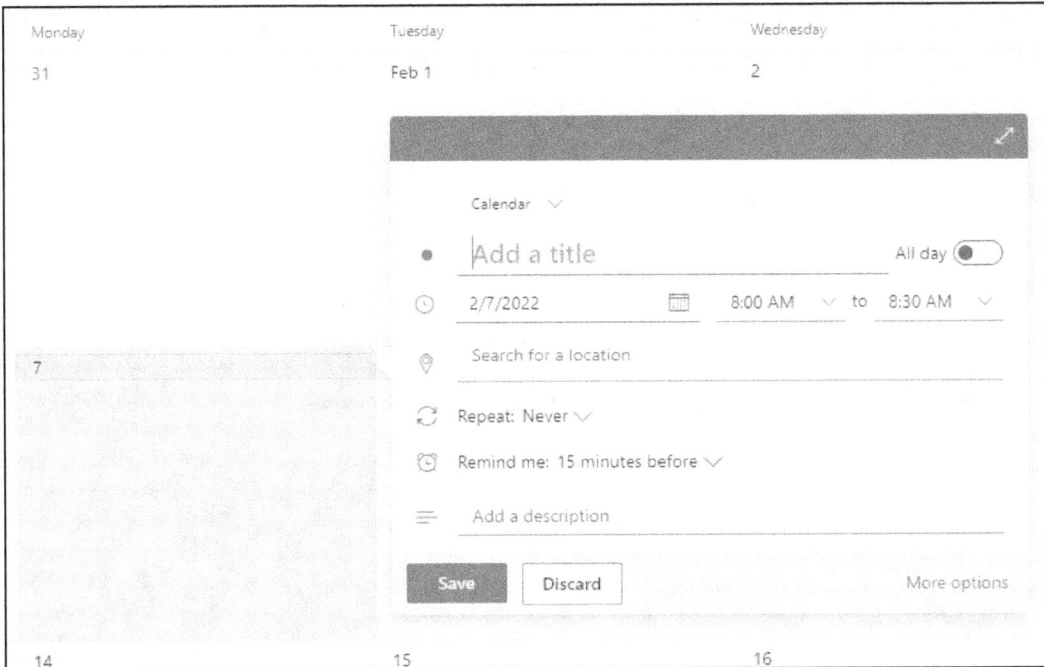

Figure 6.26

Here you can fill in the details of your meeting and add attendees as well as change response options such as having Outlook request a response from anyone you send the invitation to.

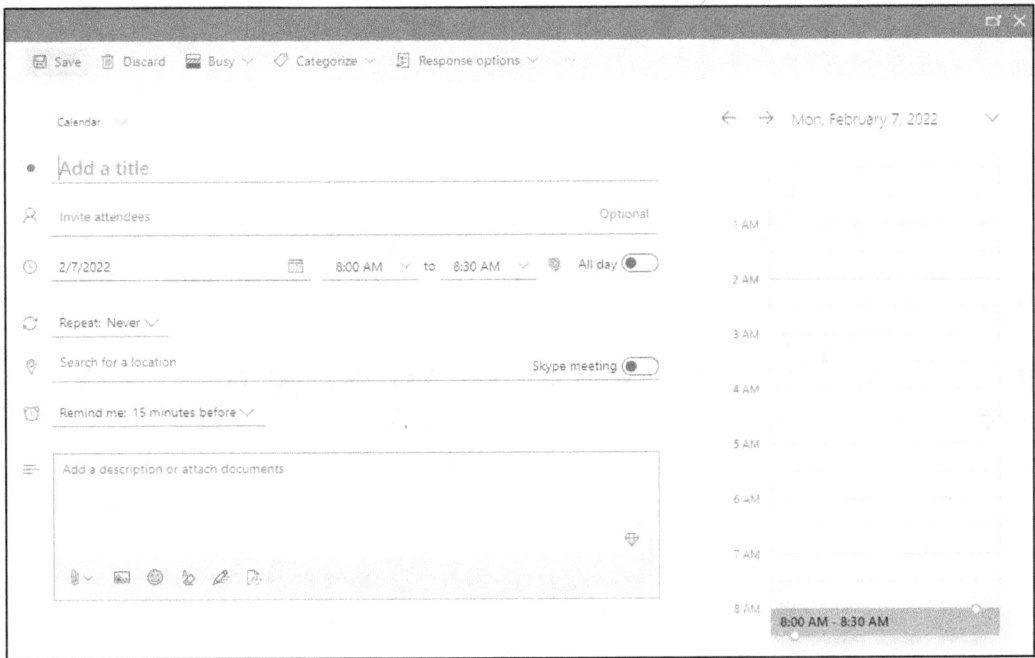

Figure 6.27

Chapter 6 – Outlook, Calendar and People

Once you have all of the information filled in you can click on *Send* to have your meeting invitation sent out to everyone on your recipient list.

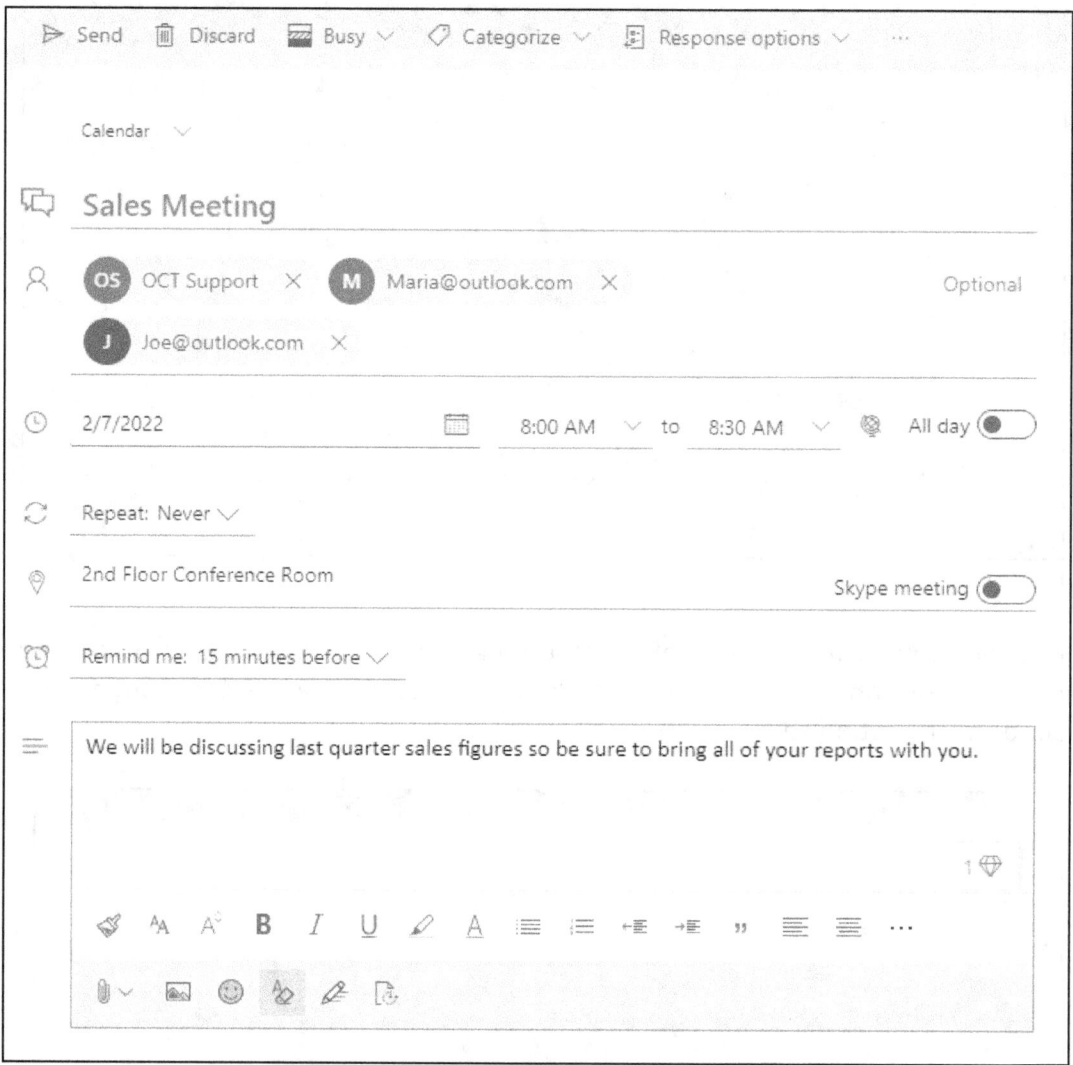

Figure 6.28

You will then see the event on your calendar and can click on it to make any changes.

Chapter 6 – Outlook, Calendar and People

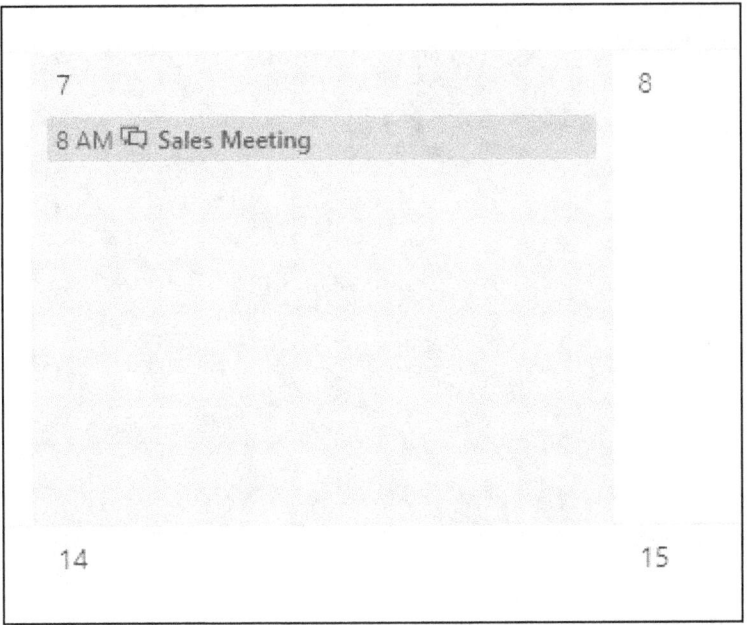

Figure 6.29

The people who you invited to the event will get an email similar to the one seen in figure 6.30. The way it looks will vary depending on their email client. They will then be able to accept or decline your invitation.

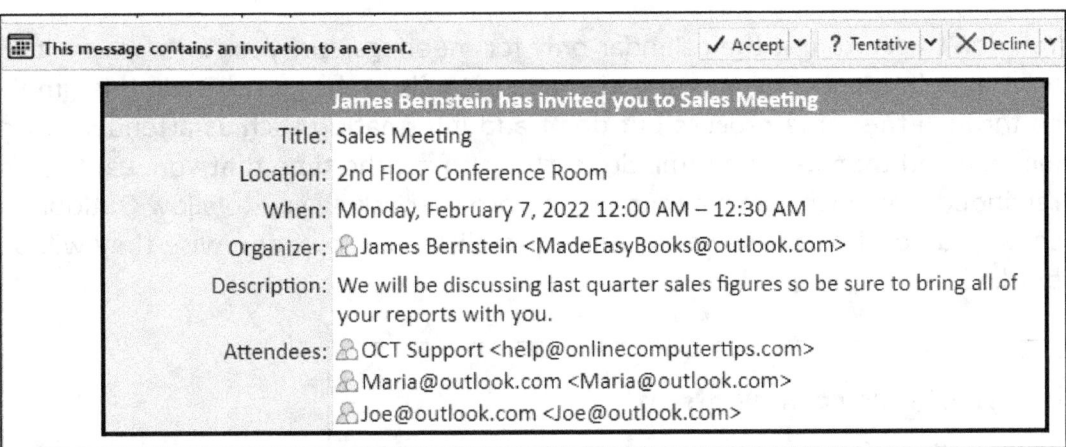

Figure 6.30

When the people on the other end accept your invitation and choose the *send a response* option, you will get an email confirmation letting you know that they have accepted the invitation.

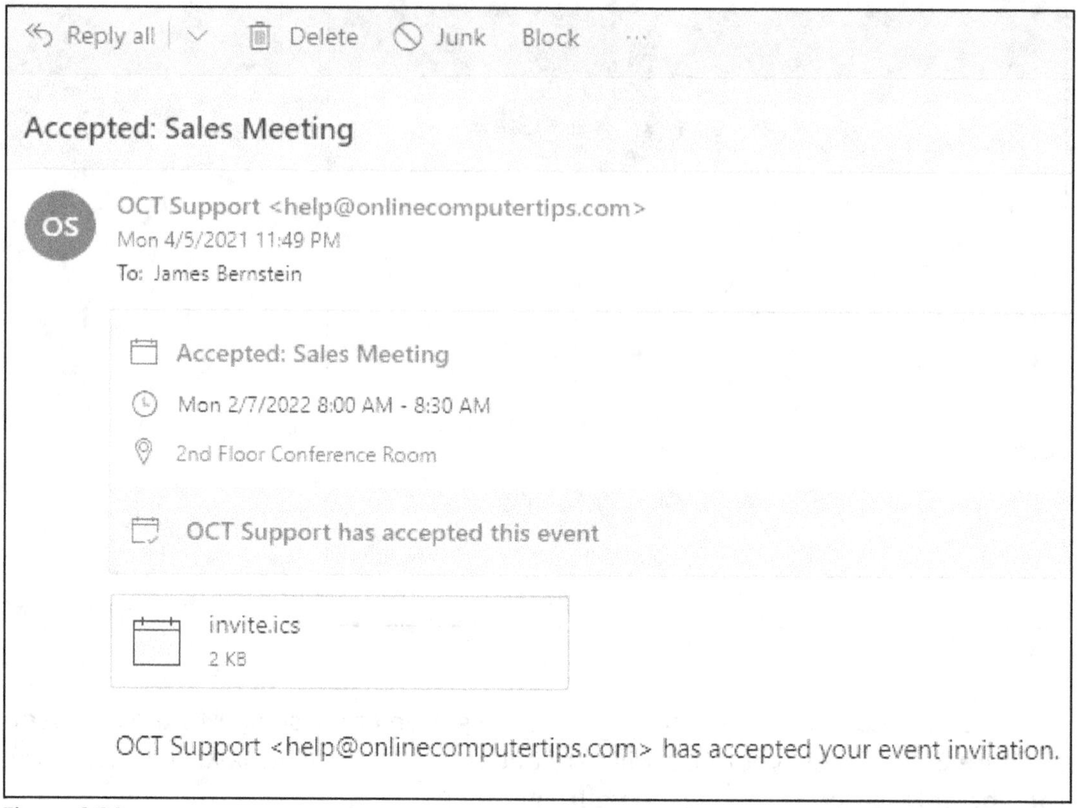

Chapter 6 – Outlook, Calendar and People

> Reply all | v   Delete   Junk   Block   ...
>
> **Accepted: Sales Meeting**
>
> OS OCT Support <help@onlinecomputertips.com>
>   Mon 4/5/2021 11:49 PM
>   To: James Bernstein
>
>   Accepted: Sales Meeting
>   Mon 2/7/2022 8:00 AM - 8:30 AM
>   2nd Floor Conference Room
>
>   OCT Support has accepted this event
>
>   invite.ics
>   2 KB
>
> OCT Support <help@onlinecomputertips.com> has accepted your event invitation.

Figure 6.31

You don't have to use the calendar only for meetings, but you can also use it to track appointments or even remind you to get milk at the store! To do this simply go through the same process but don't add information such as attendees or a location and then use the reminder settings to set the time that you want to be reminded. You might get a popup in your browser asking you to allow Outlook to show you notifications so you will need to click on *Allow* otherwise they will be blocked.

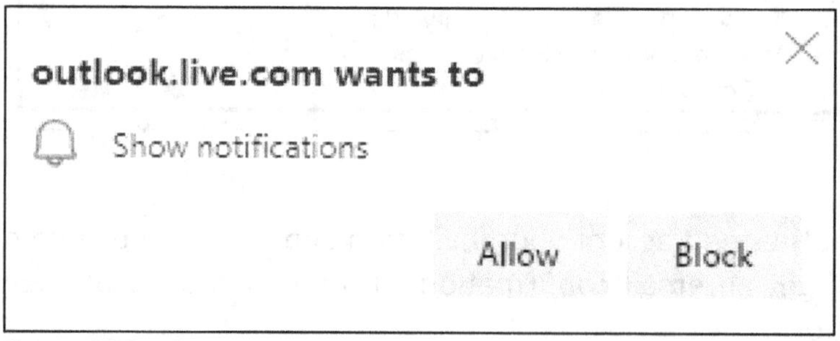

> **outlook.live.com wants to**   X
>
> 🔔 Show notifications
>
>   Allow   Block

Figure 6.32

226

Chapter 6 – Outlook, Calendar and People

To add an additional calendar you can click on the link that says *Add Calendar* and then go to the *Create blank calendar* section and give your new calendar a name. You can also choose a color and charm\icon to go with it.

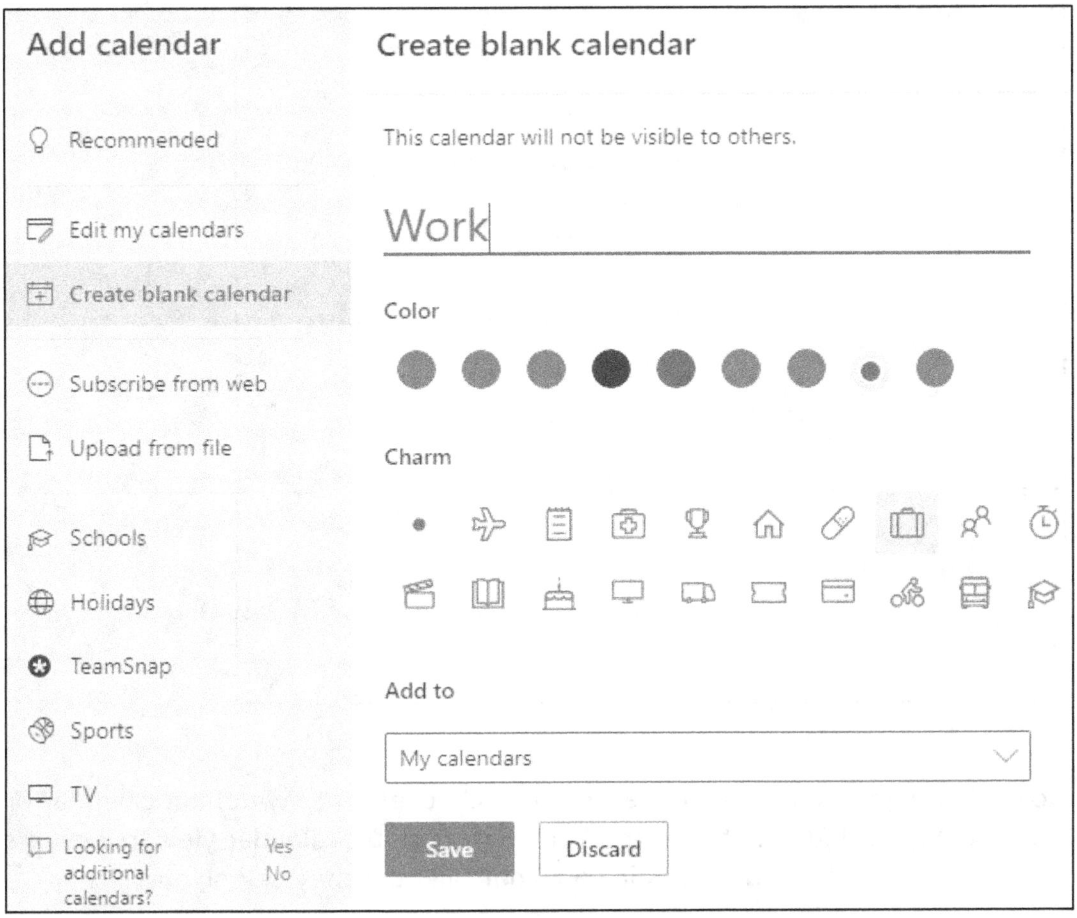

Figure 6.33

After you click on the *Save* button you will then have your new calendar listed with your default calendar. You can then click on the ellipsis to change settings such as having Outlook only show a certain calendar or if you want to change the color or charm you can do that from here. I will be discussing sharing options in Chapter 9.

Chapter 6 – Outlook, Calendar and People

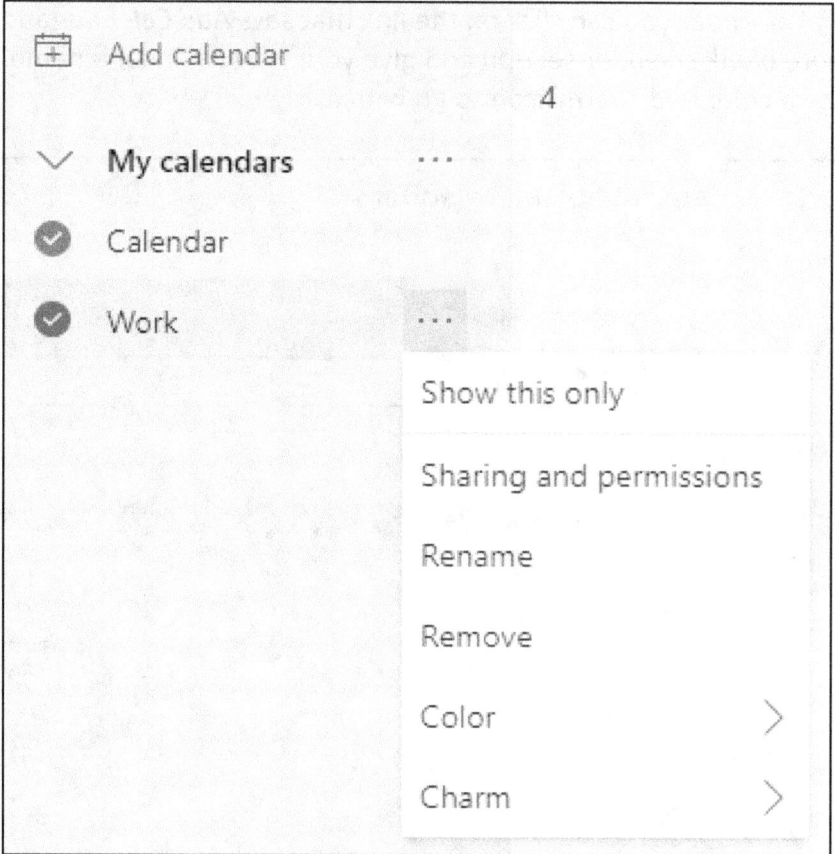

Figure 6.34

Now when I go to create a new event I can choose from my default calendar or my new Work calendar. Then when I am in my default calendar view, my events will be color coordinated depending on what calendar they belong on.

Chapter 6 – Outlook, Calendar and People

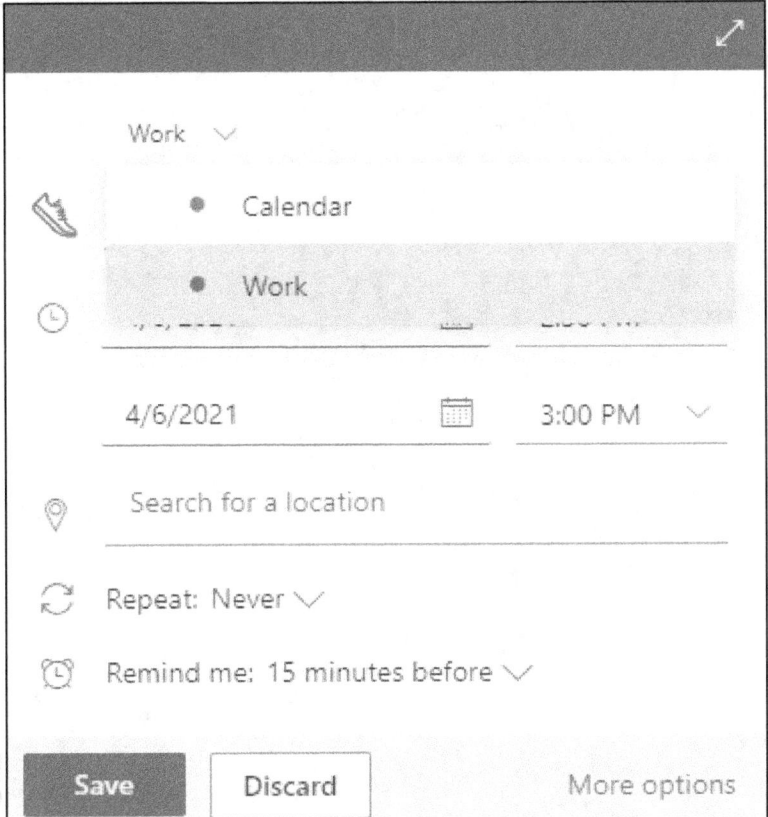

Figure 6.35

People (Contacts)
Having the ability to easily access the information related to the people you communicate with comes in really handy when doing things such as sending emails or scheduling meetings. Nobody wants to remember anyone's email address just like nobody knows anyone's phone numbers these days.

The People section of Outlook is where you can store contact information for the people that you communicate with on a regular basis. The first time you go there you will most likely see that you don't have any contacts and can click on *New contact* or *Add a contact* to add one manually.

Chapter 6 – Outlook, Calendar and People

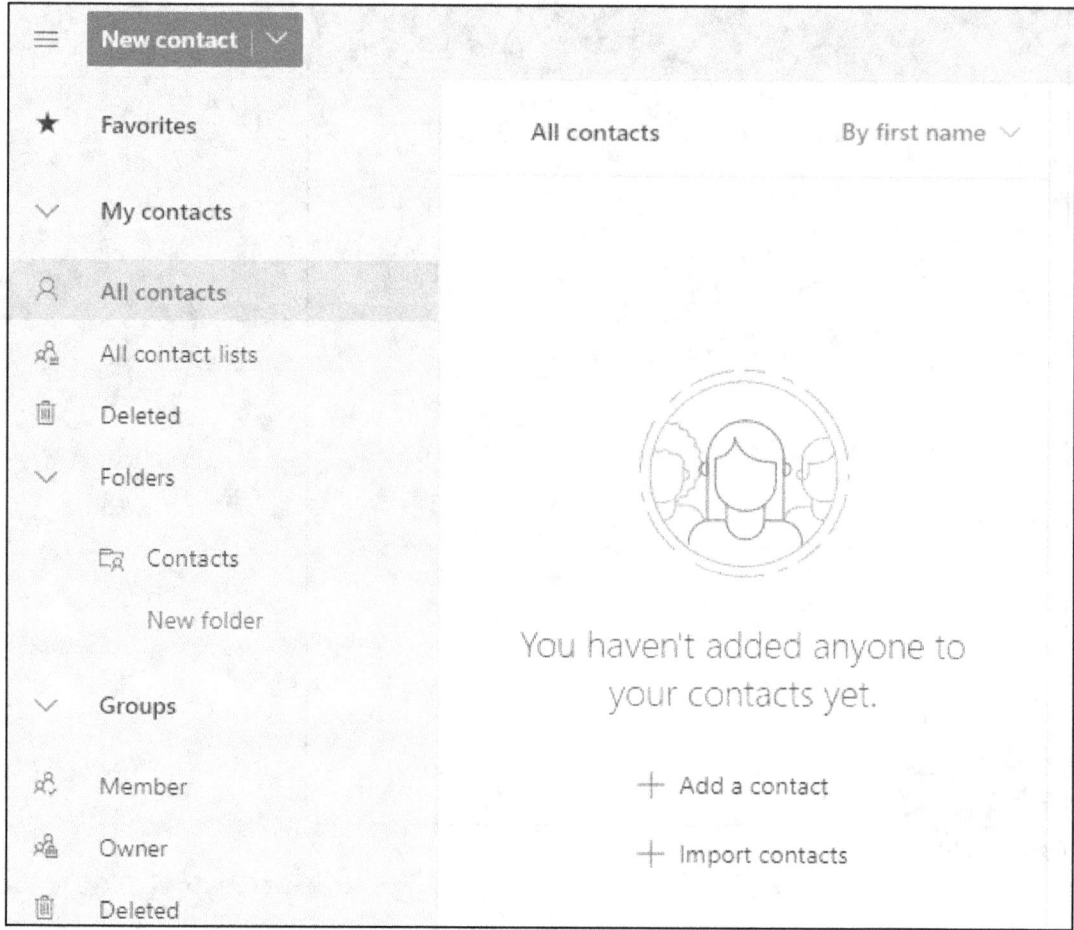

Figure 6.36

Once you start to create a new contact you will just need to fill in whatever information you would like to save for that person. You can even add a photo if you have one. If you click on *Add more*, you will be given additional fields that you can fill in for this contact.

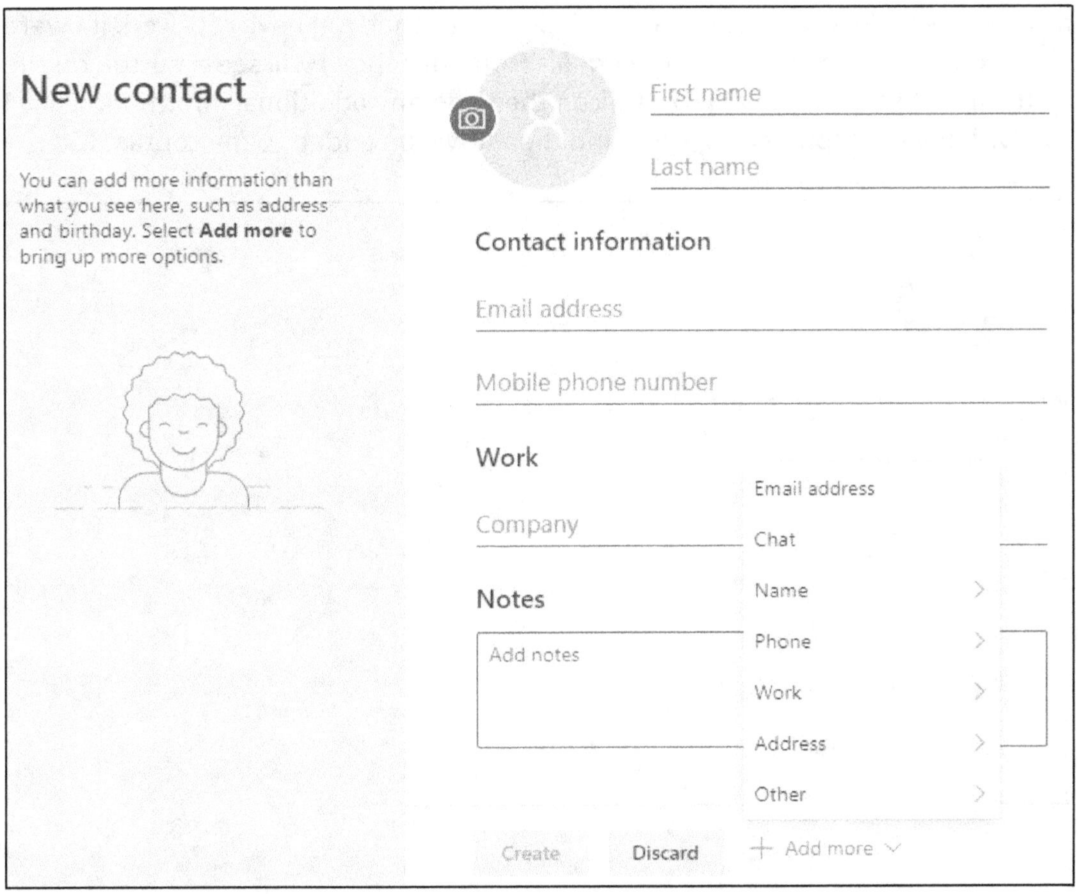

Chapter 6 – Outlook, Calendar and People

Figure 6.37

Now if I go back to my contacts, Todd will show up in my list. If I need to make changes to his contact I can click on the *Edit contact* link.

Figure 6.38

Chapter 6 – Outlook, Calendar and People

You can also add a contact from an existing email that you have received. If I were to click on the name in one of the emails from my Inbox I will see a button on the bottom that says *Add to contacts*. I can then add any additional information like I did with my new contact for Todd and then it will be added to my contact list.

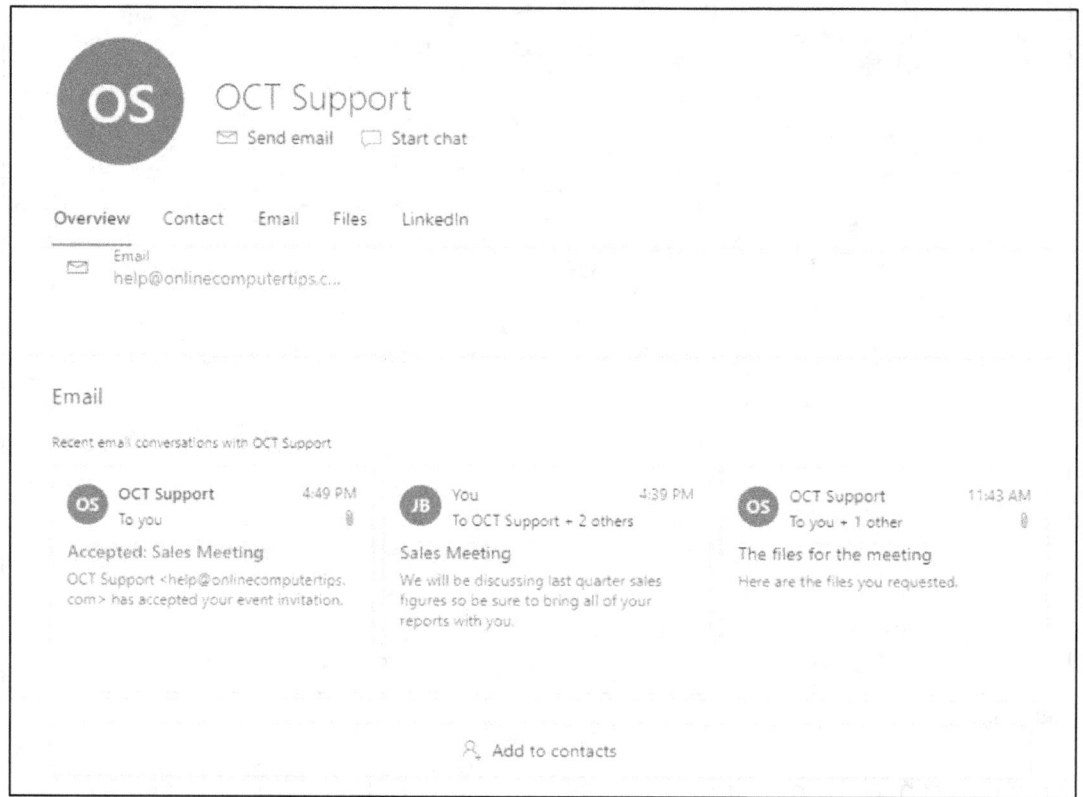

Figure 6.39

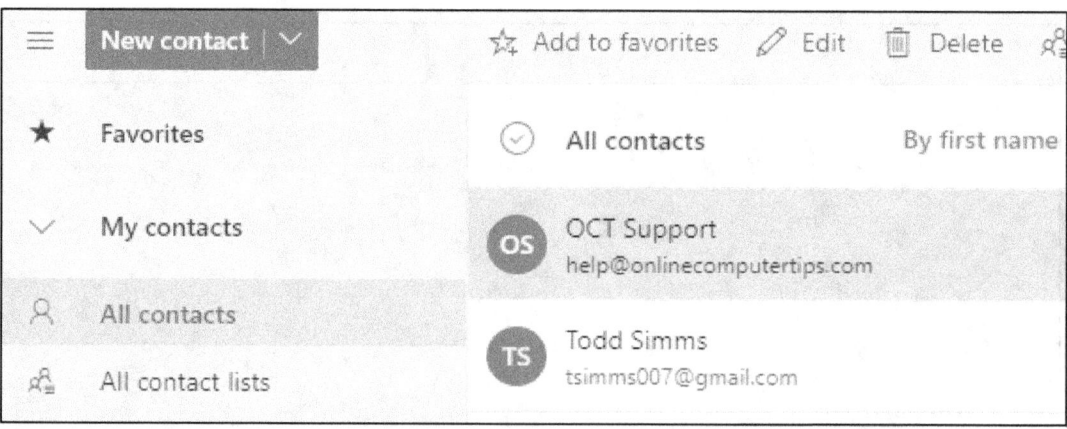

Figure 6.40

You can also create *contact lists* that consist of multiple email addresses and then you can send an email to that list without having to type in the addresses one at a time or add them from your contacts individually. This is similar to the Groups that I discussed earlier in the chapter.

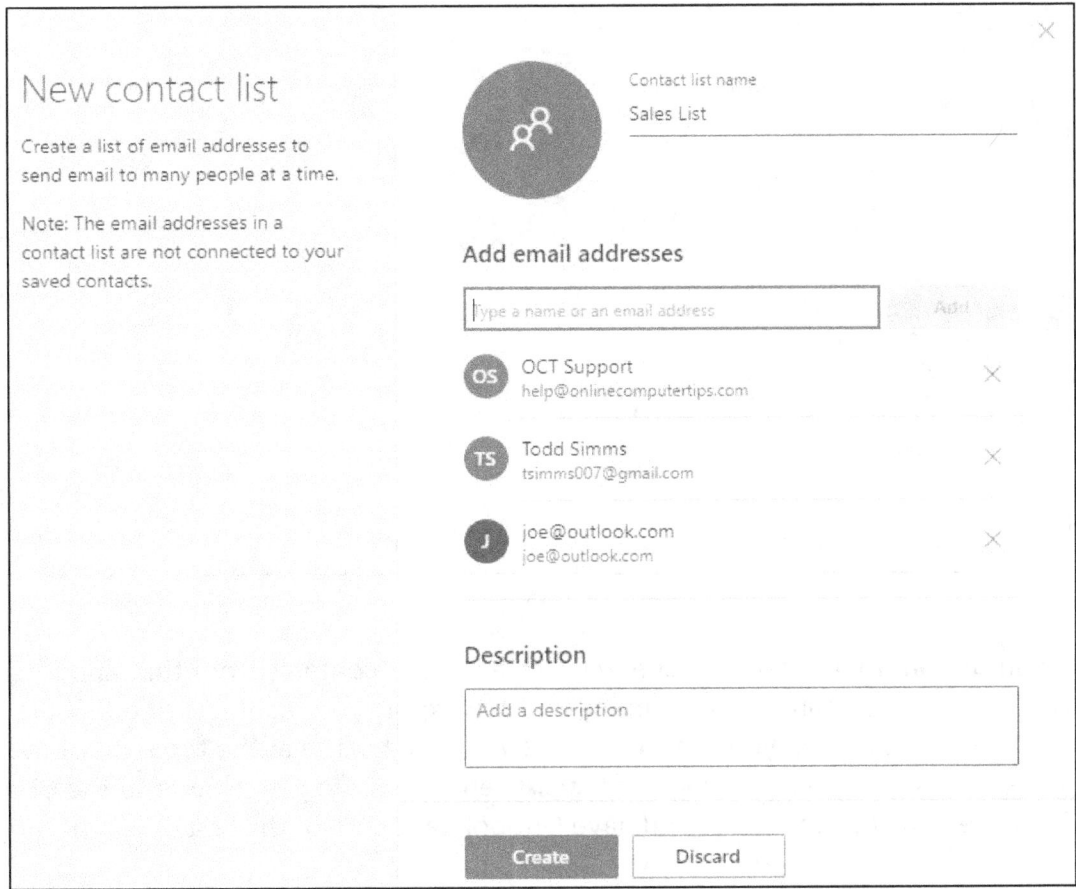

Figure 6.41

Figure 6.42 shows that when I go to this list in my contacts I have an option to send an email to everyone on the list with just one click.

Chapter 6 – Outlook, Calendar and People

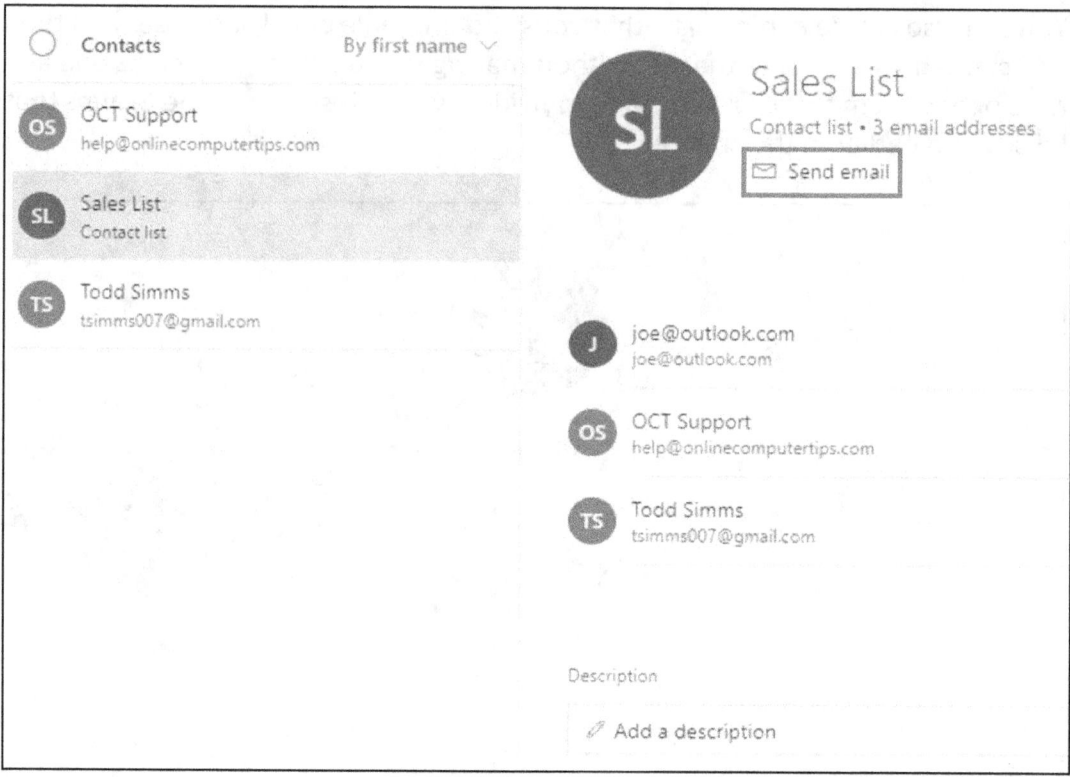

Figure 6.42

If you use another email app and want to add your contacts from that app into Outlook then you can do so assuming you can export your contacts to a CSV file. If that is the case then you can click on the *Manage* button at the top right of the screen and then choose *Import contacts*. Then you would just browse to the CSV file stored on your computer and have Outlook take care of the rest.

If you have some contacts that you use more than others, you can add them to your Favorites and then when you click on *Favorites* you will see only those marked as a favorite. These contacts will also have a star icon next to them. They will not be taken out of your regular contacts but simply added to your Favorites as well.

Chapter 6 – Outlook, Calendar and People

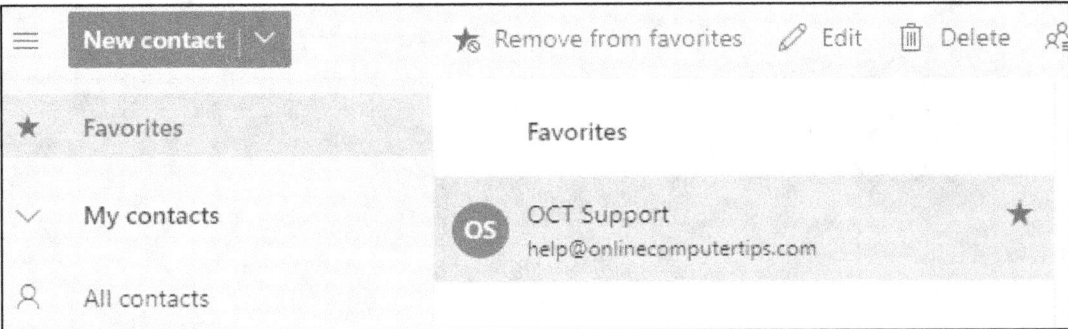

Figure 6.43

When you are looking at a particular contact you will see that there are sections within their contact where you can see information about what files they have sent you (figure 6.44) as well as a history of email conversations (figure 6.45).

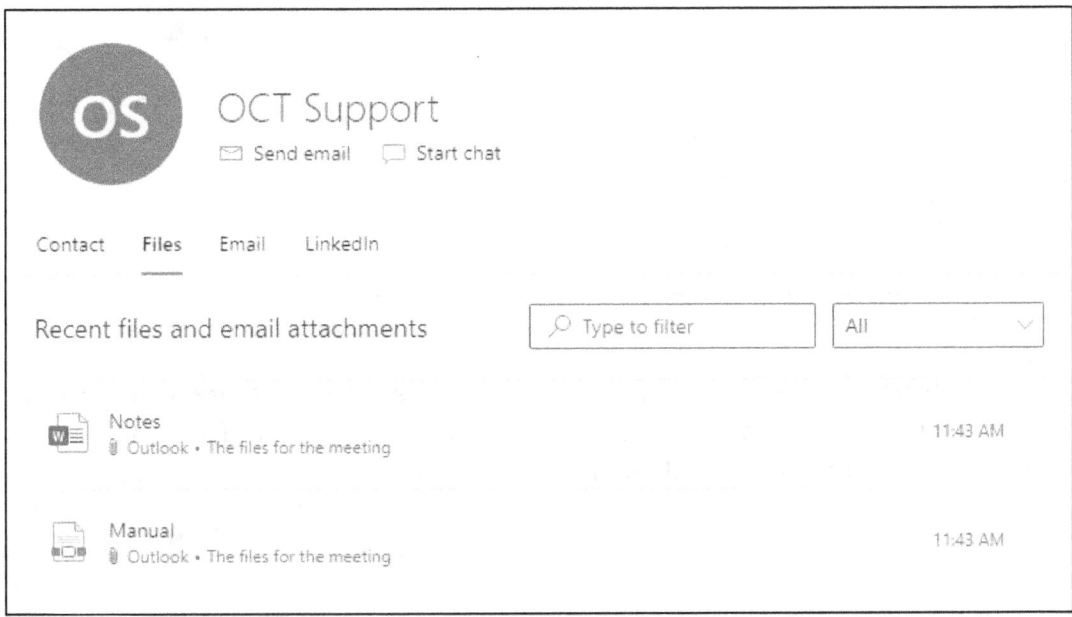

Figure 6.44

235

Chapter 6 – Outlook, Calendar and People

Figure 6.45

Once you have your contacts in Outlook you can use them next time you compose an email by clicking on the *To* button and selecting one or more from the list. You can even search for a contact if you have a long list.

Chapter 6 – Outlook, Calendar and People

Figure 6.46

Files

As you start to receive emails with attachments you might start to forget what email had the attachment you are looking for. If you don't download your attachments to your hard drive when you receive them in your email then it might be a little tough to find what you are looking for.

Fortunately, you can use the *Files* feature in Outlook to see a listing of attachments that are in your emails. You can get to the File section by clicking on the ellipsis at the lower left corner of the screen next to the People icon.

Then you will be shown what files you have as attachments in your emails and who they were sent by. You will also be able to see the subject line of the emails that contain those files and the dates they were received.

Chapter 6 – Outlook, Calendar and People

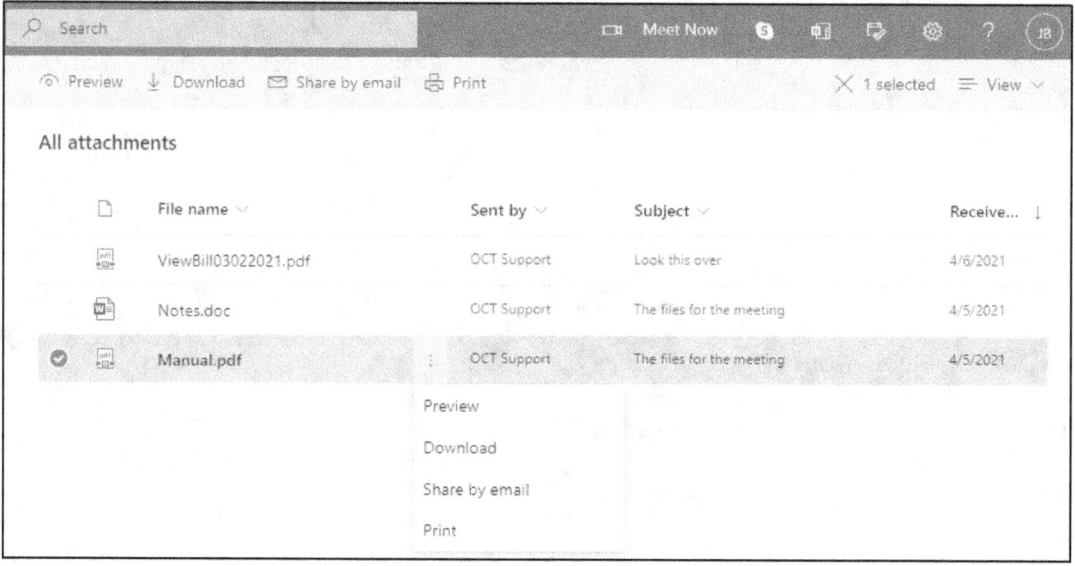

Figure 6.47

If you click on the three vertical dots next to an attachment you will have options to preview that file if possible, download the file, share it in a new email or print the contents of the file. You will also notice that the same options are at the top of the window as seen in figure 6.47.

To Do

If you are the type that likes to create lists to keep track of the things you need to get done then you might want to give the To Do tool a try. It's similar to the Tasks feature that you might have been used to using in the Outlook desktop client. One thing you will notice is that the word *task* is still used throughout your To Do list.

You can open the To Do list next to the same area you opened your Files list from. If you don't have any tasks in your list then it will be blank as seen in figure 6.48.

Chapter 6 – Outlook, Calendar and People

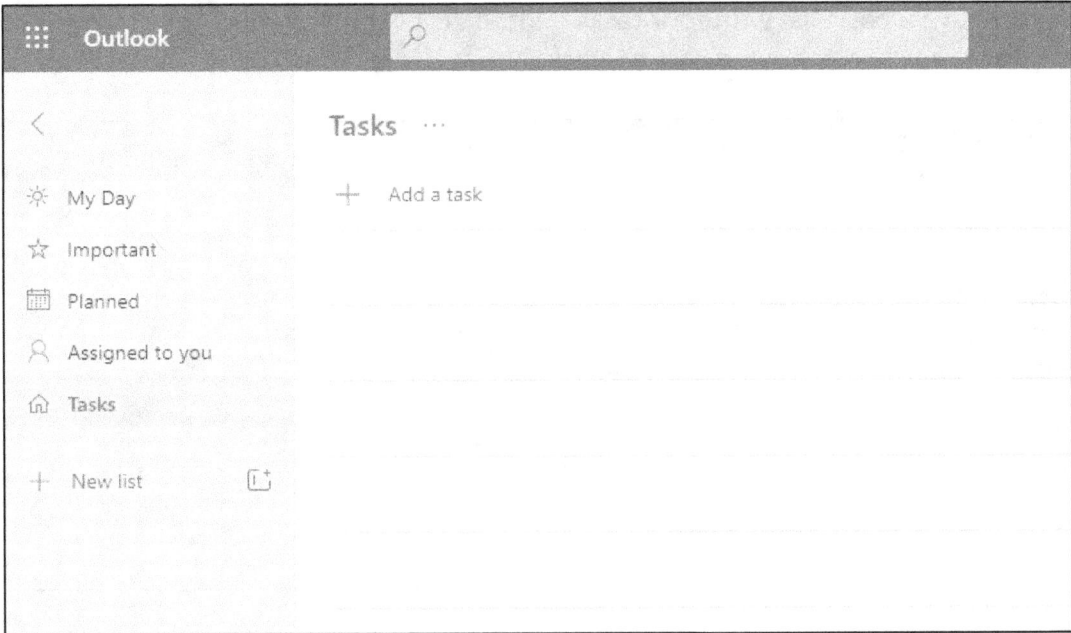

Figure 6.48

The To Do list is broken down into several components.

- **My Day** – Use this area to track tasks that you wish to complete today. You can have tasks in other areas and also referenced here. My Day is cleared at midnight every night, but the task won't be removed from its other location.

- **Important** – These are tasks that you mark as important and that need special attention.

- **Planned** – This is for tasks that have due dates or reminders but have not been marked as complete.

- **Assigned to you** – If you use Microsoft Planner (not free) you can track tasks that have been assigned to you by others.

- **Tasks** – This is where new tasks can be found.

- **New list** – Use this option to create a new task list.

I will begin by creating some new tasks by clicking on the + next to *Add a task*. Then I will just type in the task and click on *Add*.

Chapter 6 – Outlook, Calendar and People

Now I have a basic list with four tasks on it. If I click the arrows at the top right of my list I can choose how to sort my tasks.

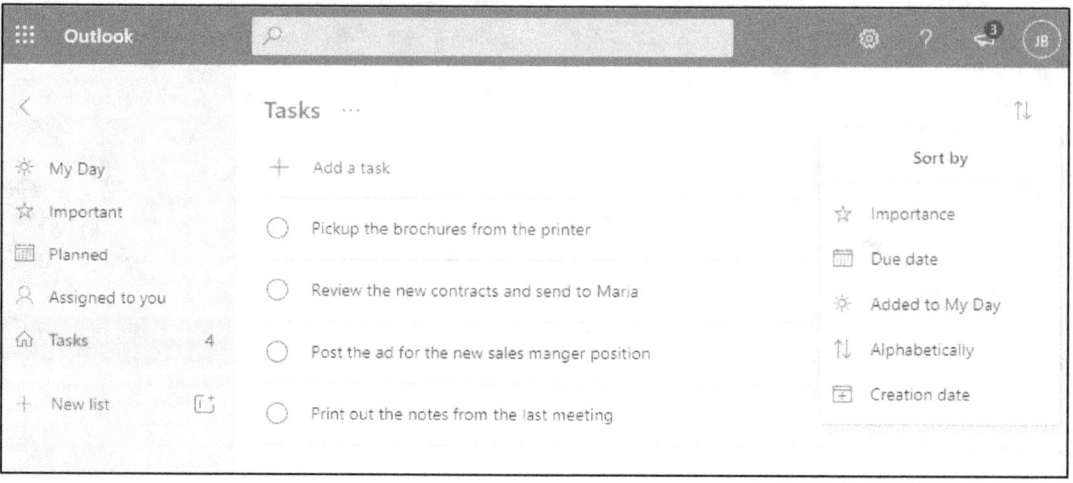

Figure 6.49

If I were to click my mouse inside the circle next to a task it would mark it as completed. If I change my mind I can click on the checkmark to mark it as not completed.

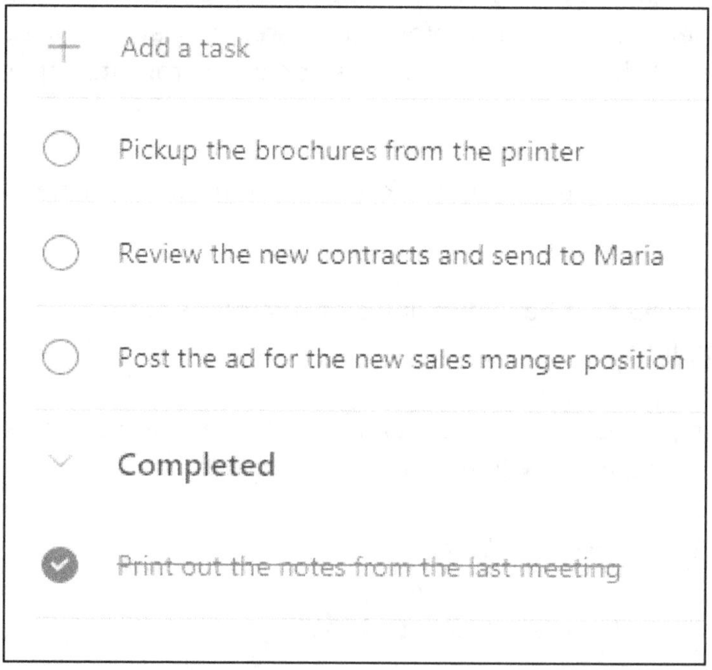

Figure 6.50

Chapter 6 – Outlook, Calendar and People

If I click on *My Day* I can either create a new task or add one of the tasks I just created to my daily to do list by clicking the + next to it. I will add my first task about picking up the brochures from the printer to my tasks that need to be completed today. I will also add a new task for the day.

Figure 6.51

If I go back to Tasks I will still have my brochure task in that list since it doesn't move it into the My Day section but rather copies it. You will also notice that my dry cleaners task is listed in the main Tasks list as well and they both have a note underneath that says My Day meaning they are assigned to be completed today.

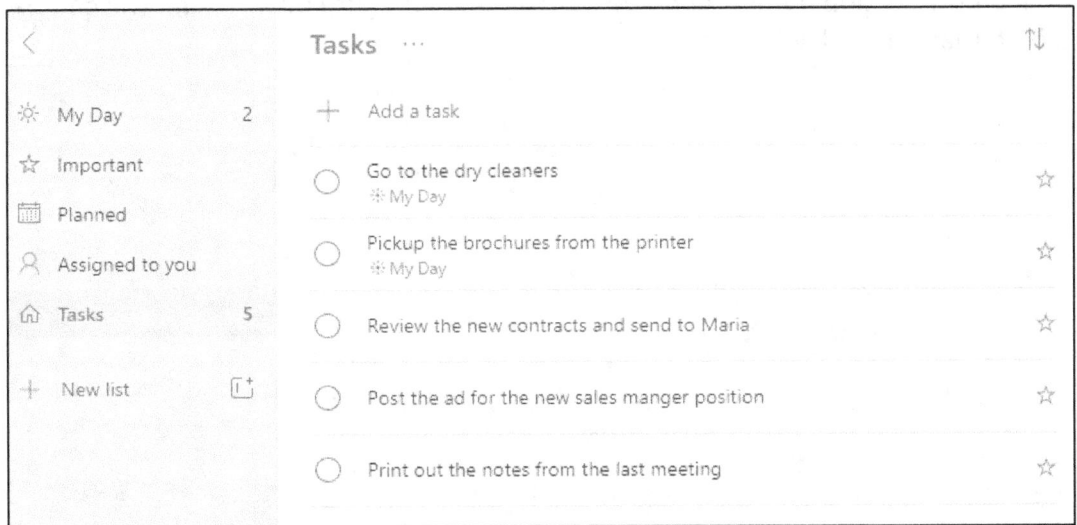

Figure 6.52

If I were to click on the star icon to the right of a task it would add it to my *Important* section yet still leave it in the Tasks section. I will do that for my last task about printing out the meeting notes.

241

Chapter 6 – Outlook, Calendar and People

Now it moved the task I marked as important to the top of the list and also added it to my Important list, and you can see that there is now a number 1 next to the Important section on the left.

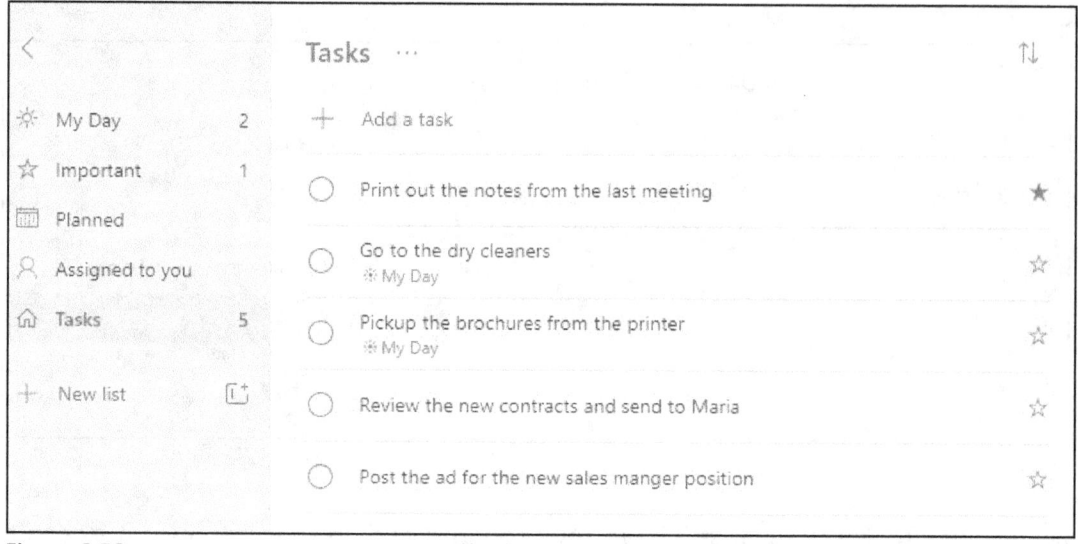

Figure 6.53

Next, I am going to add a due date to the task regarding reviewing the new contracts and sending them to Maria. To do this I will click on that task and then click on the section named *Add due date* as seen in figure 6.54. Then I will choose a date that this task will be due.

Chapter 6 – Outlook, Calendar and People

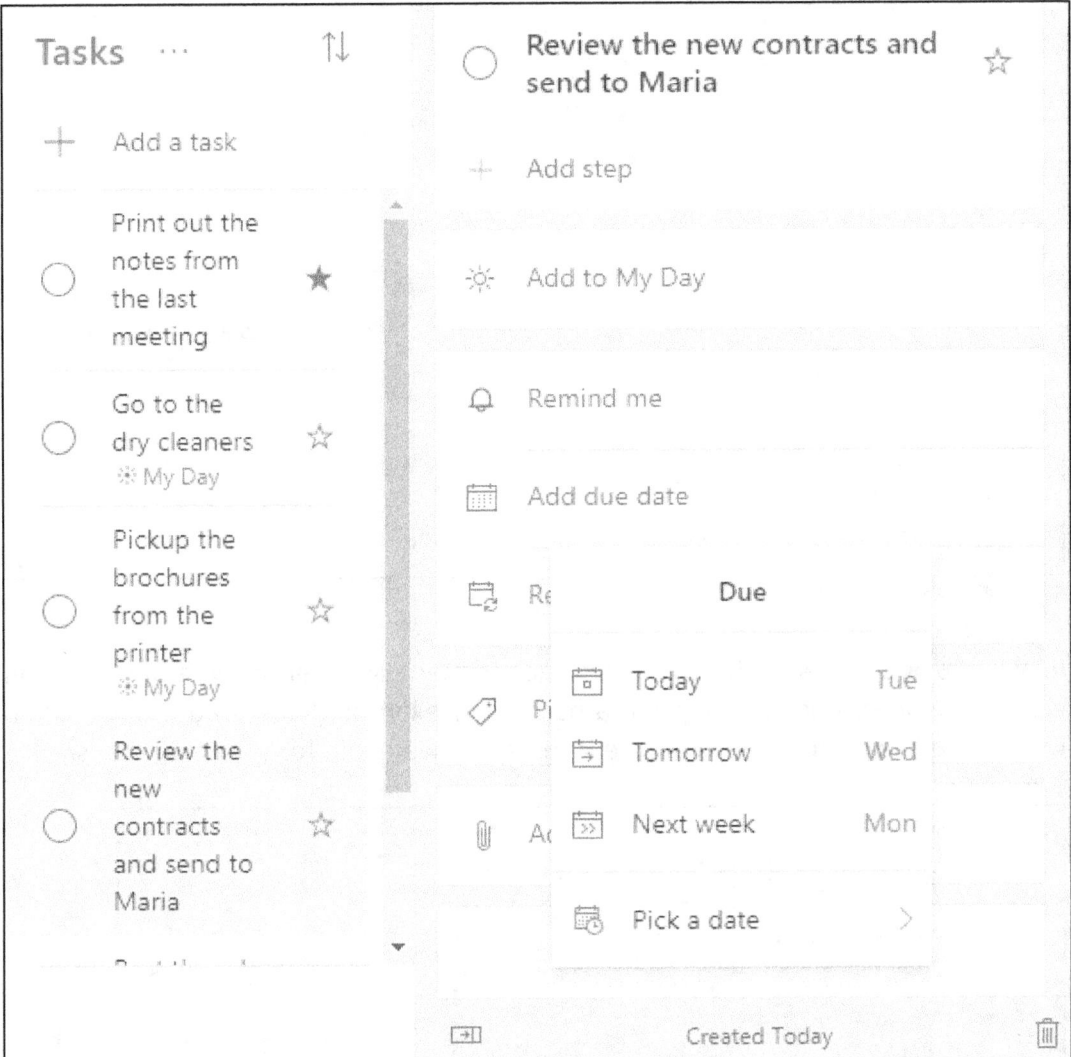

Figure 6.54

Now when I go to the *Planned* section I will see my task with its due date. It will also remain in my main Tasks area.

Chapter 6 – Outlook, Calendar and People

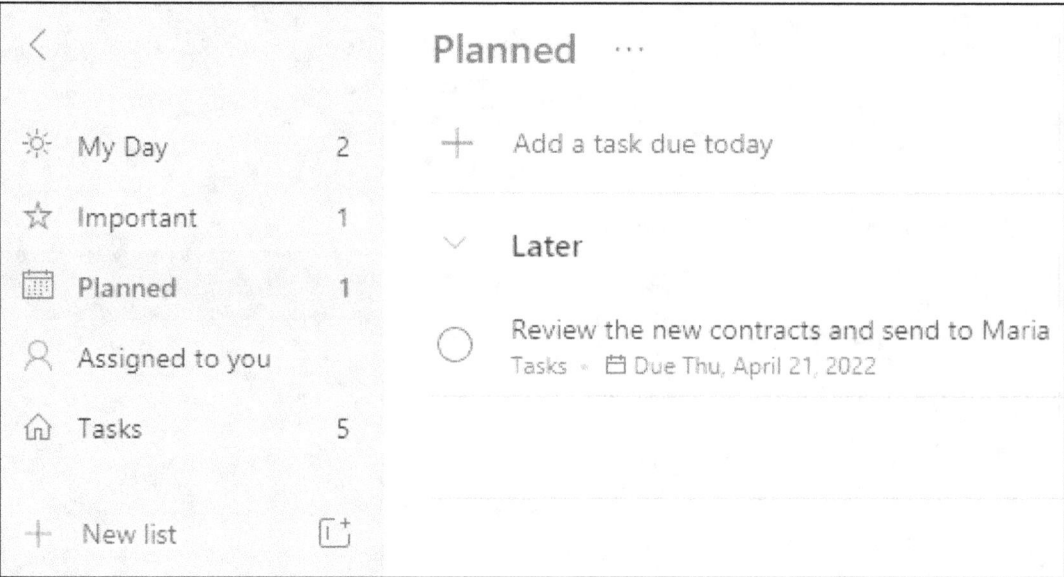

Figure 6.55

If I wish to add a new list for a different department or different type of tasks I can click on *New list* and then type in a name. For example I can create a list called **Marketing Tasks** and then I can use it the same way I did for my other tasks.

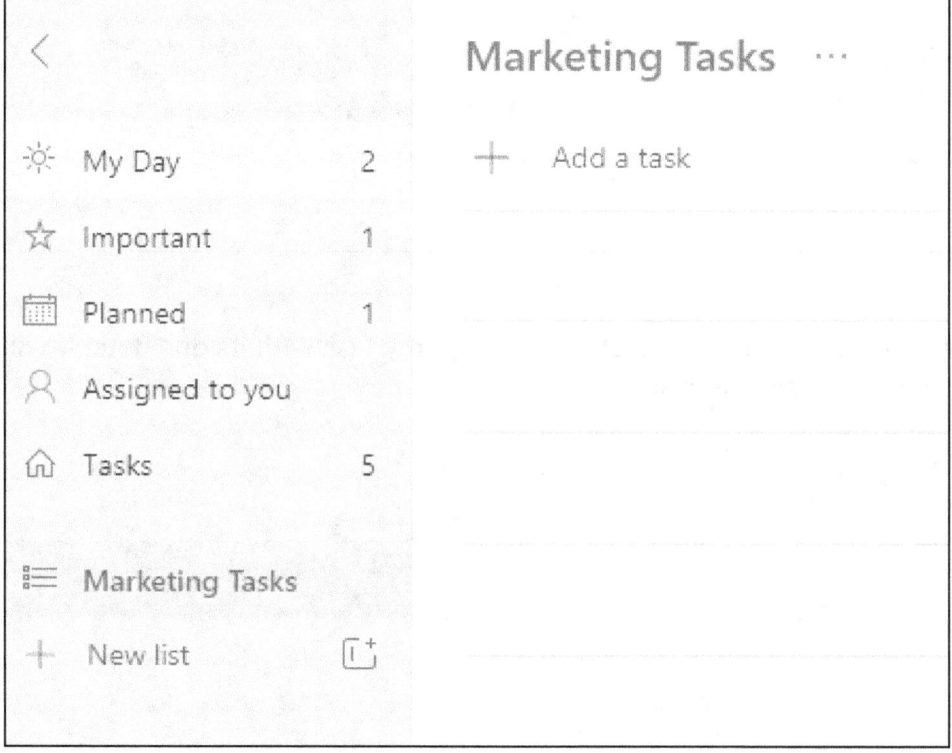

Figure 6.56

Chapter 6 – Outlook, Calendar and People

If I mark a task as important or assign a due date then it will be added to the same Important and Planned sections where my other tasks reside, but it will have the name of the list underneath it, so you know what list the task resides in.

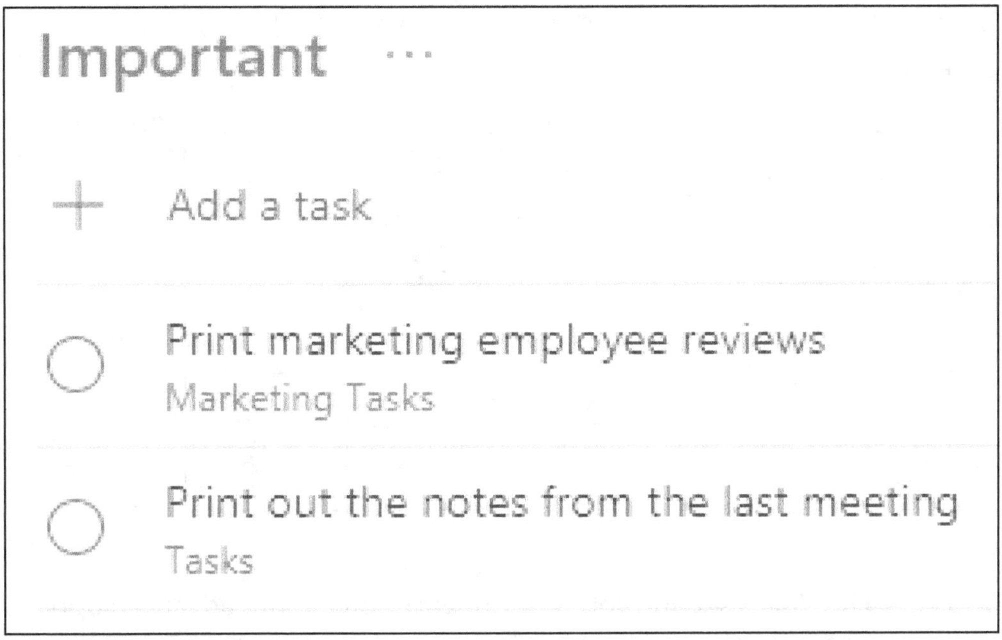

Figure 6.57

Email Rules
Email Rules are used to take specific action on emails when they arrive in your Inbox. For example, you might want any emails from a certain person to be moved to a different folder rather than your inbox. Or maybe you want certain emails to be forwarded to someone else as they arrive.

You can configure Outlook rules from the Outlook settings (discussed later in this chapter) or what I like to do is right click on the email I want to apply the rule to and then choose *Advanced options>Create rule*.

From there you can create a basic move rule where it will move all messages from a certain email address to a folder of your choosing. If you would like to configure a different type of rule then you can click on *More options*.

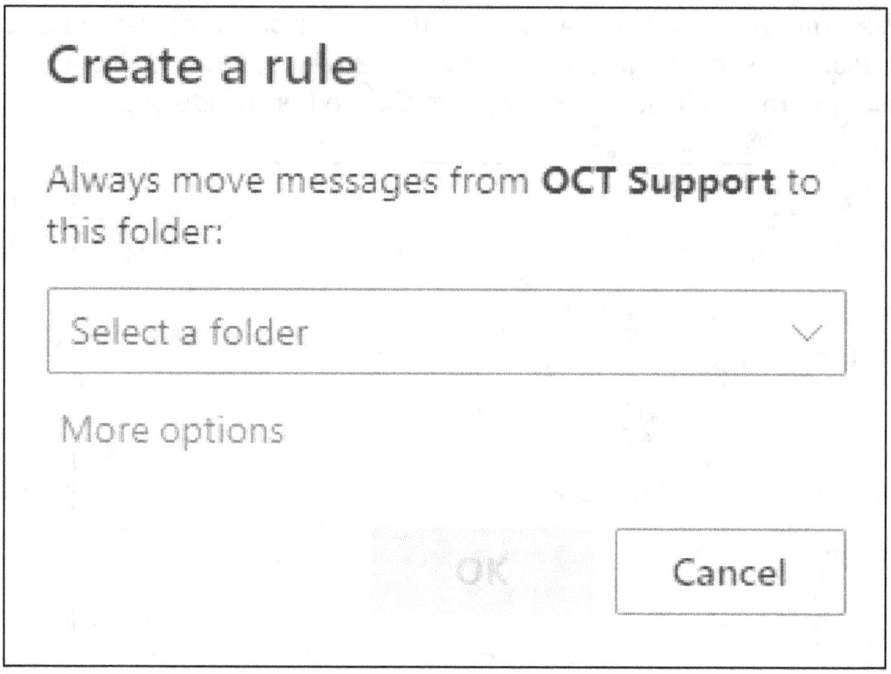

Chapter 6 – Outlook, Calendar and People

Create a rule

Always move messages from **OCT Support** to this folder:

[Select a folder ⌄]

More options

[OK]   [Cancel]

Figure 6.58

Once you get to the *Rules* section you can configure some more advanced options such as adding additional *conditions* such as applying the rule to emails with specific subjects or certain keywords.

Once you have your conditions in place then you can assign an action to be taken once those conditions are met. Figure 6.59 shows all of the actions that you can take on an email such as moving it, deleting it or forwarding it to someone else. When you have everything configured the way you like you can click the *Save* button to have that rule be active.

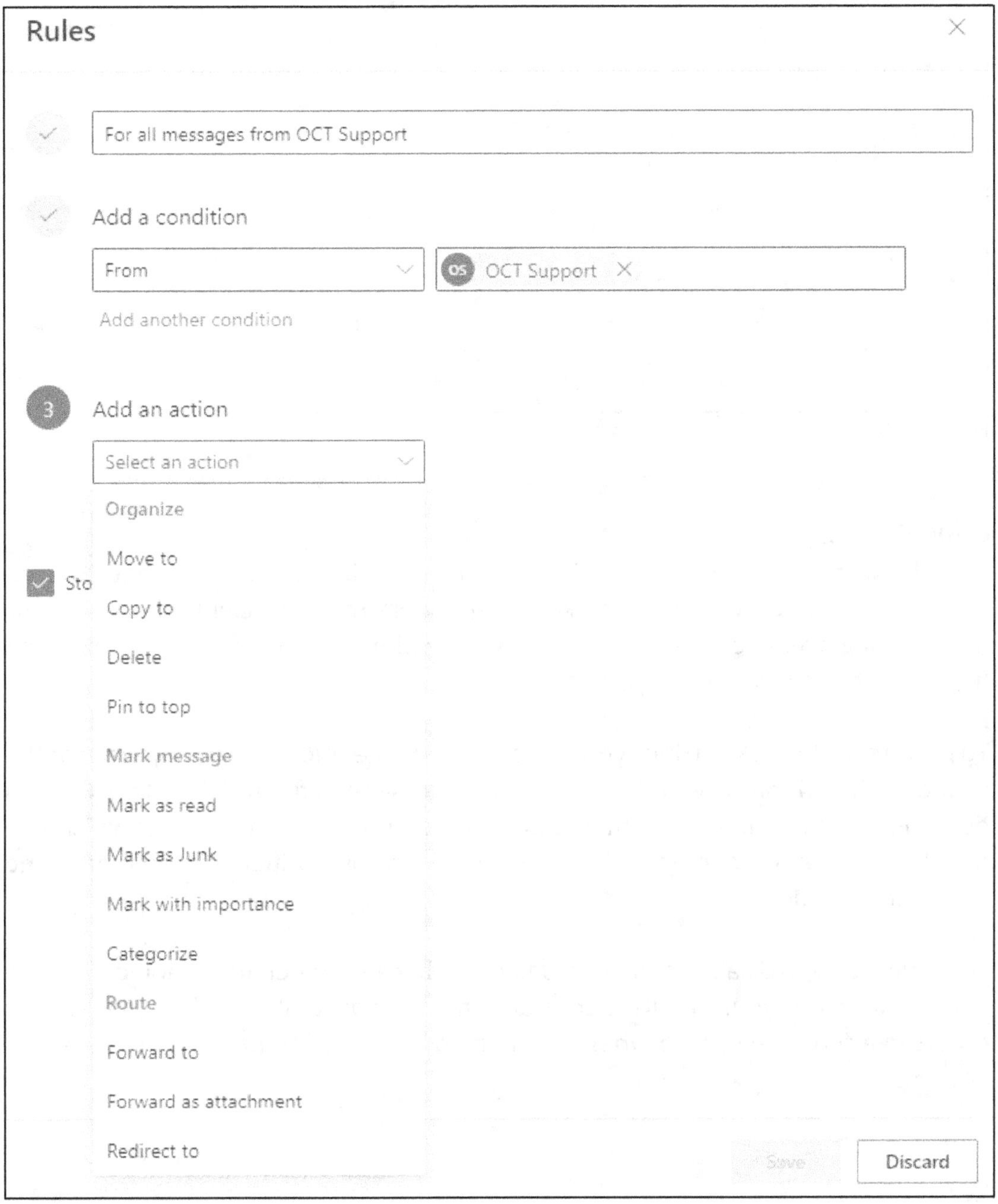

Chapter 6 – Outlook, Calendar and People

| Rules | ✕ |

✓ For all messages from OCT Support

✓ Add a condition

From ⌄   OS OCT Support ✕

Add another condition

③ Add an action

Select an action ⌄

Organize

Move to

☑ Sto

Copy to

Delete

Pin to top

Mark message

Mark as read

Mark as Junk

Mark with importance

Categorize

Route

Forward to

Forward as attachment

Redirect to

Save   Discard

Figure 6.59

Once you have your rule in place it will be listed in the Rules section and you can then go back and edit or disable the rule. If you have multiple rules you can change their order of processing by clicking the up or down arrows or run them manually by clicking on the play button.

Chapter 6 – Outlook, Calendar and People

Figure 6.60

Outlook Settings

Just like with most applications, Outlook has a variety of settings that you can configure to adjust so you can make the app work more efficiently for you. I will not be going over every single setting in this section but rather the ones I feel you might want to check out for yourself.

To get to the Outlook settings you can click on the gear icon at the top right of the window. This will show you the basic settings as seen in figure 6.60. Here you can do things such as change the theme and turn on desktop notifications which you might want to make sure is on if you would like to be notified of new emails and calendar reminders.

One thing I like to disable is the *Focused Inbox* because when it's enabled, Outlook decides which of your emails it considers more important and then places your others in a separate tab. So when it's enabled, you need to look in two places for your messages.

Chapter 6 – Outlook, Calendar and People

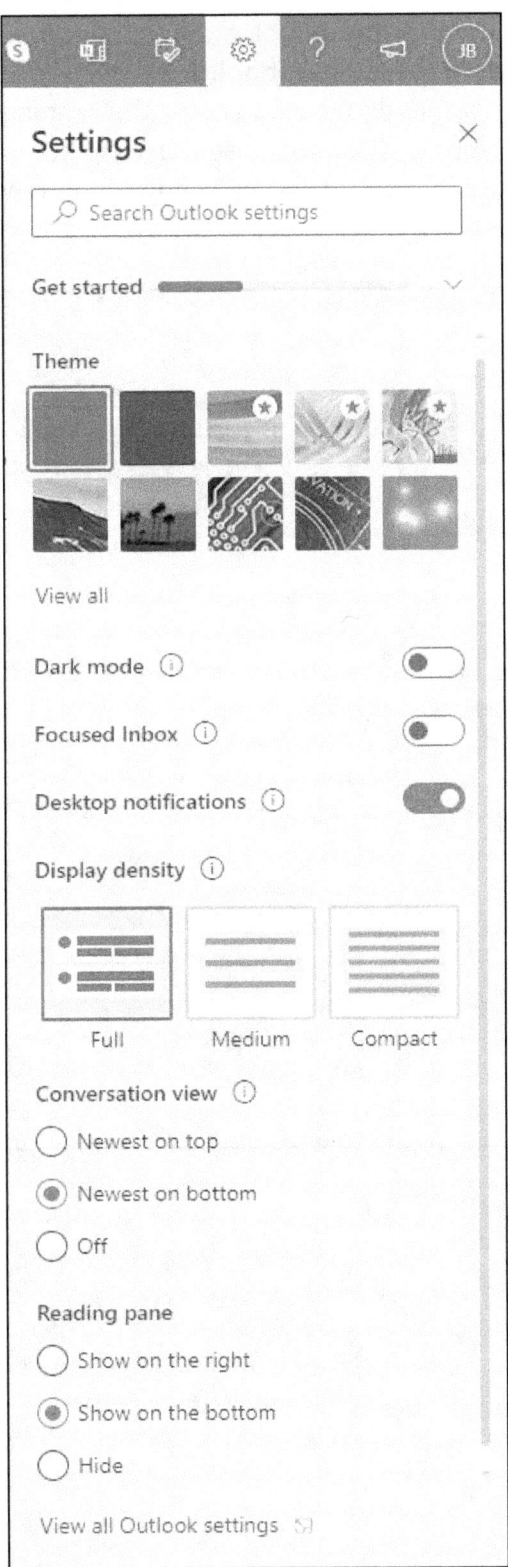

Figure 6.61

Chapter 6 – Outlook, Calendar and People

The Reading pane setting is something you might want to look at as well because that decides how you see your email previews in the main Outlook Window. Figure 6.62 shows the reading pane on the bottom while figure 6.63 shows the reading pane on the right. You can also have it off if you don't want to use this view but in order to read an email, you will need to double click it to have it open in a new window.

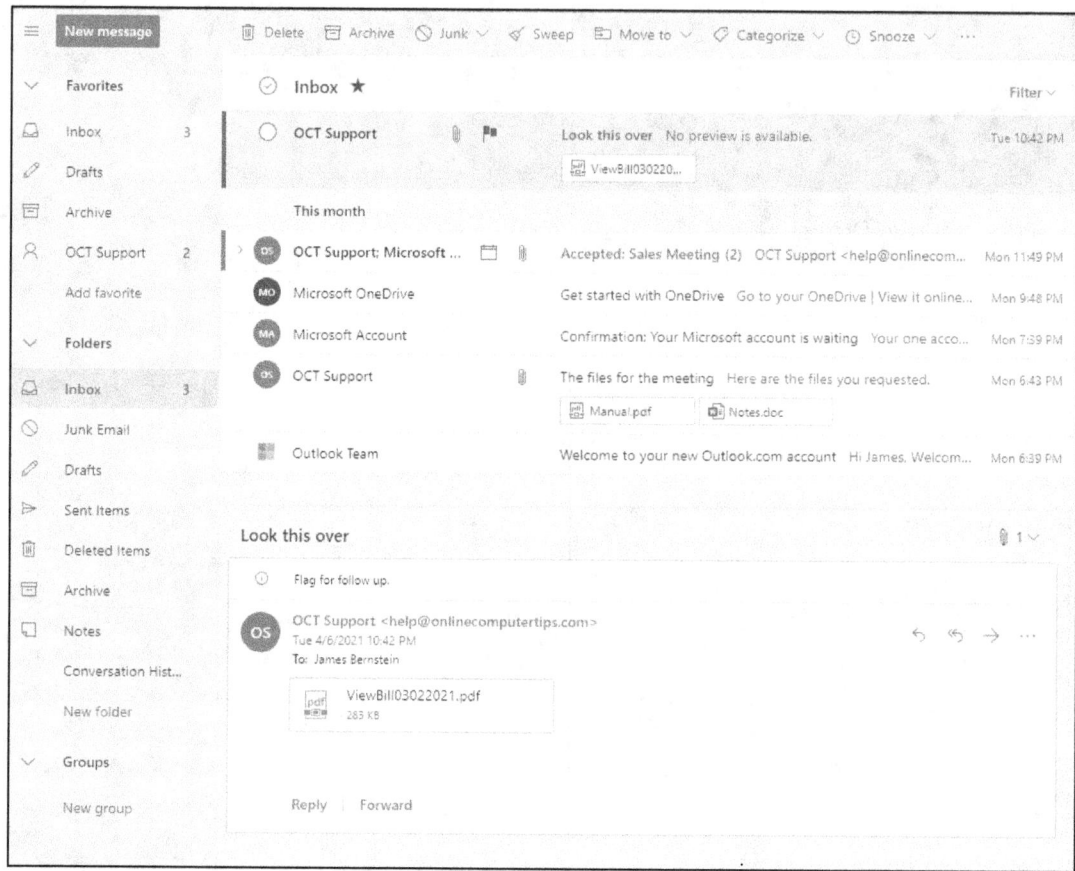

Figure 6.62

Chapter 6 – Outlook, Calendar and People

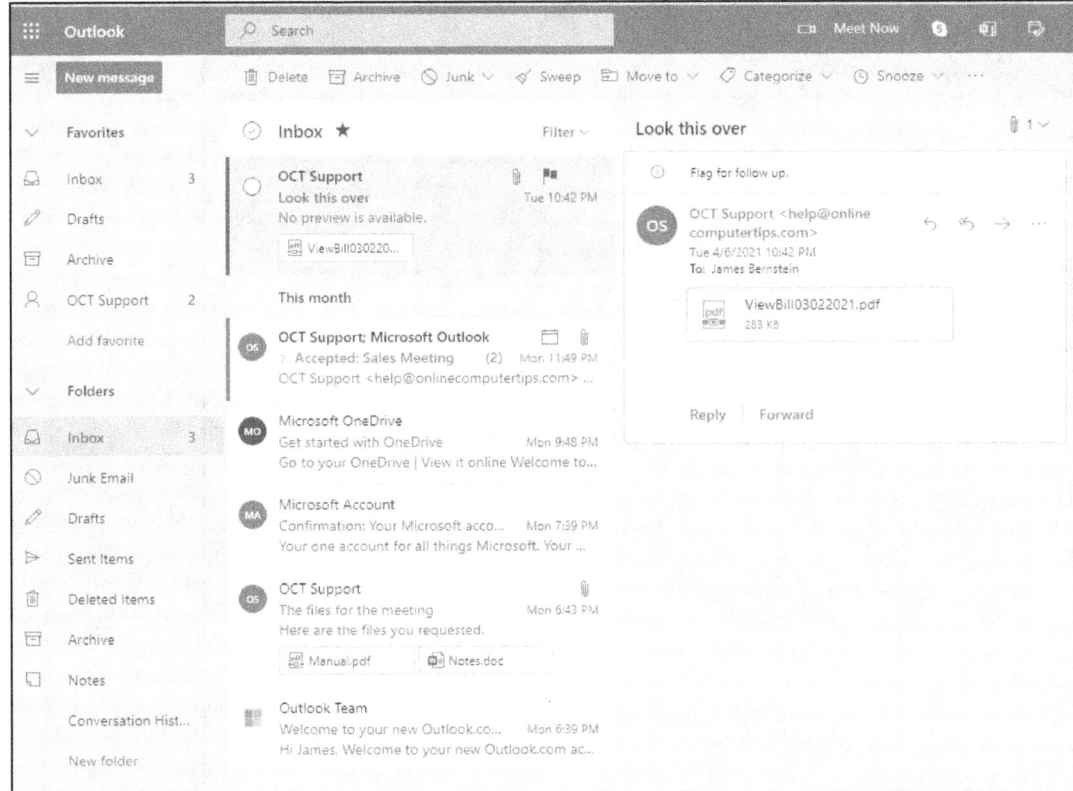

Figure 6.63

Clicking on *View all Outlook settings* will bring you to the main settings area where there are several categories of settings that you can configure.

General Settings
Here you can change things such as appearance settings, what items you receive notifications about, sync your account with your mobile device, and how much storage you are using with your account.

I would take a look at the *Notifications* section to make sure that you are being notified about things you care about and not being notified about things you don't want to be bothered with.

If you are concerned that you are getting close to using up your 15GB of allotted space that Microsoft provides you for free then you can see what exactly is using your space from the *Storage* section.

Chapter 6 – Outlook, Calendar and People

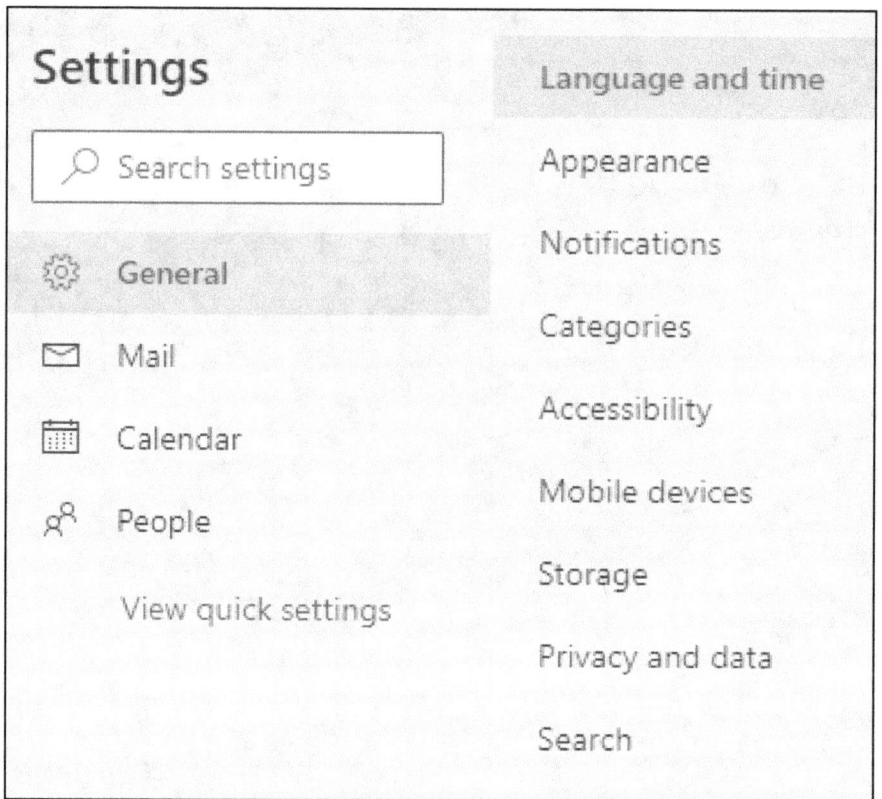

Figure 6.64

Mail Settings
This is where you will go to configure email specific settings such as how your email attachments are handled what Outlook does when you compose new emails.

If you need to set up an email signature then you can do so from the *Compose and reply* section. An email signature is text such as your company name and phone number that will automatically be added at the bottom of new emails that you compose so you don't need to type it each time. If you are looking for the BCC (blind carbon copy) box for new emails then you can enable that from here as well.

If you have marked a certain email address as junk but decide you don't want that to apply anymore then you can go to the *Junk email* section and remove it. Or you can manually add email addresses or domains to your junk list from here. A domain is the part of the address after the @ symbol such as **@microsoft.com**. If you were to add @microsoft.com to your junk list then any email coming from anyone at microsoft.com would go to your Junk folder.

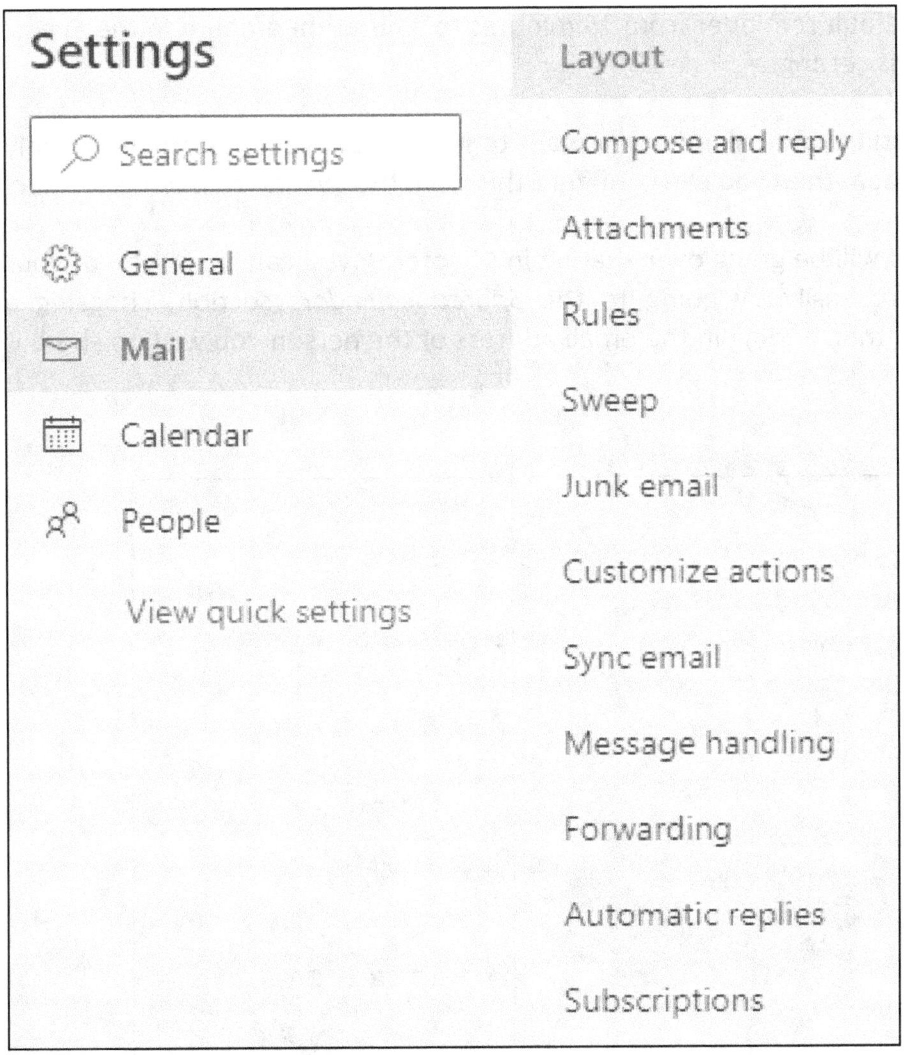

Chapter 6 – Outlook, Calendar and People

Settings	Layout
Search settings	Compose and reply
	Attachments
⚙ General	Rules
✉ Mail	Sweep
🗓 Calendar	Junk email
👥 People	Customize actions
View quick settings	Sync email
	Message handling
	Forwarding
	Automatic replies
	Subscriptions

Figure 6.65

 Many people have had issues with some of the settings here not working and have been able to resolve it by adding a phone number as a verification method. So if you are having issues and don't mind Microsoft having your phone number you can try that as well.

Calendar Settings
Here you can change calendar settings such as what day you wish to be listed as the first day of the week or what days are counted as workdays. You can also

Chapter 6 – Outlook, Calendar and People

change the default reminder from 15 minutes to a different amount in the *Events and invitations* setting.

If you are sharing your calendar and want to mark your events as private so only you can see them then you can configure this from the *Events from email* section.

Even though I will be going over sharing in Chapter 9, you can share one of your calendars very easily by going to the *Shared calendars* section, choosing a calendar, and then adding in the email address of the person you wish to share it with.

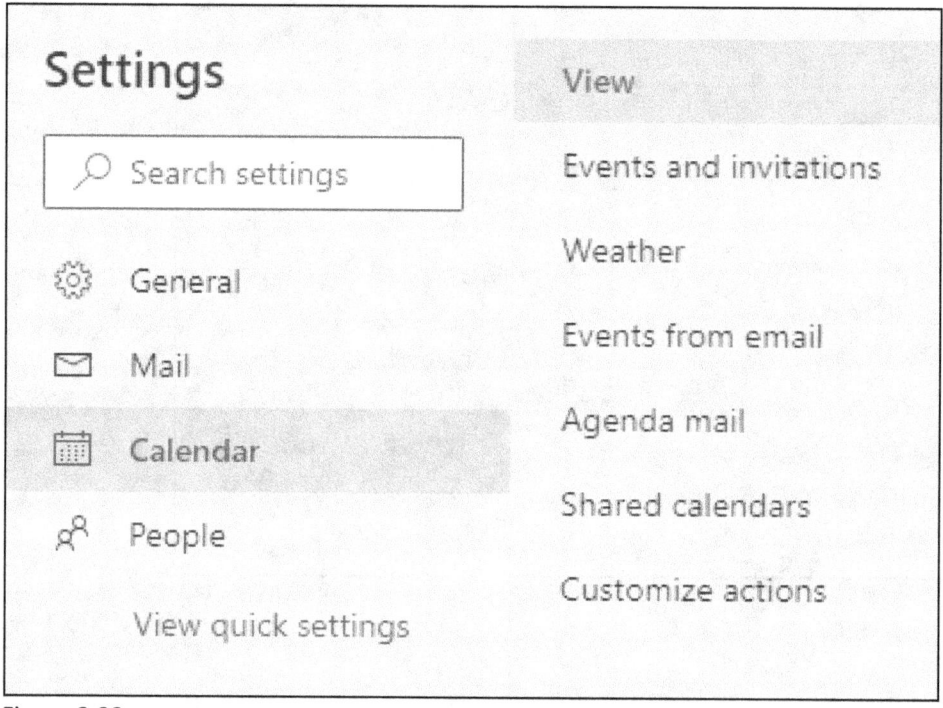
Figure 6.66

People Settings
The only thing you can change here is whether your contacts are displayed by first or last name.

Chapter 7 – OneNote

If you are not an Office power user then you might not know about OneNote or maybe you haven't even heard of it to begin with. OneNote is one of those apps that might not sound like something you would need to use until you actually use it and then you wonder how you ever managed without it.

You can think of OneNote as a virtual notebook or binder where you can have tabbed sections to store various types of information while keeping things organized at the same time. You can even include things such as pictures, audio files and website links which you would not be able to do with a paper notebook.

It's also possible to share your notebook with other users so they can access your information to help them get their work done. Plus they can then contribute to your notebook as well. Hopefully after reading this chapter you will be an official OneNote user yourself!

The OneNote Interface
If you are new to OneNote then you might be a little confused when you first open the app until you get an idea of how it works. The first time you open OneNote you most likely will be prompted to pick a notebook based on what you plan on using the app for. Your choices will be work, personal or school.

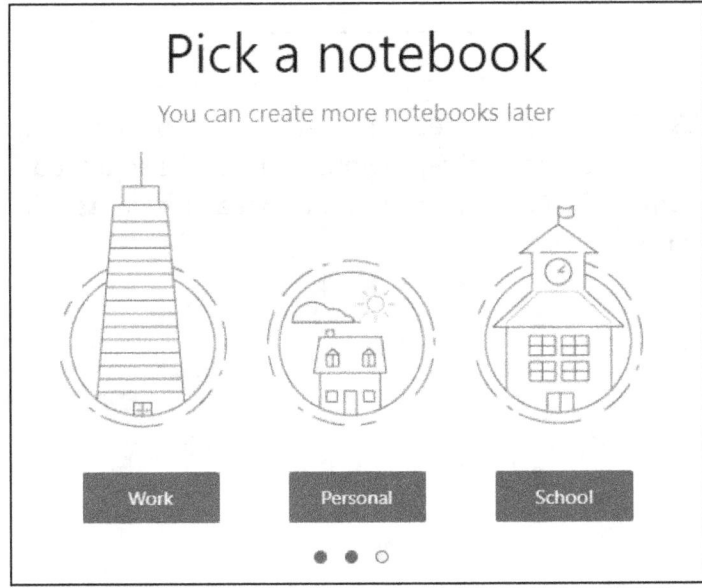

Figure 7.1

Chapter 7 – OneNote

For my example I will choose the Work option. Then OneNote gives me some suggested categories for my notebook plus the option to add my own. I will check the boxes for Meeting notes, To-do lists, Expenses and Training. Then I will add a custom category named Tasks. Once I have my selections I will click on the *Create notebook* button.

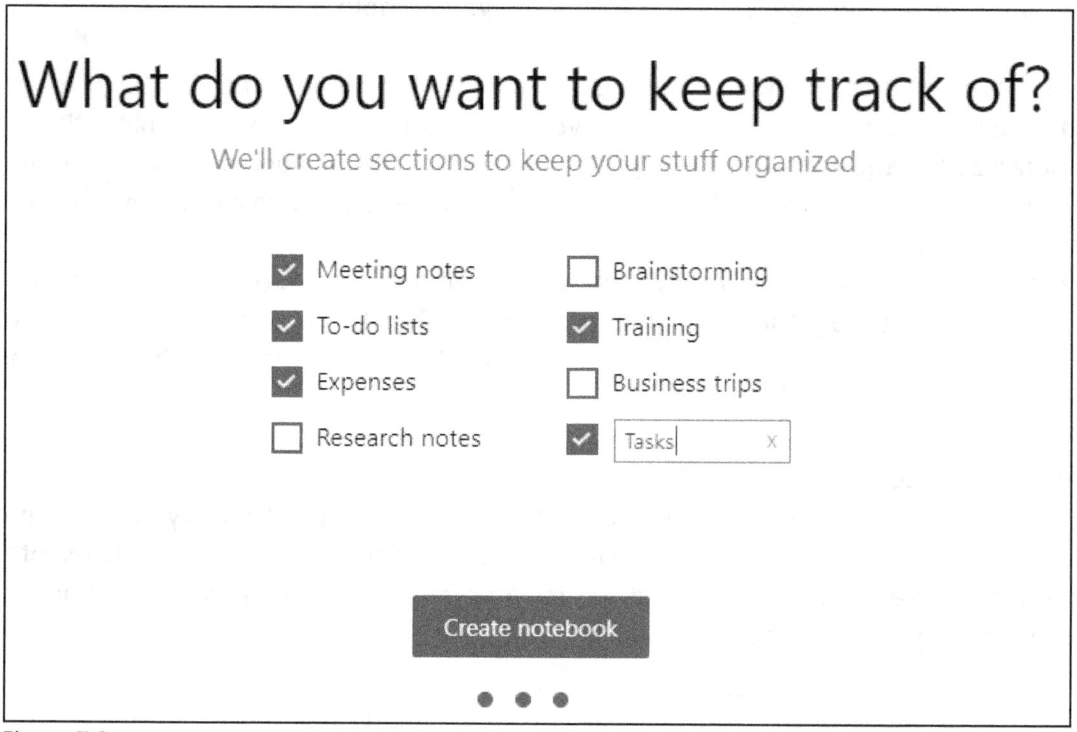

Figure 7.2

As you can see in figure 7.3, OneNote created my new notebook with the categories (referred to as sections) I chose in the previous steps and also added a *Quick Notes* section which is something you can use to jot down a quick note kind of like you would with a sticky note.

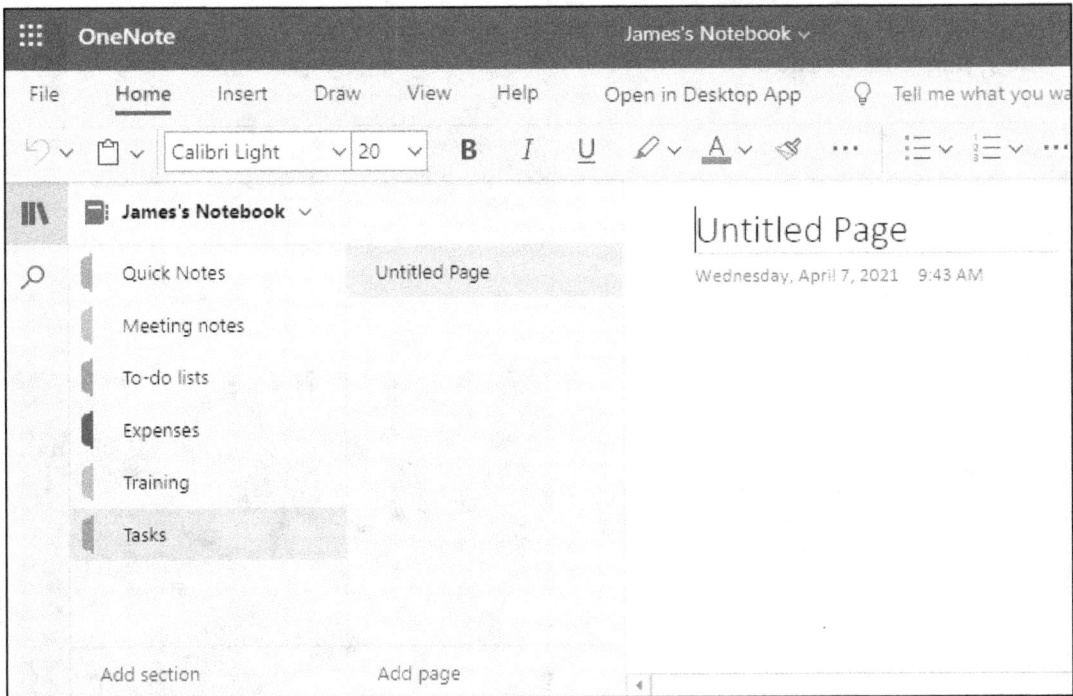

Figure 7.3

Within each section you will have pages so you can think of the sections as folders in a filing cabinet (OneNote) and then the pages are the papers inside of the folders.

I can change the default Untitled Page to say something like **New Computer Order** and it will update the page name for me. Then I can add details to this page regarding my new computers.

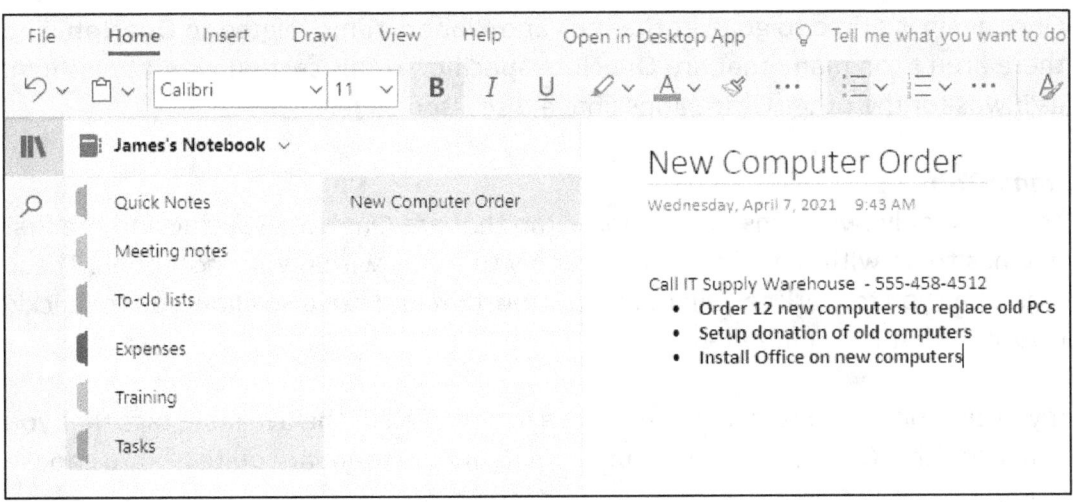

Figure 7.4

Chapter 7 – OneNote

Then I can add a new page for a different task within my Tasks section and keep adding pages as needed.

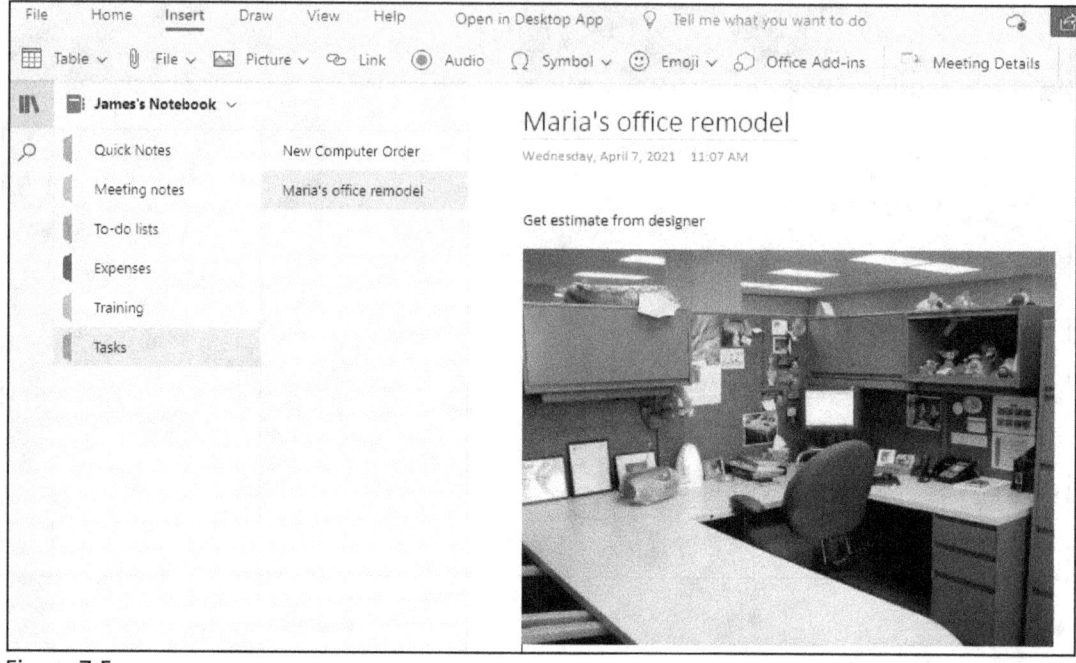

Figure 7.5

As you can see, there isn't much to the OneNote interface or even the app itself so if it's something you are interested in using, it shouldn't take you long to become an expert!

Tabs and Ribbon Items
Once again it's time to go over the tabs and Ribbon items related to OneNote and there aren't too many that are OneNote specific, so this section won't be as long as it was for the other Office apps I have discussed so far.

Home Tab
There are only two items on the Home tab that are OneNote specific and the first one has to do with tags that you can apply to items within your notebook. These tags allow you to mark certain items as important and can also allow you to quickly return to that item if needed.

If you click on the Tags icon you will get a listing of all of the available tags that you can use within OneNote. As you can see in figure 7.6 there are quite a bit to choose from.

Chapter 7 – OneNote

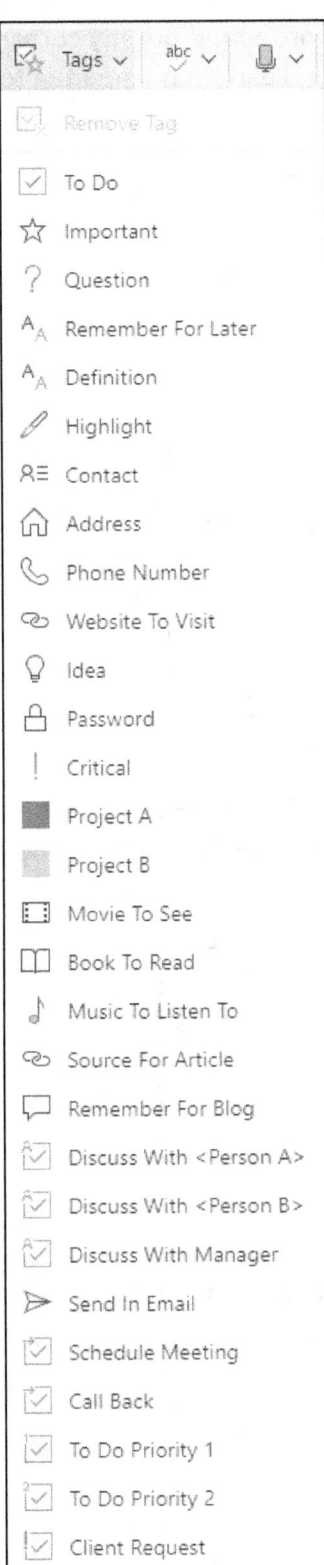

Figure 7.6

Chapter 7 – OneNote

If I were to go back to my page about the new computer order and put my cursor next to the line that says *Setup donation of old computers*, I can then add a tag to that line.

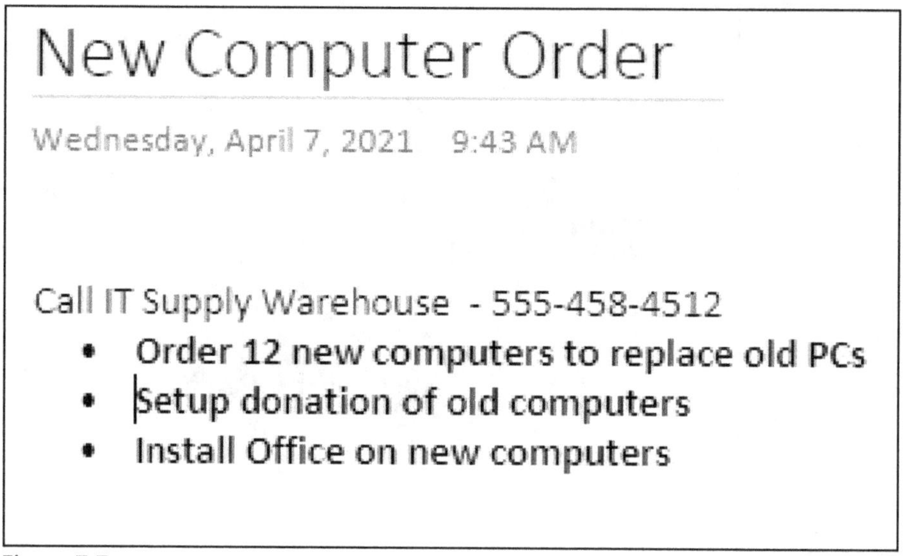

New Computer Order

Wednesday, April 7, 2021   9:43 AM

Call IT Supply Warehouse - 555-458-4512
- Order 12 new computers to replace old PCs
- Setup donation of old computers
- Install Office on new computers

Figure 7.7

I will now go to the Tags menu and select the tag that says *Discuss With Manager*. As you can see, OneNote places the same icon next to this line that corresponds with the Discuss With Manager tag.

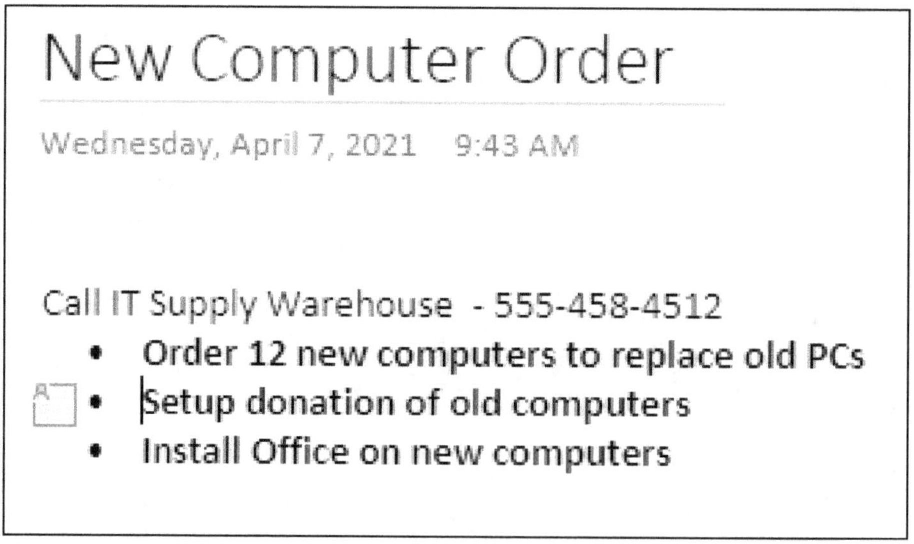

New Computer Order

Wednesday, April 7, 2021   9:43 AM

Call IT Supply Warehouse - 555-458-4512
- Order 12 new computers to replace old PCs
- Setup donation of old computers
- Install Office on new computers

Figure 7.8

Chapter 7 – OneNote

This particular tag allows you to put a checkmark in the box if you would like to mark it as complete.

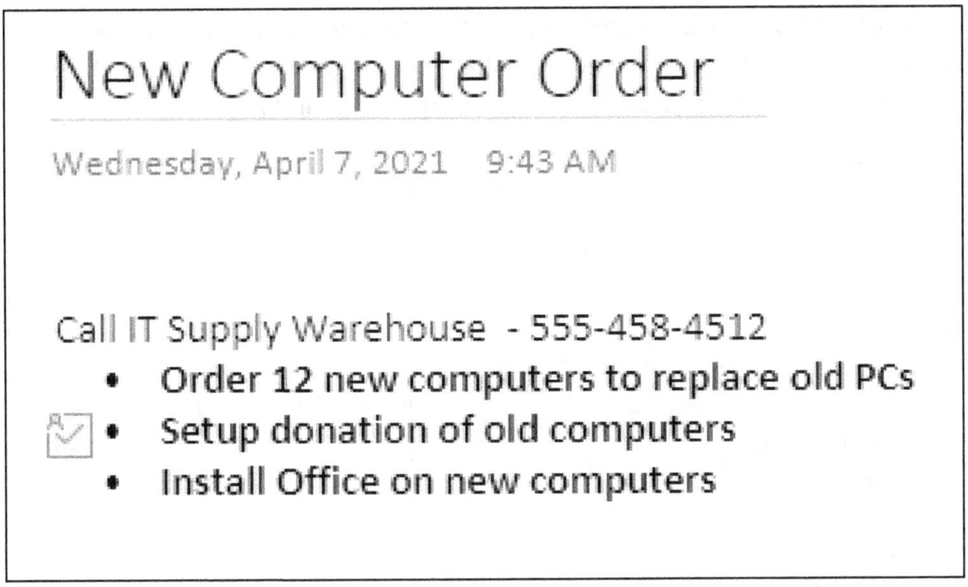

New Computer Order
Wednesday, April 7, 2021   9:43 AM

Call IT Supply Warehouse - 555-458-4512
- Order 12 new computers to replace old PCs
- 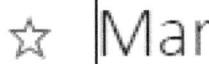 Setup donation of old computers
- Install Office on new computers

Figure 7.9

If I wanted to mark Maria's office remodel as important, I could place a star next to it.

☆ **Maria's office remodel**
Wednesday, April 7, 2021   11:07 AM

Get estimate from designer

Figure 7.10

As of this writing, tags in OneNote for the Web are pretty basic and you can't do much with them except place them throughout your pages. In the desktop version of OneNote, you can customize your tags, search for them and even create a summary page of all your tags. But if you open your OneNote for the Web notebook in the desktop version, you should be able to search for your tags.

261

Chapter 7 – OneNote

Next we have the *Feed* section which will take notes you created in other apps such as Microsoft Sticky Notes and Samsung Notes and sync them to your OneNote feed. If you don't use any of these other apps then you will not have any use for this. Even if you do use these other apps this might not be too useful. When you open your feed for the first time you will be asked to sign in. You will use the same Microsoft account that you have been using to sign in with.

Figure 7.11

I created a note using Microsoft Sticky Notes and now that note shows up in my feed within OneNote. As you can see, it's not a super useful feature but if you are a serious Sticky Notes user then you might find it helpful.

Chapter 7 – OneNote

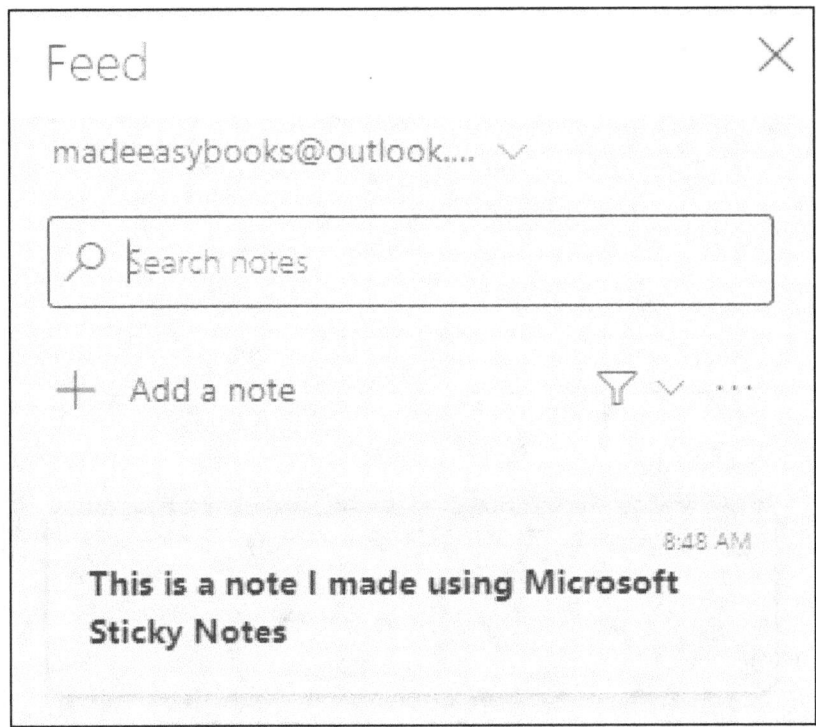

Figure 7.12

Insert Tab

The only OneNote specific item on the Insert tab is the Add Meeting Details section which is used to add meeting information from your Outlook calendar to your OneNote notebook.

Figure 7.13 shows a Sales meeting that I set up in my Outlook calendar.

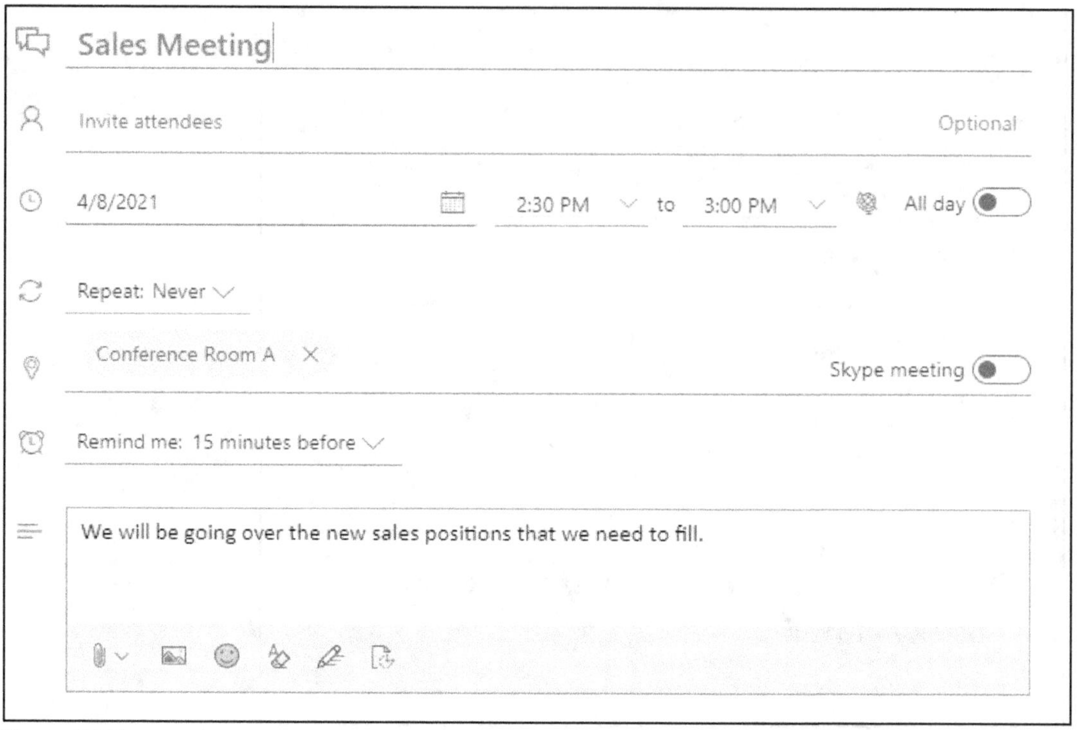

Chapter 7 – OneNote

Figure 7.13

Now I will go to *Add Meeting Details* and the first time I click on it I will be prompted to sign in with my Microsoft account once again.

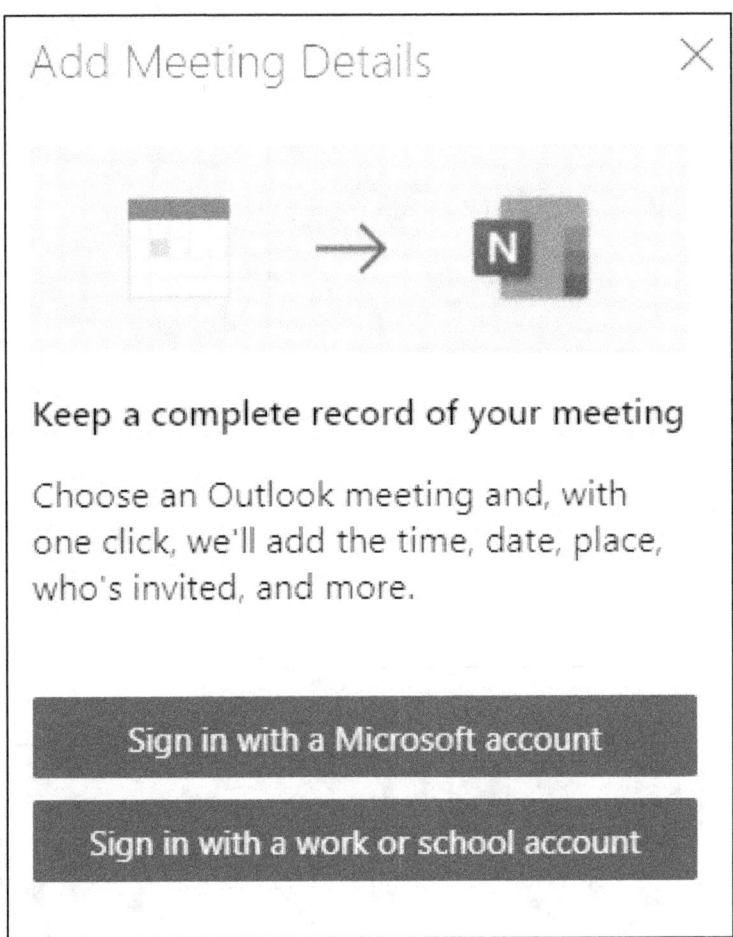

Figure 7.14

Then I will be shown any meetings that I have scheduled for today (figure 7.15) and If I click on a particular meeting, it will be inserted into my notebook on whatever page I happen to be on (figure 7.16).

Chapter 7 – OneNote

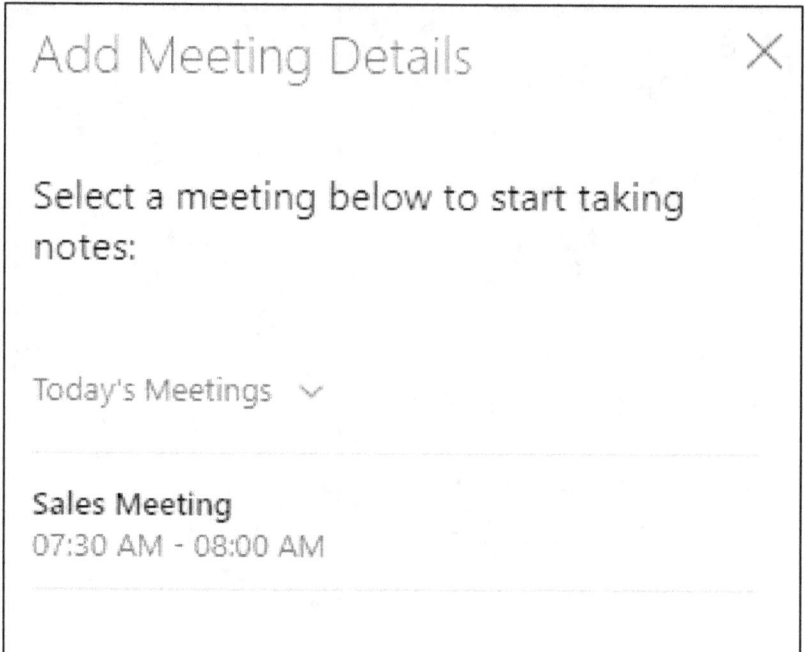

Figure 7.15

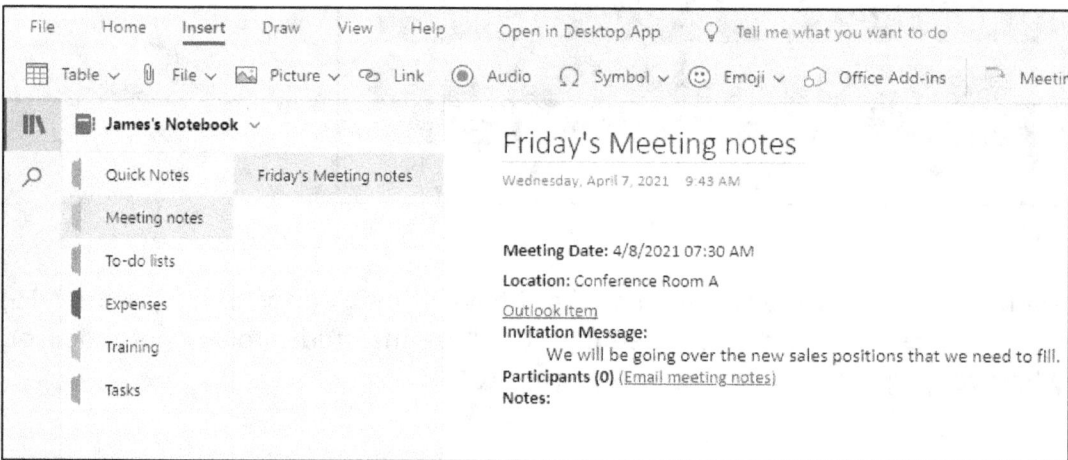

Figure 7.16

When it inserts the meeting details into my OneNote page it will have a link (Outlook Item) that will take me directly to my Outlook calendar for this particular day. There will also be a link (Email meeting notes) that will open up a new email with links to my OneNote notebook and OneDrive location so that others can see the related material. Keep in mind that only those who have shared access to these items will be able to see them.

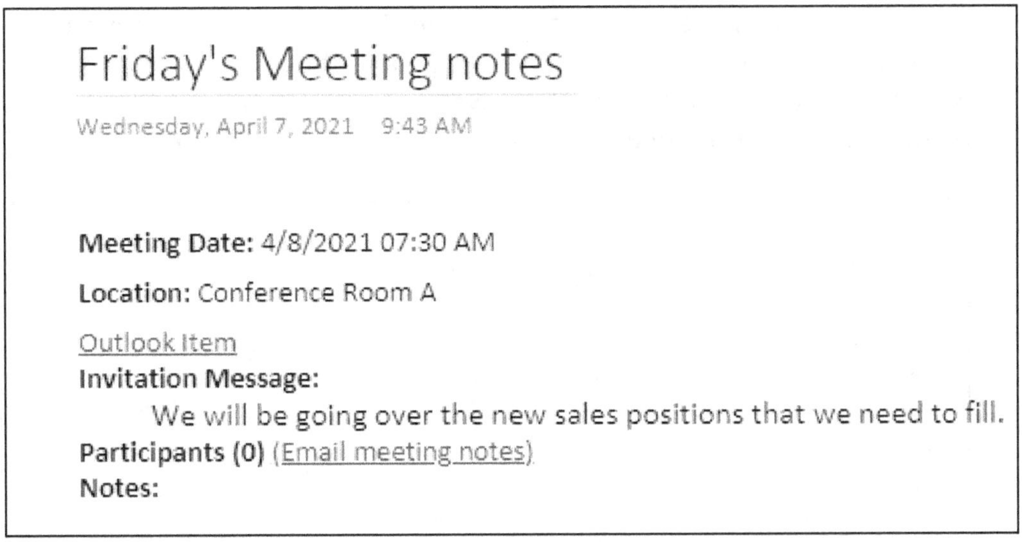

Chapter 7 – OneNote

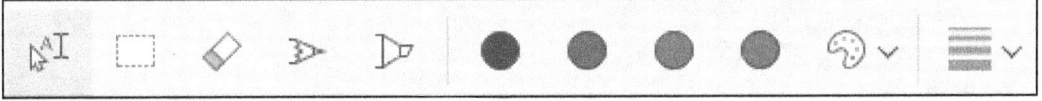

Figure 7.17

Draw Tab
The Draw tab has the same markup tools that we have already seen such as a pencil, highlighter, eraser and custom color options.

Figure 7.18

View Tab
Here we will find a few OneNote specific items that you should know about.

Page Color, Page Versions, Show Authors and Deleted Notes

Figure 7.19

- **Page Color** – The default background page color is white for your notebooks, but you can change it to another color if you like.

- **Page Versions** – OneNote will keep track of changes you make to your pages and you can use the Page Version selection to view and restore older versions of your pages as needed. Figure 7.19 shows that I have three versions of my New Computer Order page and if I click on one of them I will get a yellow bar at the top that says the version number and that I can restore or delete this version or copy the content to the main page.

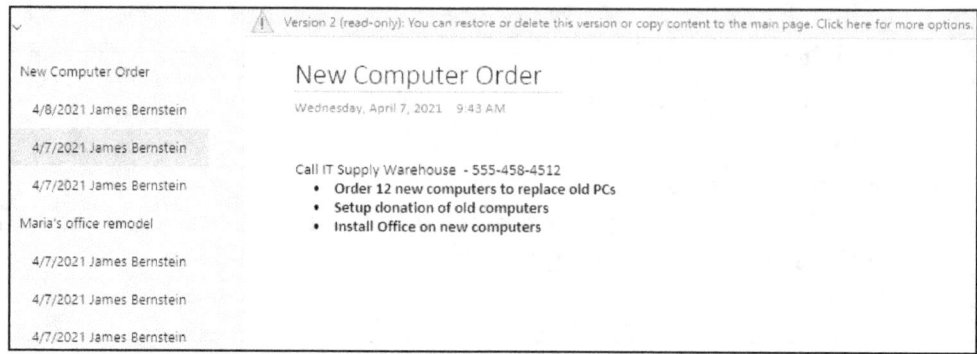

Figure 7.20

If I click on the yellow bar I will be given the option to hide my older versions, restore this version or delete this version.

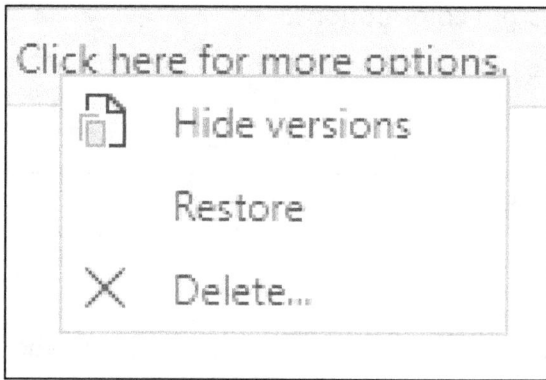

Figure 7.21

- **Show Authors** – If you have multiple people working on your notebook then you can use this feature to see who added what notes.

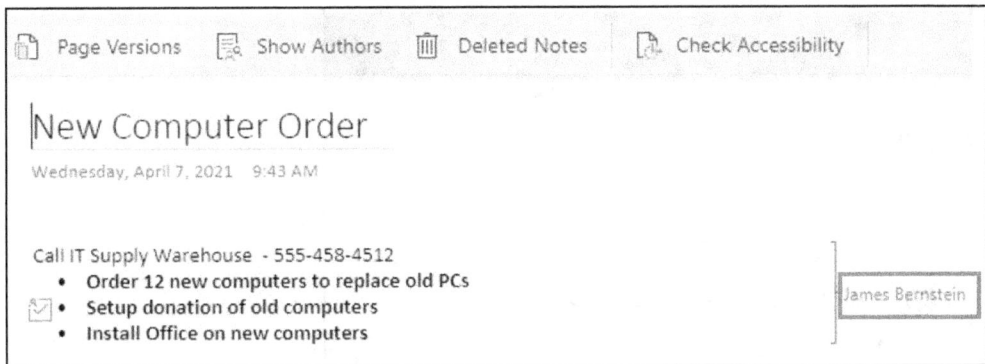
Figure 7.22

- **Deleted Notes** – If you deleted a note or a page you can go to the Deleted Notes section to see your deleted items. You can then right click on an item and choose *Restore* and then choose which section you want to restore the item to. It doesn't have to be restored back to its original location if you would like to have it somewhere else.

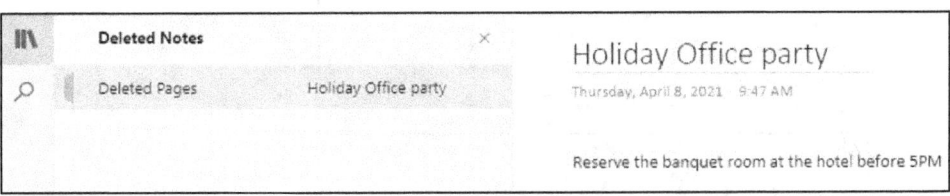
Figure 7.23

Adding Sections and Pages
Like you saw at the beginning of this chapter, OneNote will give you an option to automatically add some preconfigured sections based on what type of notebook you wish to create. But as you start becoming a OneNote power user you will most likely want to add additional sections with their own associated pages.

Fortunately, this is a very easy process, and you can quickly add new sections and pages as needed. To add a new section, all you need to do is right click on an existing section and choose *New Section* and give it a name.

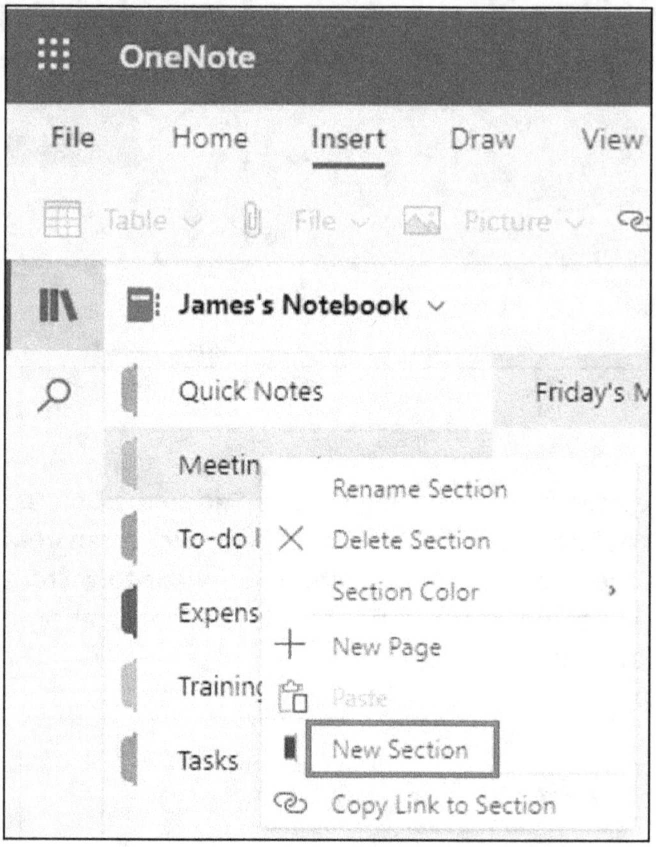

Figure 7.24

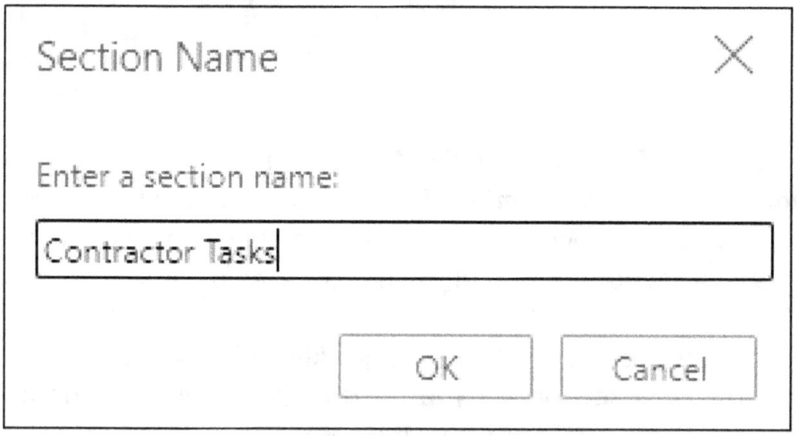

Figure 7.25

Then your new section will be created with a default page named *Untitled Page*. If you would like to change the order of any of your sections, all you need to do is click on one and drag it to its new location.

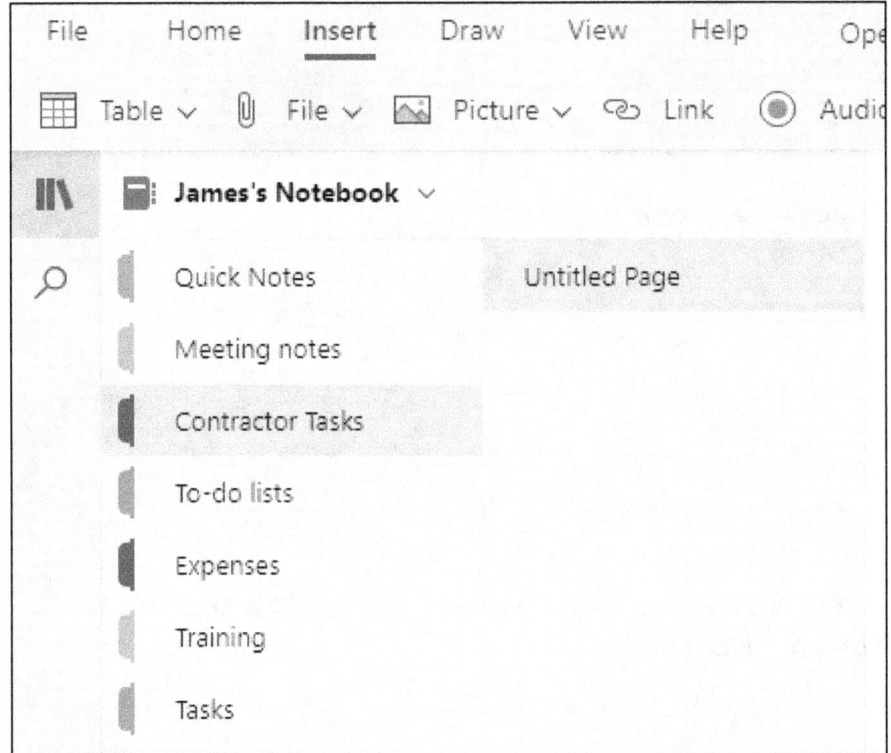

Figure 7.26

 You might have noticed the choice named *Copy Link to Section* in figure 7.24. This will allow you to copy a link to that particular section that you can then paste into something like an email to send off to another person. Then when they click on the link they will be taken to that section in your notebook assuming they have permission to view it.

If you need to add additional pages to your sections then all you need to do is right click in the page list area for that section and choose *New Page*.

Chapter 7 – OneNote

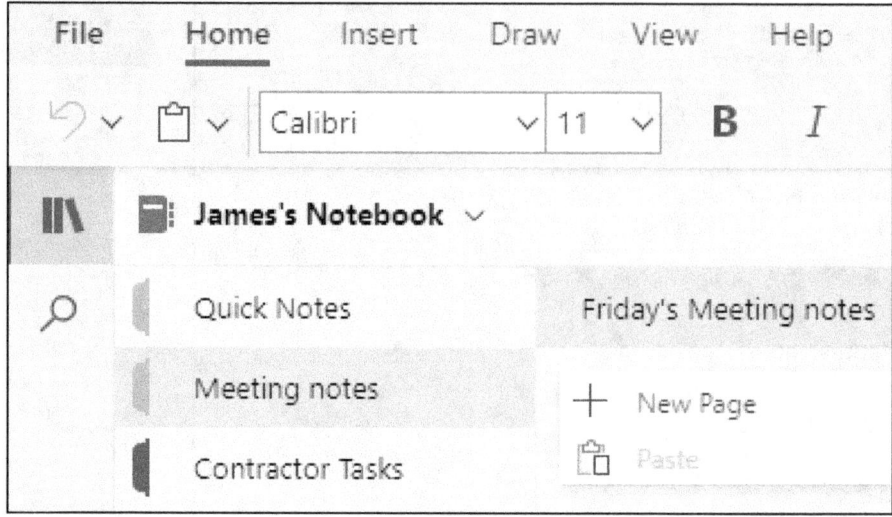

Figure 7.27

Then you can type in a name for your new page, and it will be listed with your other pages for that particular section.

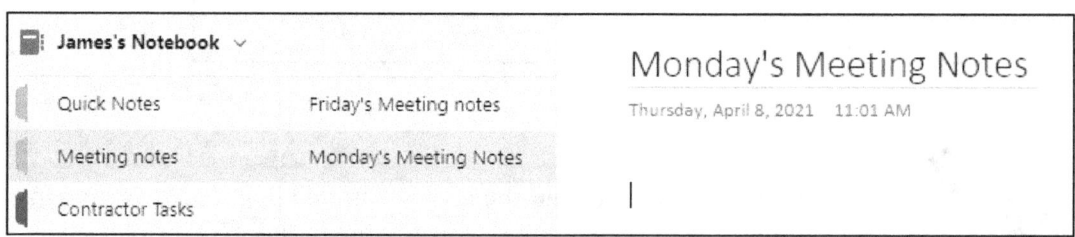

Figure 7.28

Adding Content to Your Pages
A OneNote notebook without any content is not very useful so once you have some sections and pages in place you will need to add some useful information to these pages to create a useful notebook.

Adding content to OneNote is a little different than adding content to Word for example because you can simply click anywhere you like and start typing and there is no real page structure like these is with Word.

If I were to go back to my New Computer Order page and hover my mouse over the text within it you would see that it shows a box around the text.

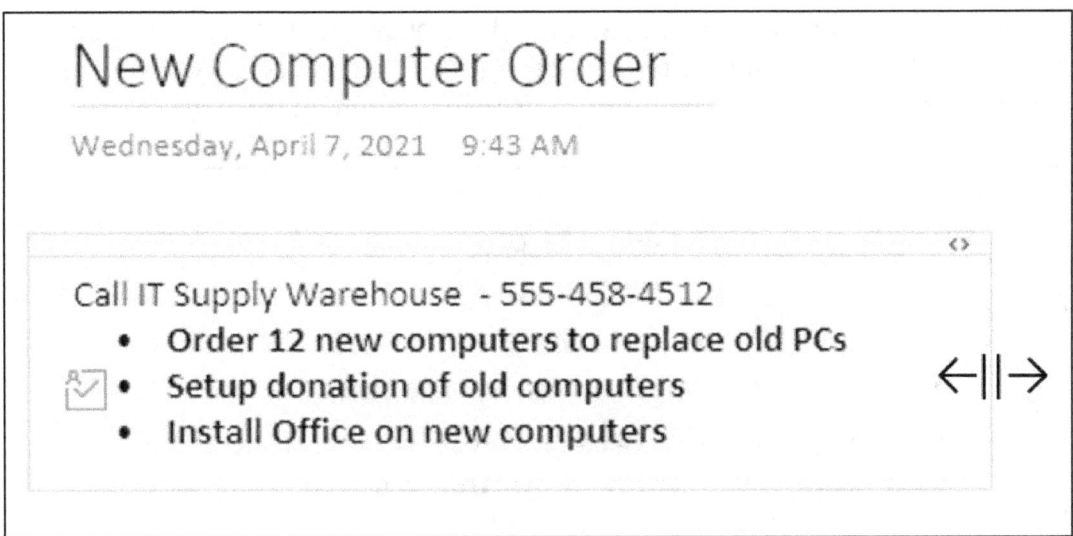

Figure 7.29

If I hold my mouse at the edge of the box it makes a double sided arrow cursor that I can then use to shrink or enlarge the size of this box. This comes in handy if you have text that is being placed on the next line down and you want the text to be on the same line. An example of this can be seen in figure 7.30.

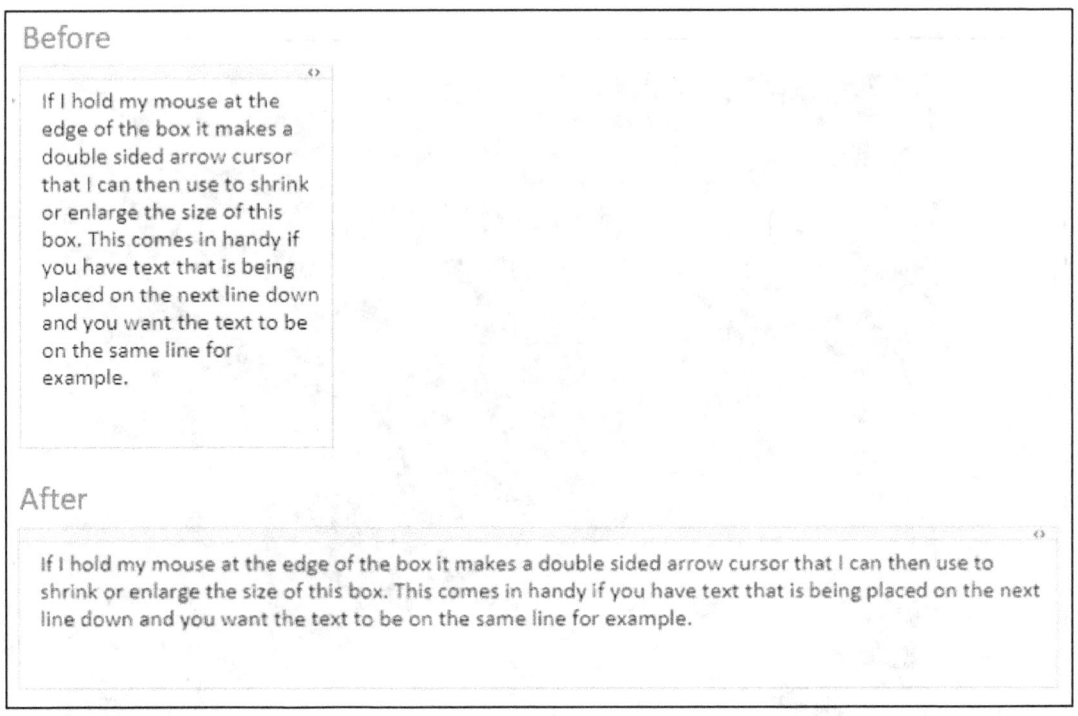

Figure 7.30

Chapter 7 – OneNote

To move an object on a page you can hold the mouse over the grey bar at the top of the box that is surrounding the object to get a 4 sided cursor and then you can simply drag that box and its contents to its new location on the page.

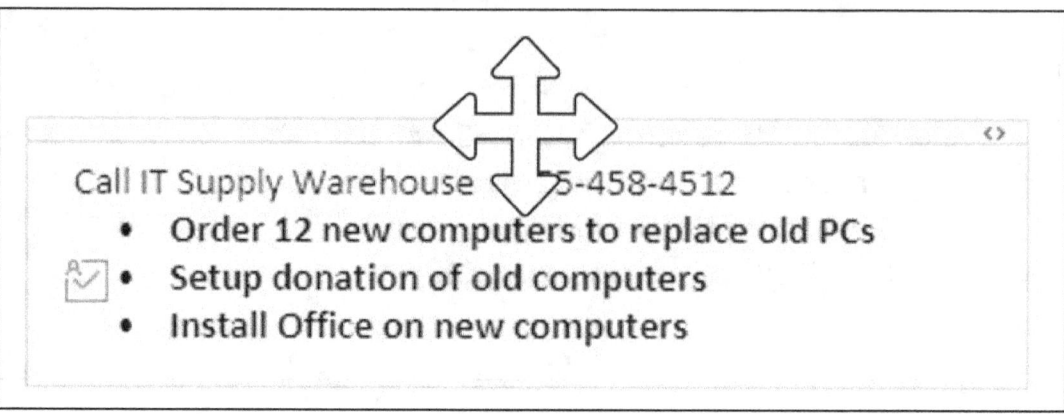

Figure 7.31

You will find that some objects like pictures will not have this box around them when you hover your mouse over them but instead they will have a marker to the left of them as seen in figure 7.32. You can click on this marker to drag your objects around the page in this scenario.

Figure 7.32

Chapter 7 – OneNote

Just like with most other Office apps or any apps for that matter, right clicking on objects will give you additional options such as copying, moving or resizing that object. If the object contains text then you will have text formatting options as well.

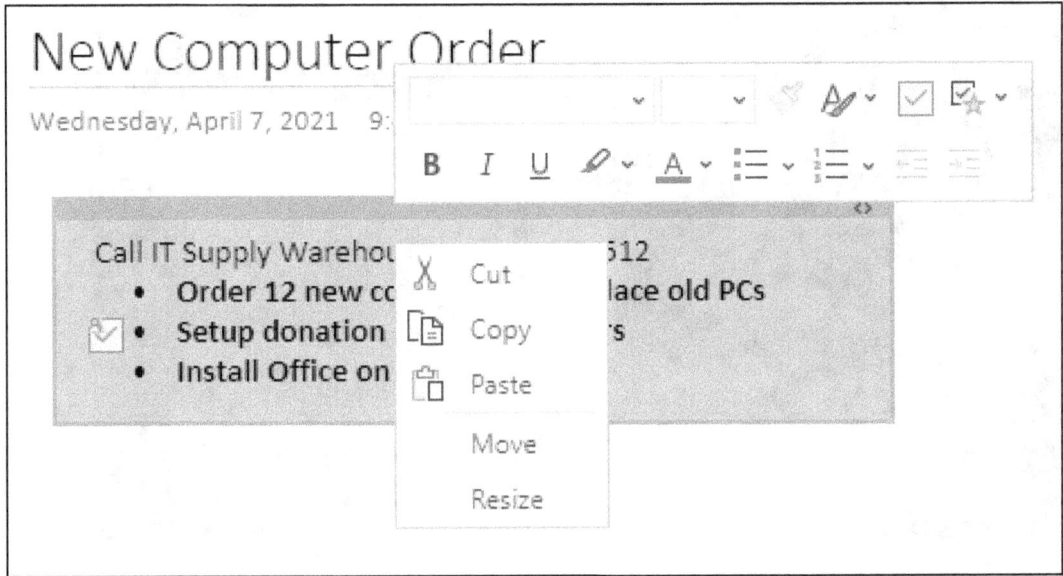

Figure 7.33

Right clicking on a picture will give you a different set of options.

Chapter 7 – OneNote

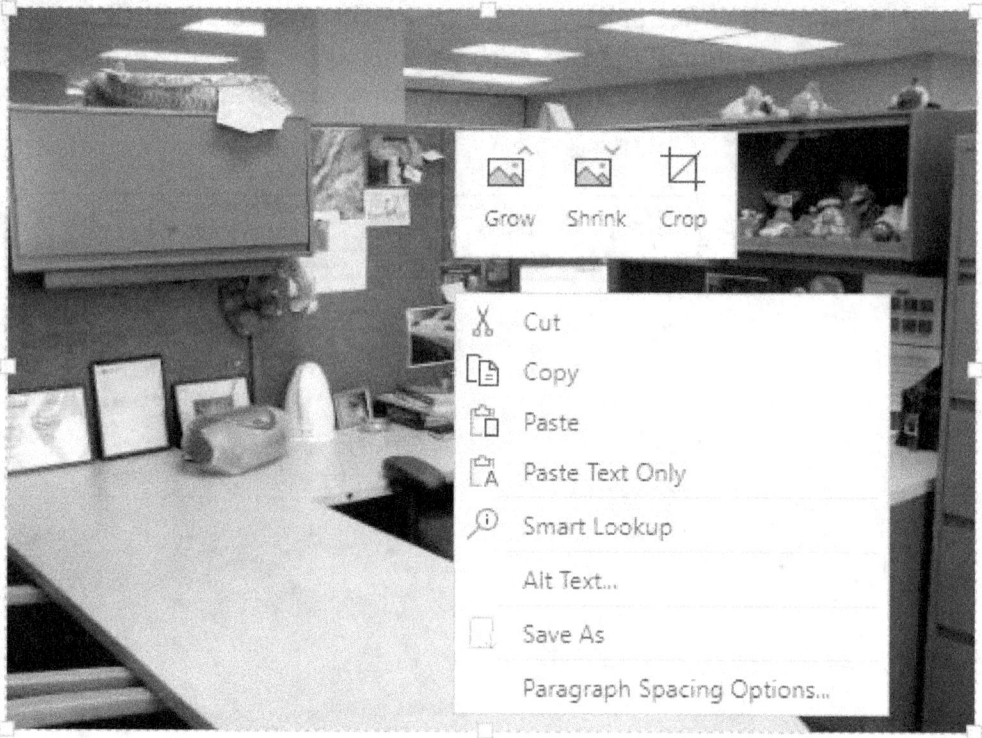
Figure 7.34

Selecting a picture will also make the *Picture* tab active with additional picture formatting tools.

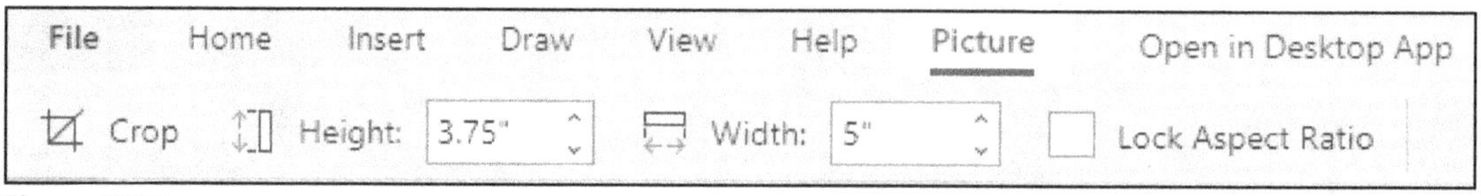

Figure 7.35

Adding Additional Notebooks
If you have some other information that is not related to your current notebook then you can add a new notebook to the OneNote app that you can easily switch over to when needed.

If you click on the dropdown arrow next to your notebook name you will have an option called *Add notebook* and also an option called *More notebooks*.

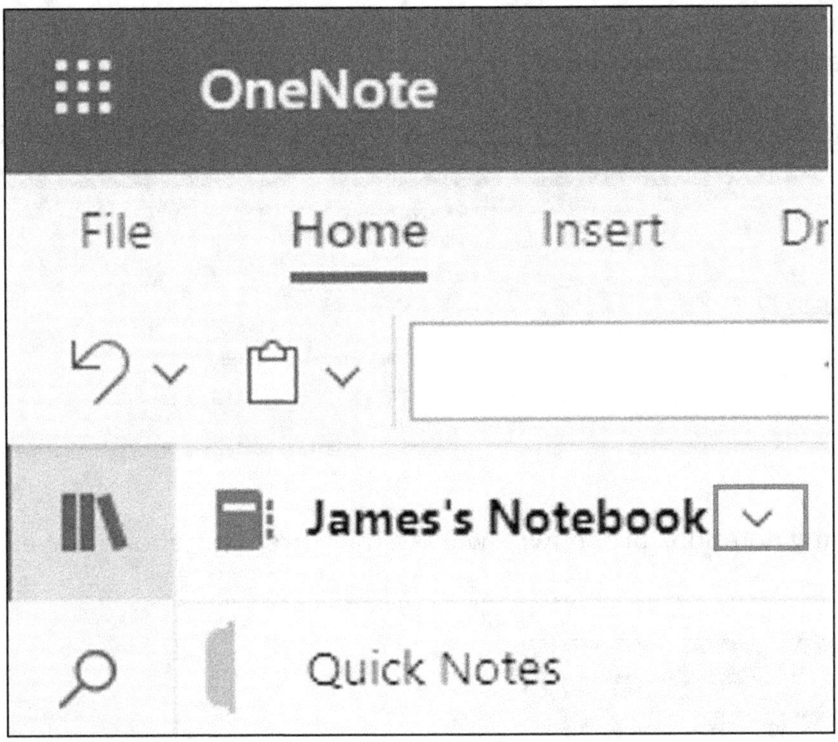

Chapter 7 – OneNote

Figure 7.36

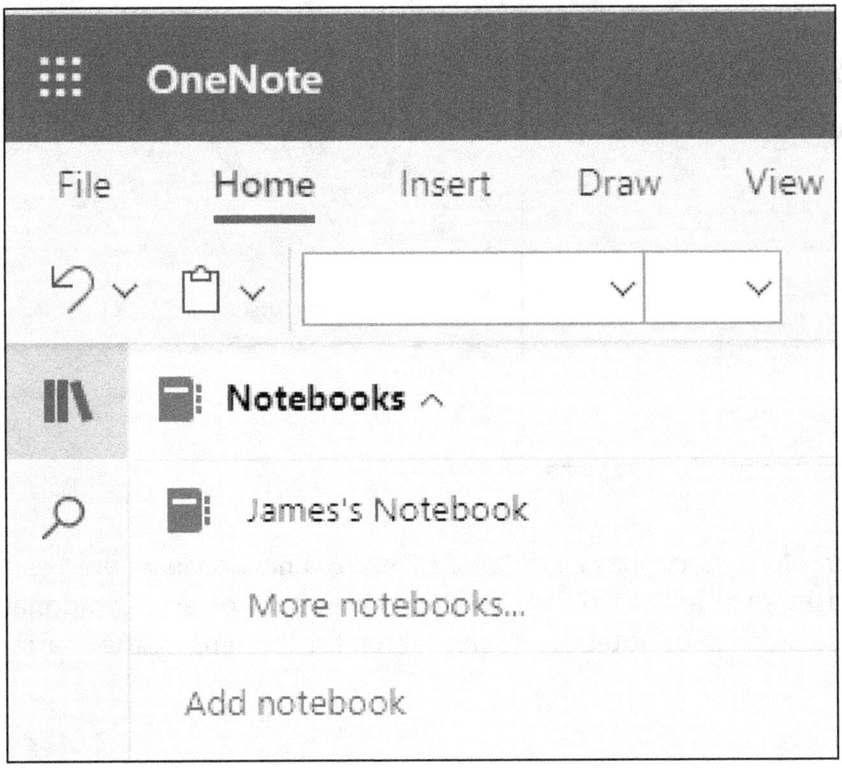

Figure 7.37

Clicking on *Add notebook* will prompt me to enter the name for my new notebook which I will call **New Site Construction**.

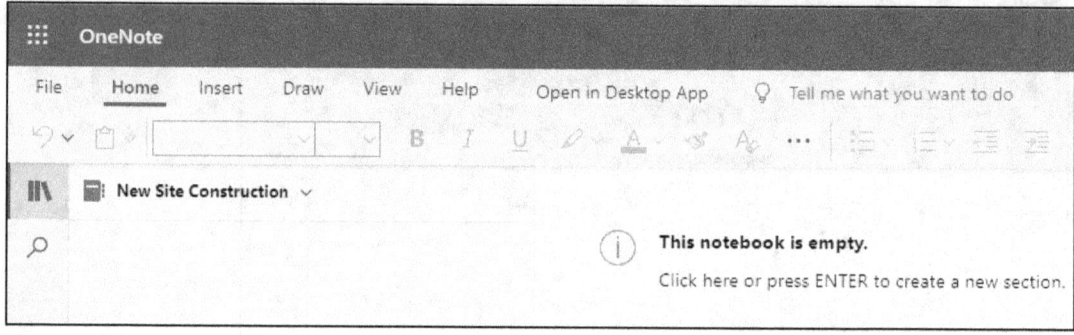

Figure 7.38

Now when I go to my notebook dropdown I will see my current notebook as well as my new one.

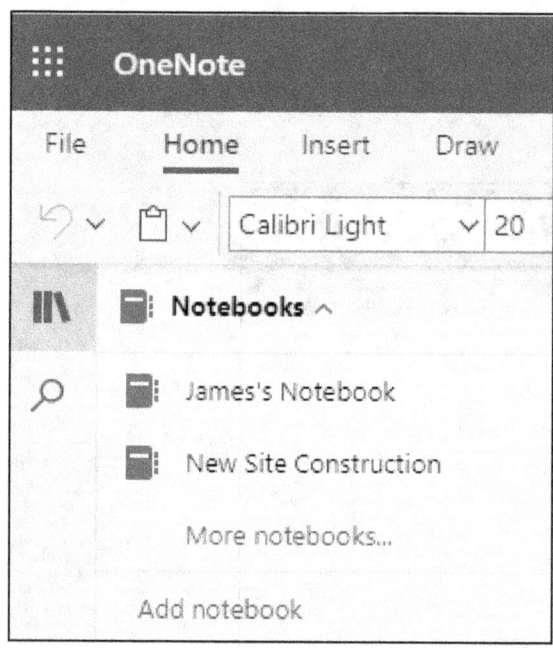

Figure 7.39

If I were to click on *More notebooks* I would be taken to a new page where I can perform similar tasks such as switch between my notebooks or add additional notebooks. If I have a bunch of notebooks I can search for them using the search box.

Chapter 7 – OneNote

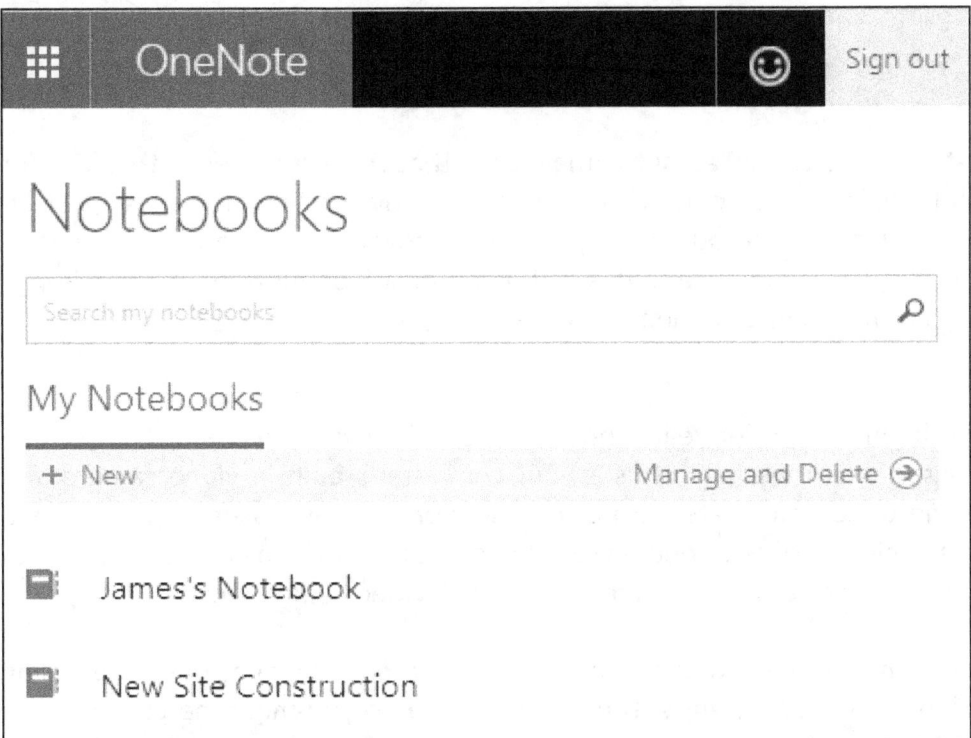

Figure 7.40

Chapter 8 – Additional Apps

Now that I have discussed all of the main apps that come included with Office for the Web I would like to spend a little time going over some of the less popular apps (depending on who you ask) so you can see how they work and decide if they are something you would like to use. This chapter will be more of an overview of these apps rather than an in depth discussion.

Skype
Skype has been around for years and it is used to hold one on one or group video or text based chat meetings. It uses your computer's built in video camera and microphone to communicate with other users on the call, assuming you have a camera and microphone connected to your computer. You can also use Skype with your smartphone or tablet which most likely has video capabilities.

You can sign in to Skype with the same Microsoft account that you have been using for all of the other Office apps. The first time you do you might be prompted to allow notifications from Skype so you will know when you have an incoming call or message.

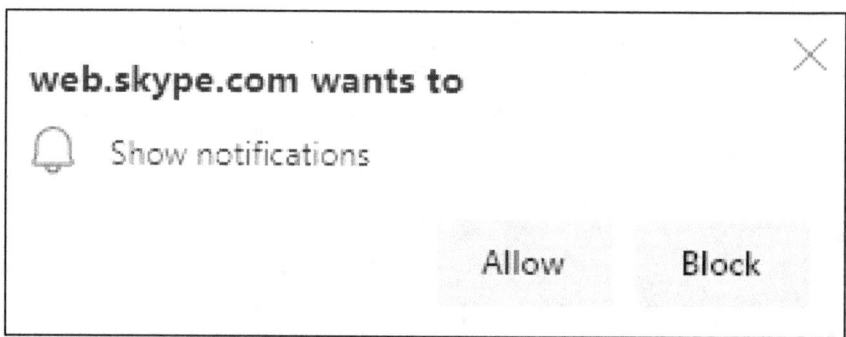
Figure 8.1

Then you will be asked to upload a picture for your profile which is optional.

Chapter 8 – Additional Apps

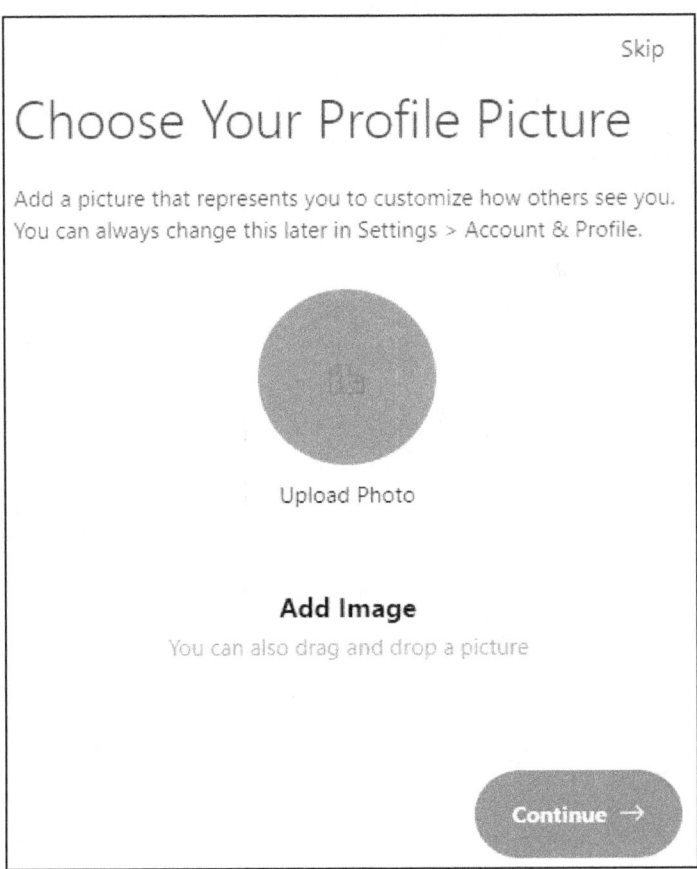

Figure 8.2

You might also get a prompt from your web browser asking you to give Skype permission to use your microphone which you will need to do otherwise it will be blocked.

Figure 8.3

Next, you will be able to test your computer's audio capabilities as well as make a test call to make sure your computer is able to use Skype properly.

Chapter 8 – Additional Apps

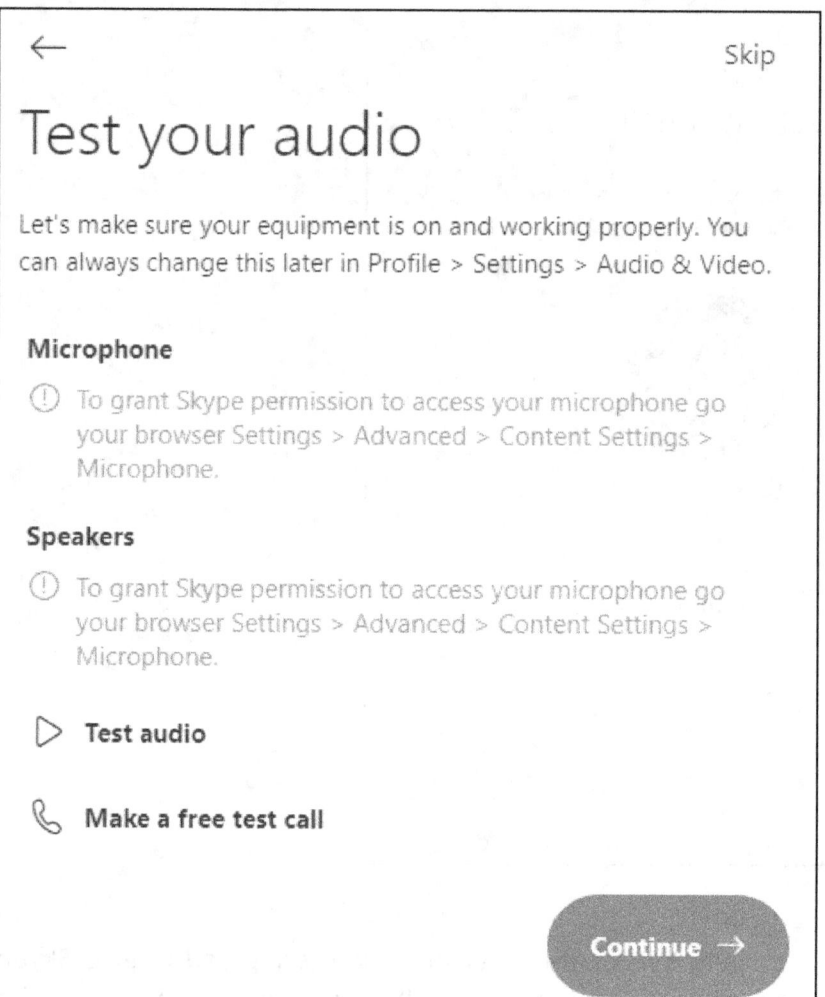

Figure 8.4

Finally, Skype will want to access your contacts to make it easier to initiate calls and chats with others.

Chapter 8 – Additional Apps

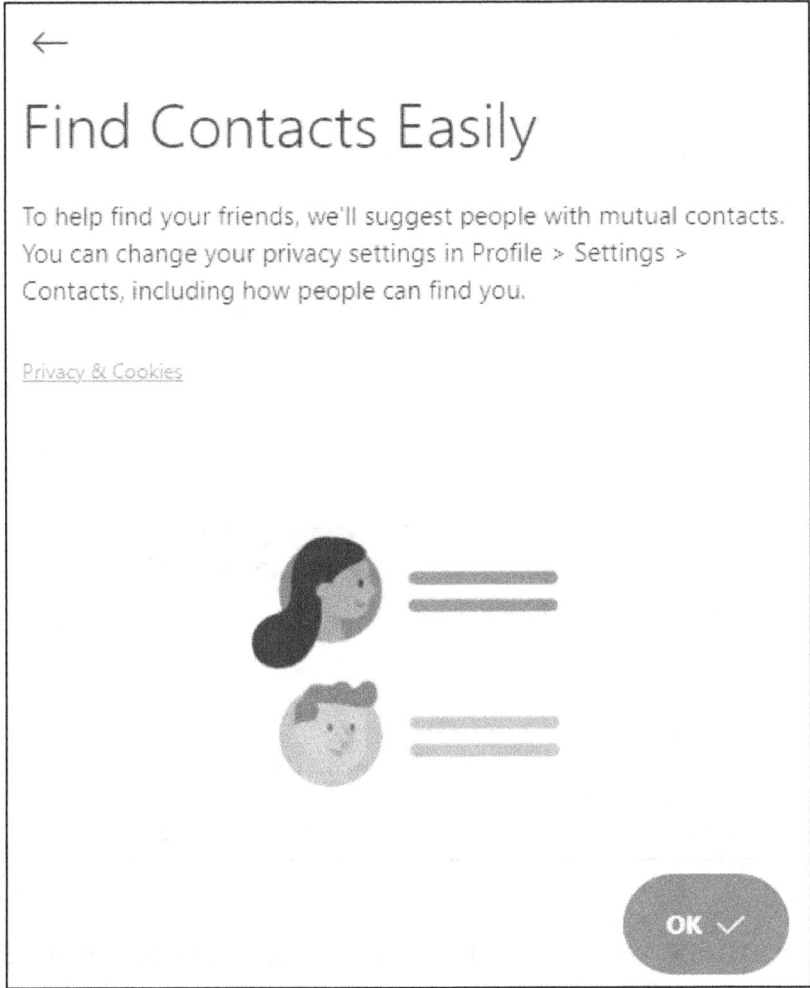

Figure 8.5

Once you have everything configured you will be taken to the main Skype screen where you will be shown your conversation history which you won't have if it's the first time you have used Skype with this account.

The main Skype window is broken up into Chats, Calls, Contacts and Notifications and you can click on each one of these categories to see your history or initiate a new call.

Chapter 8 – Additional Apps

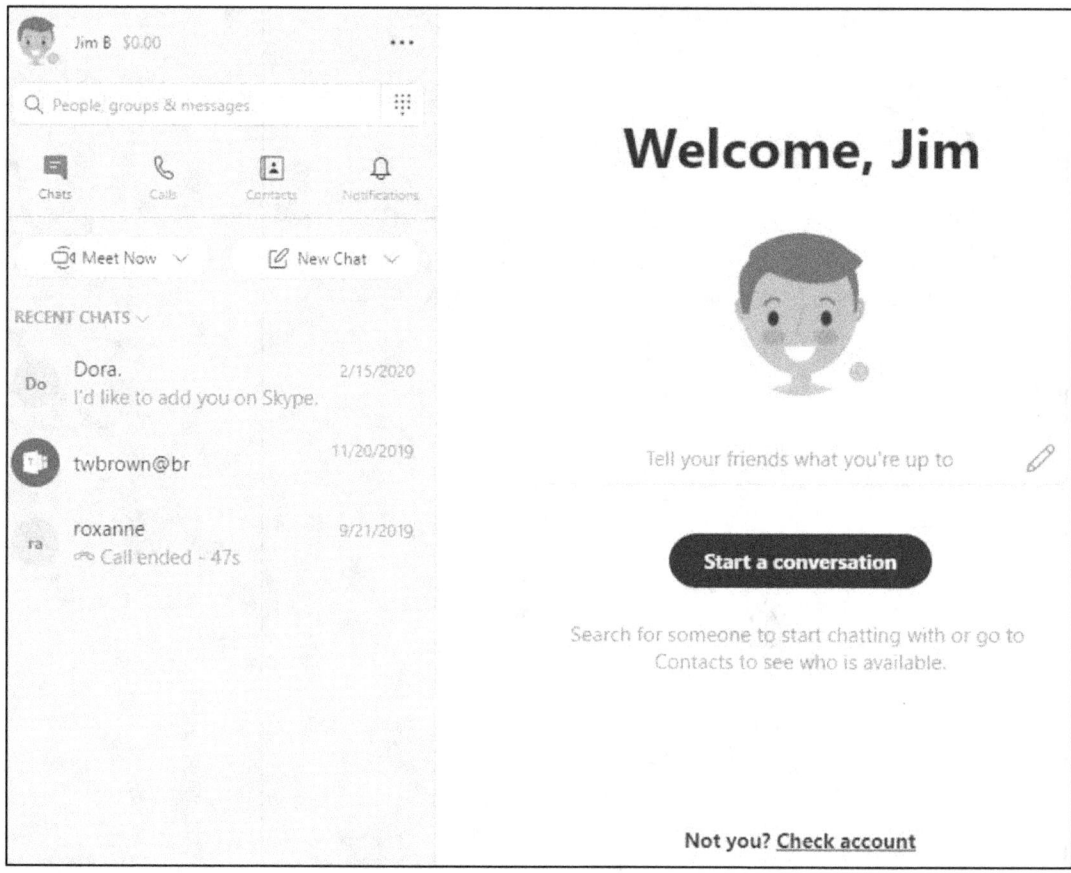

Figure 8.6

You can also click on the 10 dot phone dial pad icon next to the search box to bring up the phone dialer and manually dial a phone number to initiate a call. The main thing to remember when using this feature is that it's not free and you will need to buy Skype Credits to use it.

Chapter 8 – Additional Apps

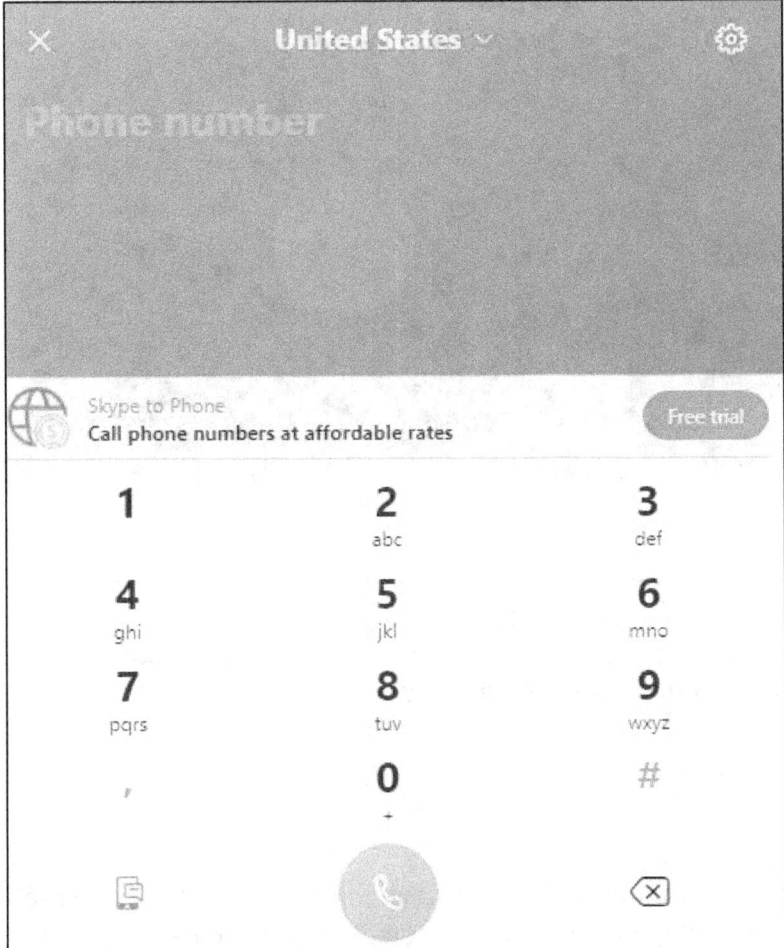

Figure 8.7

Clicking on the *Meeting* button will allow you to either join someone's meeting in progress or host your own meeting. To join an existing meeting you will need to type or paste in the code that should be provided by the person hosting the meeting.

If you would like to host your own meeting then simply click on *Host a meeting* and you will be presented with a meeting configuration screen where you can type in the subject of the meeting and will also be given a link that you can send out to invite others to your meeting. If you don't have a video camera connected to your computer or choose not to enable it then your attendees will see your profile picture instead assuming you have uploaded one.

Chapter 8 – Additional Apps

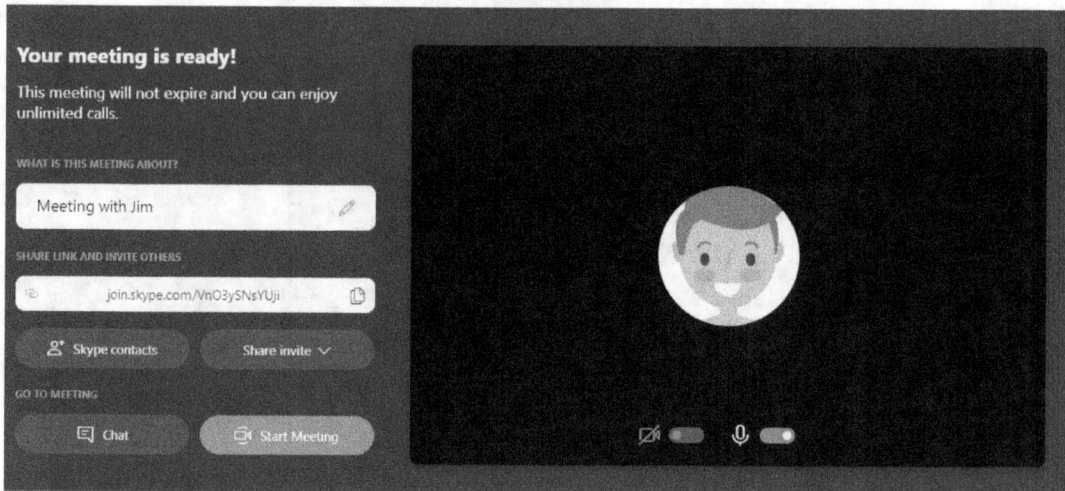

Figure 8.8

 If you would like to learn about the more popular video conferencing apps then check out my books titled **Zoom Made Easy** and **Google Meet Made Easy**.
https://www.amazon.com/dp/B088B96YNK
https://www.amazon.com/dp/B08DFQPSD7

Once you have started the meeting and others have joined you will see a screen similar to figure 8.9. My meeting only has two people, but you can have up to 100 participants with the free version. You will also notice how you have a variety of tools such as the ability to record the meeting, share your screen, raise your hand, start a chat and so on.

If you want to leave the meeting simply click on the red phone hang-up icon. And if you want to enable or disable audio or video you can do that with the microphone and camera buttons.

Chapter 8 – Additional Apps

Figure 8.9

If you have used other meeting apps such as Zoom or Google Meet then you should have no problem getting the hang of Skype.

Forms
If you are or have been a Google Apps user then you might have heard of Google Forms which is used to create things like surveys or quizzes. Well, Microsoft has the same kind of app and it's called Forms as well.

When you open Forms for the first time you will be shown any recent or pinned forms you have created in the past. But if it's your first time using Forms then you will have the option to create a new form, quiz or course evaluation survey. And of course you will have the option to use some premium templates that will require you to pay for an Office 365 subscription.

 If you would like to learn about all of the free Google Apps available for you to use online then check out my book titled **Google Apps Made Easy**.
https://www.amazon.com/dp/1798114992

Chapter 8 – Additional Apps

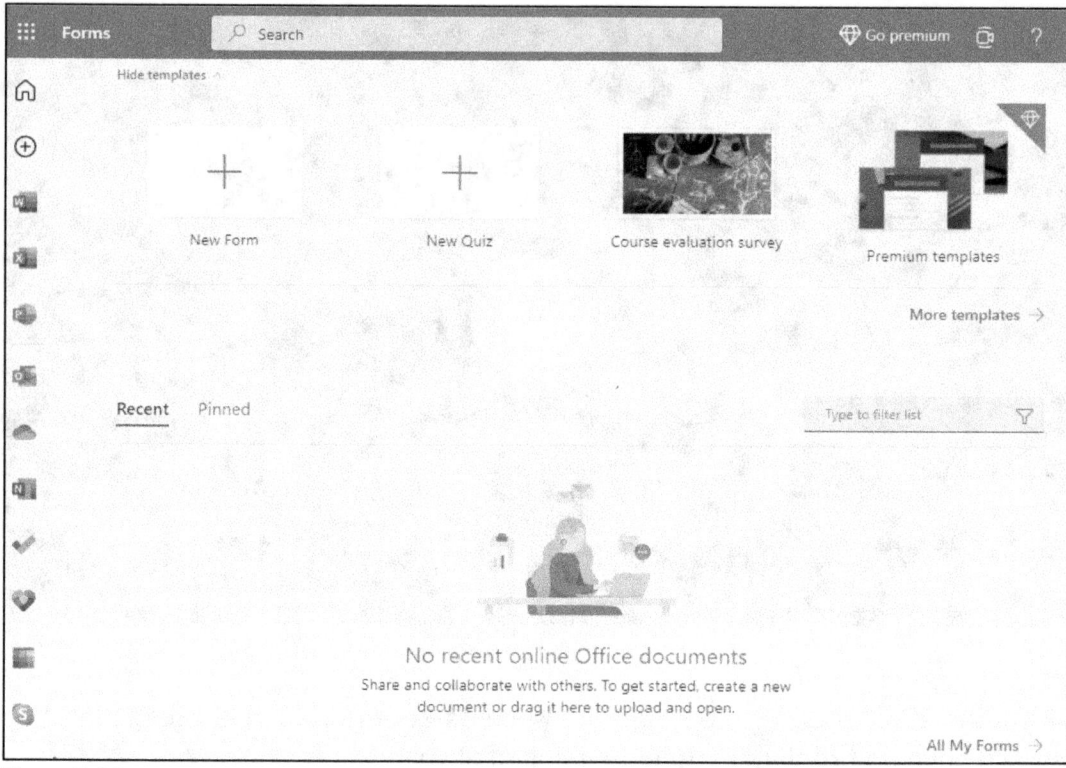

Figure 8.10

Forms does come with some free templates that you can access by clicking on *More templates*.

Chapter 8 – Additional Apps

Figure 8.11

Let's start by opening the *Event registration* template and see how it looks. As you can see in figure 8.12, this template comes with some preconfigured sections and questions that might not work for what you are trying to accomplish.

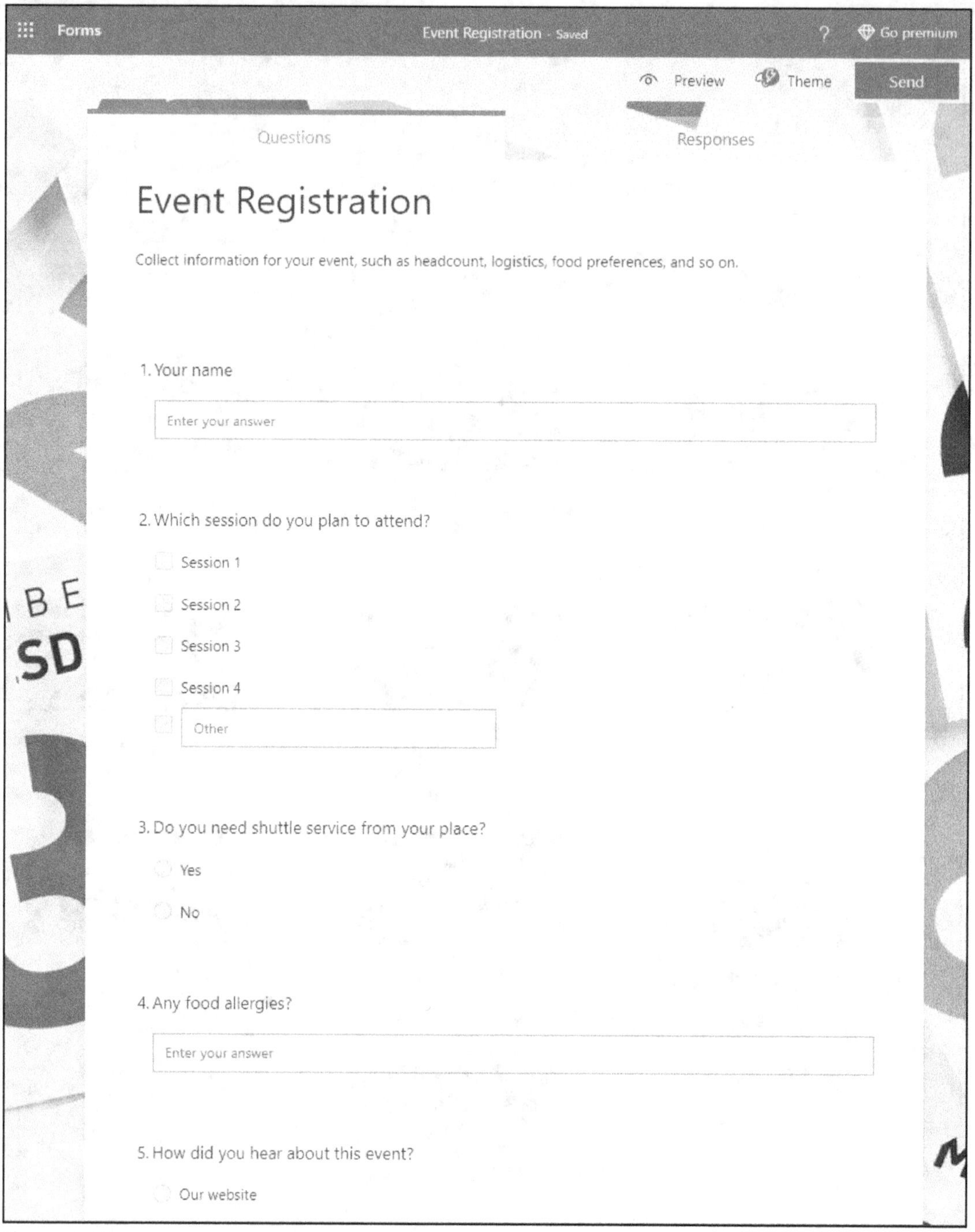

Chapter 8 – Additional Apps

Figure 8.12

Fortunately, you do not have to stick with the default configuration and can click on any of the sections to customize it to suit your needs. If I click on the section with the question "Which session do you plan to attend?" I can then change the

Chapter 8 – Additional Apps

questions and answers as seen in figure 8.14. I can also set the response to be required.

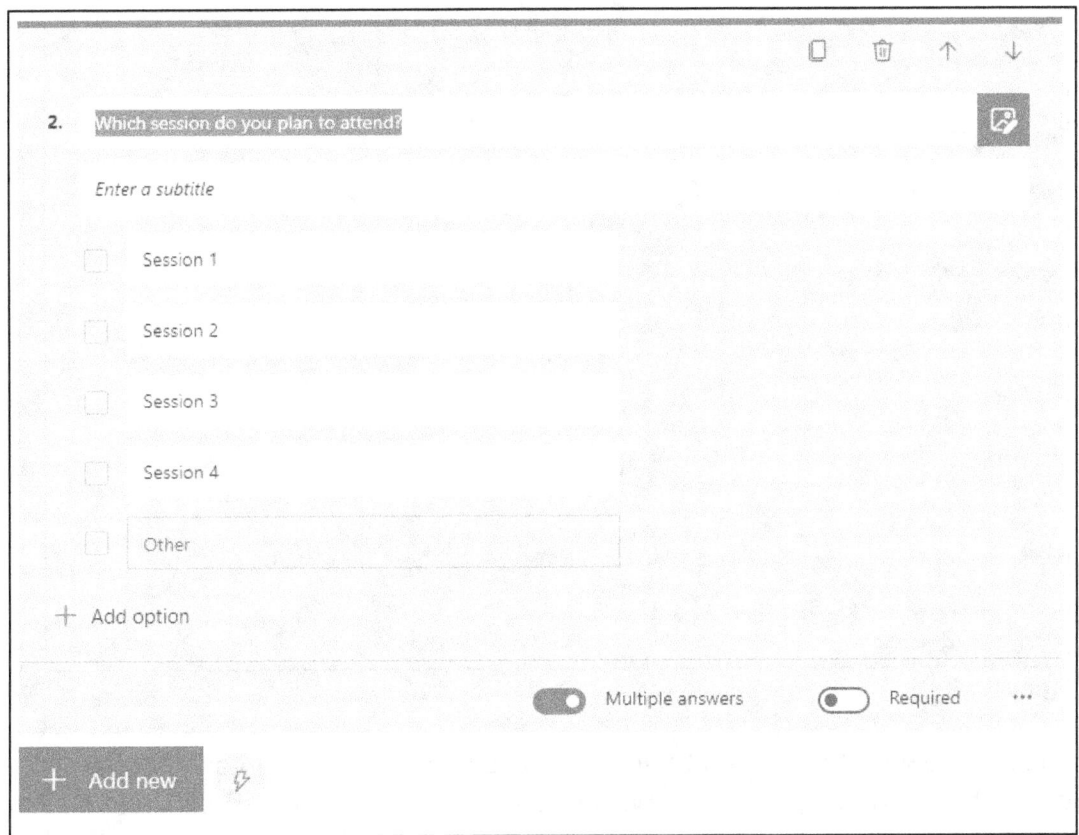

Figure 8.13

Chapter 8 – Additional Apps

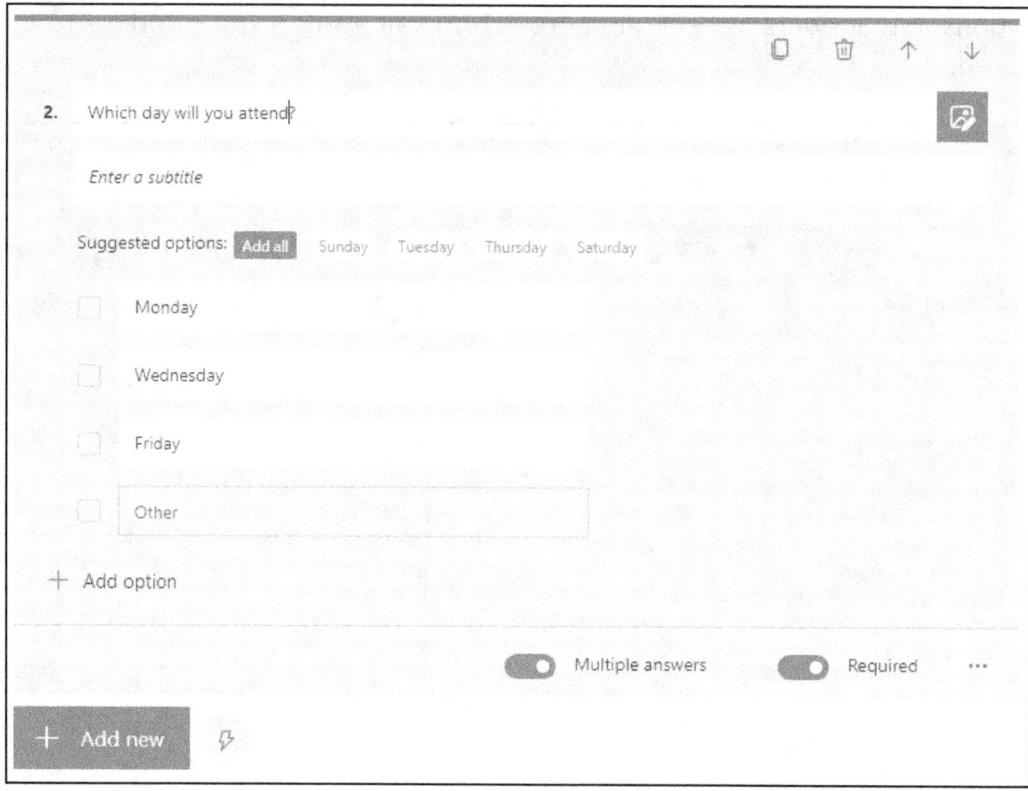

Figure 8.14

The Add new button is used to add a new section to your form and choose from one of the section types. Forms will even give you some suggestions that you can use for your form.

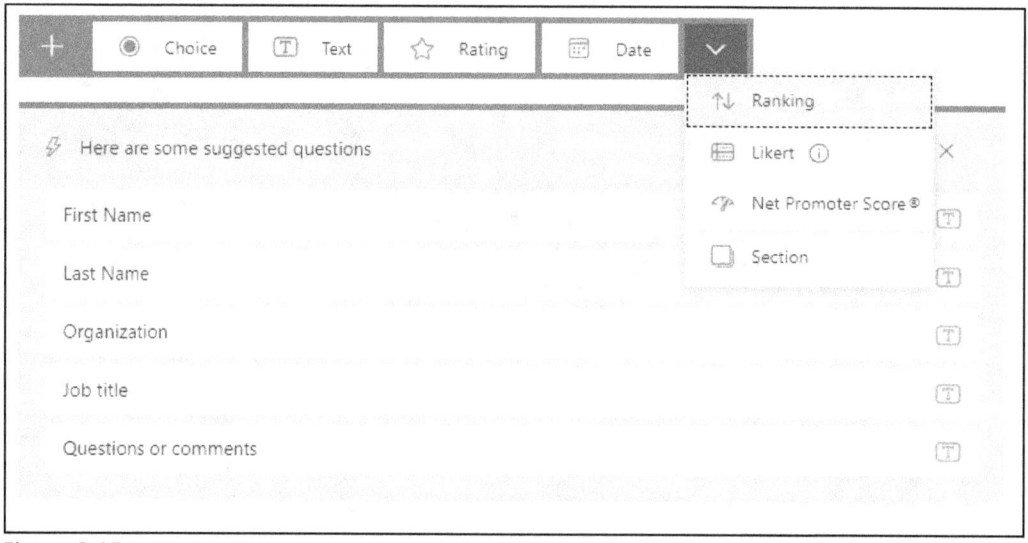

Figure 8.15

Chapter 8 – Additional Apps

I will use the *Rating* choice and create a rating question for my form.

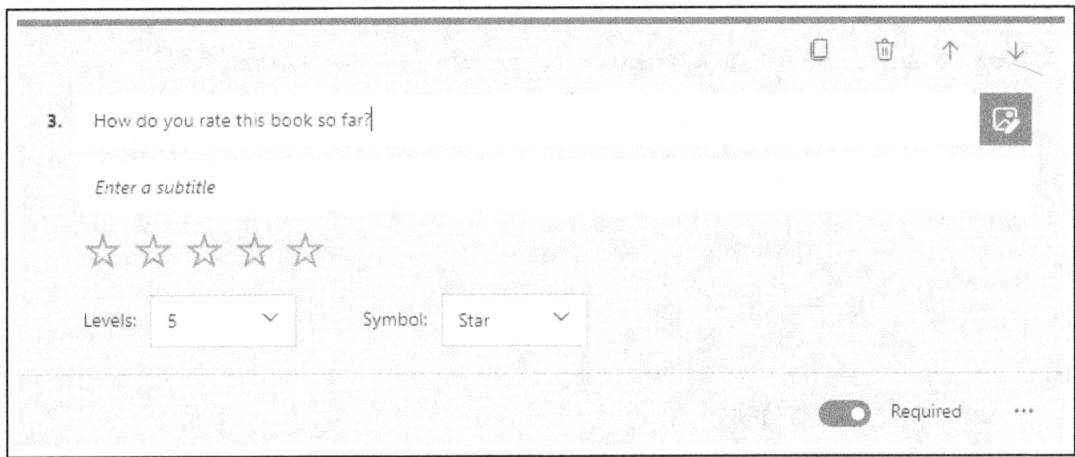

Figure 8.16

Now when I go back and look at my form I can see my changes and new section.

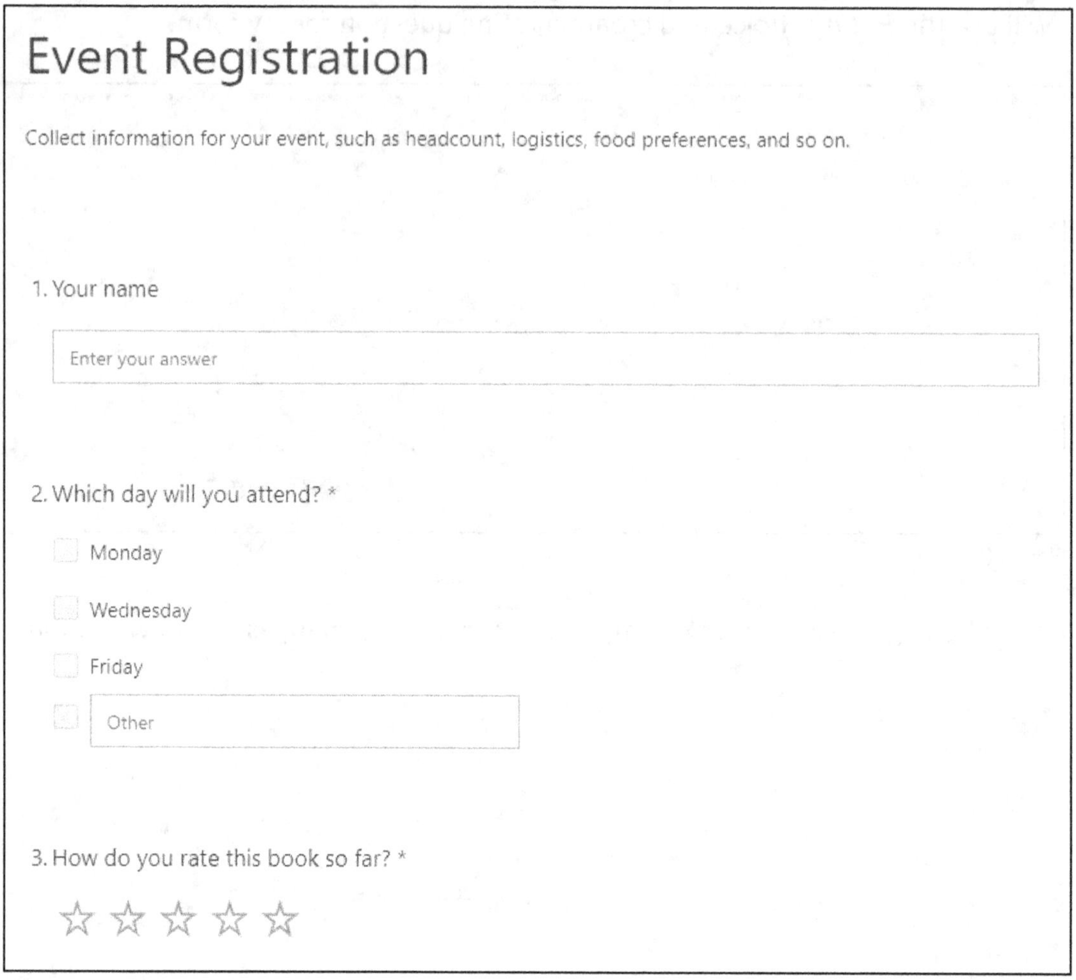

Chapter 8 – Additional Apps

Event Registration

Collect information for your event, such as headcount, logistics, food preferences, and so on.

1. Your name

   [Enter your answer]

2. Which day will you attend? *

   ☐ Monday
   ☐ Wednesday
   ☐ Friday
   ☐ Other

3. How do you rate this book so far? *

   ☆ ☆ ☆ ☆ ☆

Figure 8.17

To have others fill out your form you can send it to them via email, shared link, QR code, or have it embedded into your website by clicking on the *Send* button.

Chapter 8 – Additional Apps

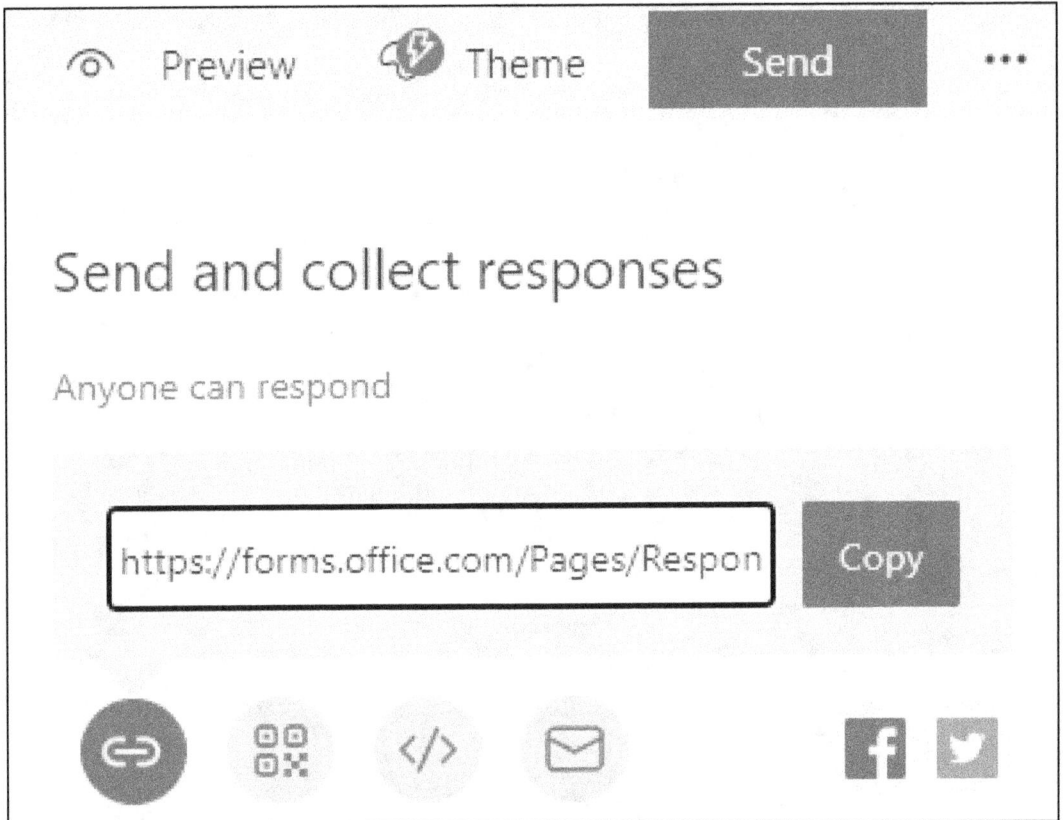

Figure 8.18

When the people on the receiving end of your form fill out the form it will look similar to figure 8.19.

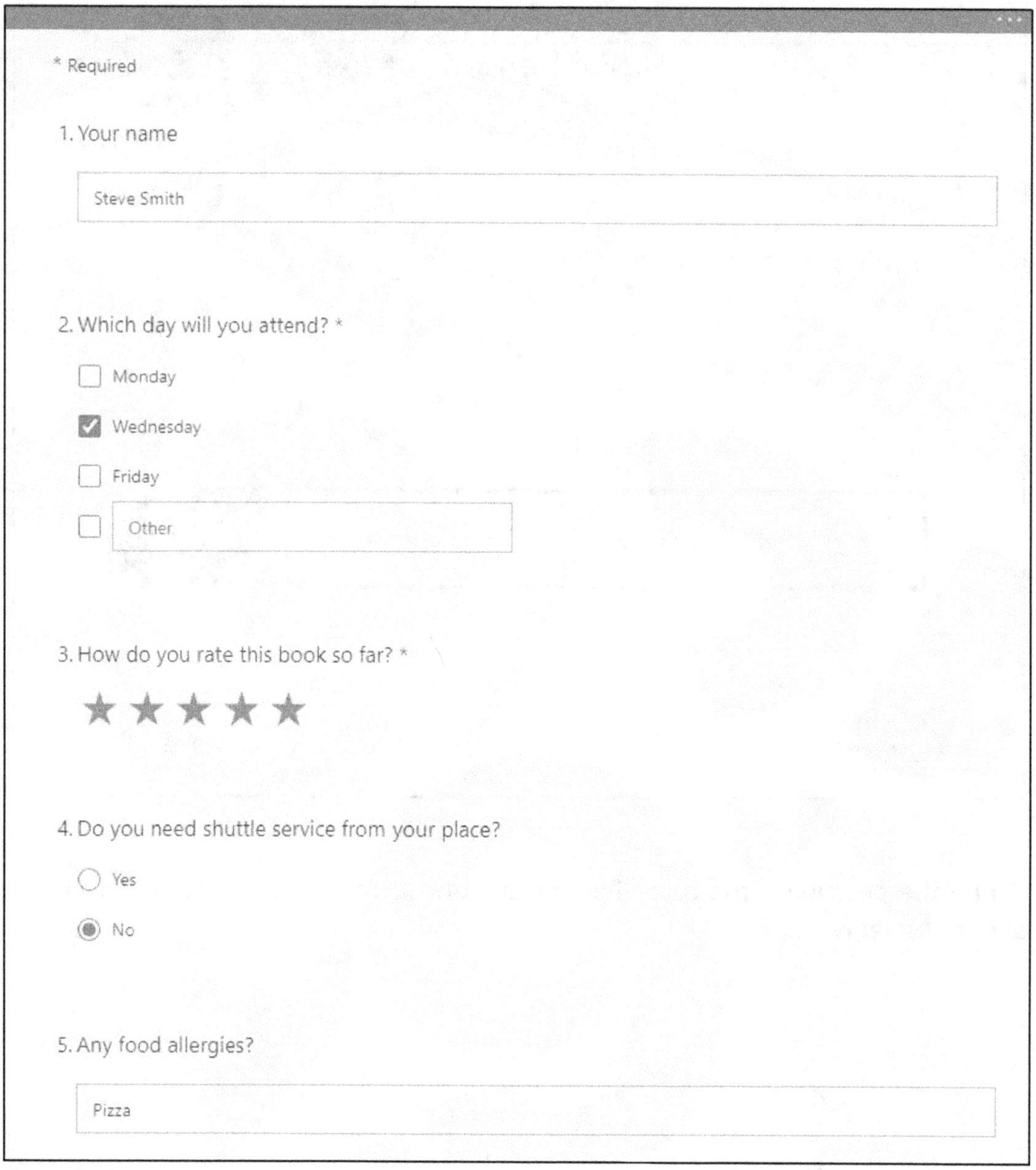

Chapter 8 – Additional Apps

* Required

1. Your name

   [Steve Smith]

2. Which day will you attend? *
   - [ ] Monday
   - [x] Wednesday
   - [ ] Friday
   - [ ] Other

3. How do you rate this book so far? *

   ★ ★ ★ ★ ★

4. Do you need shuttle service from your place?
   - ( ) Yes
   - (•) No

5. Any food allergies?

   [Pizza]

Figure 8.19

Now I can go to the *Responses* tab of my form and see the entries added by those who filled out my form.

Chapter 8 – Additional Apps

Figure 8.20

Chapter 8 – Additional Apps

When you create a new form or quiz from scratch you will go through the same process but rather than edit existing sections, you will add new sections for each type of question or survey you want to add.

Sway

Microsoft Sway is a newer Office app and is used to create presentations similar to PowerPoint, but these are more multimedia based with animations, videos and pictures. It will be difficult to show you exactly how it works since I cannot run a Sway show within a book but I will rather go over the basics so you can try it out for yourself.

When you first open Sway you will see some options for starting your Sway from a template, from a topic, from a document or from scratch.

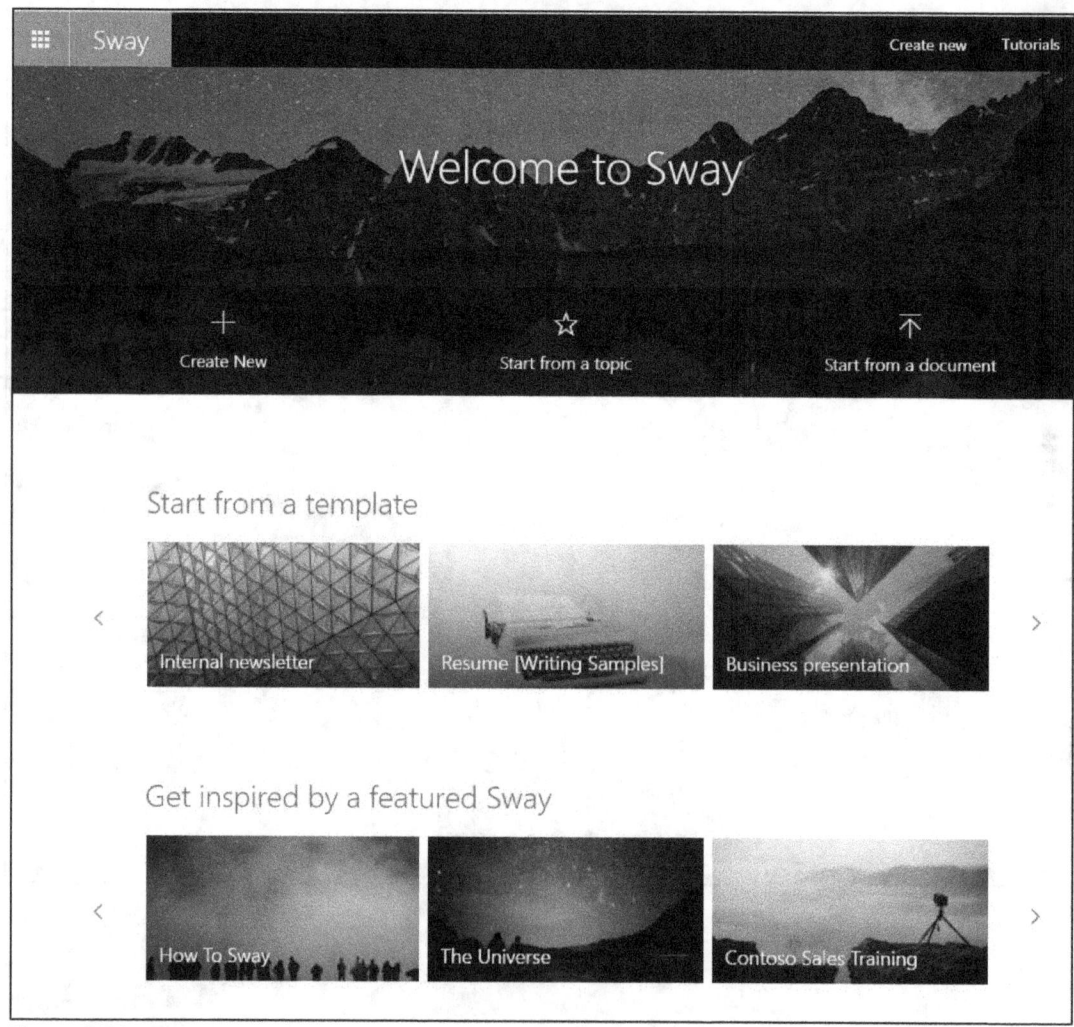

Figure 8.21

Chapter 8 – Additional Apps

Let's see what happens if I create a Sway from a topic such as *smartest dog breeds* and then click on *Create outline*.

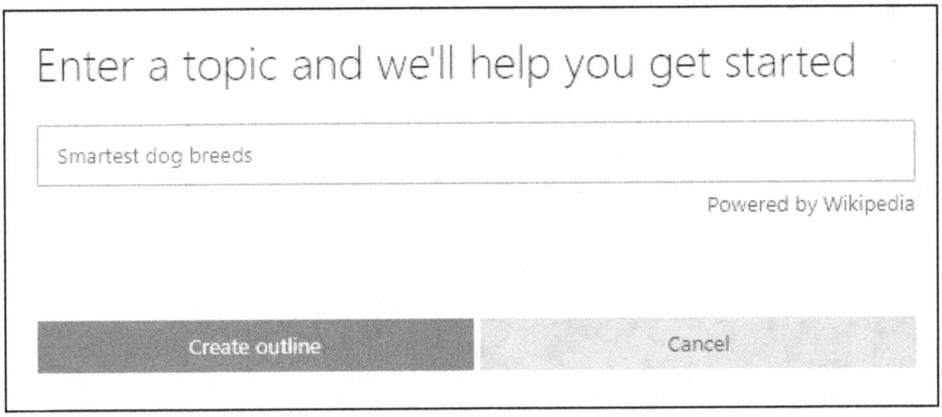

Figure 8.22

When I type in my topic subject, Sway will ask me to get more specific by offering me some suggestions. I will choose *Dog intelligence* and then click on *Create Outline*.

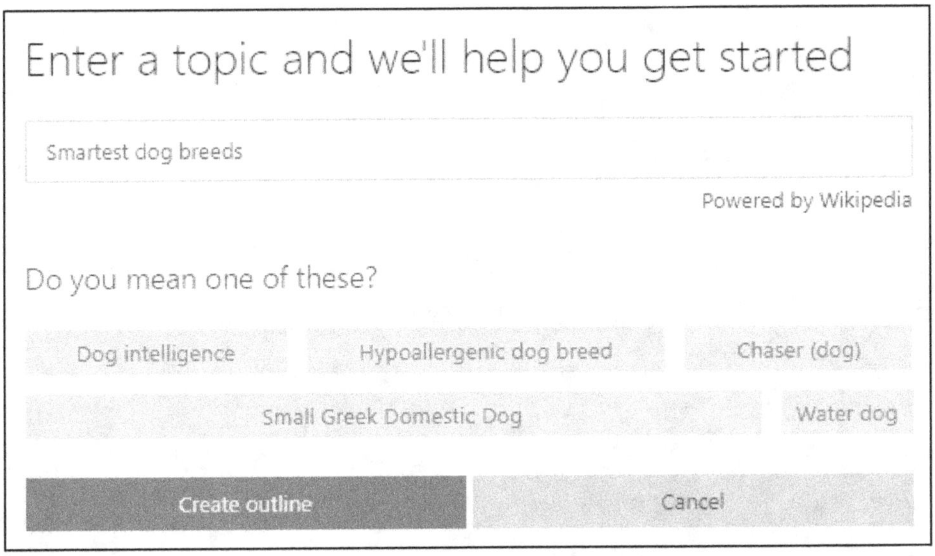

Figure 8.23

Sway will then create an outline for me based on the information I provided, and it did a fairly good job for my topic. Figure 8.24 shows part of the outline that Sway created for me. Now I can do things such as enter information about intelligent dog breeds and add pictures, movies, links to relevant websites and so on as shown in figure 8.25.

299

Chapter 8 – Additional Apps

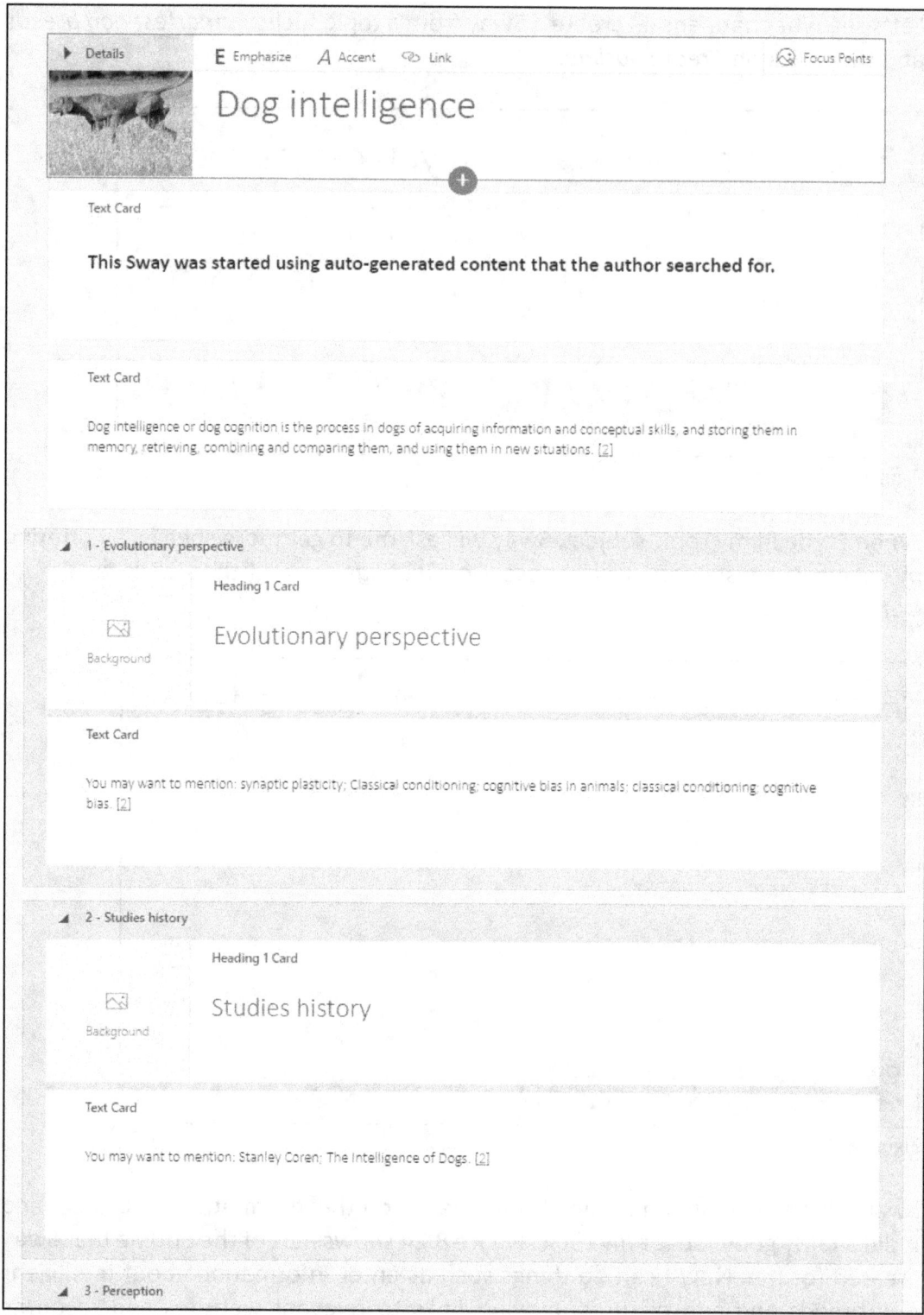

Figure 8.24

Chapter 8 – Additional Apps

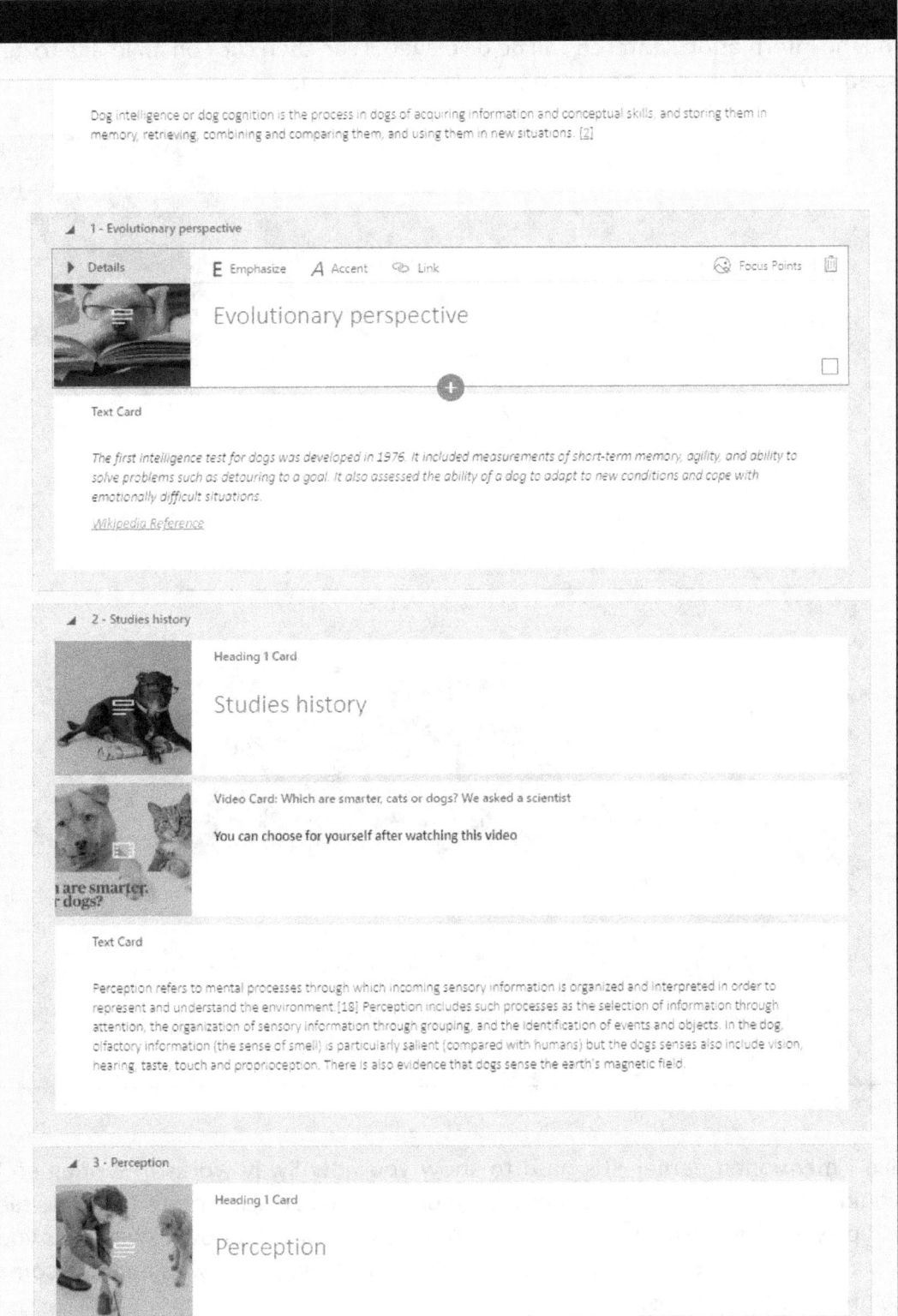

Figure 8.25

Chapter 8 – Additional Apps

When I click on Play at the top right of the screen then my Sway show will play out and the information I entered will be displayed. I can then click on an image to get a better view of it or on my video to have it play for me.

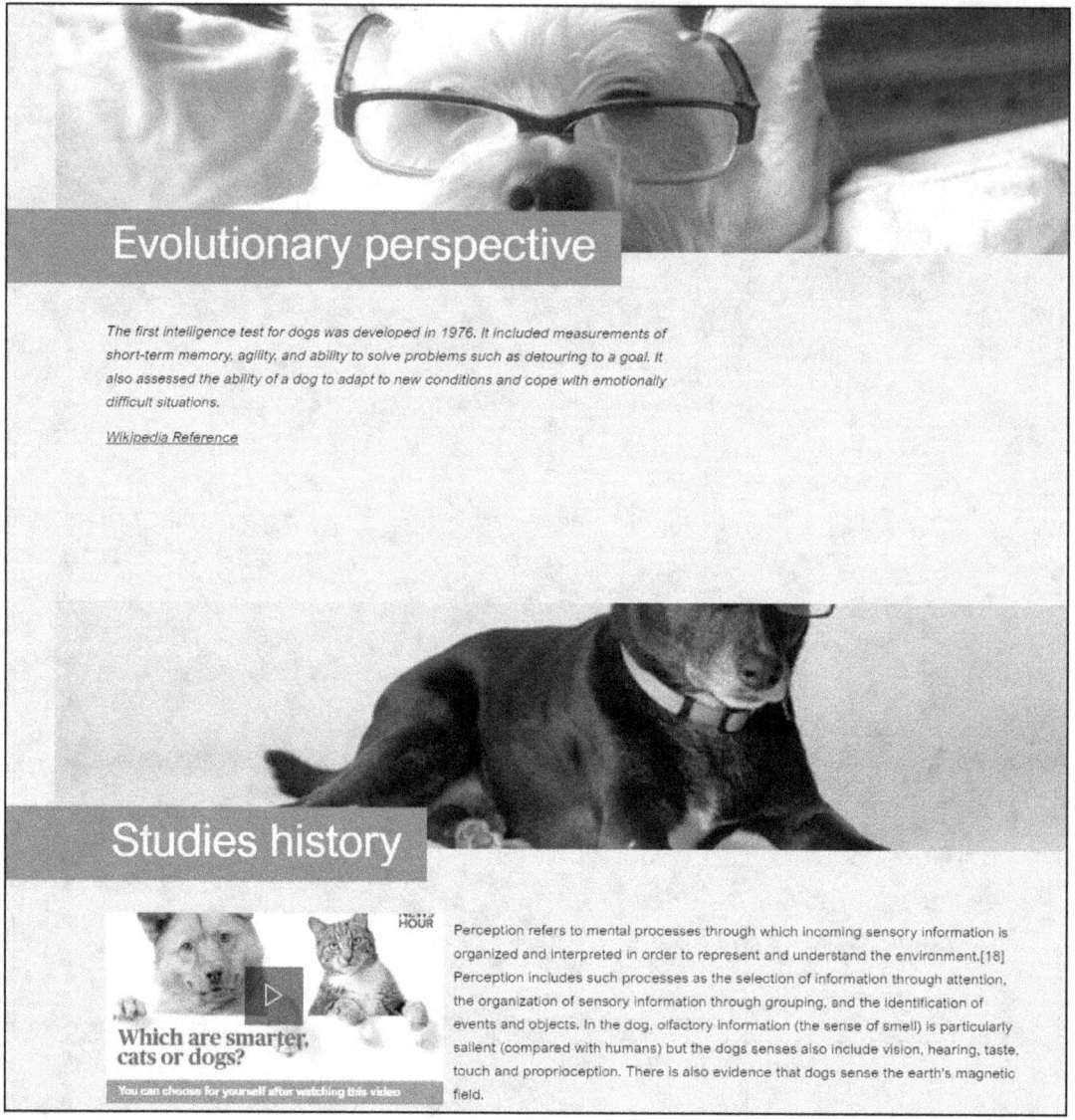

Figure 8.26

Like I mentioned earlier, it's hard to show you how Sway works in writing so I would recommend just trying it out for yourself. You can also open a template file and play it to see how it would look if you were to create your own Sway. Plus you can always go on YouTube and search for *Microsoft Sway examples* and find some helpful demonstrations.

Chapter 8 – Additional Apps

Family Safety

We all know that the internet can be a dangerous place and there is always some kind of trouble around the corner. This might not be a big deal if you are only looking out for yourself but if you have kids at home then you might want to look into keeping them safe while they are online.

There are many programs and apps that will help you keep your kids safe while online and some are better than others and of course some are free, and some are not.

The Microsoft Family Safety app can be used on your computer as well as on your mobile device. It can do things such as restrict websites, control which apps and games your kids can use, and also how long they can use them for. When running on their smartphones it can track their location and send your reports of their daily activities.

When you first go to the app online you will be prompted to create a *family group*.

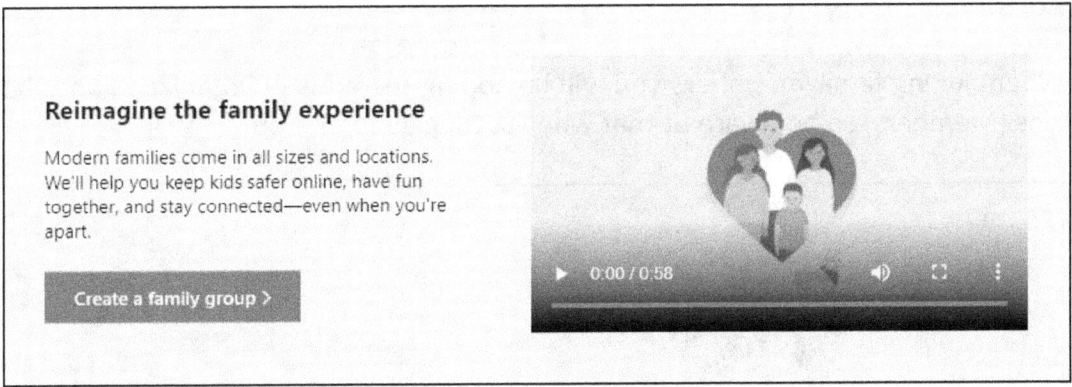

Figure 8.27

To add family members they will need to have a Microsoft account just like you do for everything else.

Chapter 8 – Additional Apps

Figure 8.28

When adding family members you will be adding the adults (Organizers) and the kids (Members) so be aware of that when setting everyone up.

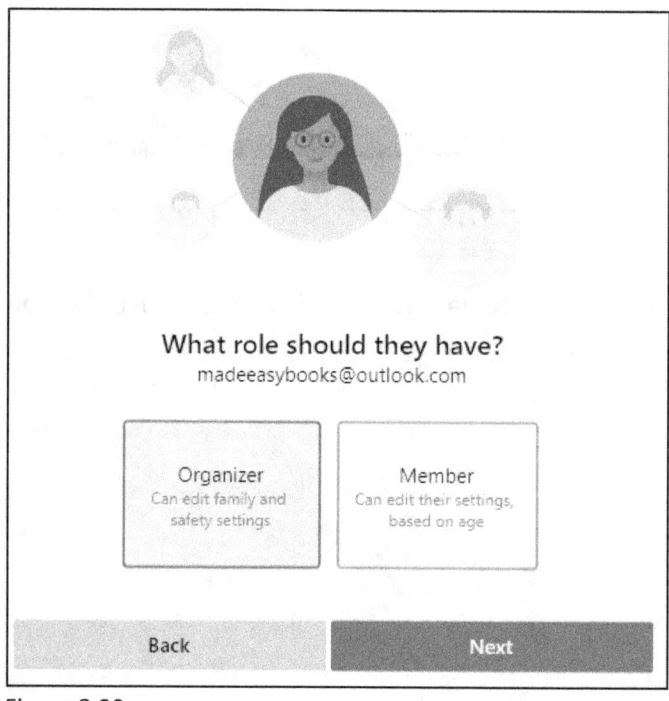

Figure 8.29

Chapter 8 – Additional Apps

Microsoft will then send that person an invitation and they can then accept the invitation to be added to the family group.

You're invited

jimb@onlinecomputertips.com invited you to join their Microsoft family group.

Join now

This invitation expires on April 22.

Figure 8.30

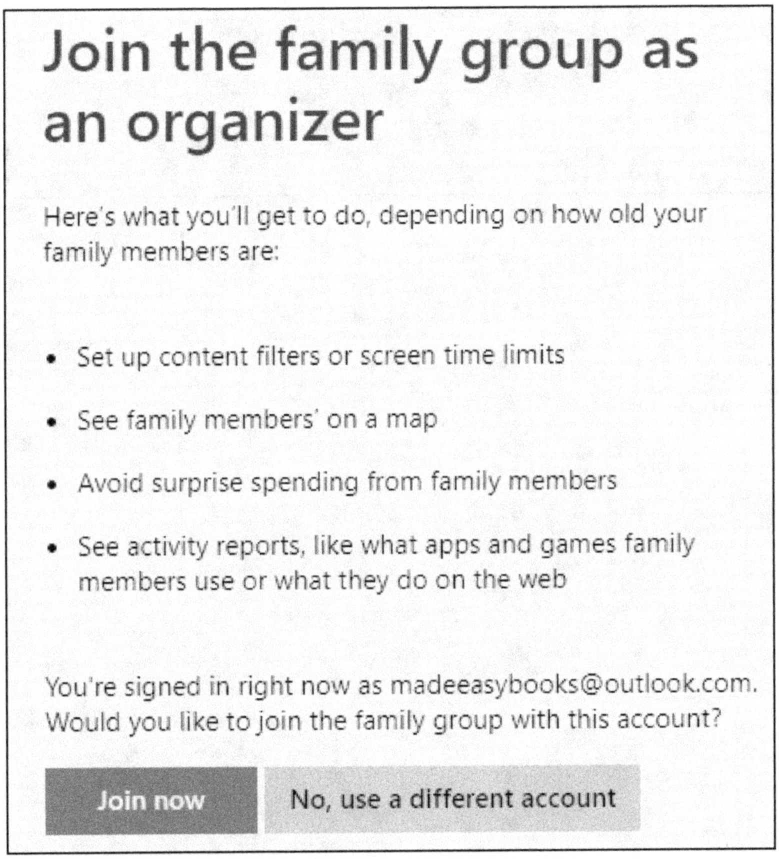

Join the family group as an organizer

Here's what you'll get to do, depending on how old your family members are:

- Set up content filters or screen time limits
- See family members' on a map
- Avoid surprise spending from family members
- See activity reports, like what apps and games family members use or what they do on the web

You're signed in right now as madeeasybooks@outlook.com. Would you like to join the family group with this account?

Join now   No, use a different account

Figure 8.31

Chapter 8 – Additional Apps

Now that I have an organizer (adult) and a member (child), I can start configuring my restrictions or access levels by clicking on *More options* under the user's name.

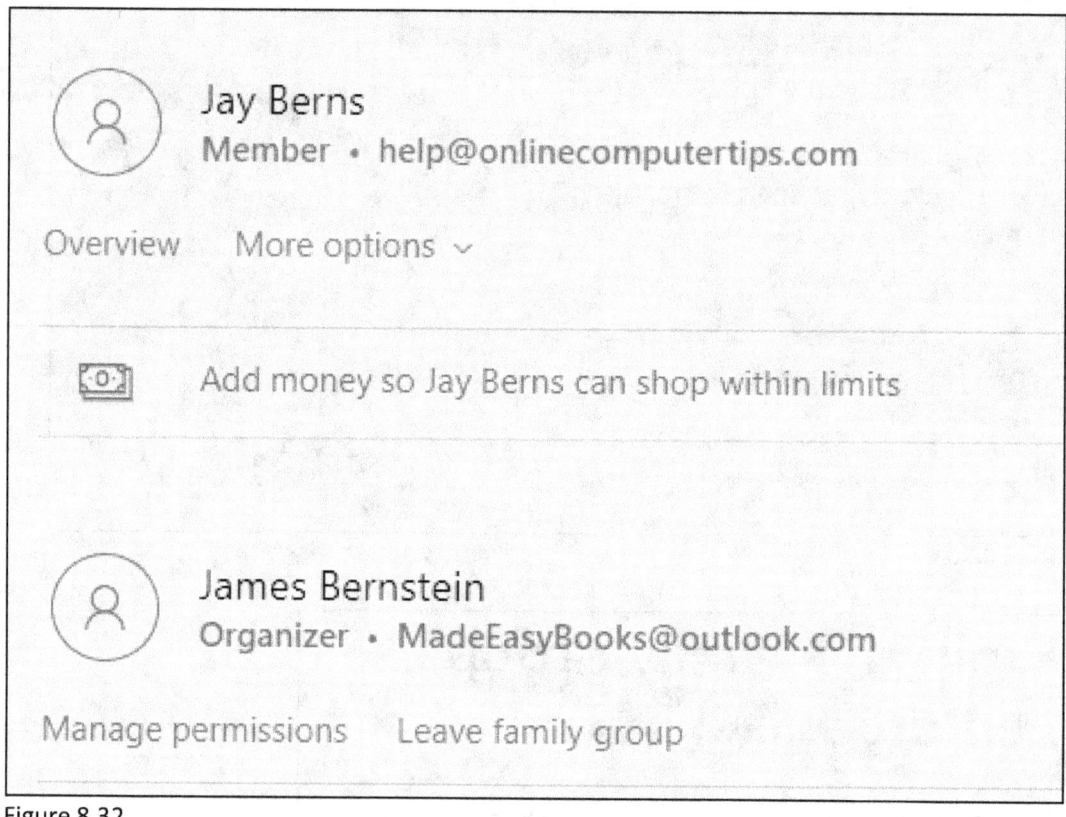

Figure 8.32

Chapter 8 – Additional Apps

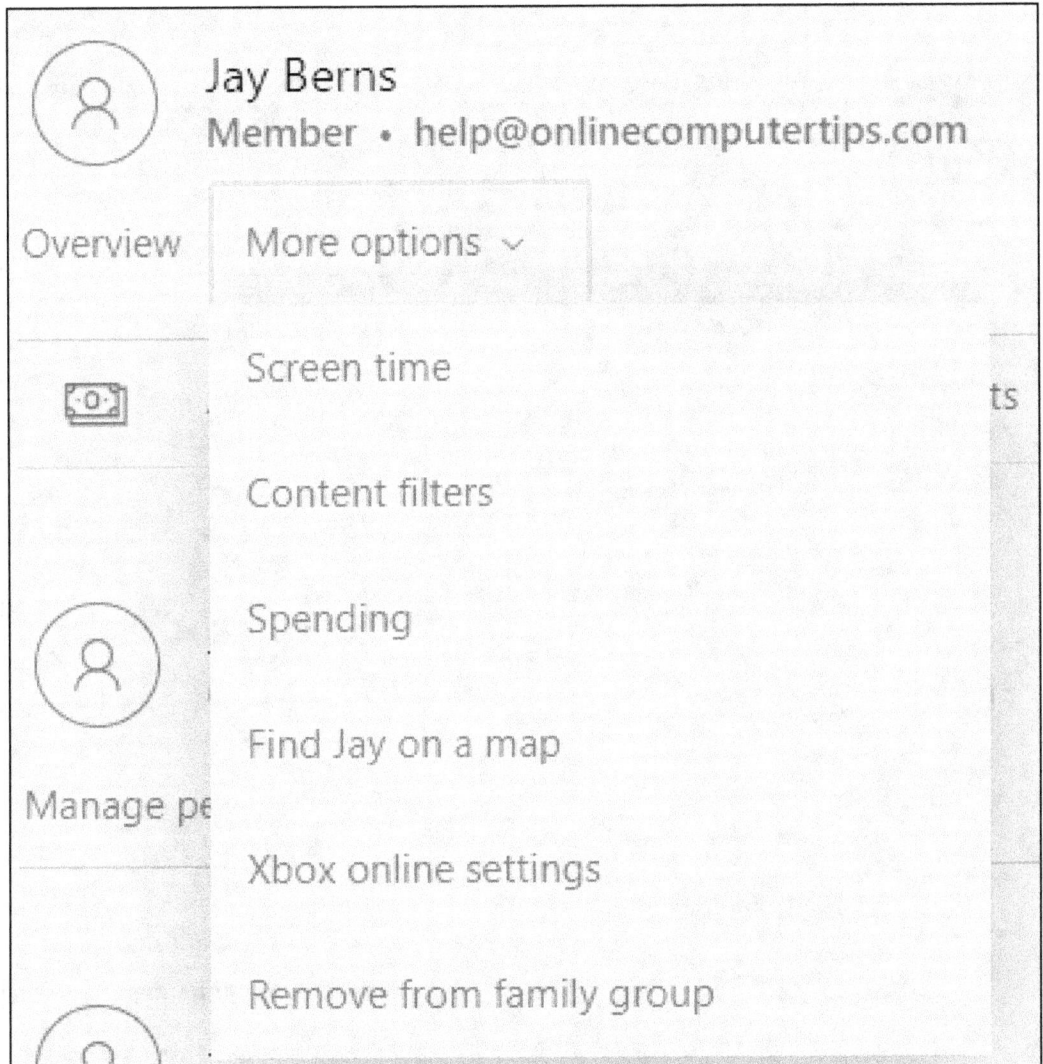

Figure 8.33

In order to get the maximum benefit out of Family Safety, you will need to set up your kid's devices so your changes can be applied to them.

Chapter 8 – Additional Apps

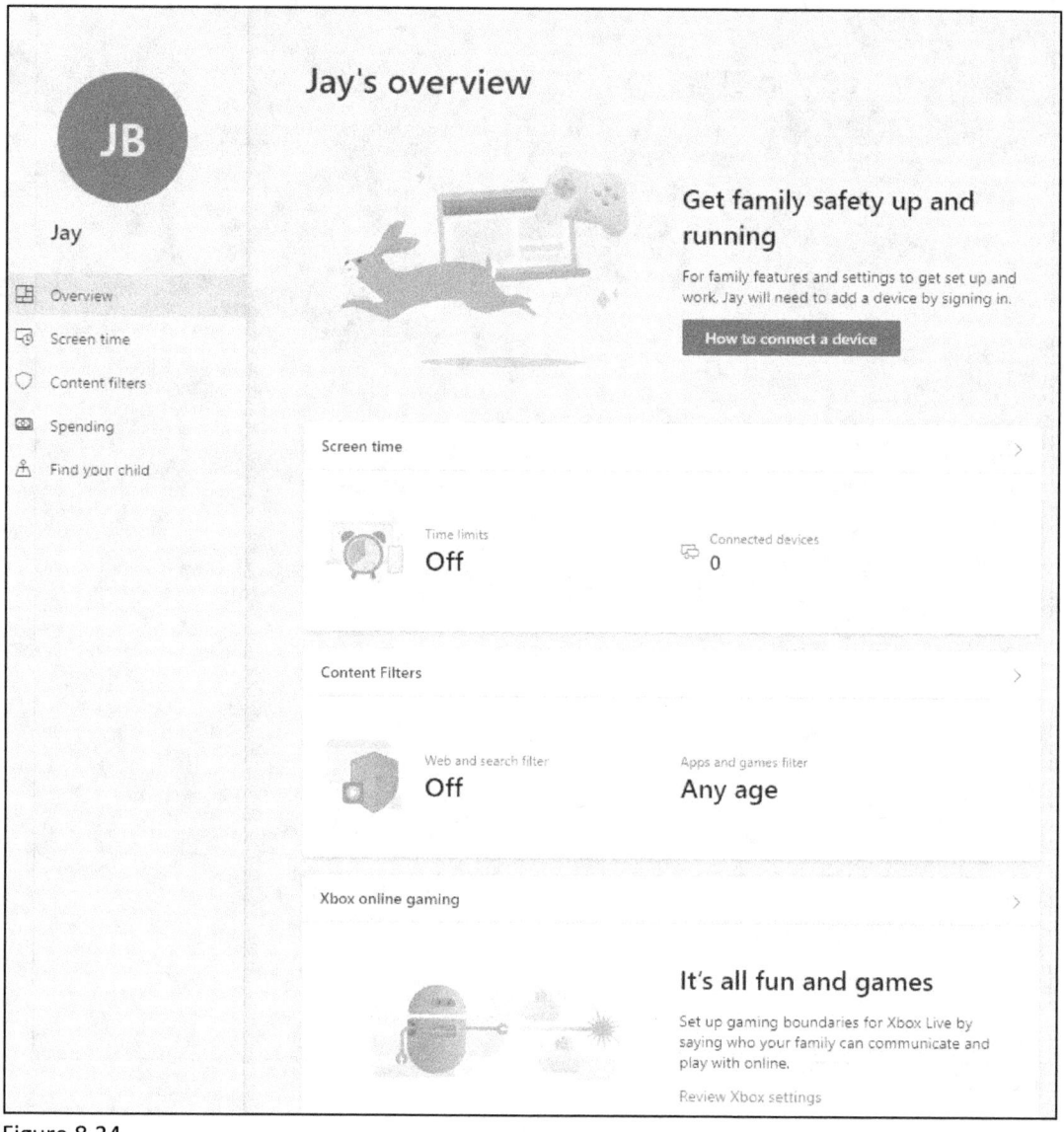

Figure 8.34

Chapter 9 – Sharing, Downloading and Printing Your Files

Now that you have an understanding of how all of the Office for the Web applications work it's time to get into the processes you can perform in all of the apps which will allow you to share your work with others, keep a copy of your work on your own computer and of course print copies of your work.

Sharing and Collaboration
One of the main reasons to use online cloud based applications is to make it easier to share your files with others so they can contribute to them and so you can see their changes without needing to have multiple copies of the same file floating around your Inbox.

Almost all of the Office apps have some sort of sharing functionality and for the most part, it works the same. You share your work and invite others to either view or edit your files based on your needs. You can share your files within the app or from the actual file itself in your OneDrive account.

To share a file from your OneDrive account all you need to do is select the file and then click on *Share*. From there you can type in the email address of the person you wish to share your file with and also change the default access level from edit to view if needed. If you look at figure 9.1 you will see that my newly created family members from Family Safety are available as a choice to share with.

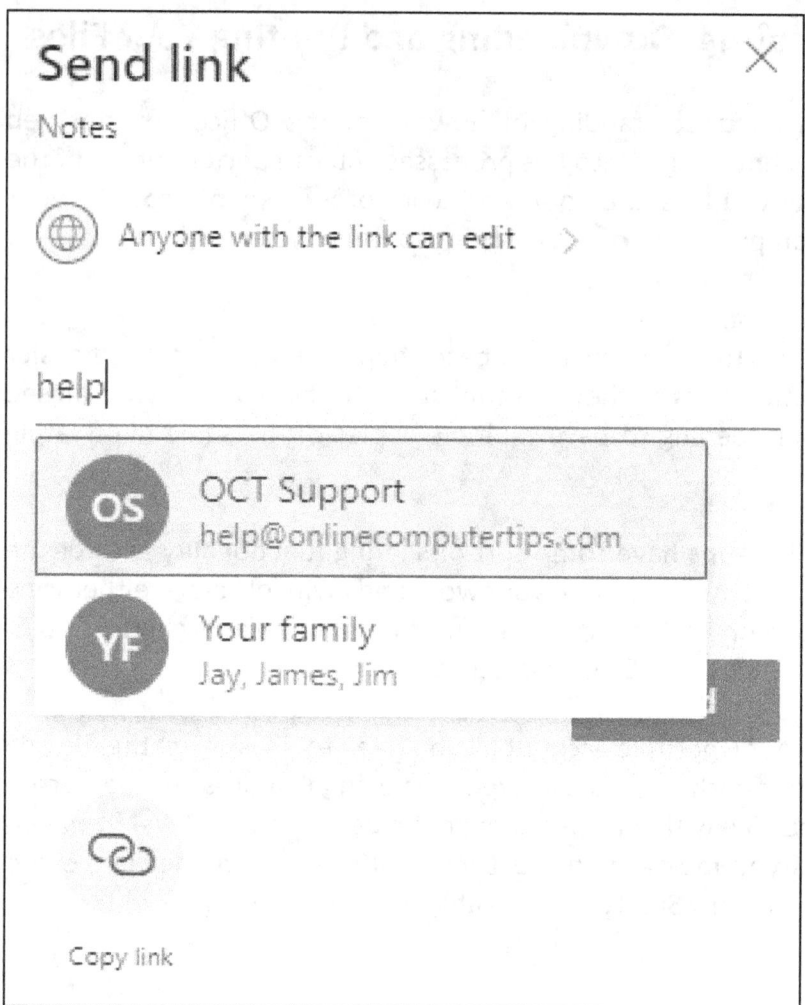

Figure 9.1

If I do click on *Anyone with the link can edit* to change the link settings I will get the options as seen in figure 9.2. I can then uncheck the box to allow editing and set an expiration date and assign a password to open the file. By default the link will work for anyone who has it but if you would like it to only apply to certain people then you can click on *Specific people*.

Chapter 9 – Sharing, Downloading and Printing Your Files

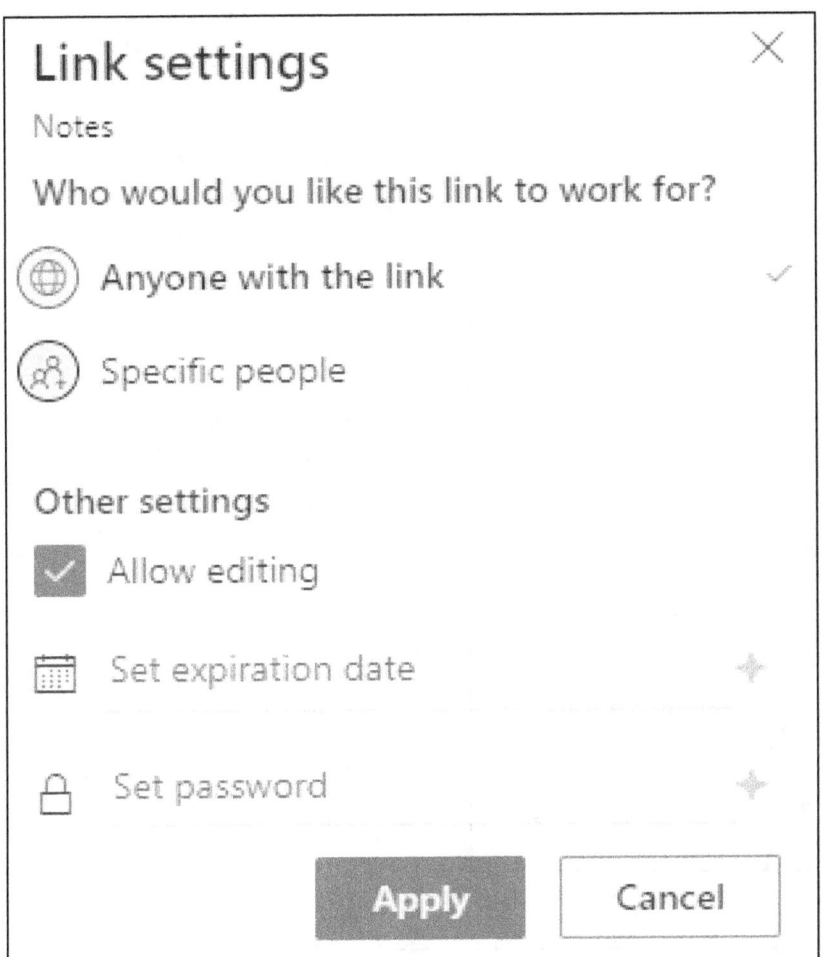

Figure 9.2

You can then right click on the file and choose *Details* to see who has access to that file (figure 9.3). Then you can click on *Manage access* to change permission levels or remove access to your file (figure 9.4). From here you can also click on *Grant Access* to give additional people access to your file.

Chapter 9 – Sharing, Downloading and Printing Your Files

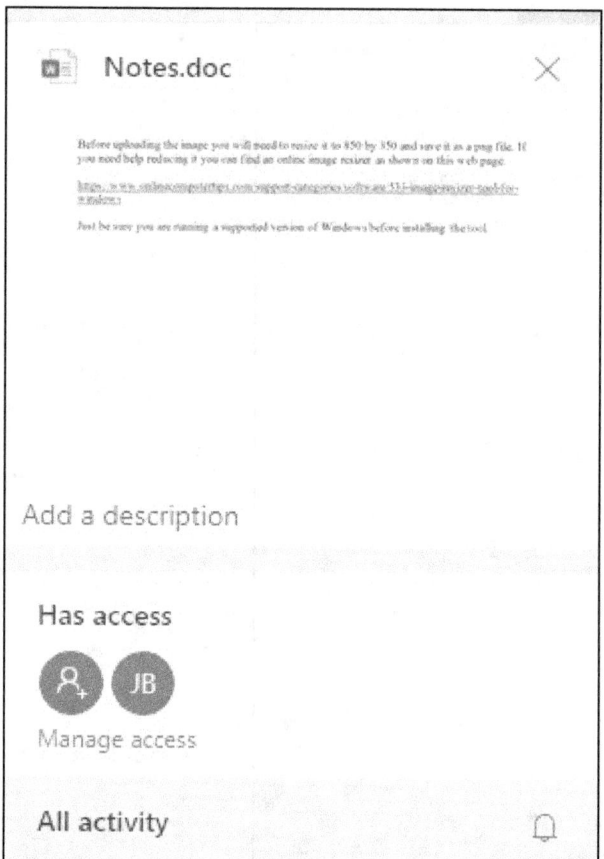
Figure 9.3

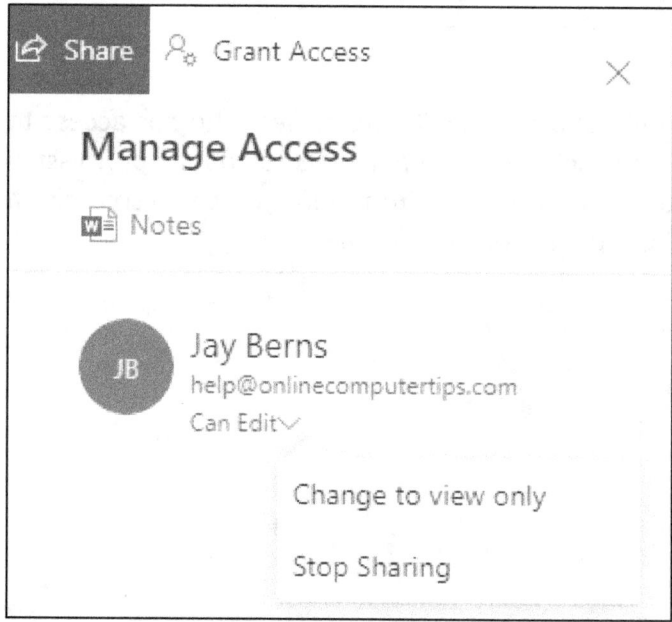
Figure 9.4

Chapter 9 – Sharing, Downloading and Printing Your Files

Another way to share your files is to go to the File menu within the app itself. Figure 9.5 shows the file menu for Word which will look the same for Excel, PowerPoint and OneNote. From here you can click on *Share with People* to bring up the same share dialog box as seen in figure 9.1.

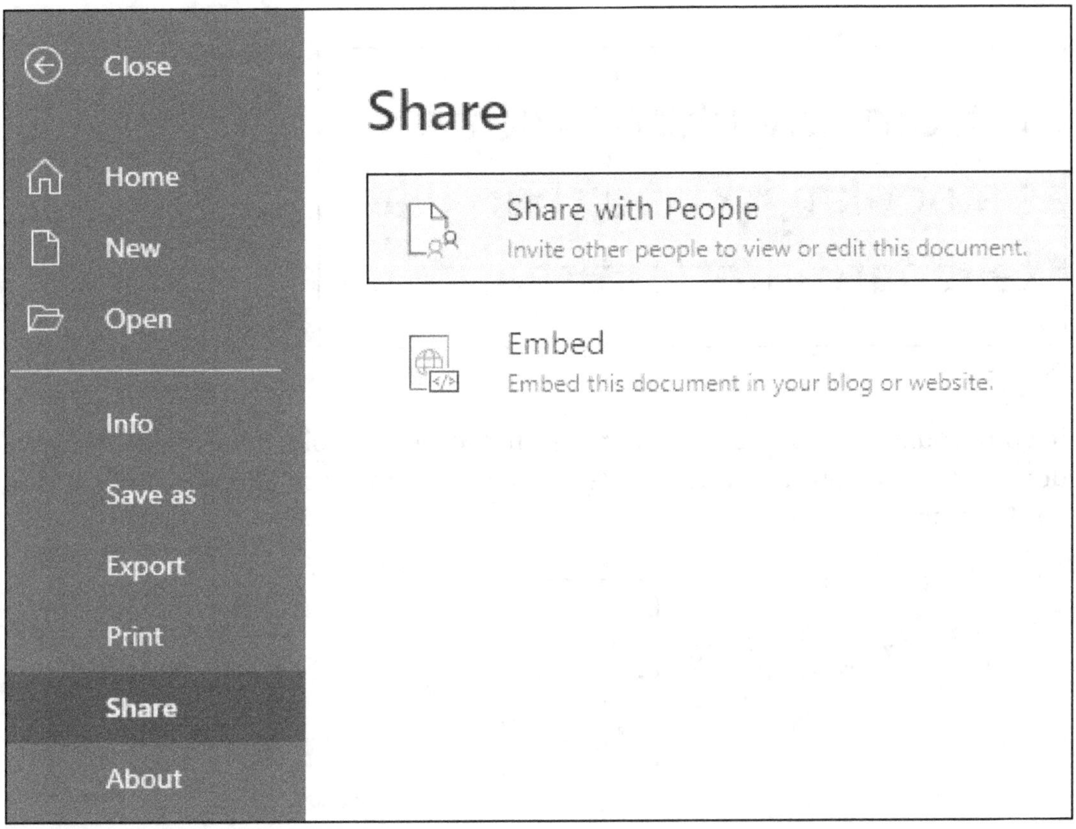

Figure 9.5

You should also see a Share button in the Ribbon of each app as well that will allow you to do the same thing.

Figure 9.6

Chapter 9 – Sharing, Downloading and Printing Your Files

Once you share a file (a Word document in my example) you will know when someone else has your file open because you will see their initials by the share button as seen in figure 9.6. You will also have a marker in your document that shows where in the document they are working as seen in figure 9.7. This is just an estimate and is based on where their mouse cursor currently resides.

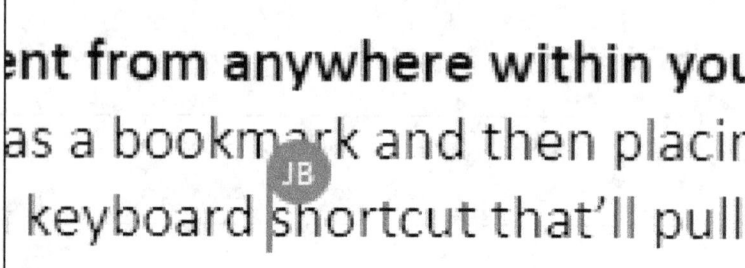

Figure 9.7

If you would like to see the changes that other people have made to your document then you can go to the *Review* tab click on *Track Changes* and set it to *For Everyone*.

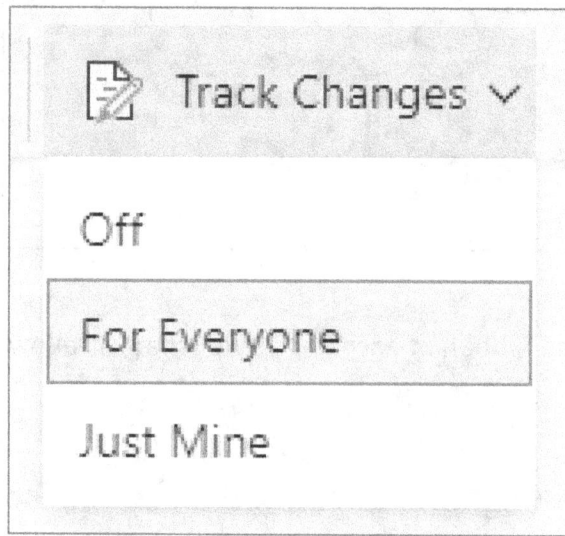

Figure 9.8

Then if you refresh the page you will see markups on the page that show what was changed. For example, figure 9.9 shows that the number 24 was changed to 23, the number 25 was changed to 24 and an exclamation point was added to the end of the last sentence. You can also see vertical lines off to the left of the paragraphs that have been changed by other people.

Chapter 9 – Sharing, Downloading and Printing Your Files

> 24~~3~~. **Start a new document from anywhere within your browser** by adding docs.google.com/create as a bookmark and then placing it in your bookmarks bar—or creating a custom keyboard shortcut that'll pull the link up on demand.
>
> 2~~5~~4. Don't limit yourself to Docs' list of default fonts. You can **add dozens of fonts into your word processing setup**—and once their added, they'll always be available in the regular font dropdown menu. All you have to do are open that dropdown menu and look for the "More fonts" optioned at the top. Click it and browse or search Google's web font archive to find the style that meets your needs—then write away with the right look for every project you tackle.

Figure 9.9

If you hover your mouse over one of these changes you can see who made the change as well as the date and time it was made.

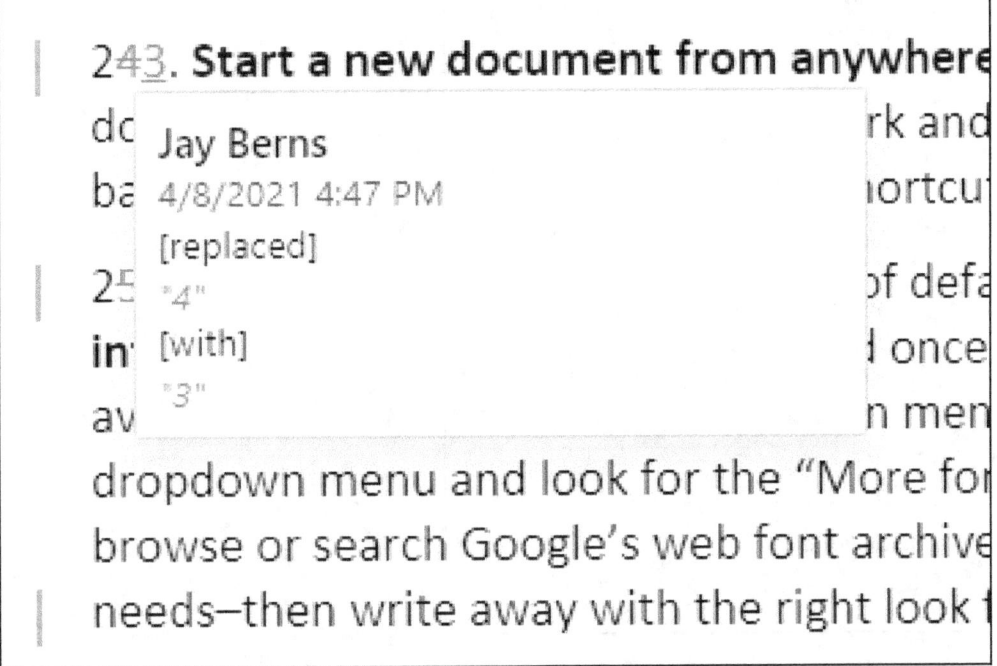

Figure 9.10

Now if I were to go back to the file in OneDrive, right click on it and choose *Details* I would see who has edited the file and when.

Chapter 9 – Sharing, Downloading and Printing Your Files

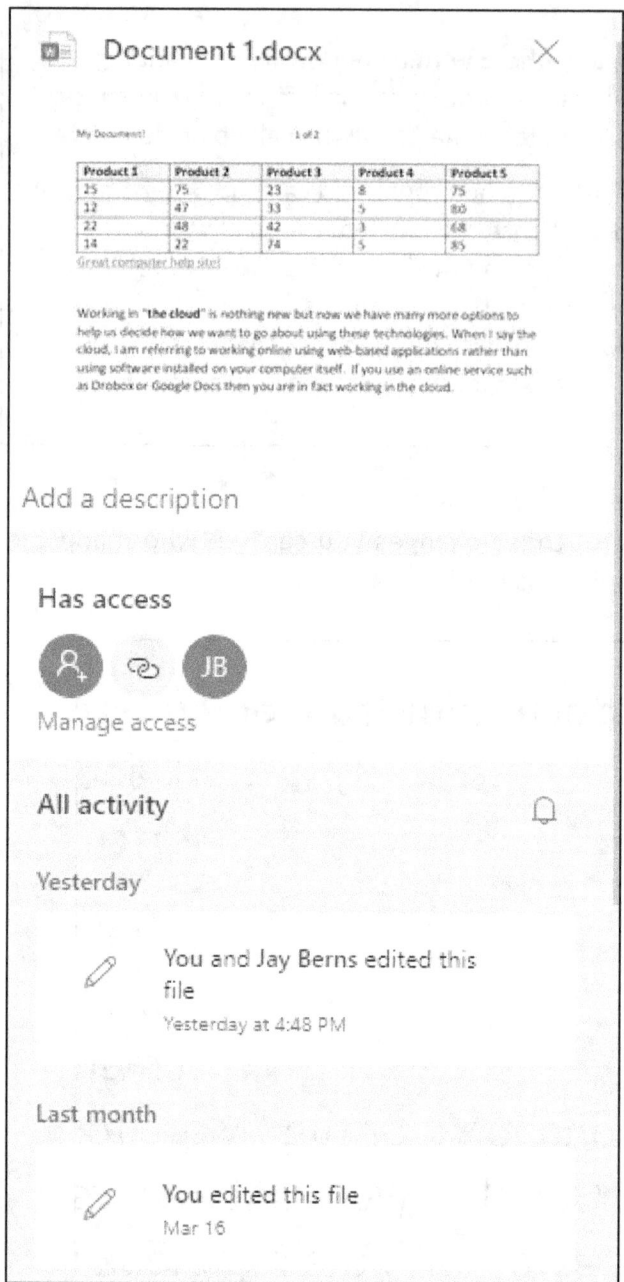

Figure 9.11

Sharing works the same for all of the Office apps for the most part, but I do want to show you how to share a calendar in Outlook. Let's say I created a new calendar called **Sales Shared Calendar**. You remember how to create a new calendar right?

Chapter 9 – Sharing, Downloading and Printing Your Files

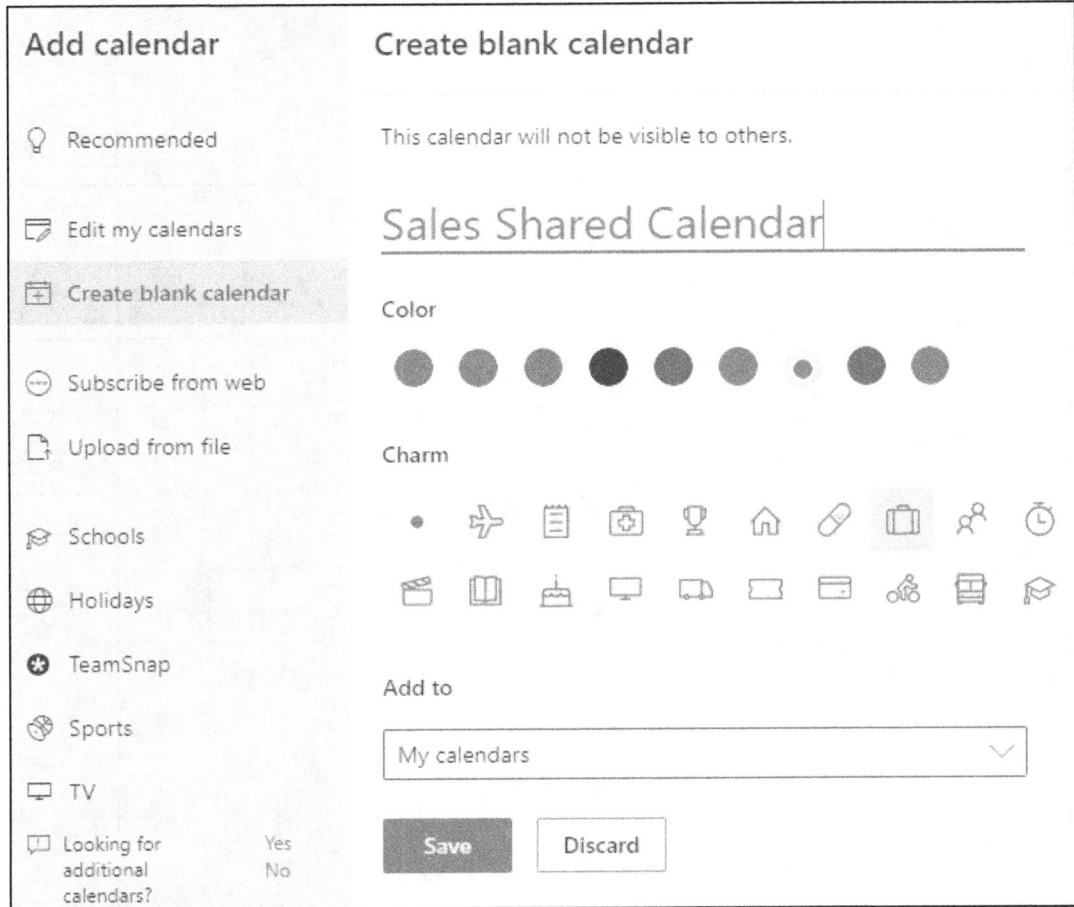

Figure 9.12

Then from the calendar itself I will click on the ellipsis and choose *Sharing and Permissions*.

Chapter 9 – Sharing, Downloading and Printing Your Files

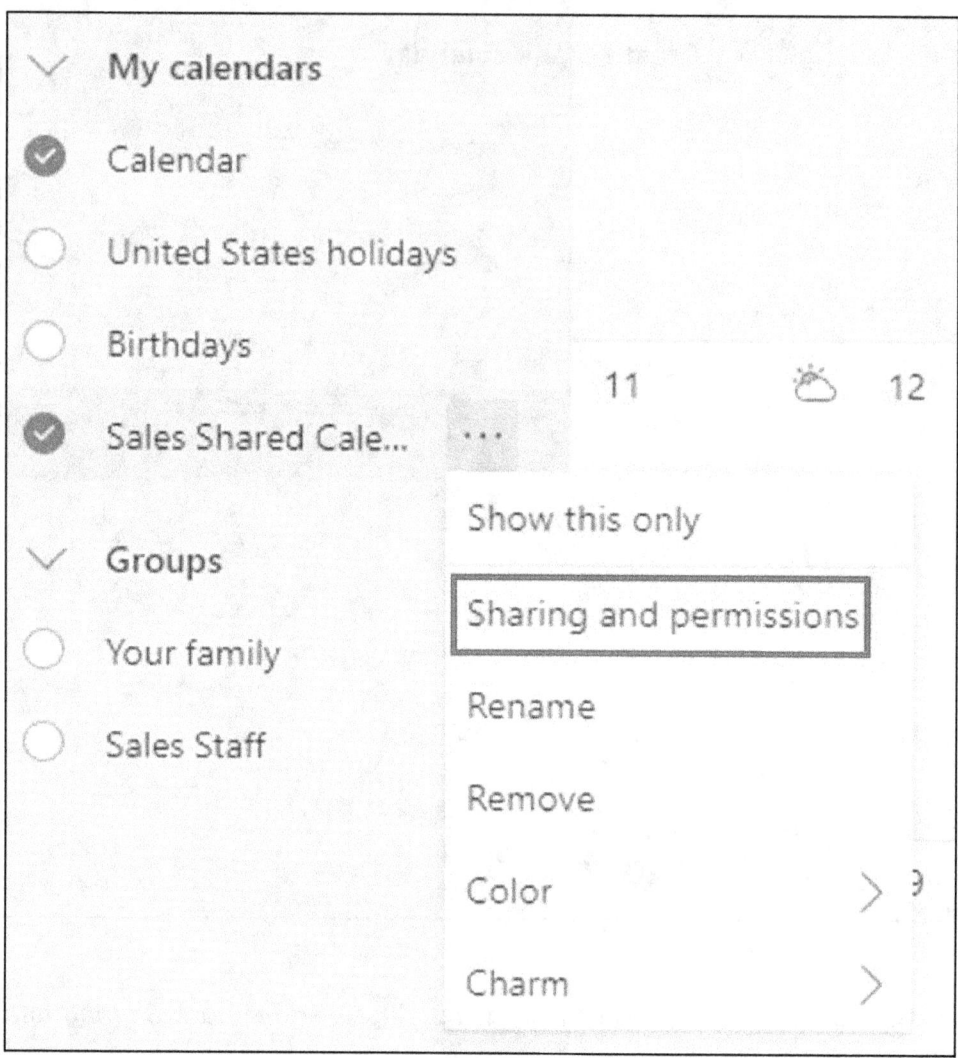

Figure 9.13

Then I would enter the email addresses of the people I want to share it with and choose whether they can edit my calendar or just view the details and then click on *Share*.

Chapter 9 – Sharing, Downloading and Printing Your Files

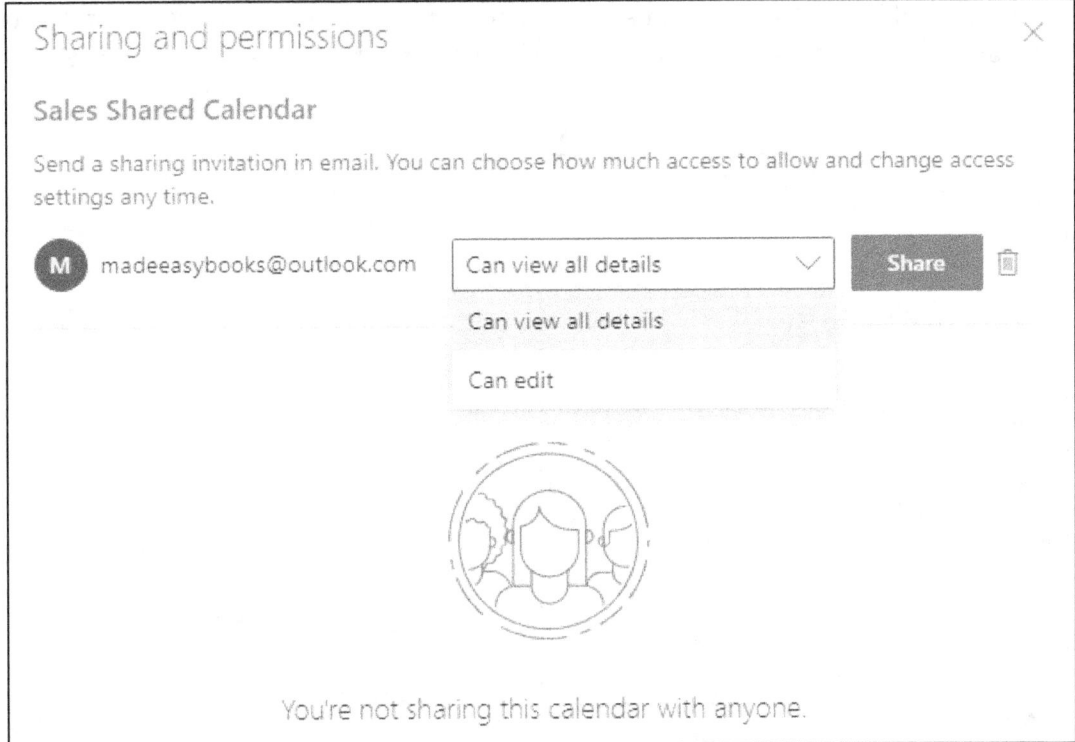

Figure 9.14

Then the person you shared the calendar with will get an email inviting them to access your calendar.

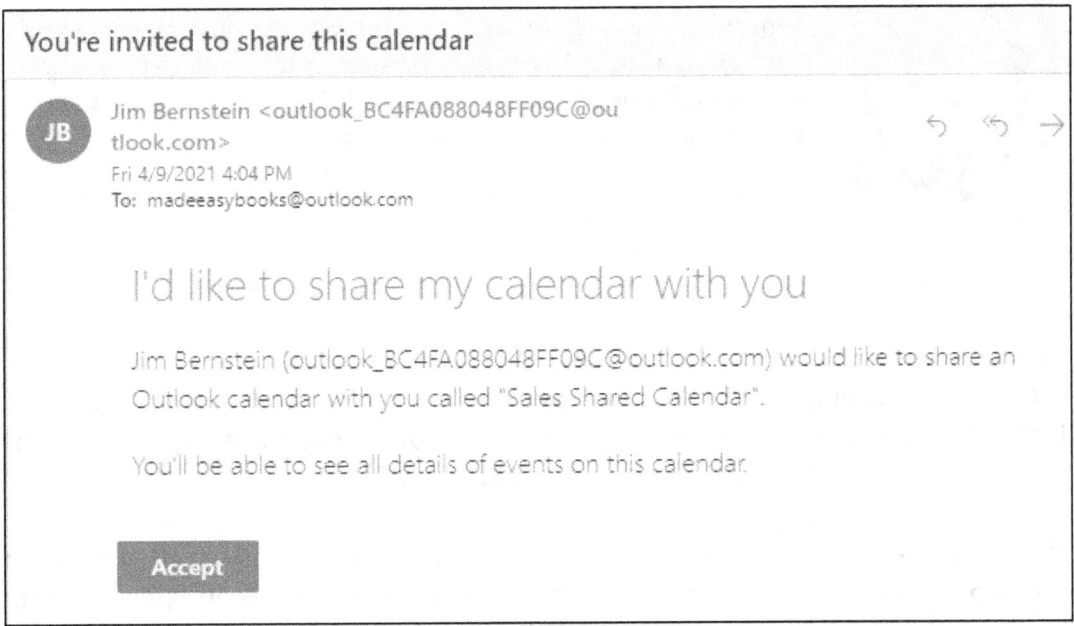

Figure 9.15

Then you will have that shared calendar added to your list of calendars and you can turn it off or on as needed, as well as change the name or color of those calendar events.

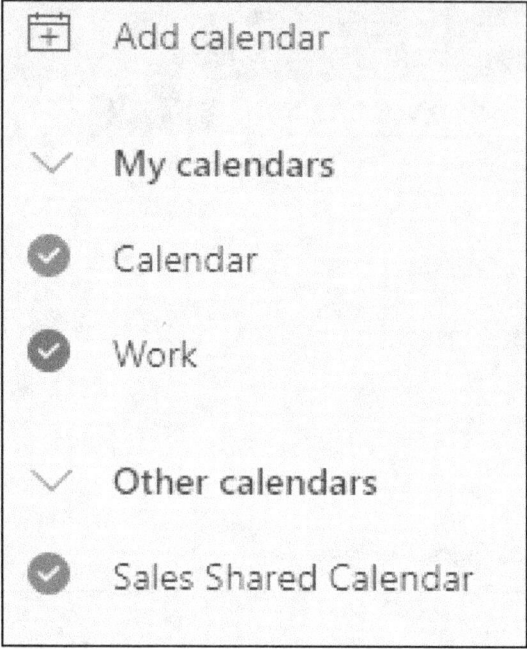

Figure 9.16

 If you want to you share your calendar with non outlook.com users (such as Gmail users), they will only be able to accept the invitation using an outlook.com or a Microsoft 365 account so keep that in mind before sending out the invitation.

Downloading and Exporting Your Files
After you use Office for the Web for a while, you might start to notice some of the limitations it has compared to the desktop version or even the pay for versions such as Office 365 if you use them at work for example.

If you have access to the desktop version or a paid online version then you can download your files from the Office for the Web version and then open them up in one of those other versions. Or maybe you want to backup your files on an

Chapter 9 – Sharing, Downloading and Printing Your Files

external hard drive or work on them offline or even in another app such as Google Apps.

Fortunately, it's easy to download or export your files so you can work with them elsewhere if needed. The process is very similar between the different Office apps with the exception of a few different exporting options that are application specific.

If I were to go into the Word app and then to the File tab I would see the options as shown in figure 9.17

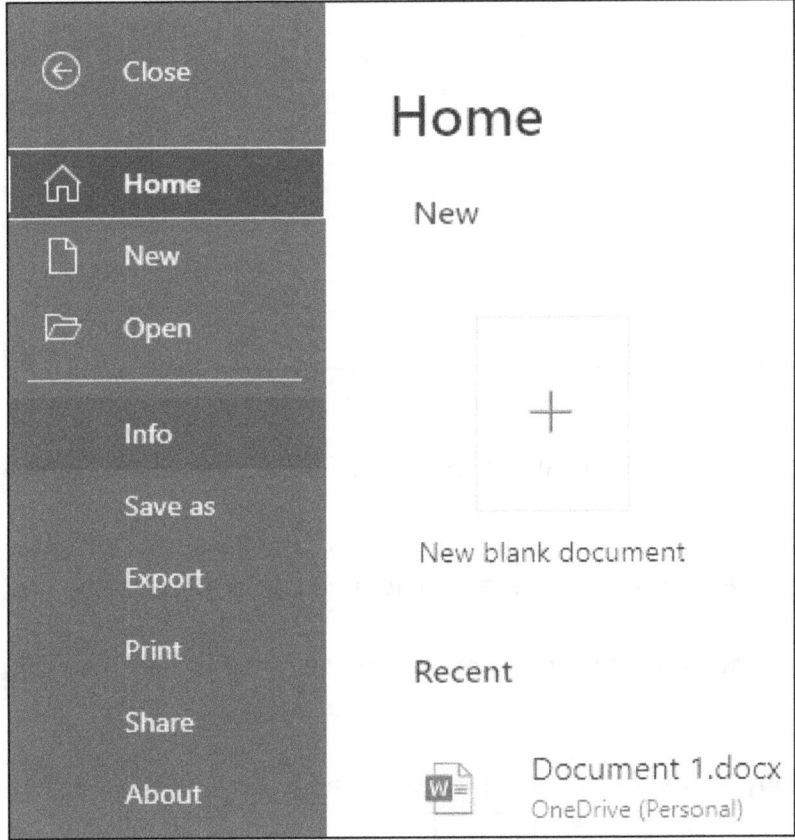

Figure 9.17

You can see that there is a *Save as* choice and also an *Export* choice. If I were to click on Save as I would be given several choices as to how I want to save my file.

321

Chapter 9 – Sharing, Downloading and Printing Your Files

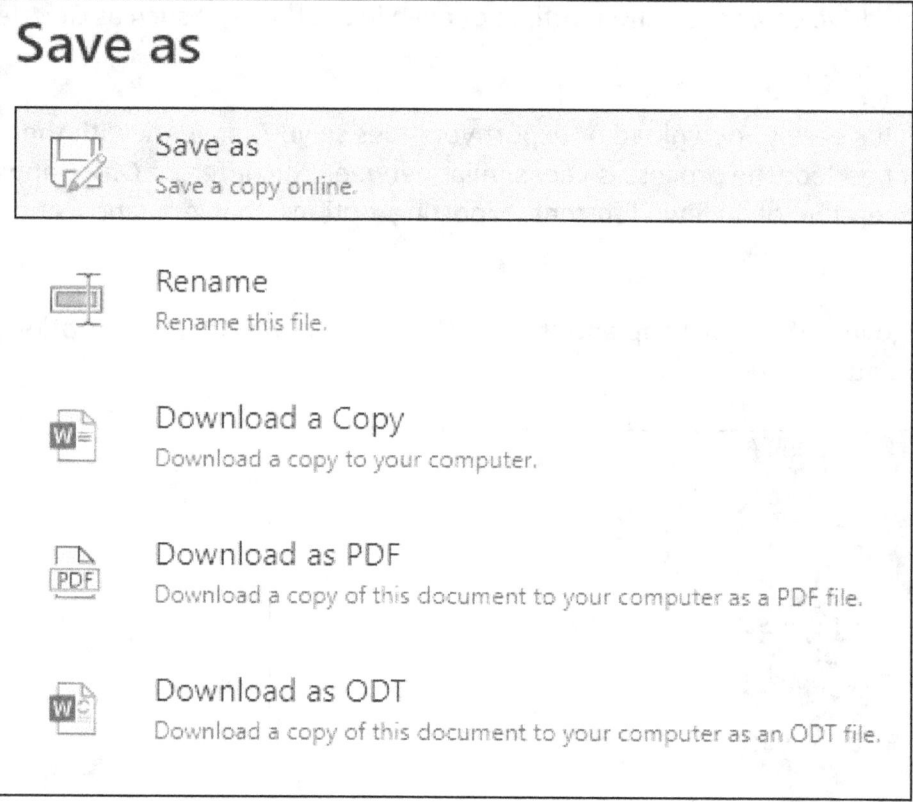

Figure 9.18

Here is what each one of these options will allow me to do.

- **Save as** – This will allow me to save another copy of my file with a different name or in a different location leaving me with two copies of the same file.

- **Rename** – If I want to change the name of the current file I can use this option.

- **Download a Copy** – This will allow me to download a copy of my file to the hard drive of my computer in Word format.

- **Download as PDF** – If I need my file in a PDF version I can choose this option and then save the new PDF file to my hard drive.

- **Download as ODT** – This will allow me to download a copy of my file in OpenDocument Text format which can then be opened in a variety of different word processing software.

Chapter 9 – Sharing, Downloading and Printing Your Files

If I choose the *Download a Copy* option, I will be prompted to choose the location on my hard drive where I would like the file to be downloaded to. It's important to select the proper location or at least remember where you downloaded your file to so you can find it later.

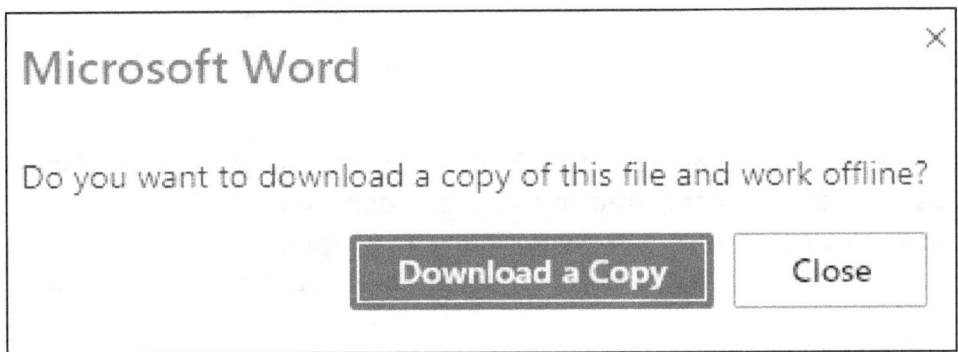
Figure 9.19

The way you get prompted to download the file will differ depending on what web browser you use. Figure 9.20 shows how the process will look in the Microsoft Edge browser where I would click on *Save as* and then choose a location on my computer.

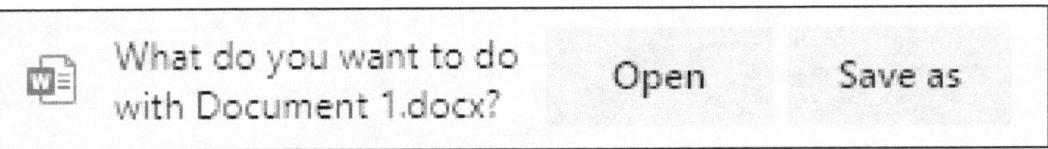
Figure 9.20

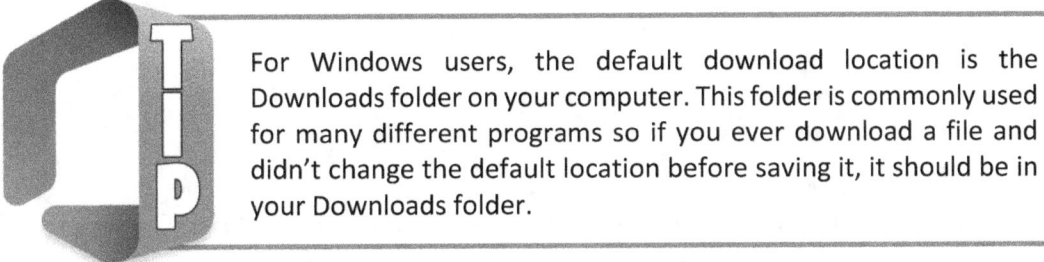

For Windows users, the default download location is the Downloads folder on your computer. This folder is commonly used for many different programs so if you ever download a file and didn't change the default location before saving it, it should be in your Downloads folder.

If I were to choose the *Export* version I would be able to export my Word file to a PowerPoint presentation, but Word would decide how it would be laid out and it might not be the way you would want it to look.

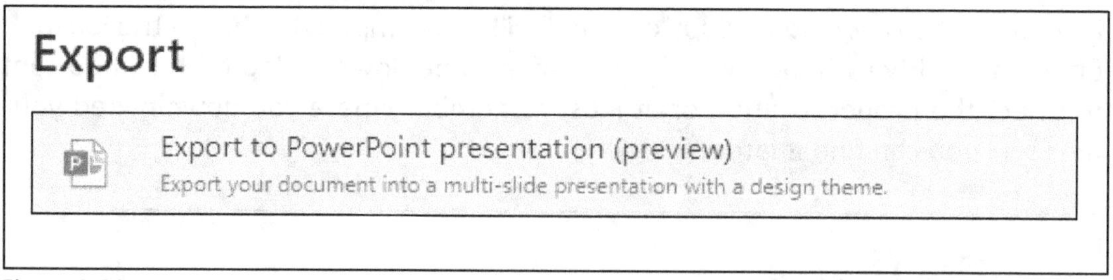

Chapter 9 – Sharing, Downloading and Printing Your Files

Export

 Export to PowerPoint presentation (preview)
Export your document into a multi-slide presentation with a design theme.

Figure 9.21

As you can see in figures 9.22 and 9.23, PowerPoint and Excel have slightly different Save as options compared to Word and don't have an Export option. PowerPoint will let you save your presentation as an *OpenDocument Presentation* file and Excel will let you save your spreadsheet as an *OpenDocument Spreadsheet* file.

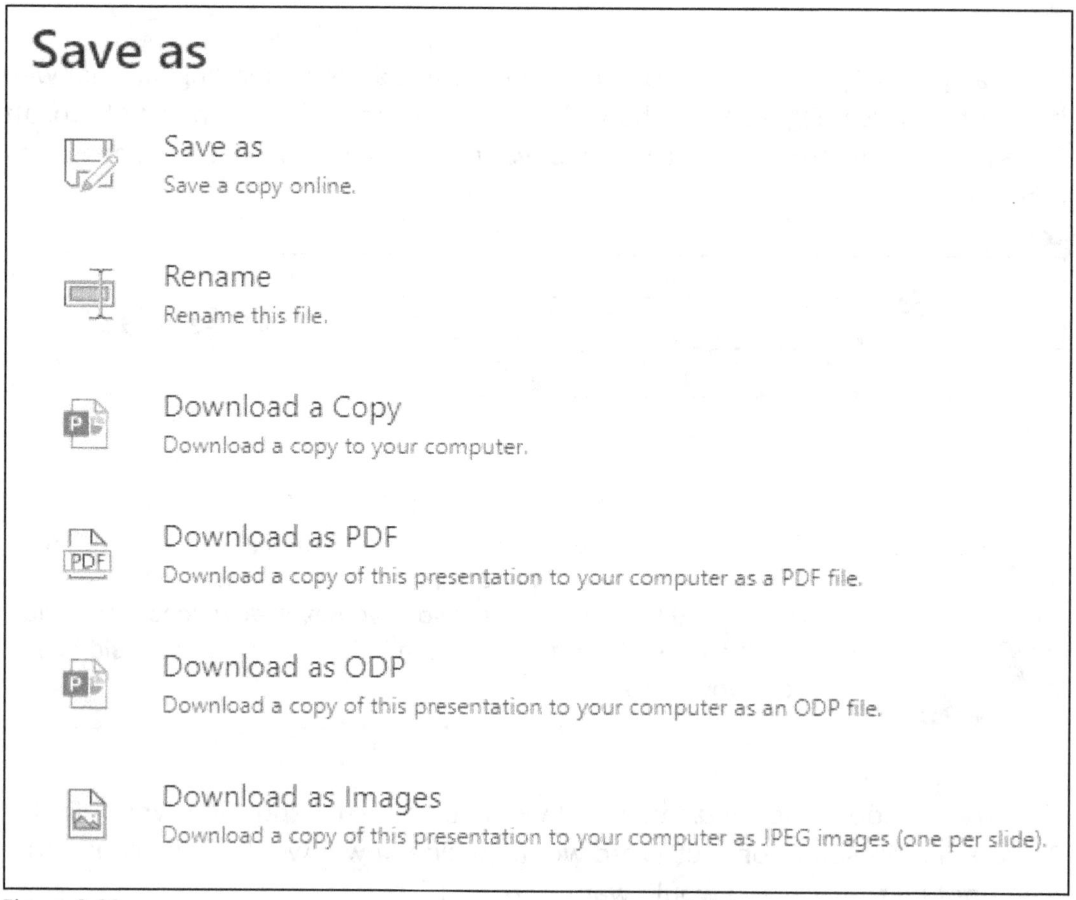

Save as

Save as
Save a copy online.

Rename
Rename this file.

Download a Copy
Download a copy to your computer.

Download as PDF
Download a copy of this presentation to your computer as a PDF file.

Download as ODP
Download a copy of this presentation to your computer as an ODP file.

Download as Images
Download a copy of this presentation to your computer as JPEG images (one per slide).

Figure 9.22

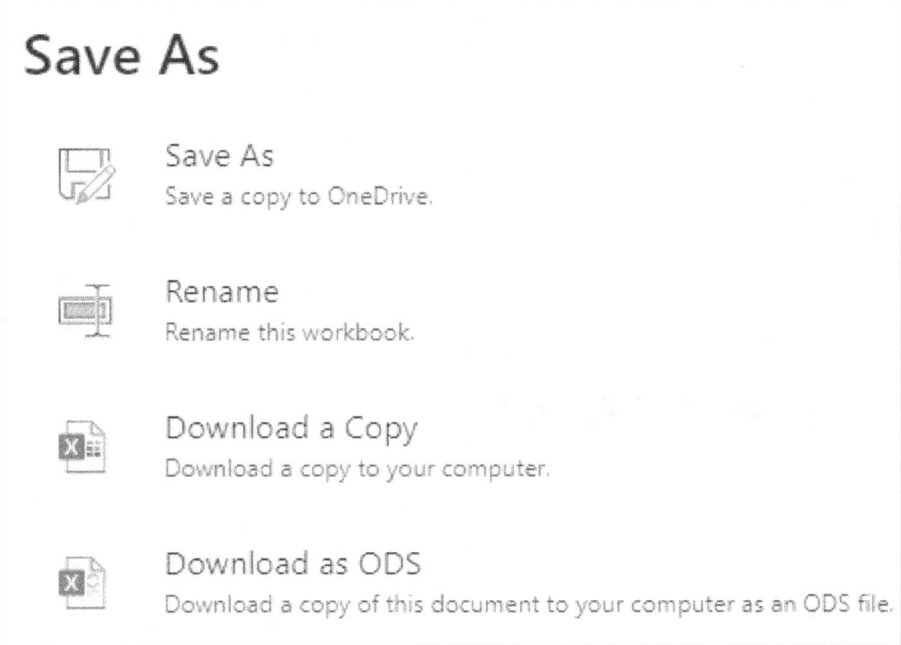

Figure 9.23

Printing and Page Setup
Even though paper printouts are becoming a thing of the past and all of our documents are being maintained digitally, you will still need to print out your work once in a while so it's good to know how to accomplish this.

Before you print out your work you should make sure that your page setup is correct so your copy will look the same way on paper as it does on the screen. When you go to the File menu and then click on Print you will be able to change some of the page setup options but you should also check things like page size and margin widths before you even start the printing process.

For Word documents, you should go to the Layout tab, for Excel files you should go to the Page Layout tab, and for PowerPoint files the Design tab and then Slide Size.

When you are ready to print you can adjust any other settings as needed and the setup options will vary depending on what app you are printing from.

Chapter 9 – Sharing, Downloading and Printing Your Files

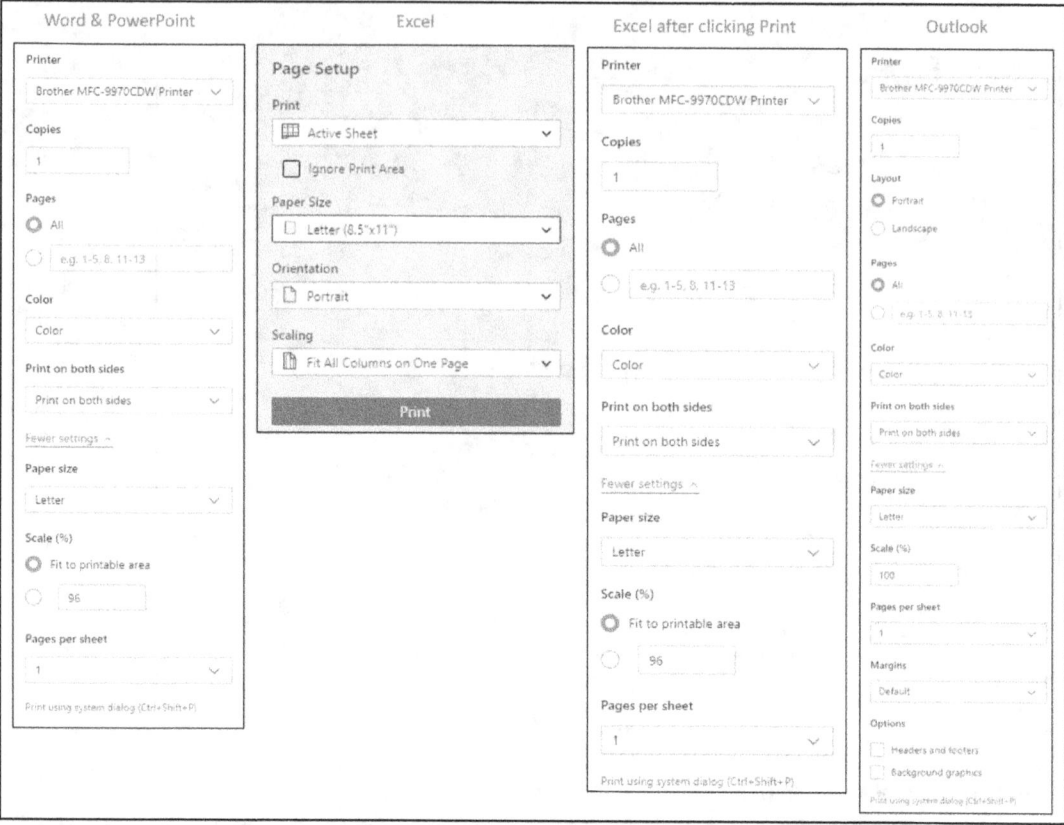

Figure 9.24

I will now take some time to discuss the various printing options.

- **Printer** – Here is where you can choose what printer to send the print job too assuming you have more than one.

- **Copies** – Enter the number of copies you wish to print. If you have a 3 page document and choose 2 copies, you will end up printing 6 sheets of paper.

- **Pages** – This tells the app which pages to print. You can choose all of the pages or a range such as **2-5** or even a range and individual pages such as **2-5, 7, 9** to have it print pages 2 through 5 plus pages 7 and 9.

- **Color** – If you want your printout to be in black and white only then choose the *Black and White* option, otherwise it will print in color assuming you have a color printer.

- **Print on both sides** – If your printer supports duplexing (printing on both sides) then you can save paper by using this option.

- **Paper Size** – This tells the app what size to format your print job for. Just make sure that your printer uses the size of paper that you set this to.

- **Scale** – Here you can shrink or enlarge your print job to take up less or more of the page. Just make sure you don't make it too large where parts of it get cut off.

- **Pages per sheet** – This will allow you to print out multiple pages on one sheet of paper. Just keep in mind that the more pages you add to a sheet, the smaller each page will be printed.

- **Margins** – This is an Outlook only option where you can change your margin size from default to none, minimum or custom to make your email fit the page for printing.

- **Headers and footers** – If your email has headers or footers and you want them to print out then check this box. This is another Outlook only option.

- **Background graphics** – If your email has a background graphic and you want it to print out then check this box. Just be aware that it might make the email harder to read on paper. This is another Outlook only option.

Speaking of printing emails, in order to find the print option for your emails you can go to the ellipsis within that email and then select the Print choice.

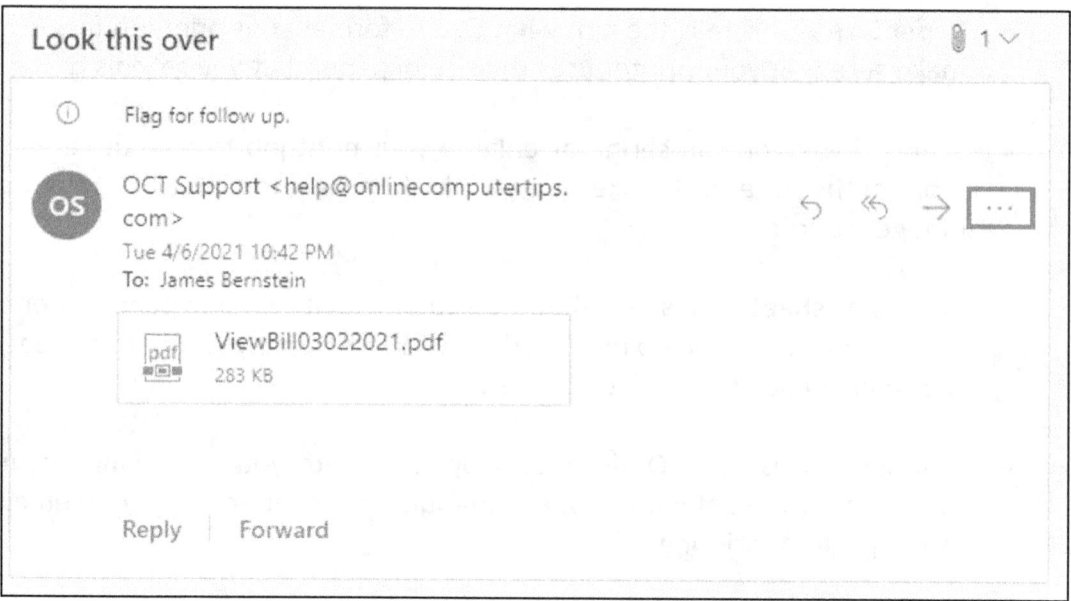

Figure 9.25

One thing you might have noticed in the print configuration box is the *Print using system dialog* link. This will allow you to use the printing options that come with Windows (or Mac) rather than the web based options that come with Office.

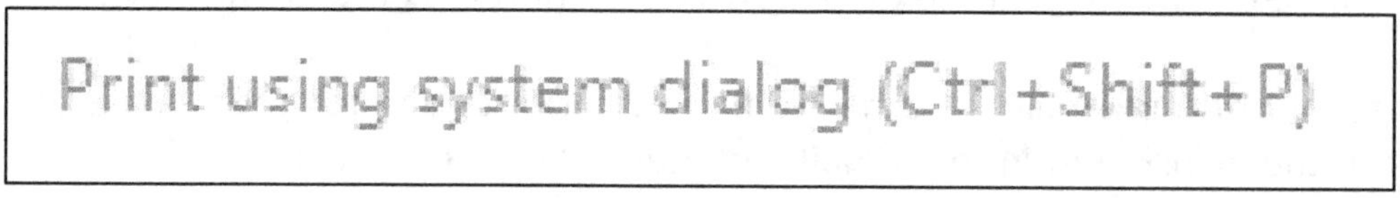

Print using system dialog (Ctrl+Shift+P)

Figure 9.26

You might be more used to seeing this type of printer screen than the ones that you will see within the Office apps.

Chapter 9 – Sharing, Downloading and Printing Your Files

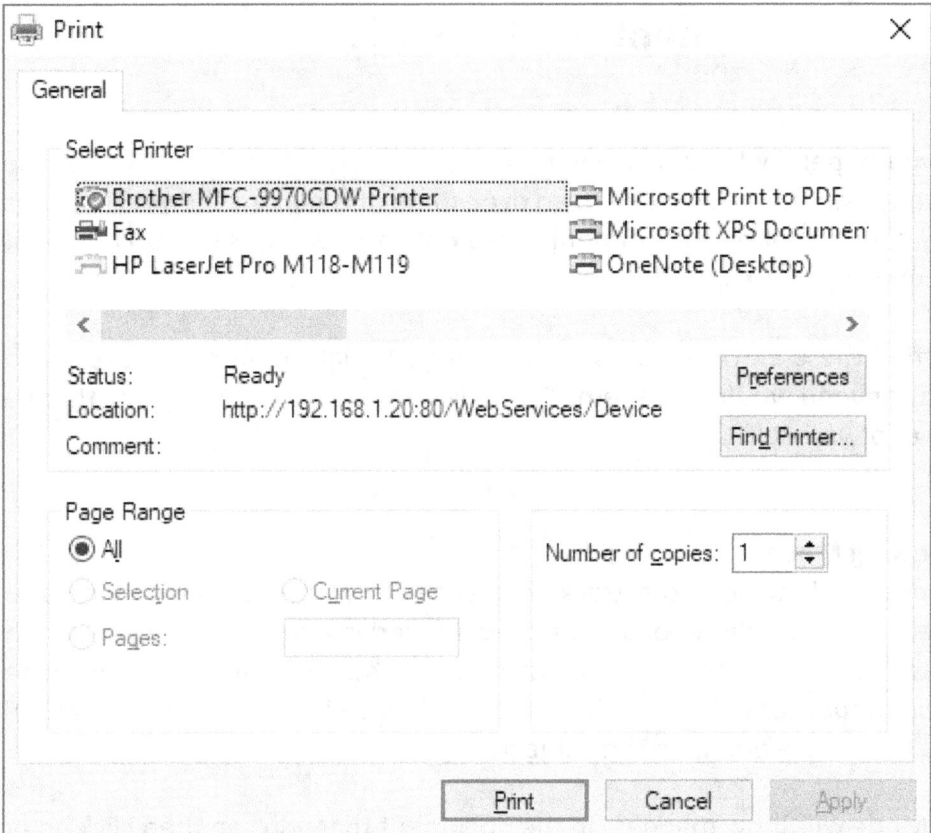

Figure 9.27

Chapter 10 - Extras

Now that you hopefully have a really good idea of how all of the Office for the Web applications work, I would like to go over some of the extra "bonus" features of Office that might not be as commonly used but can be just as helpful as any of the more popular features.

You might find these extra features helpful, or you might read about them and wonder why anyone would use them. The only way to find out is to give them a shot and see for yourself!

Word Reviewing Mode
In the last chapter I talked about tracking changes to your shared documents so you can see what your fellow collaborators were working on. In order to see what changes have been made by who you will need to change your document mode to *Reviewing Mode*. Some of this information will be a bit repetitive but I wanted to go into a little more detail on the subject.

Reviewing Mode will show markups in the document that you can then click on or hover your mouse over to see who made the changes. To enter Reviewing Mode you will need to go to the mode menu which should be on Editing by default and change it to Reviewing.

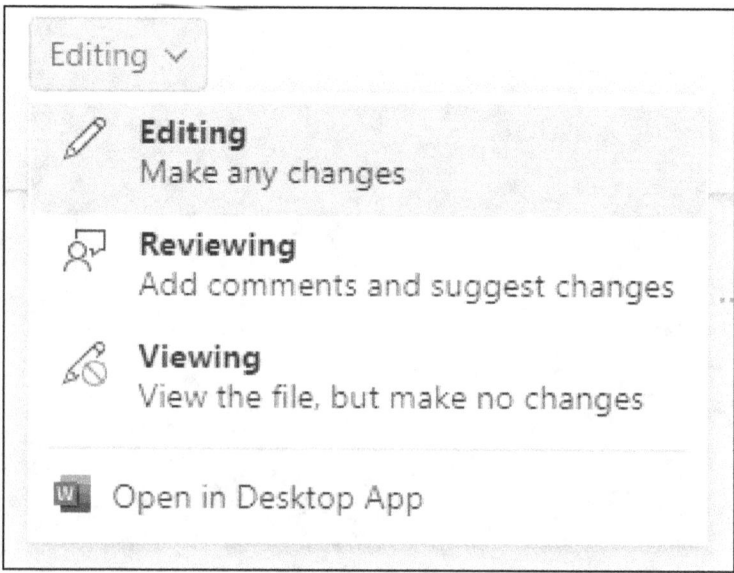

Figure 10.1

Chapter 10 - Extras

You will also need to enable the *Track Changes>For Everyone* mode on the Review tab to see others changes.

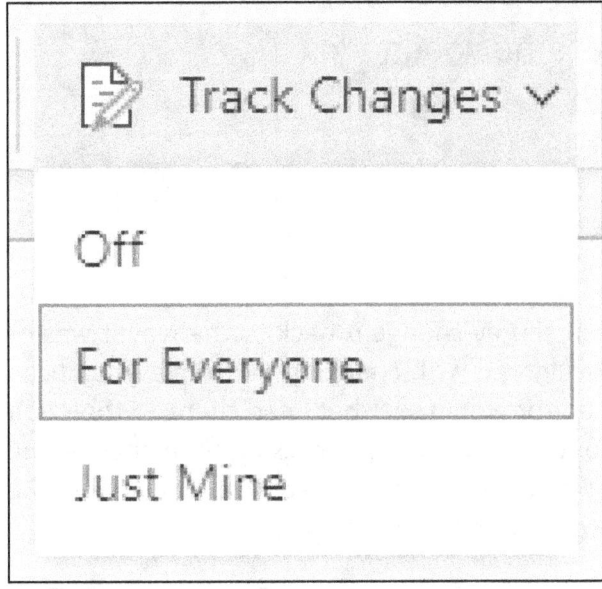

Figure 10.2

If someone else is in your document when you enable change tracking they will see a popup in their Word window.

Figure 10.3

Once you do that you will be able to see the changes made by others. If they are currently working on your shared document you will be able to see where they are at and the changes they made but you can also see this in Editing mode.

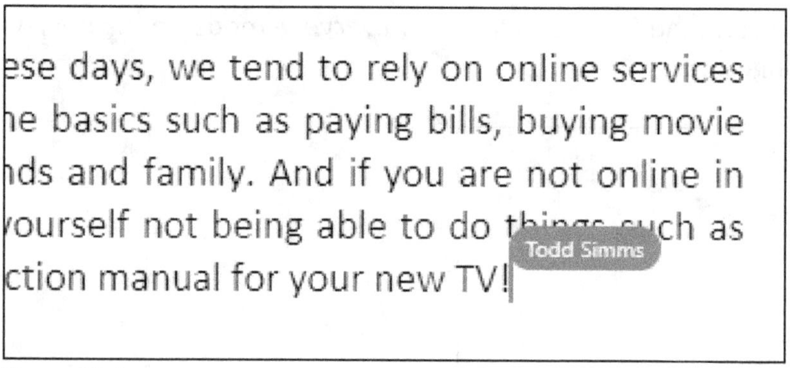

Chapter 10 - Extras

> ese days, we tend to rely on online services
> e basics such as paying bills, buying movie
> ds and family. And if you are not online in
> ourself not being able to do things such as   *Todd Simms*
> ction manual for your new TV!

Figure 10.4

If you disagree with a change you can simply change it back to the way it was or change it to something else. So if I disagreed with changing TV to television I can simply change it back and the other editor would see that I had changed their edit and their change would be crossed out. Or you can right click on their change and choose *Reject Format Change* or *Reject Replacement* etc. depending on the change and have the change reverted back to the way it was.

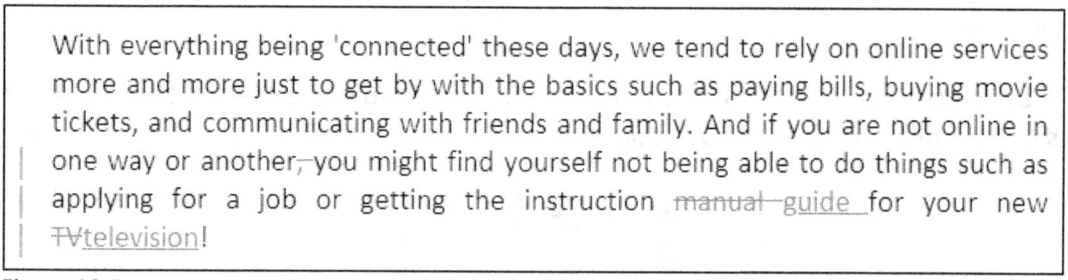

> With everything being 'connected' these days, we tend to rely on online services more and more just to get by with the basics such as paying bills, buying movie tickets, and communicating with friends and family. And if you are not online in one way or another, you might find yourself not being able to do things such as applying for a job or getting the instruction ~~manual~~ guide for your new ~~TV~~television!

Figure 10.5

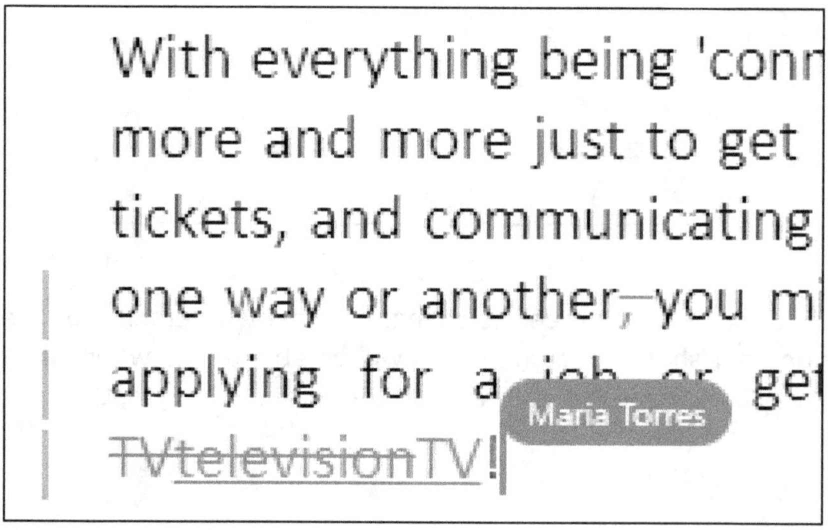

> With everything being 'conn
> more and more just to get
> tickets, and communicating
> one way or another, you m
> applying for a ~~job or~~ ge   *Maria Torres*
> ~~TV~~television~~TV~~!

Figure 10.6

They can also hover their mouse over the change to see details such as when it was done and by whom.

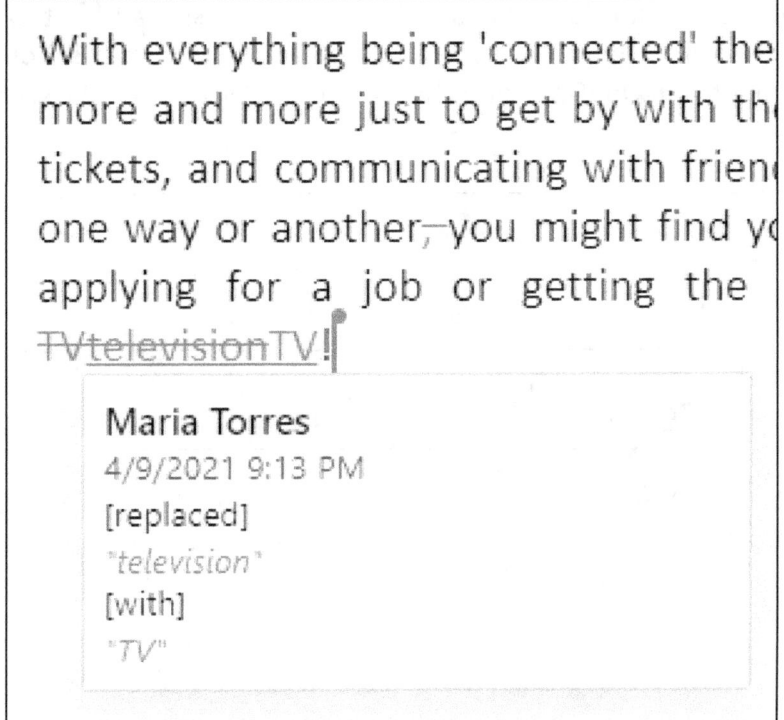

Figure 10.7

If you don't want to see tracking mode you can go back to Editing or Viewing mode, but you will be warned that turning off tracking will turn off change tracking for everyone until you turn it back on again.

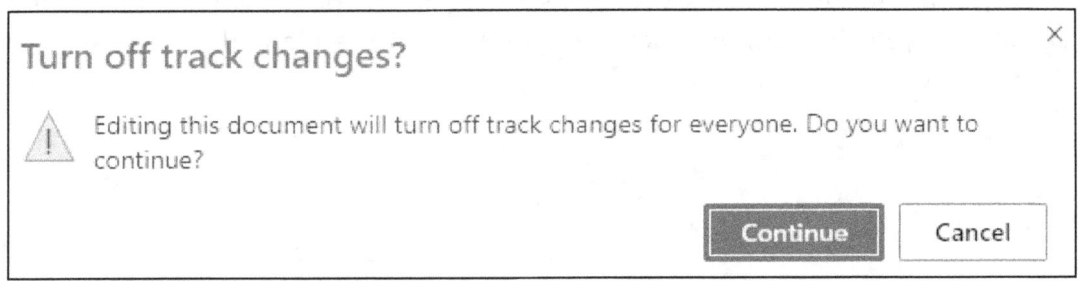

Figure 10.8

Previous Versions
One great thing about working online in the cloud besides having a reputable company backing up your files is the ability to revert back to different versions of

Chapter 10 - Extras

your files if needed. If you keep backups of your files on your computer then you can do the same thing depending on the method you use for your backups.

If you need to view or restore an older version of a document, spreadsheet or presentation you can go to the *File* tab and then click on *Previous Versions*. You can also right click on your file in OneDrive and choose *Version History* to take you to the same place.

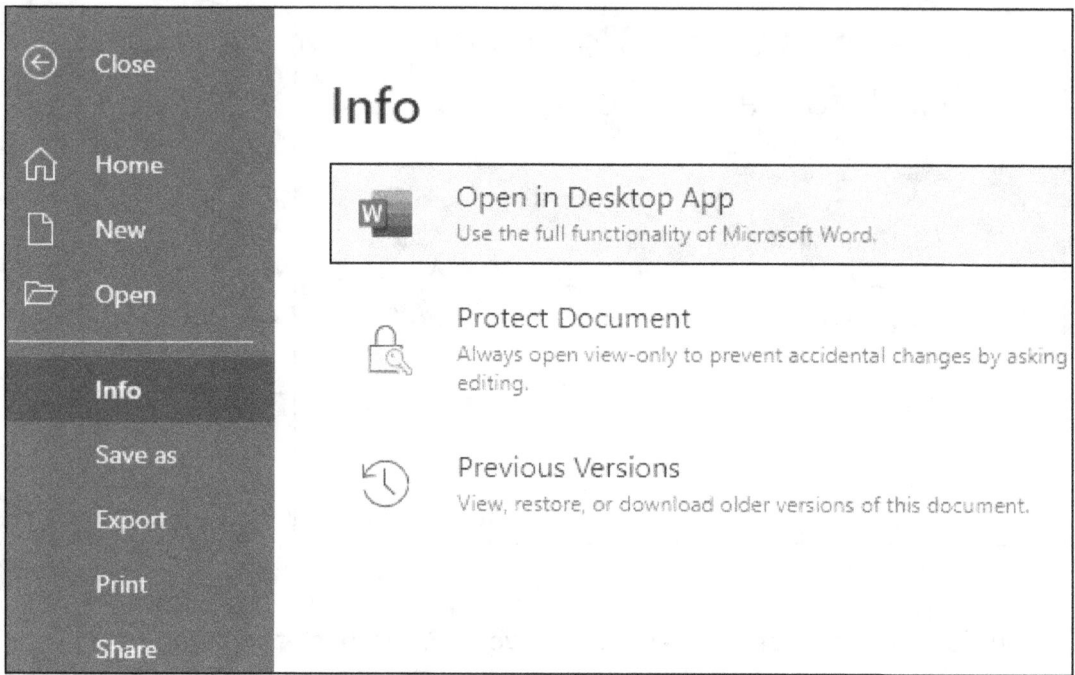

Figure 10.9

Once you are in the Previous Versions screen you will be shown all of the older versions of your file with its date and a preview of the file and time as seen in figure 10.10.

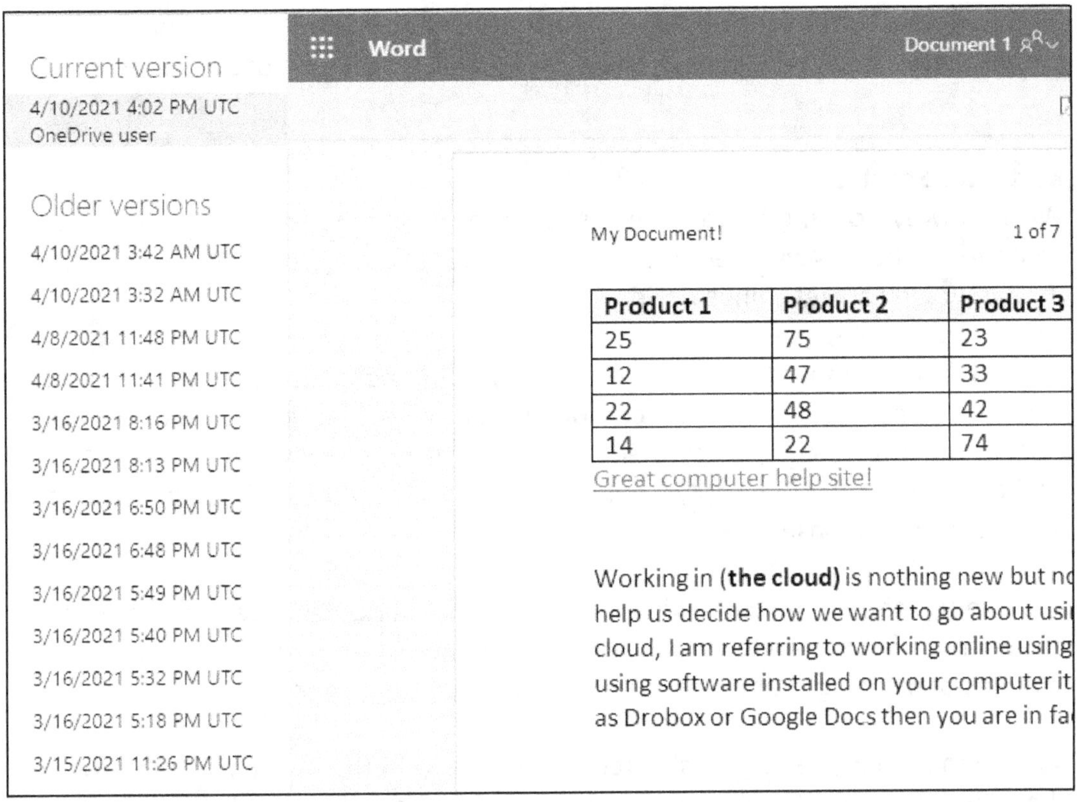

Chapter 10 - Extras

[Figure showing OneDrive version history panel with current version 4/10/2021 4:02 PM UTC by OneDrive user, and list of older versions dating from 4/10/2021 3:42 AM UTC back to 3/15/2021 11:26 PM UTC, alongside a document preview showing "My Document!" with a table of Product 1, Product 2, Product 3 values and text about working in the cloud]

Figure 10.10

If you were to click on an older date then you would see a preview of that file from that date and be given an option to restore or download the file to your computer. If you are using a personal Microsoft account, you can retrieve the last 25 versions of a file.

Figure 10.11

335

Chapter 10 - Extras

If you choose the *Restore* option then that version of the file will become your current version so make sure this is what you want to do before doing so.

Keyboard Shortcuts
We are always looking for faster ways to do things and when it comes to using our computers, the less we need to take our hands off the keyboard to use the mouse, the faster we can get things done.

This is where keyboard shortcuts can help you be more efficient with your work. Keyboard shortcuts consist of a combination of keys that you press to perform a certain function such as copy or make your text bold. Windows has a bunch of keyboard shortcuts that apply to many different programs and the same goes for Apple Macintosh based computers.

You can use these shortcuts while working in the various Office apps to help you get your work done a little quicker. Once you get them memorized you will find that you start using them without even thinking about them.

For the most part, keyboard shortcuts are written in the order you need to press the keys. You might be used to pressing Ctrl-Alt-Del when logging into your computer at work and you press the keys in that order to do so. On a standard keyboard, you will have two *Ctrl*, *Alt* and *Shift* keys and it usually doesn't matter which one you use.

There are more keyboard shortcuts available than anyone will ever want to learn so here are some of the more common and useful shortcuts that I think you should know about.

Find text	CTRL+F, or F3
Hide the Search pane	ESC
Switch to Zoom control	CTRL+Z
Switch to page-number control	CTRL+G
Print	CTRL+P
Right one character	RIGHT ARROW
Left one character	LEFT ARROW
Right one word	CTRL+RIGHT ARROW

Chapter 10 - Extras

Left one word	CTRL+LEFT ARROW
Up one line	UP ARROW
Down one line	DOWN ARROW
Up one paragraph	CTRL+UP ARROW
Down one paragraph	CTRL+DOWN ARROW
Beginning of line	HOME
End of line	END
Beginning of page	CTRL+HOME
End of page	CTRL+END
Cut	CTRL+X
Copy	CTRL+C
Paste	CTRL+V
Insert hyperlink	CTRL+K
Undo	CTRL+Z
Redo	CTRL+Y
Move between misspelled words	ALT+F7
Bold	CTRL+B
Italics	CTRL+I
Underline	CTRL+U
Bulleted list	CTRL+PERIOD
Align left	CTRL+L
Align right	CTRL+R
Align centered	CTRL+E

Add-Ins

Office has a way for you to add extra functionality to your apps in the form of add-ins. These add-ins are additional software that integrates into your apps and

Chapter 10 - Extras

essentially become part of them. There are add-ins for all types of things from video players to additional clipart to emoji keyboards. Not all add-ins are made for all apps so you will need to read the description to see what Office apps they will work for.

To get to the add-ins section you can go to the *Insert* tab from your Office app and then click on *Add-ins*. You most likely won't have any add-ins unless you have added some in the past. To view the available add-ins you can click on the Office Store button to view what is available to add to your apps.

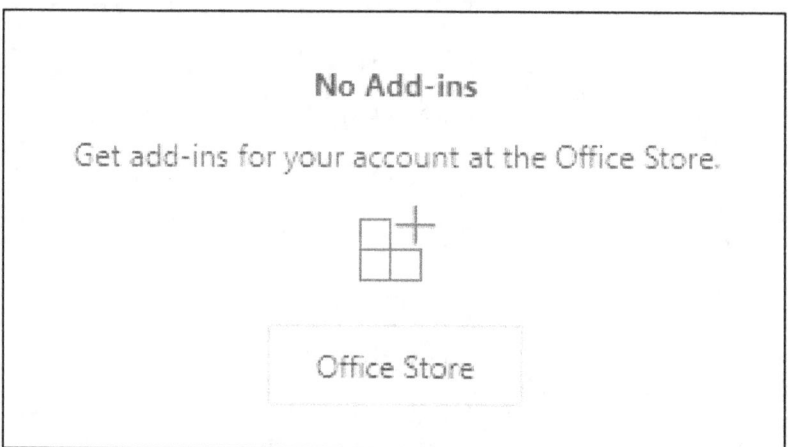

Figure 10.12

The add-ins will be sorted by suggested for you, rating or name depending on what option you choose. You will also see categories on the left if you want to narrow down your search or you can even type in a word or phrase in the search box to search for related apps. Once you find something you like all you need to do is click on the *Add* button. I will install the Pickit add-in which gives you high quality images to add to your PowerPoint presentations and Word documents.

Chapter 10 - Extras

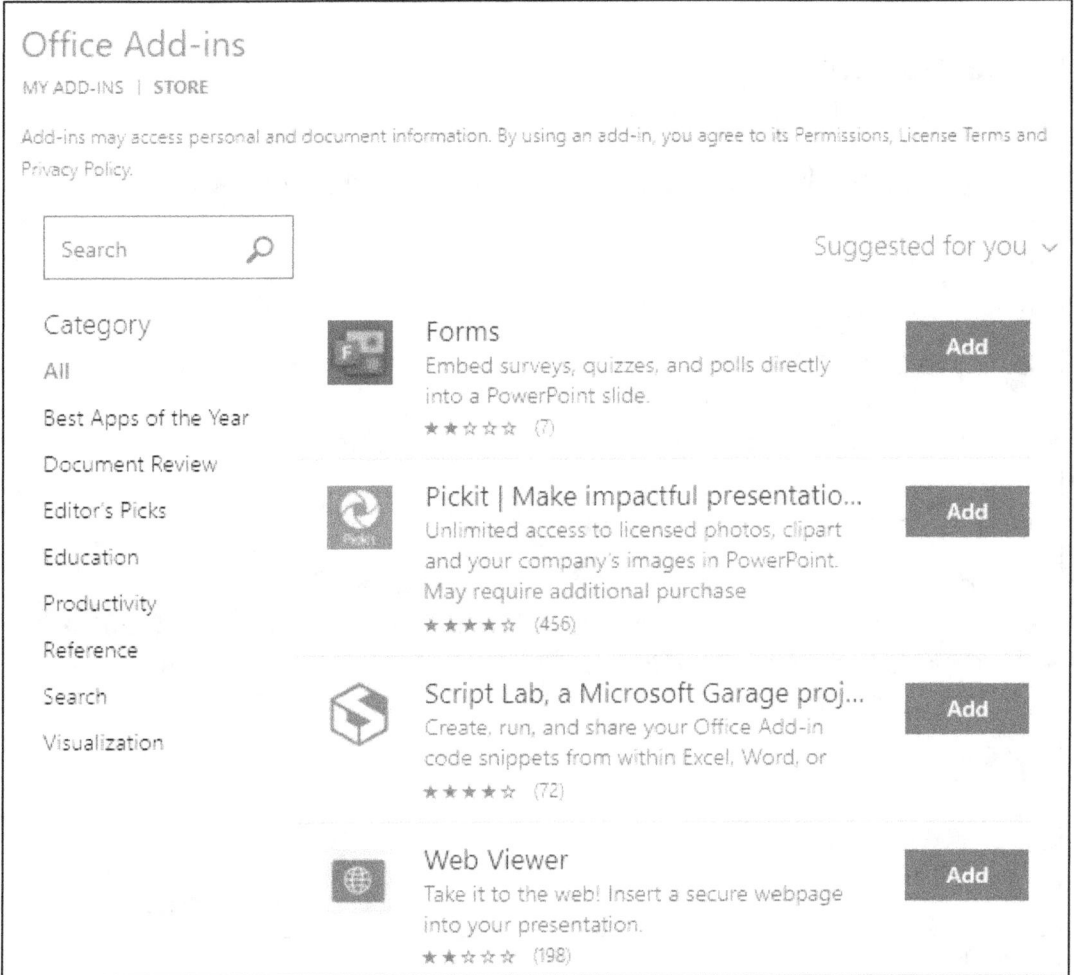

Figure 10.13

Then you will most likely get some type of license agreement that you will have to agree to in order to continue with the installation.

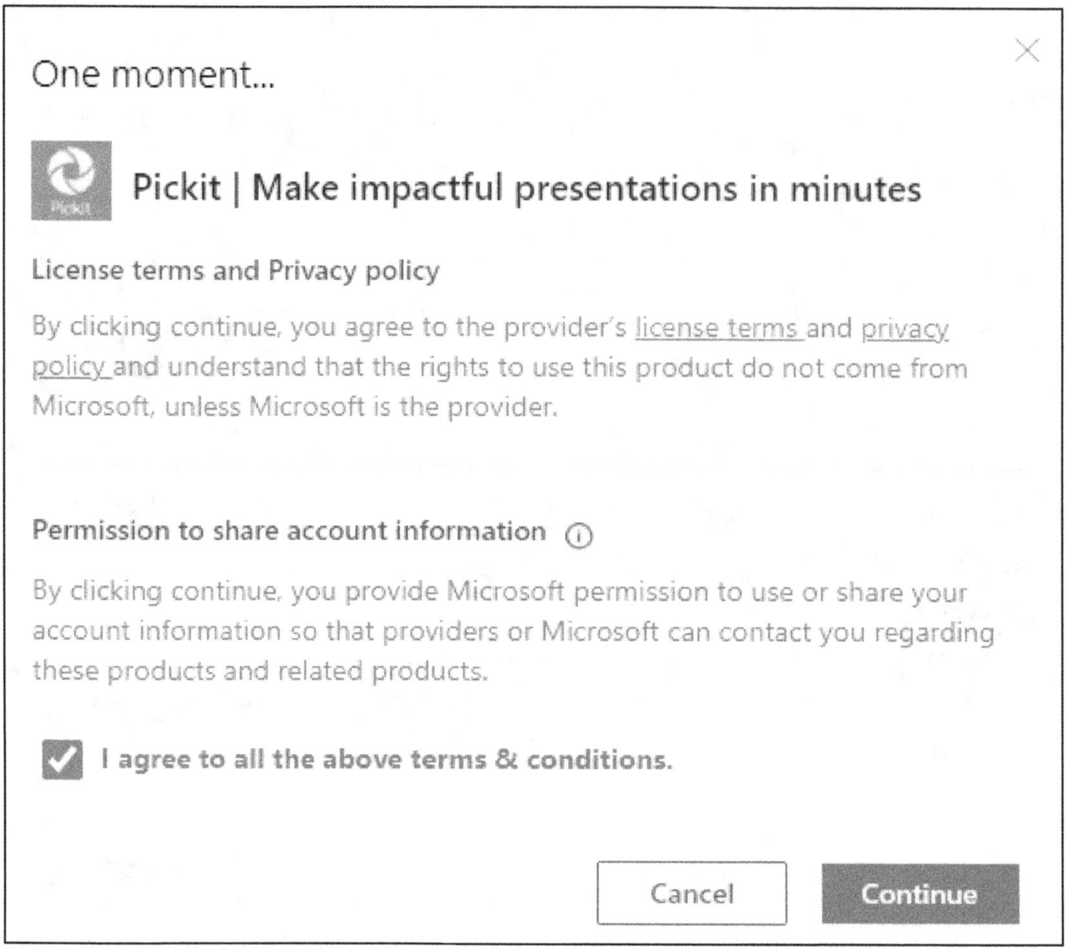

Chapter 10 - Extras

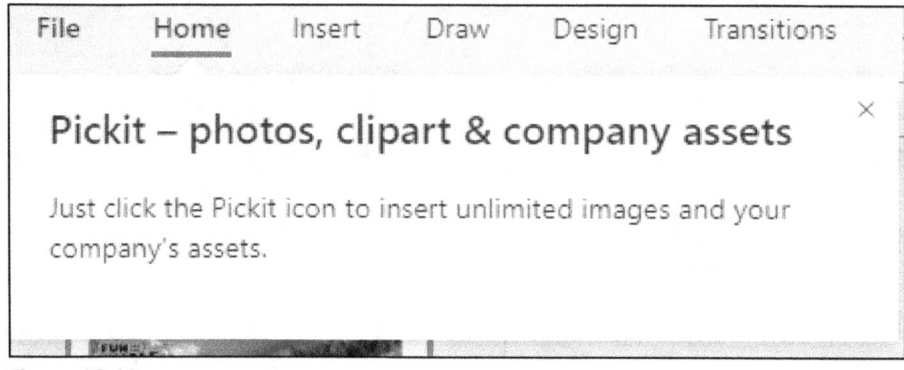

Figure 10.14

Next, the add-in might give you a popup telling you where to find it. This will vary between add-ins.

Figure 10.15

Chapter 10 - Extras

Now when I go to my Home tab as instructed by the app in figure 10.5 I will see my new Pickit group that I can click on to open the add-in.

Figure 10.16

Some add-ins will want you to sign up before using them while others will not. In this case, I will sign in with my Microsoft account.

Figure 10.17

You may also get a popup from Office asking you if it is ok for the add-in to access your information.

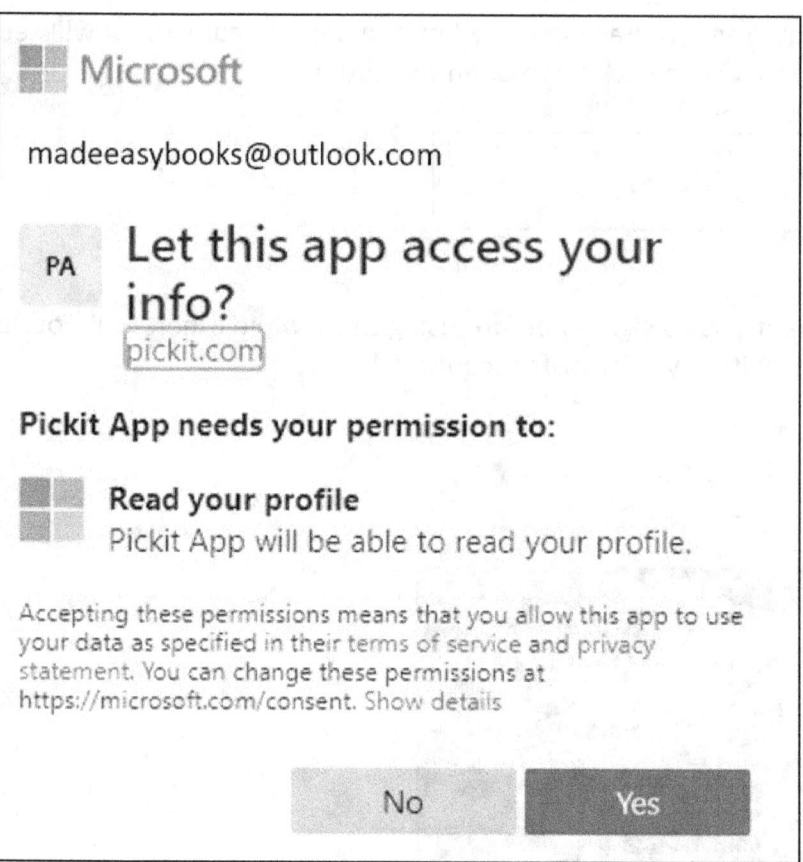

Figure 10.18

Once I agree to everything and open the add-in I can see that it is only a trial and I have 6 days left to use it before I will either have to buy it or it will stop working. Figure 10.19 shows the categories that I can choose from on the left and then on the right shows the results if I were to do an image search for dogs. When I find something I like, all I need to do is insert it into my presentation or document.

Chapter 10 - Extras

Figure 10.19

Chapter 10 - Extras

If you decide that you do not want a certain add-in installed in Office you can go back to your add-ins, click on the ellipsis and choose *Remove*.

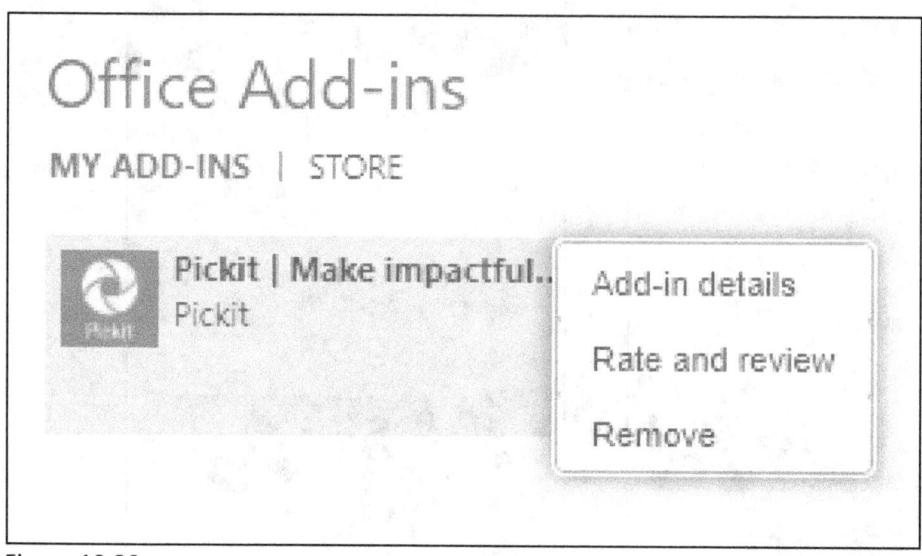

Figure 10.20

Office Apps on Your Mobile Devices
Since many people use their smartphones and tablets more than their computers at home, it makes sense that you should be able to use the same Office apps that you use on your PC on these devices.

Microsoft provides versions of many of their Office applications as mobile device apps that you can install from the Google Play Store or Apple App Store so you can then work on your files while outside of your home or office. You would install these apps just like you would any other app on your phone or tablet. Just be sure you are installing the official Microsoft app so look for Microsoft Corporation as the app developer when searching.

Chapter 10 - Extras

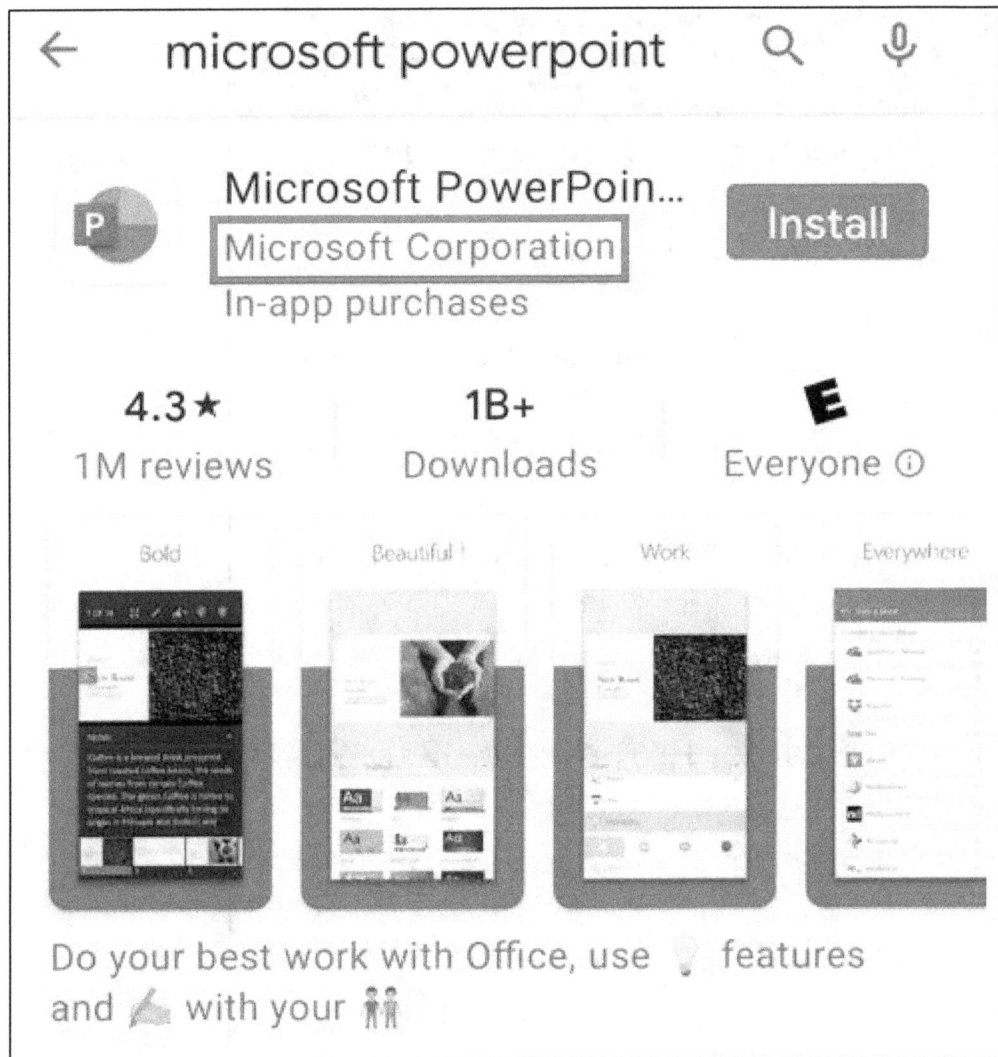

Figure 10.21

Once you have your app downloaded, you can log in with the same Microsoft account you use on your computer and you will be able to open the same documents you did on your computer, assuming they are stored in your OneDrive account. There is also a OneDrive app by the way. Figures 10.22 through 10.25 show some examples of Office apps on a smartphone.

Chapter 10 - Extras

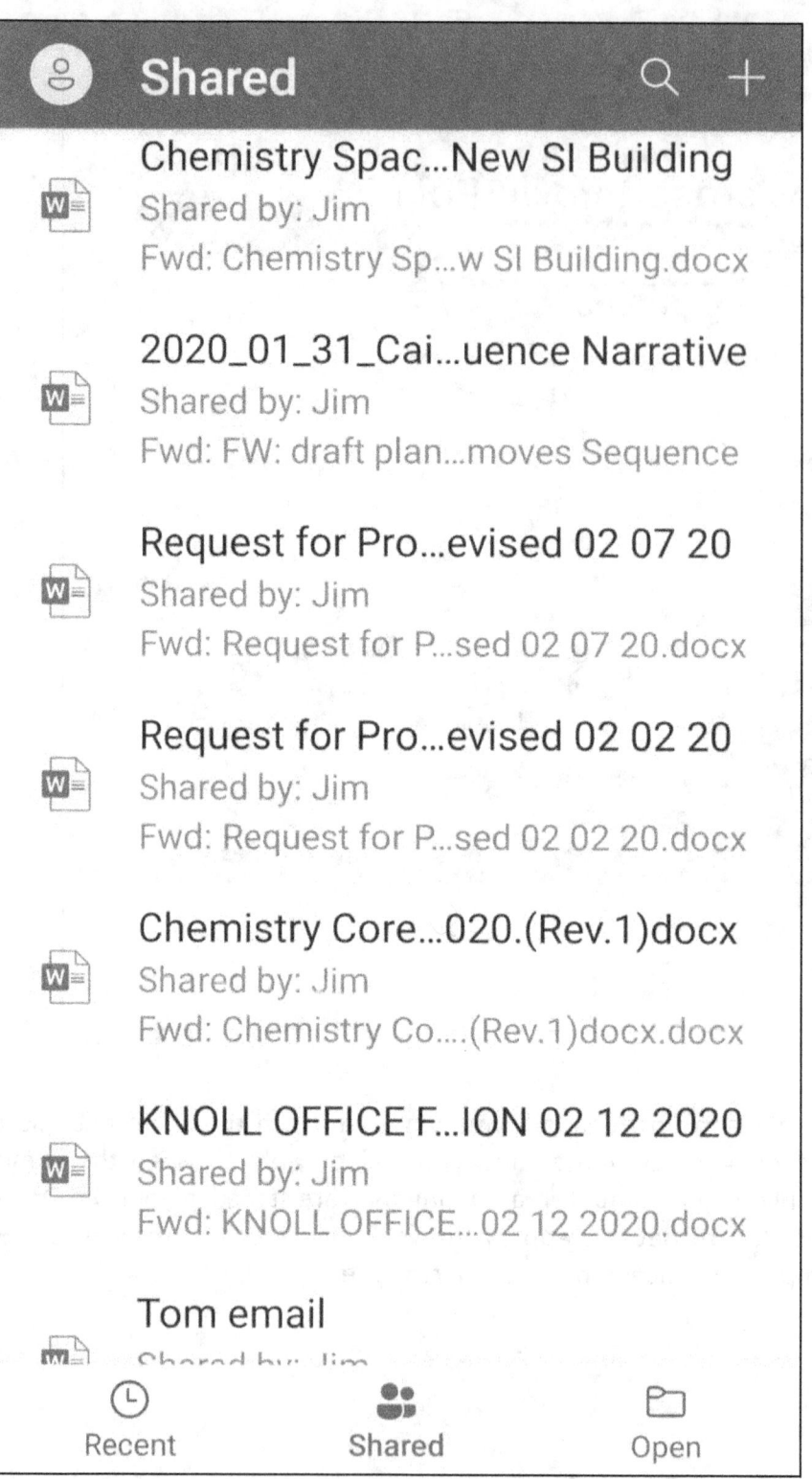

Figure 10.22

Chapter 10 - Extras

If you are interested in learning about how Windows 10 works to improve your overall Windows skills then check out my book titled **Windows 10 Made Easy**.
https://www.amazon.com/dp/B08RZDL5CP

If you do have a Microsoft account that you use to sign into your computer but don't want to use that account for Office then you have the option to make a new account to use instead. Simply open your browser and type in the following URL in your address bar.

https://signup.live.com/

You will then be asked to create an account if you don't have one to sign in with.

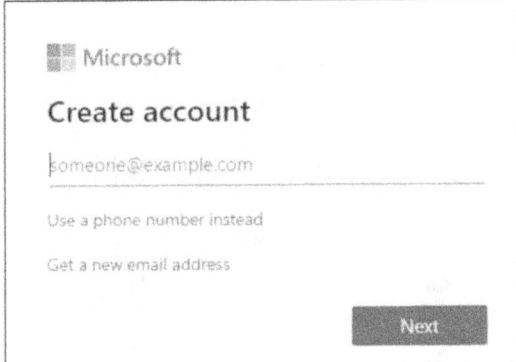

Figure 1.1

You don't need to use a Microsoft email such as joe@outlook.com to sign up for a Microsoft account. You can simply use any email address that you might have. You will then need to create a password and enter your name and date of birth. You don't need to add the real information here if you want a little privacy, but you might want to for file sharing purposes. You will then be sent a code to that email address that you will need to type in to verify your email address.

Once you supply all the information Microsoft asks for and verify you email address, you will be taken to the main Microsoft user account portal where you can do things such as add family members, connect additional devices to your account or change your password. There is even a place to sign up for a Microsoft 365 account (more on that later).

Figure 10.23

Chapter 10 - Extras

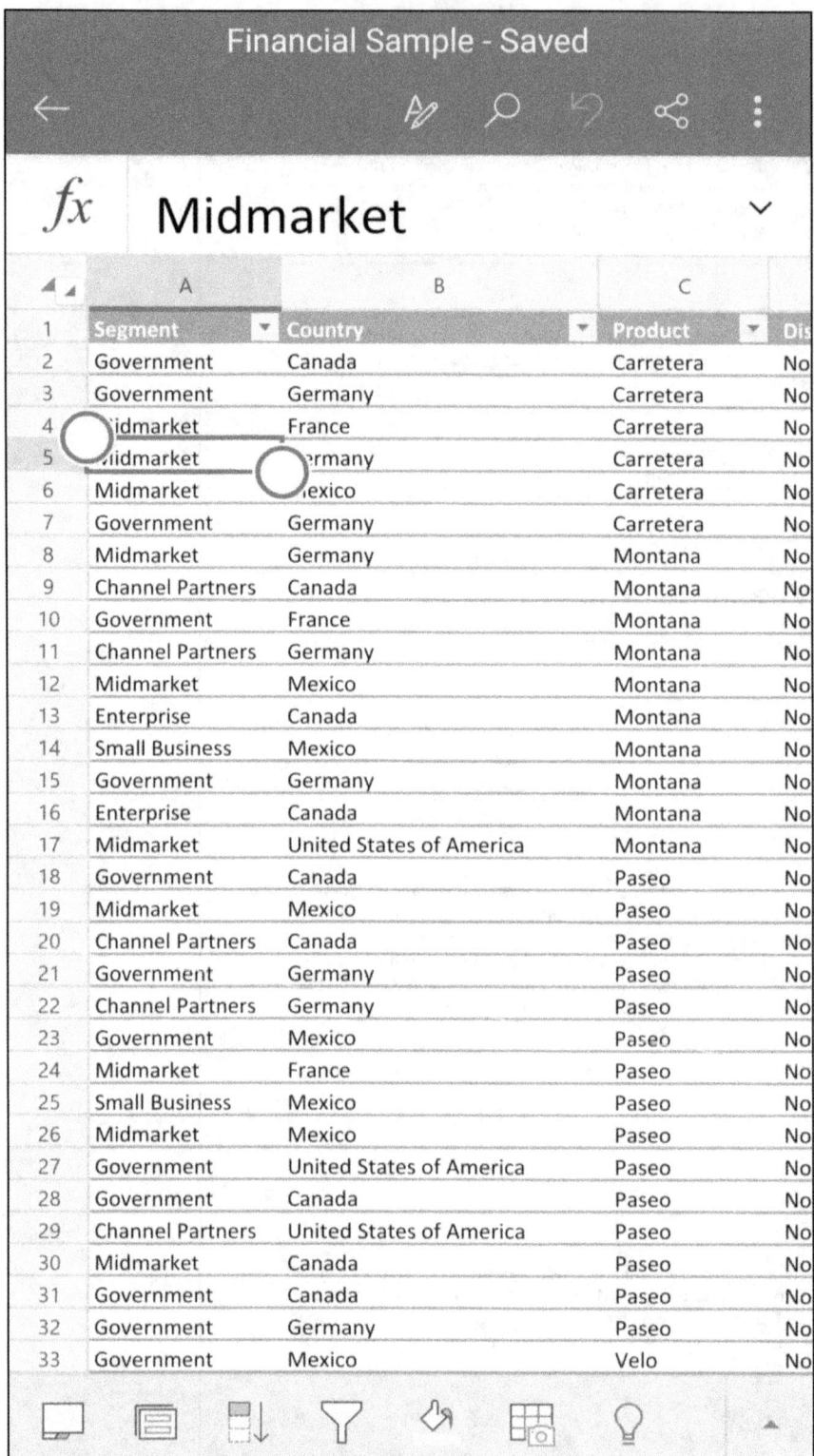

Figure 10.24

Chapter 10 - Extras

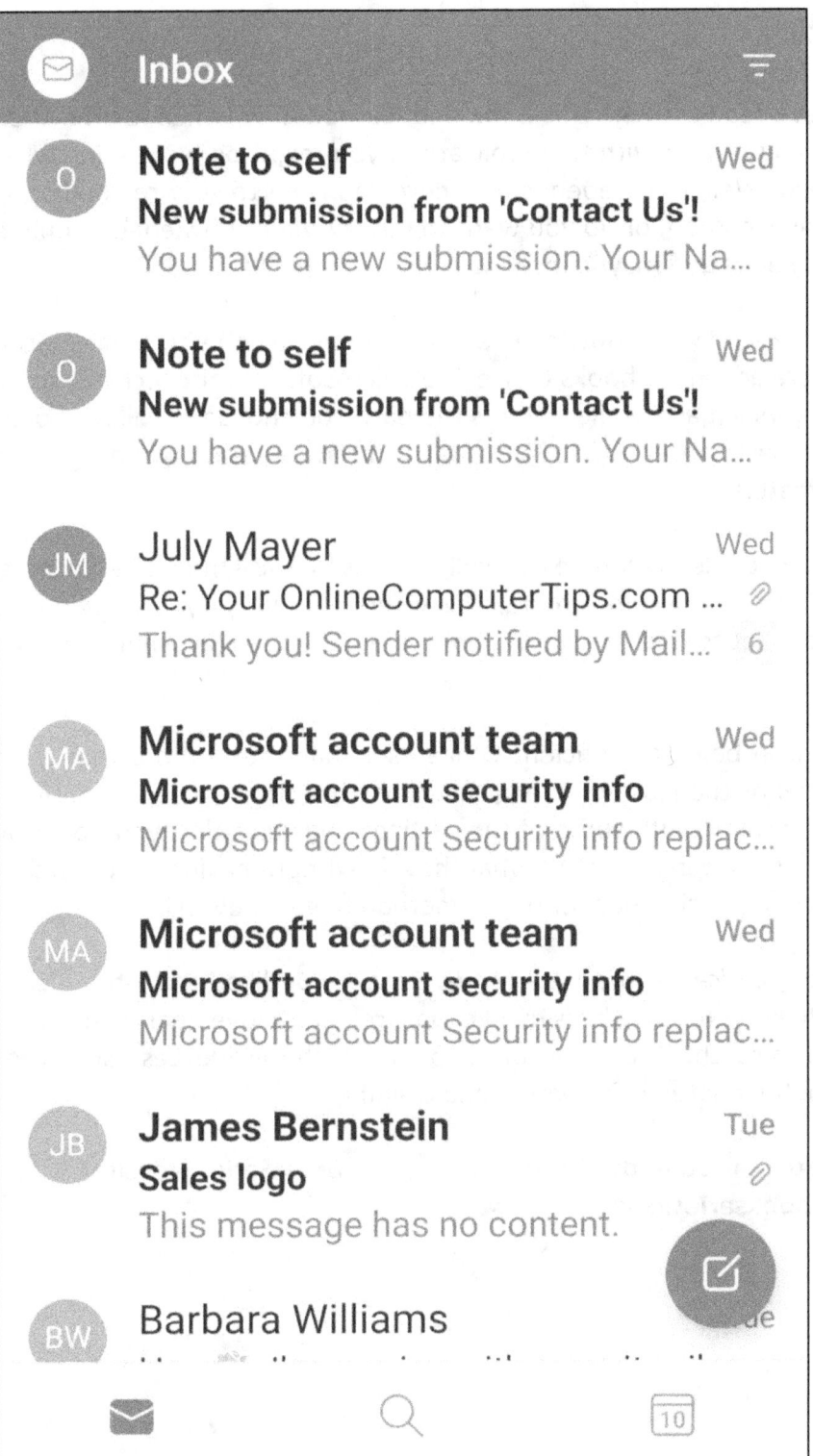

Figure 10.25

What's Next?

Now that you have read through this book and learned how Office for the Web works and what you can do with the application, you might be wondering what you should do next. Well, that depends on where you want to go. Are you happy with what you have learned, or do you want to further your knowledge of online office productivity apps and maybe look into upgrading to Office 365?

If you do want to expand your knowledge and computers in general, then you can look for some more advanced books Office 365\Microsoft 365 or check out some other vendors apps such as Google if that's the path you choose to follow. Focus on mastering the basics, and then apply what you have learned when going to more advanced material.

There are many great video resources as well, such as Pluralsight or CBT Nuggets, which offer online subscriptions to training videos of every type imaginable. YouTube is also a great source for instructional videos if you know what to search for.

If you are content in being a proficient Office user that knows more than your coworkers and friends then just keep on practicing what you have learned. Don't be afraid to poke around with some of the settings and tools that you normally don't use and see if you can figure out what they do without having to research it since learning by doing is the most effective method to gain new skills.

Thanks for reading *Office for the Web Made Easy*. If you liked this title, please leave a review. Reviews help authors build exposure. Plus, I love hearing from my readers! You can also check out the other books in the Made Easy series for additional, computer-related information and training.

And don't forget to stay up to date on my Made Easy Book Series website!
www.madeaseybookseries.com

What's Next?

You should also check out my computer tips website, as well as follow it on Facebook to find more information on all kinds of computer topics.

www.onlinecomputertips.com
https://www.facebook.com/OnlineComputerTips/

About the Author

James Bernstein has been working with various companies in the IT field for over 20 years, managing technologies such as SAN and NAS storage, VMware, backups, Windows Servers, Active Directory, DNS, DHCP, Networking, Microsoft Office, Photoshop, Premiere, Exchange, and more.

He has obtained certifications from Microsoft, VMware, CompTIA, ShoreTel, and SNIA, and continues to strive to learn new technologies to further his knowledge on a variety of subjects.

He is also the founder of the website onlinecomputertips.com, which offers its readers valuable information on topics such as Windows, networking, hardware, software, and troubleshooting. James writes much of the content himself and adds new content on a regular basis. The site was started in 2005 and is still going strong today.

www.ingramcontent.com/pod-product-compliance
Lightning Source LLC
Chambersburg PA
CBHW080450220526
45465CB00006B/2222